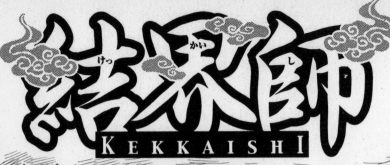

結界師
KEKKAISHI

田辺イエロウ
YELLOW TANABE PRESENTS

15

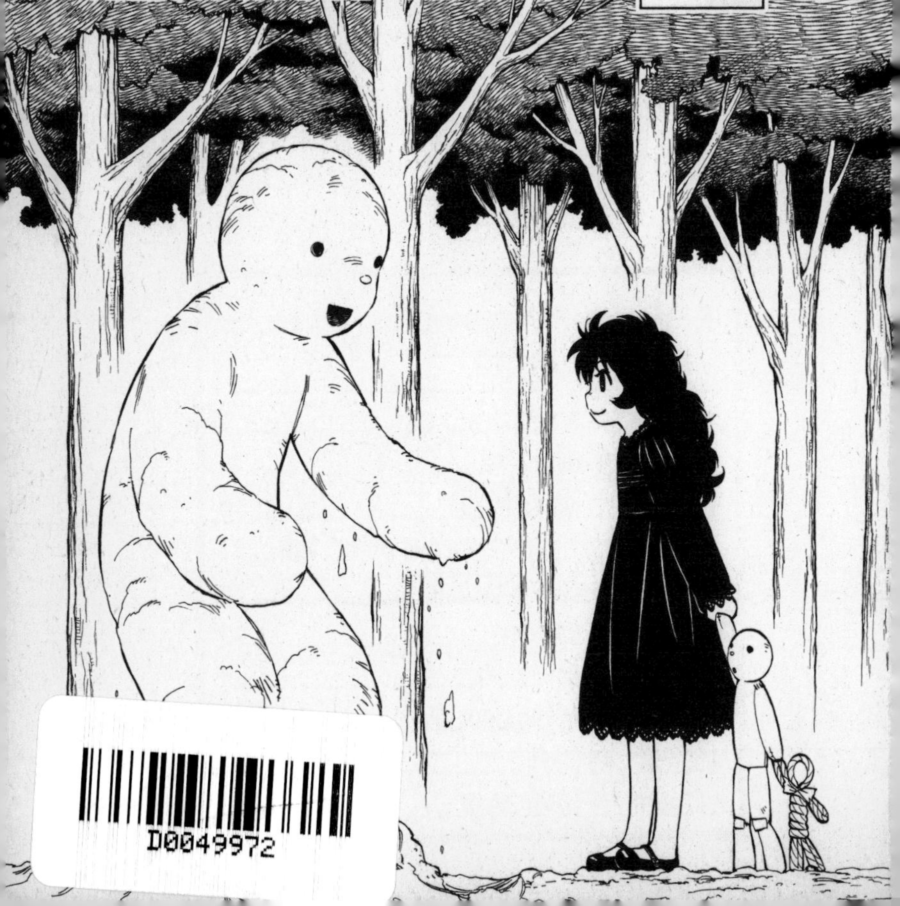

THe Story THUS Far

Yoshimori Sumimura and Tokine Yukimura have an ancestral duty to protect the Karasumori Forest from supernatural beings called ayakashi. People with their gift for terminating ayakashi are called kekkaishi, or "barrier masters."

Ichiro Ogi, the eighth member of the Shadow Organization's Council of Twelve, accuses Masamori of botching the battle against the Kokuboro. In hopes of discrediting Masamori, Ogi initiates a council inspection of the Karasumori Site.

The council's ninth member, Okuni, is assigned to oversee the inspection. But just before Okuni arrives at the Karasumori Site, a mysterious black box is delivered to the headquarters of Masamori's night troops, and Misao, a young night trooper, is sucked inside! And then an identical box appears at the Karasumori Site...

Is all this a cowardly conspiracy against Yoshimori and Masamori... or the start of something even more menacing?

KEKKAISHI VOL. 15
TABLE OF CONTENTS

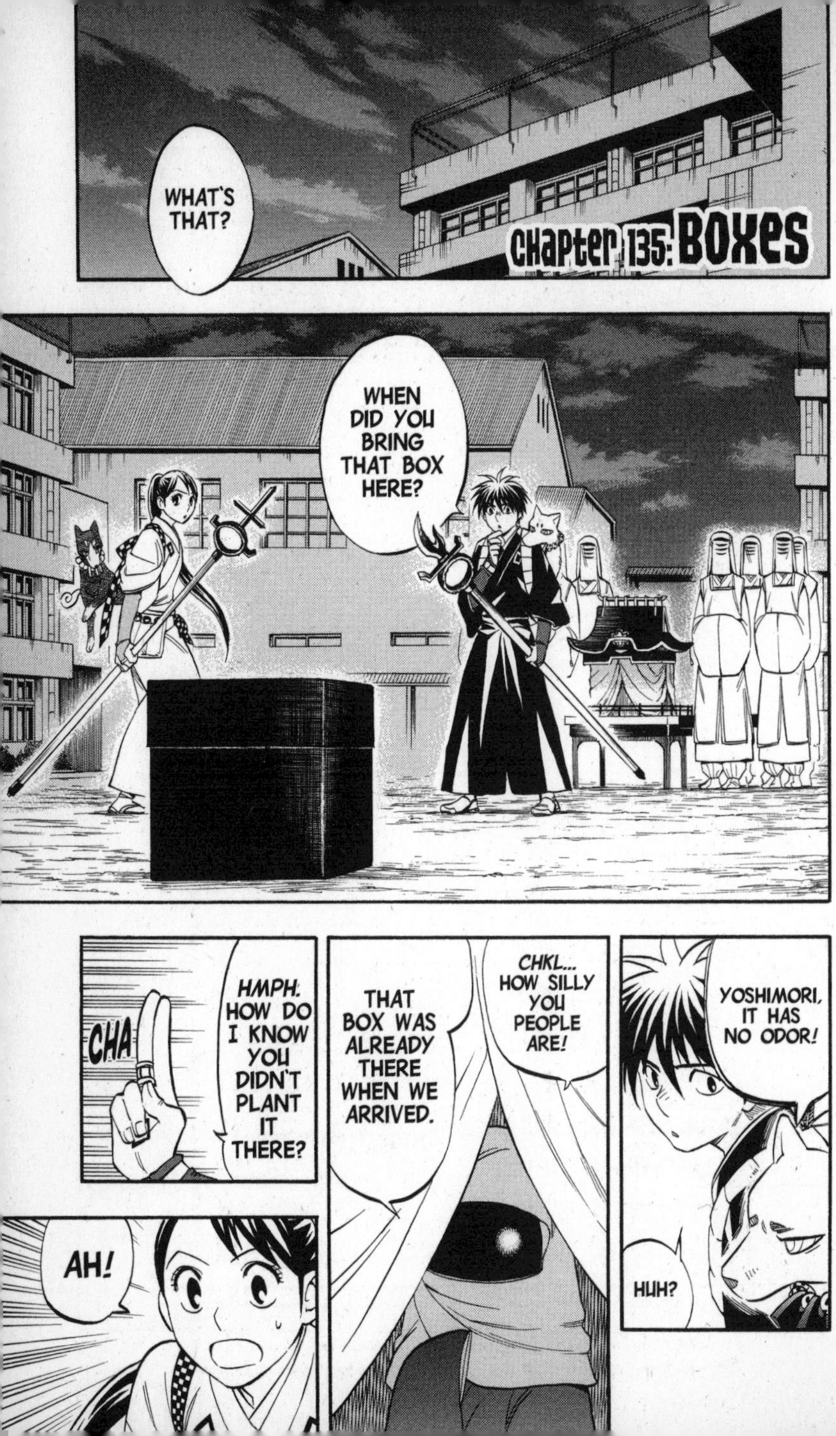
Chapter 135: Boxes
WHAT'S THAT?
WHEN DID YOU BRING THAT BOX HERE?
YOSHIMORI, IT HAS NO ODOR!
HUH?
CHKL... HOW SILLY YOU PEOPLE ARE!
THAT BOX WAS ALREADY THERE WHEN WE ARRIVED.
CHA
HMPH. HOW DO I KNOW YOU DIDN'T PLANT IT THERE?
AH!

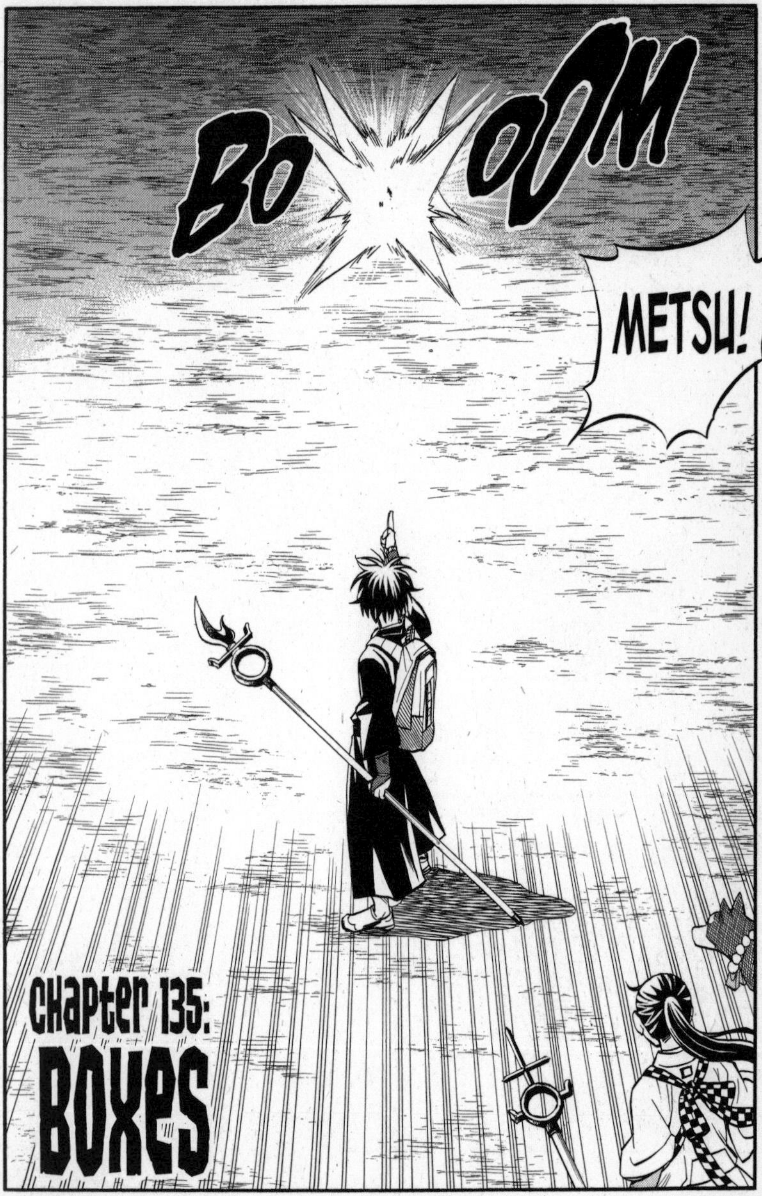
BOOOM
METSU!
Chapter 135:
Boxes

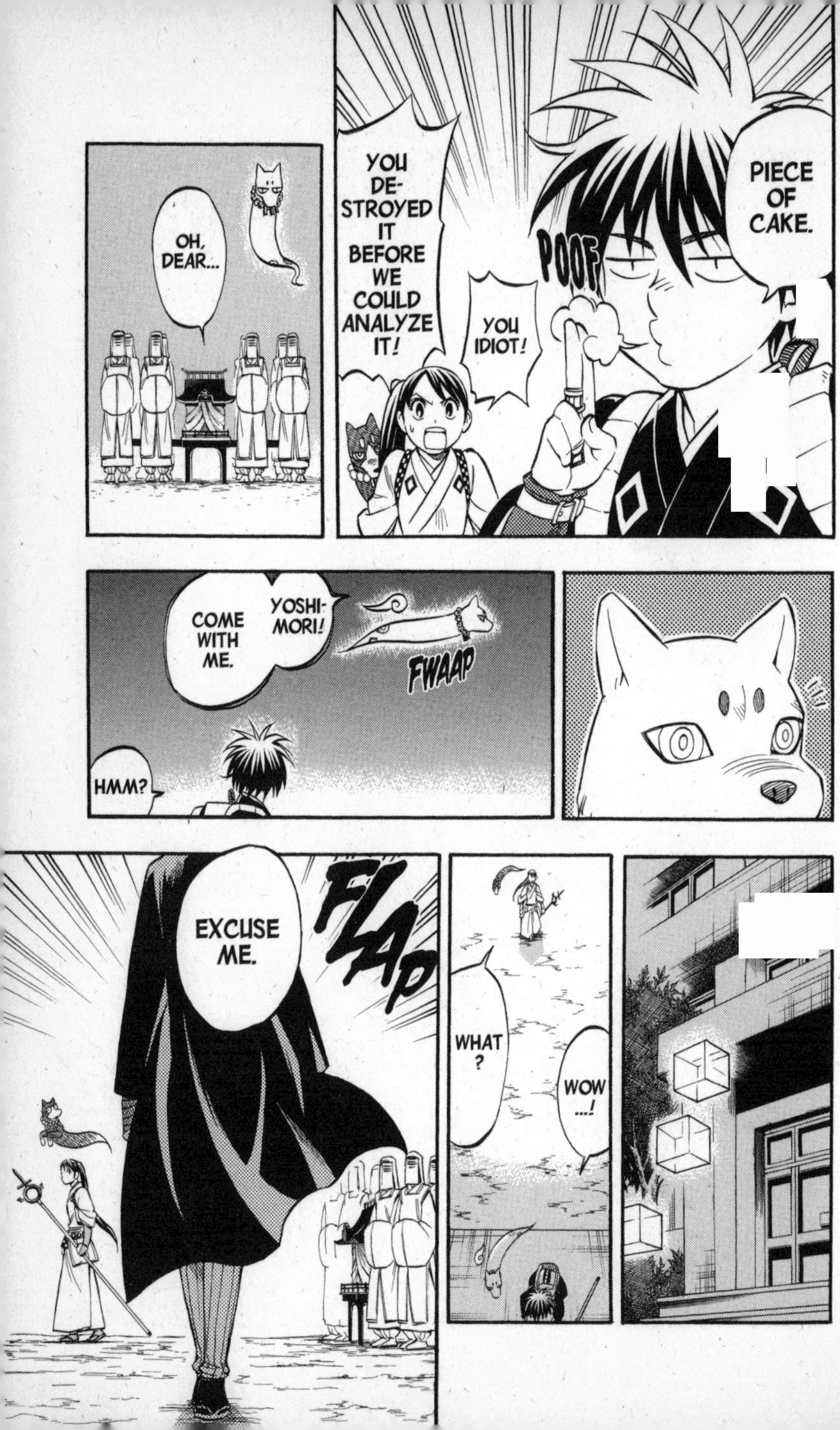
PIECE OF CAKE.
POOF
YOU IDIOT!
YOU DE-STROYED IT BEFORE WE COULD ANALYZE IT!
OH, DEAR...
YOSHI-MORI!
COME WITH ME.
FWAAP
HMM?
WOW...!
WHAT?
EXCUSE ME.
FLAP

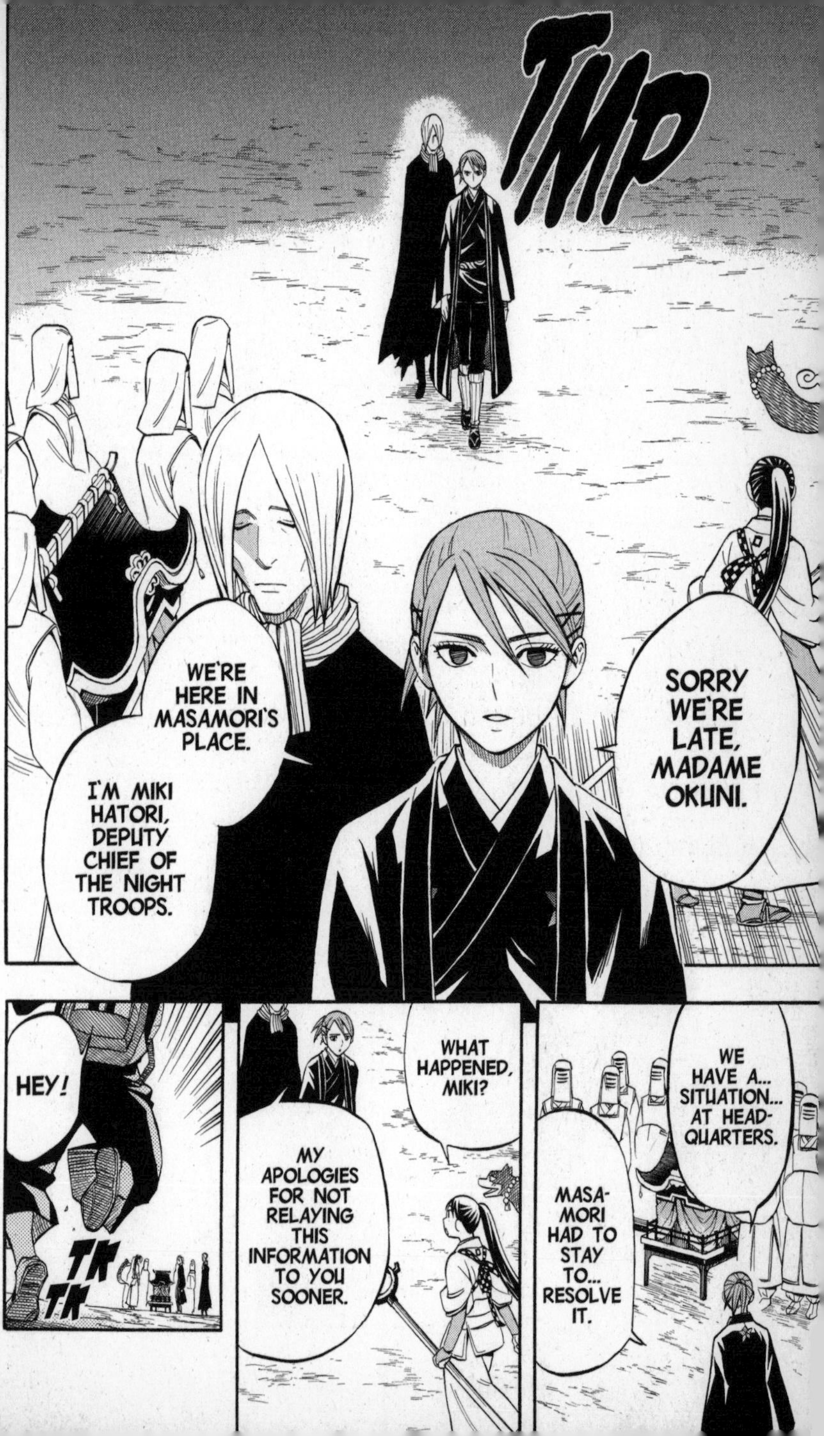
TMP
SORRY WE'RE LATE, MADAME OKUNI.
WE'RE HERE IN MASAMORI'S PLACE.
I'M MIKI HATORI, DEPUTY CHIEF OF THE NIGHT TROOPS.
WE HAVE A... SITUATION... AT HEAD-QUARTERS.
MASA-MORI HAD TO STAY TO... RESOLVE IT.
WHAT HAPPENED, MIKI?
MY APOLOGIES FOR NOT RELAYING THIS INFORMATION TO YOU SOONER.
HEY!
TK TK

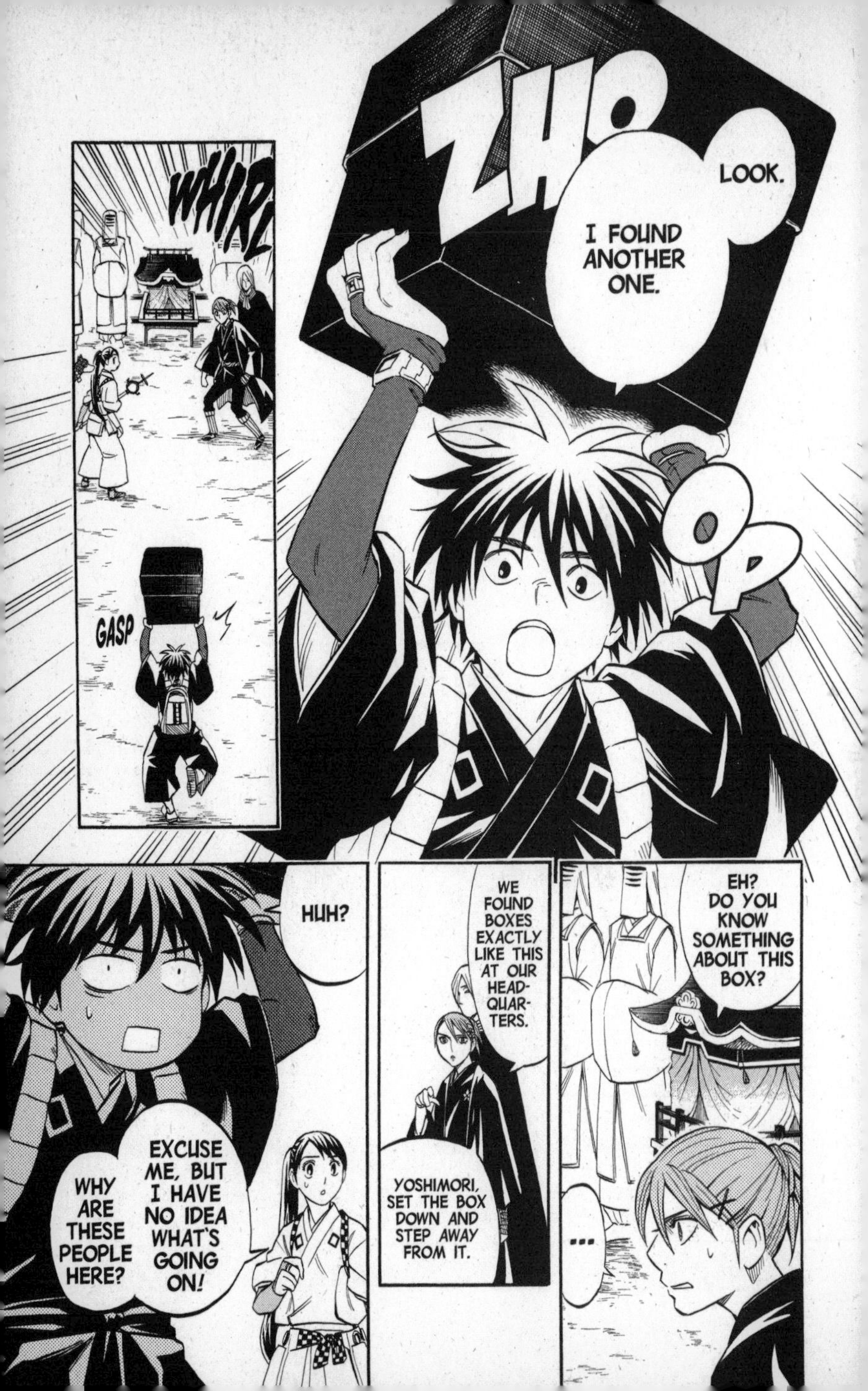
ZHO
LOOK.
I FOUND ANOTHER ONE.
OP
WHIRL
GASP
EH? DO YOU KNOW SOMETHING ABOUT THIS BOX?
...
WE FOUND BOXES EXACTLY LIKE THIS AT OUR HEAD-QUARTERS.
YOSHIMORI, SET THE BOX DOWN AND STEP AWAY FROM IT.
HUH?
EXCUSE ME, BUT I HAVE NO IDEA WHAT'S GOING ON!
WHY ARE THESE PEOPLE HERE?

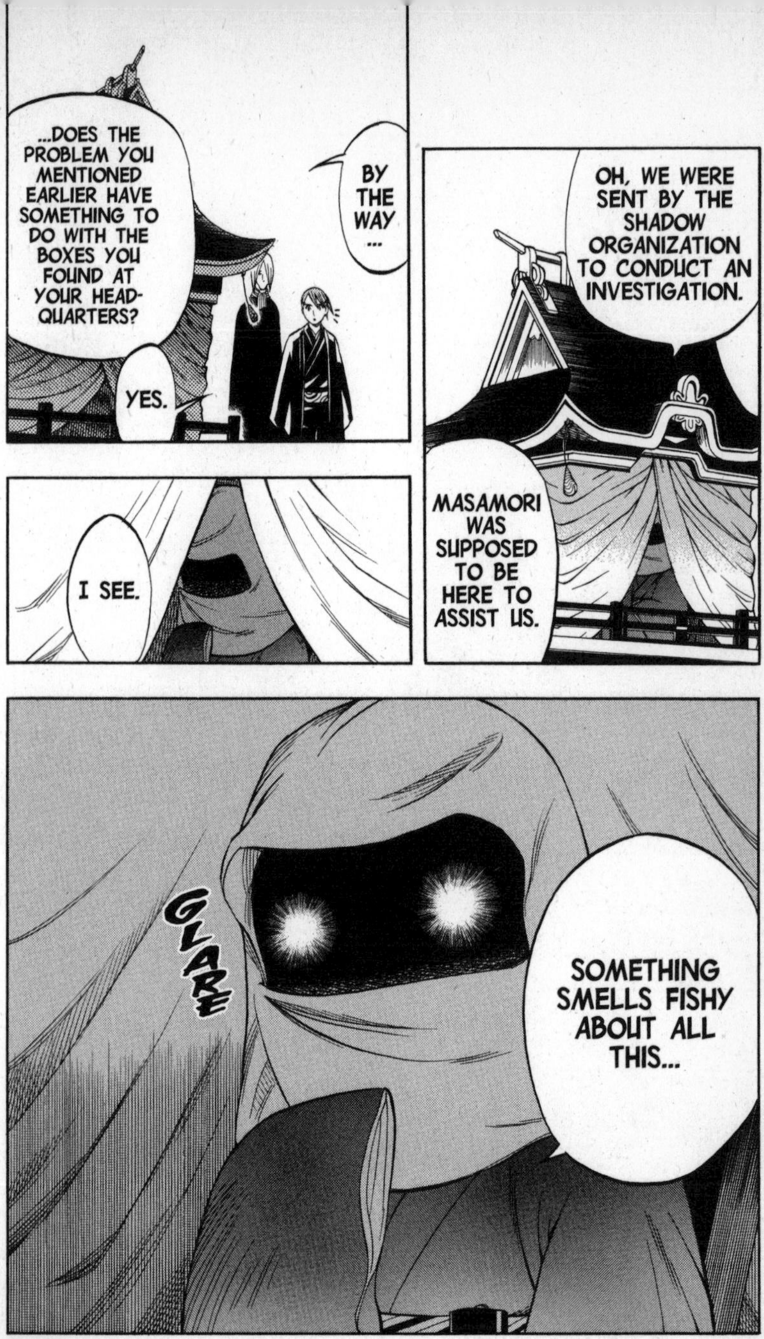
OH, WE WERE SENT BY THE SHADOW ORGANIZATION TO CONDUCT AN INVESTIGATION.
MASAMORI WAS SUPPOSED TO BE HERE TO ASSIST US.
BY THE WAY...
...DOES THE PROBLEM YOU MENTIONED EARLIER HAVE SOMETHING TO DO WITH THE BOXES YOU FOUND AT YOUR HEAD-QUARTERS?
YES.
I SEE.
SOMETHING SMELLS FISHY ABOUT ALL THIS...
GLARE

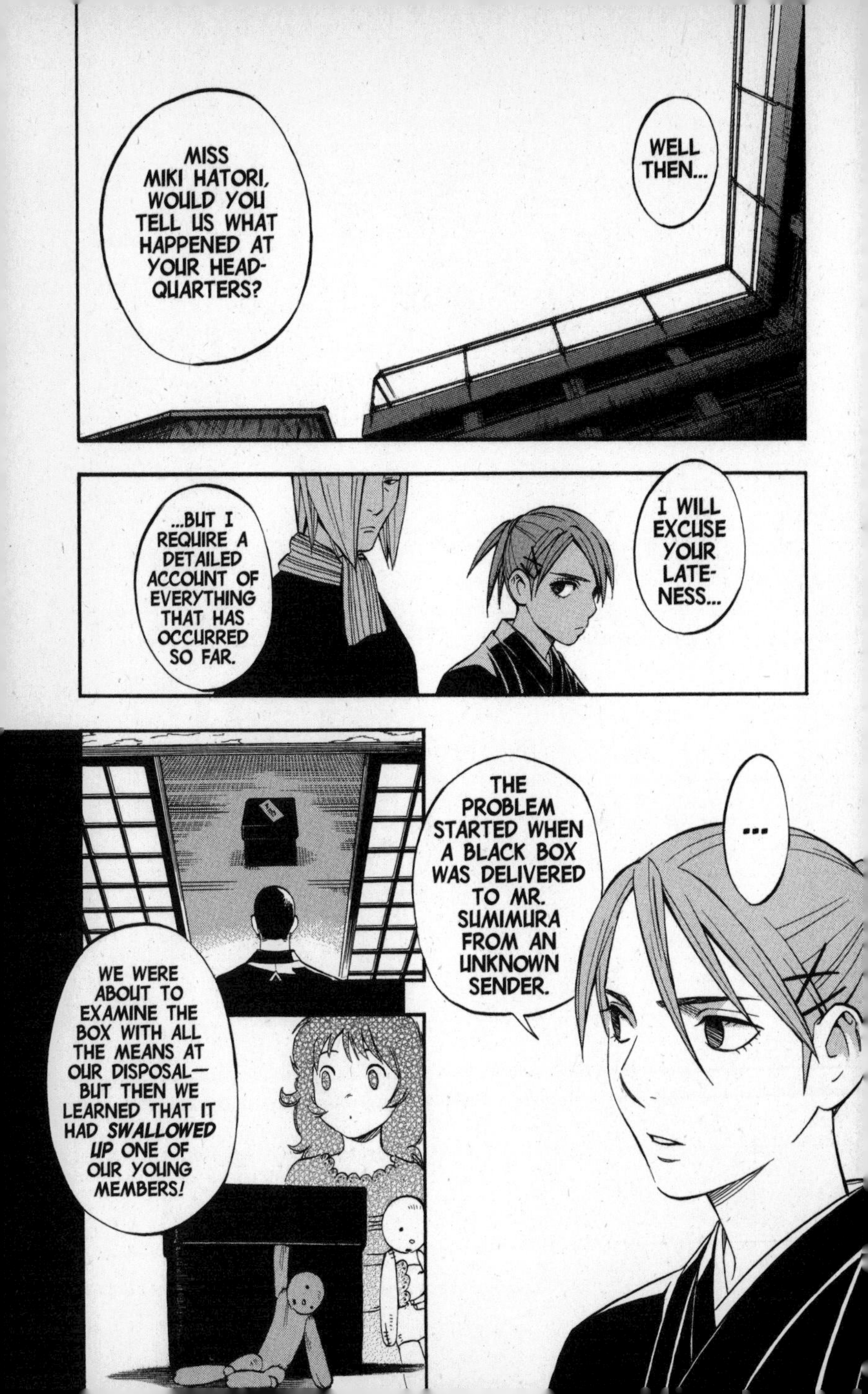
WELL THEN...
MISS MIKI HATORI, WOULD YOU TELL US WHAT HAPPENED AT YOUR HEAD-QUARTERS?
I WILL EXCUSE YOUR LATE-NESS...
...BUT I REQUIRE A DETAILED ACCOUNT OF EVERYTHING THAT HAS OCCURRED SO FAR.
...
THE PROBLEM STARTED WHEN A BLACK BOX WAS DELIVERED TO MR. SUMIMURA FROM AN UNKNOWN SENDER.
WE WERE ABOUT TO EXAMINE THE BOX WITH ALL THE MEANS AT OUR DISPOSAL— BUT THEN WE LEARNED THAT IT HAD *SWALLOWED UP* ONE OF OUR YOUNG MEMBERS!

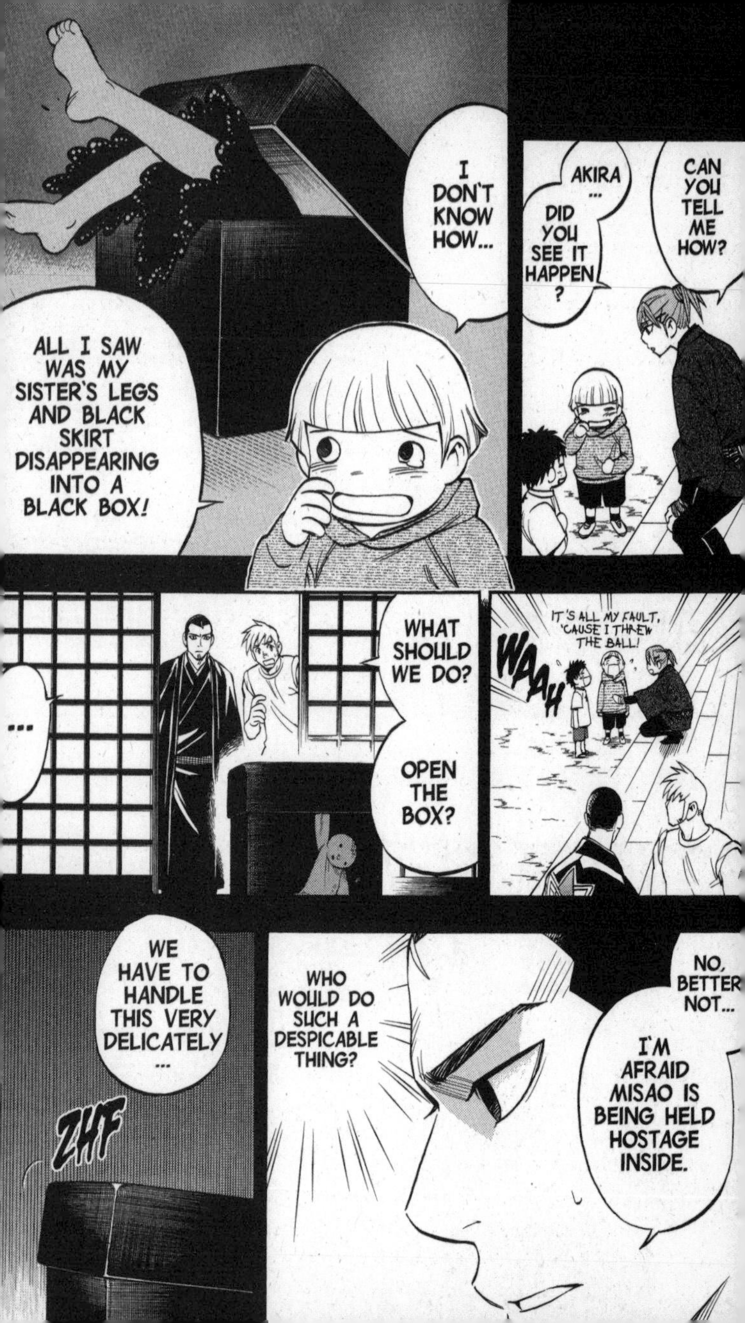
CAN YOU TELL ME HOW?
AKIRA... DID YOU SEE IT HAPPEN?
I DON'T KNOW HOW...
ALL I SAW WAS MY SISTER'S LEGS AND BLACK SKIRT DISAPPEARING INTO A BLACK BOX!
WAAAH
IT'S ALL MY FAULT, 'CAUSE I THREW THE BALL!
WHAT SHOULD WE DO?
OPEN THE BOX?
...
NO, BETTER NOT...
I'M AFRAID MISAO IS BEING HELD HOSTAGE INSIDE.
WHO WOULD DO SUCH A DESPICABLE THING?
WE HAVE TO HANDLE THIS VERY DELICATELY...
ZHF

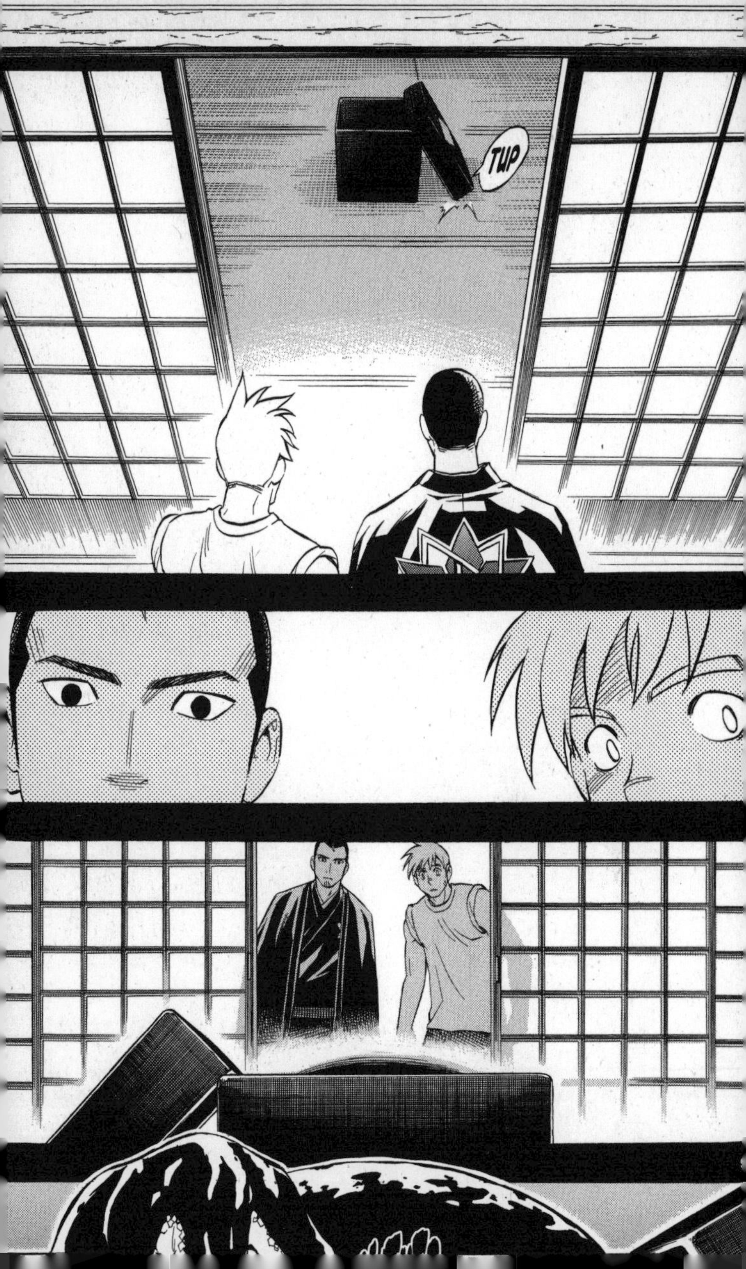
TUP

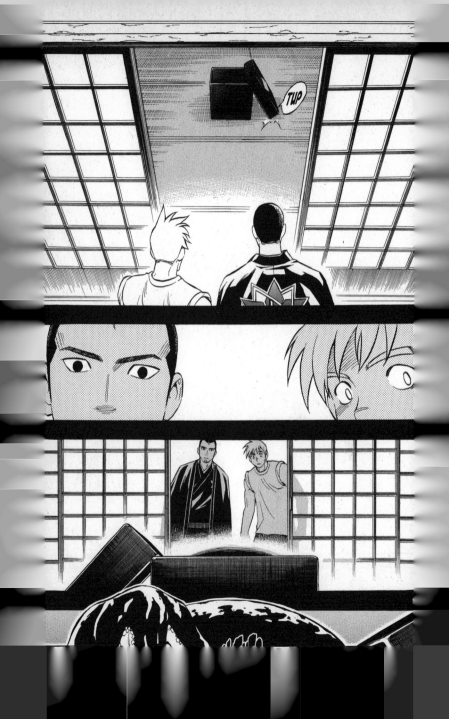

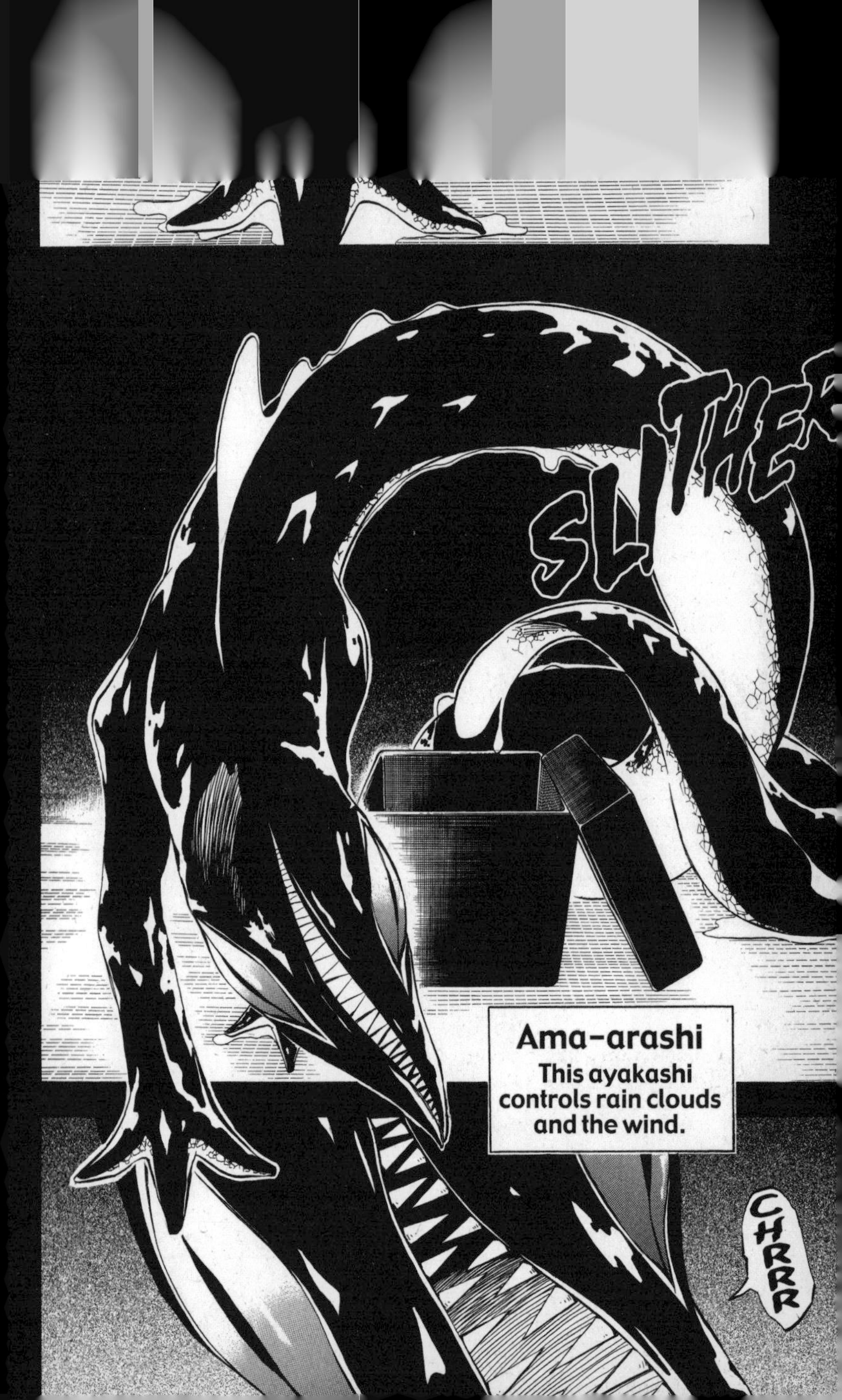
SLITHER
Ama-arashi
This ayakashi controls rain clouds and the wind.
CHRRR

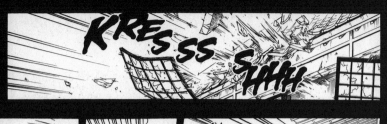

KRESSSSSHHH
SLTH SLTH SLTH
HE'S ESCAPING!
CAPTURE HIM!
!
WHAT ABOUT THE BOX ...?!
WRITHE
WRITHE
HE'S OBVIOUSLY A VERY POWERFUL AYAKASHI... SO WHY DID HE RUN FROM US?
WHAT IS IT HE'S AFTER?

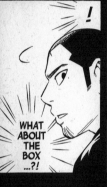

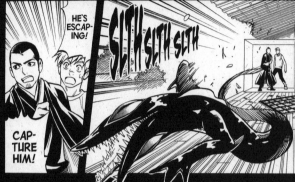

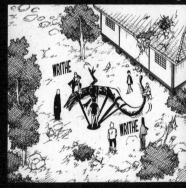

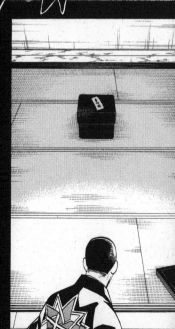

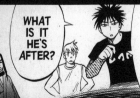

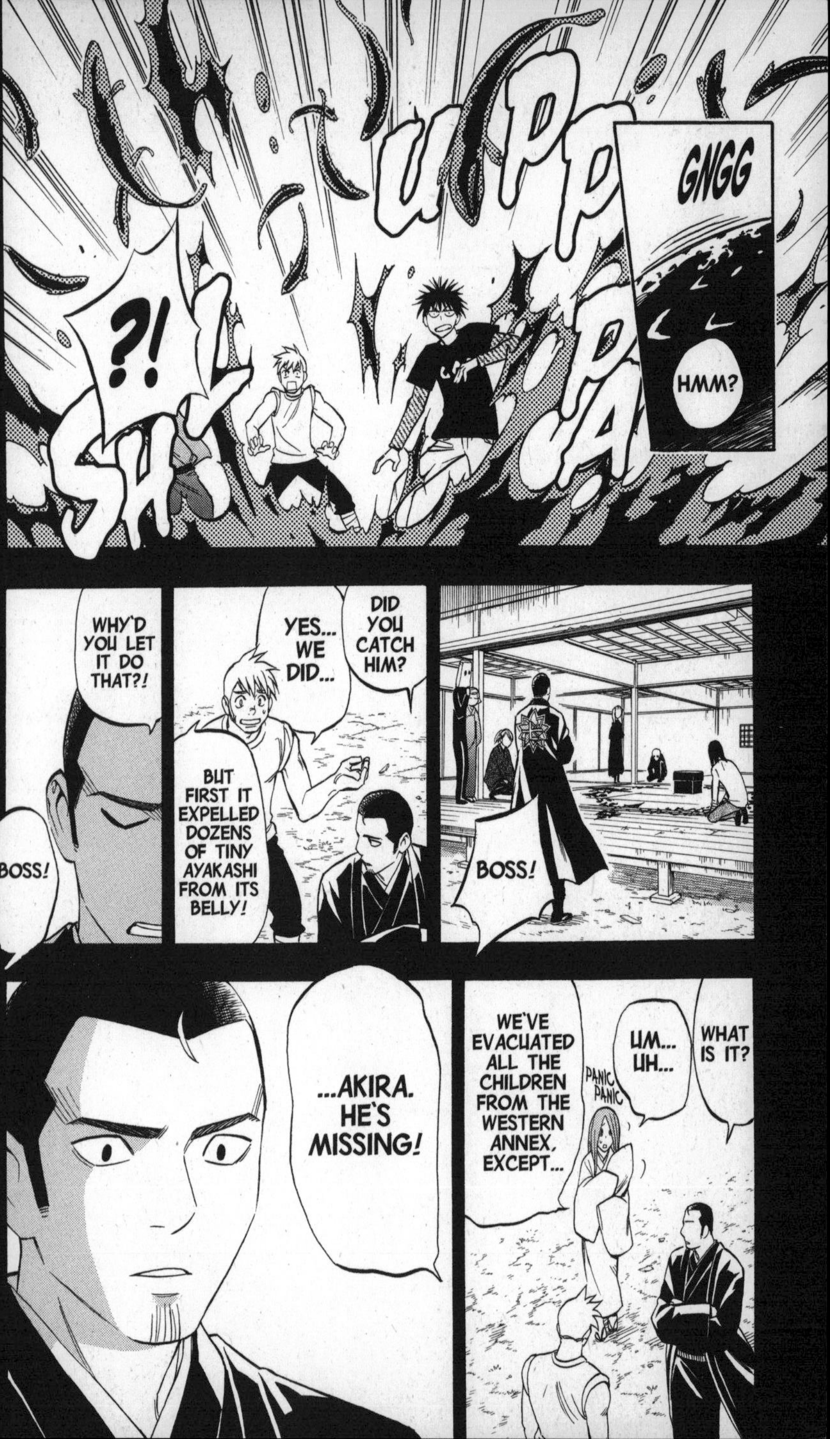
GNGG
HMM?
?!
BOSS!
DID YOU CATCH HIM?
YES... WE DID...
BUT FIRST IT EXPELLED DOZENS OF TINY AYAKASHI FROM ITS BELLY!
WHY'D YOU LET IT DO THAT?!
BOSS!
WHAT IS IT?
UM... UH...
PANIC PANIC
WE'VE EVACUATED ALL THE CHILDREN FROM THE WESTERN ANNEX, EXCEPT...
...AKIRA. HE'S MISSING!

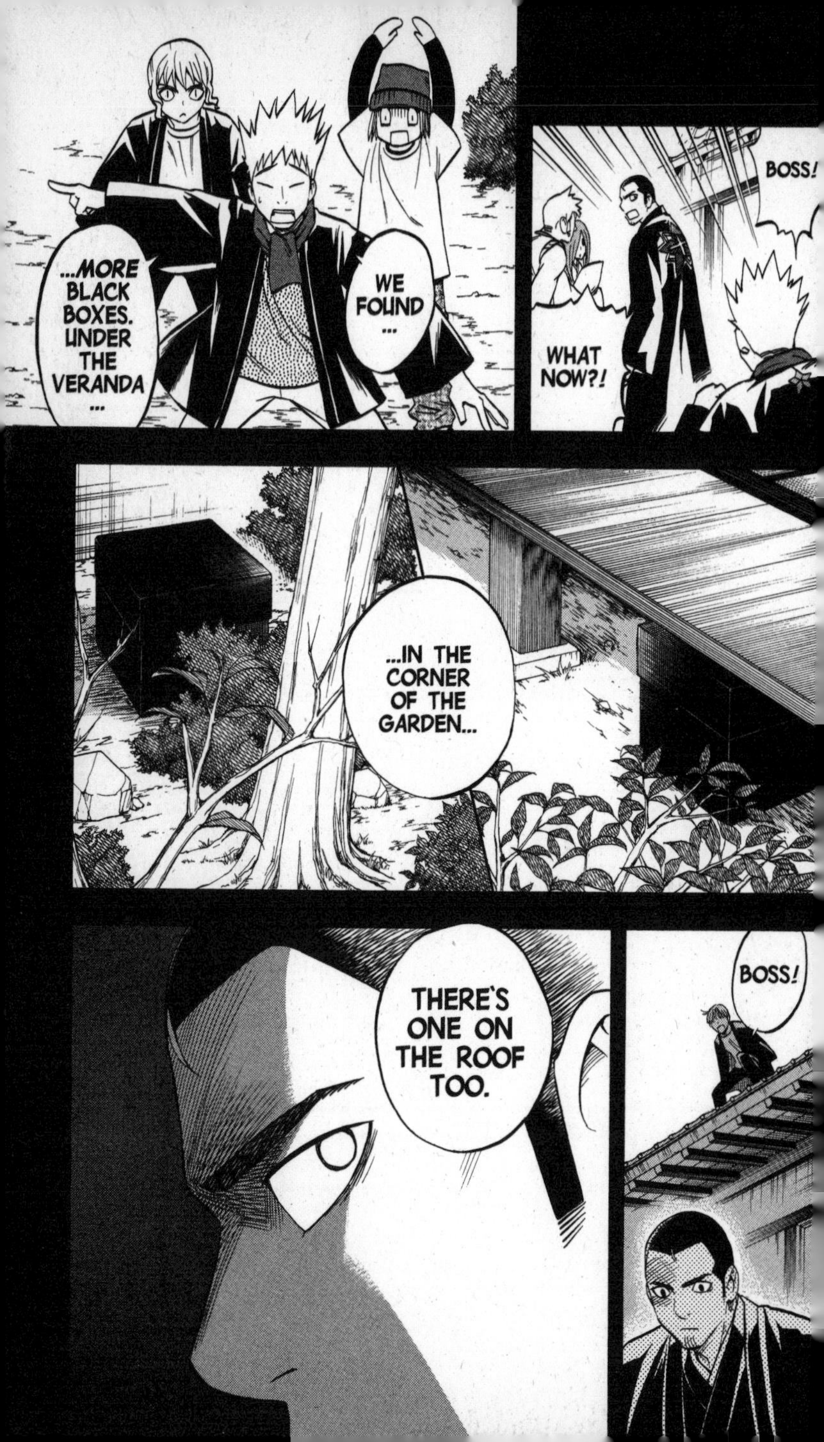
BOSS!
WHAT NOW?!
WE FOUND ...
...MORE BLACK BOXES. UNDER THE VERANDA ...
...IN THE CORNER OF THE GARDEN...
BOSS!
THERE'S ONE ON THE ROOF TOO.

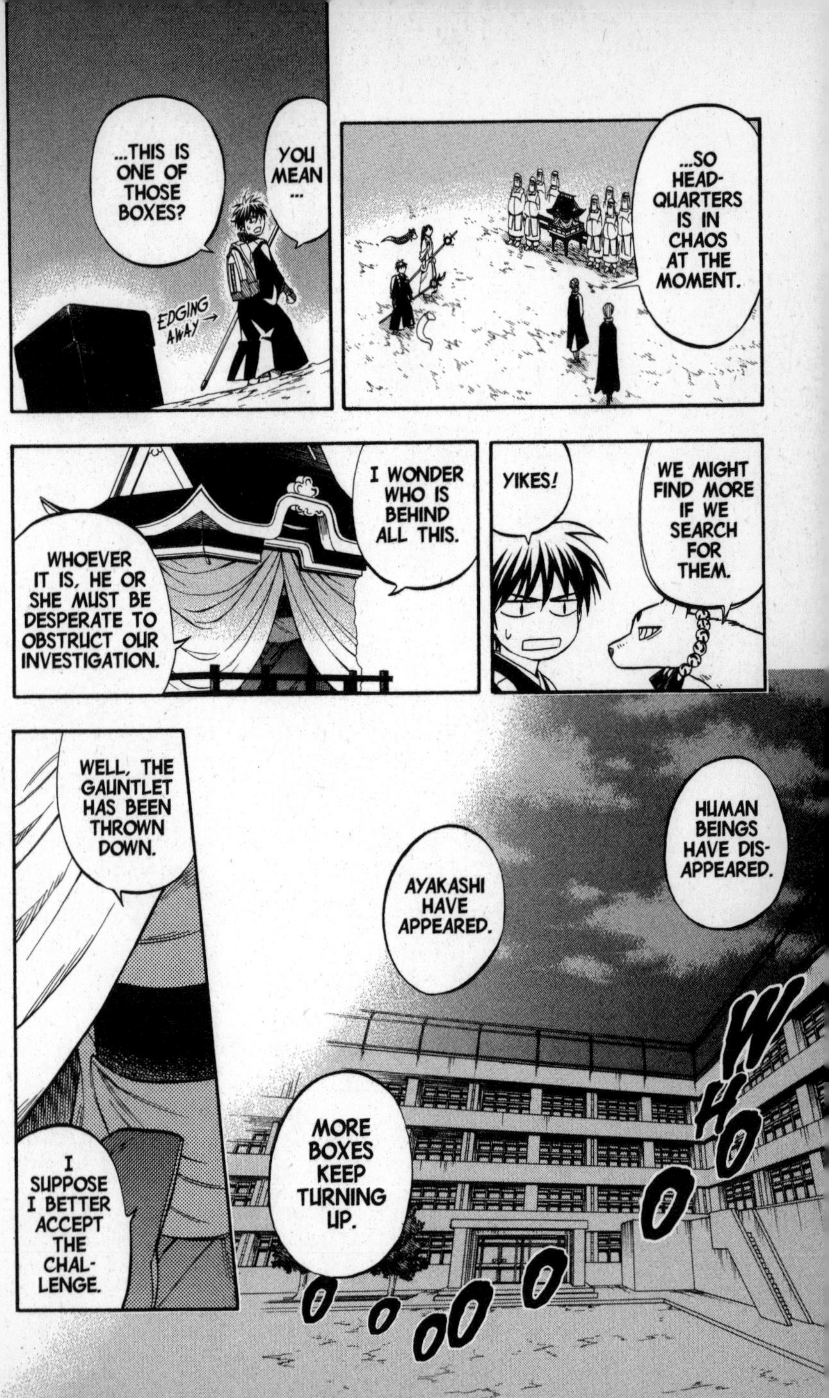
...SO HEADQUARTERS IS IN CHAOS AT THE MOMENT.
YOU MEAN...
...THIS IS ONE OF THOSE BOXES?
EDGING AWAY
WE MIGHT FIND MORE IF WE SEARCH FOR THEM.
YIKES!
I WONDER WHO IS BEHIND ALL THIS.
WHOEVER IT IS, HE OR SHE MUST BE DESPERATE TO OBSTRUCT OUR INVESTIGATION.
HUMAN BEINGS HAVE DISAPPEARED.
AYAKASHI HAVE APPEARED.
WHOOOOOOOOO
MORE BOXES KEEP TURNING UP.
WELL, THE GAUNTLET HAS BEEN THROWN DOWN.
I SUPPOSE I BETTER ACCEPT THE CHALLENGE.

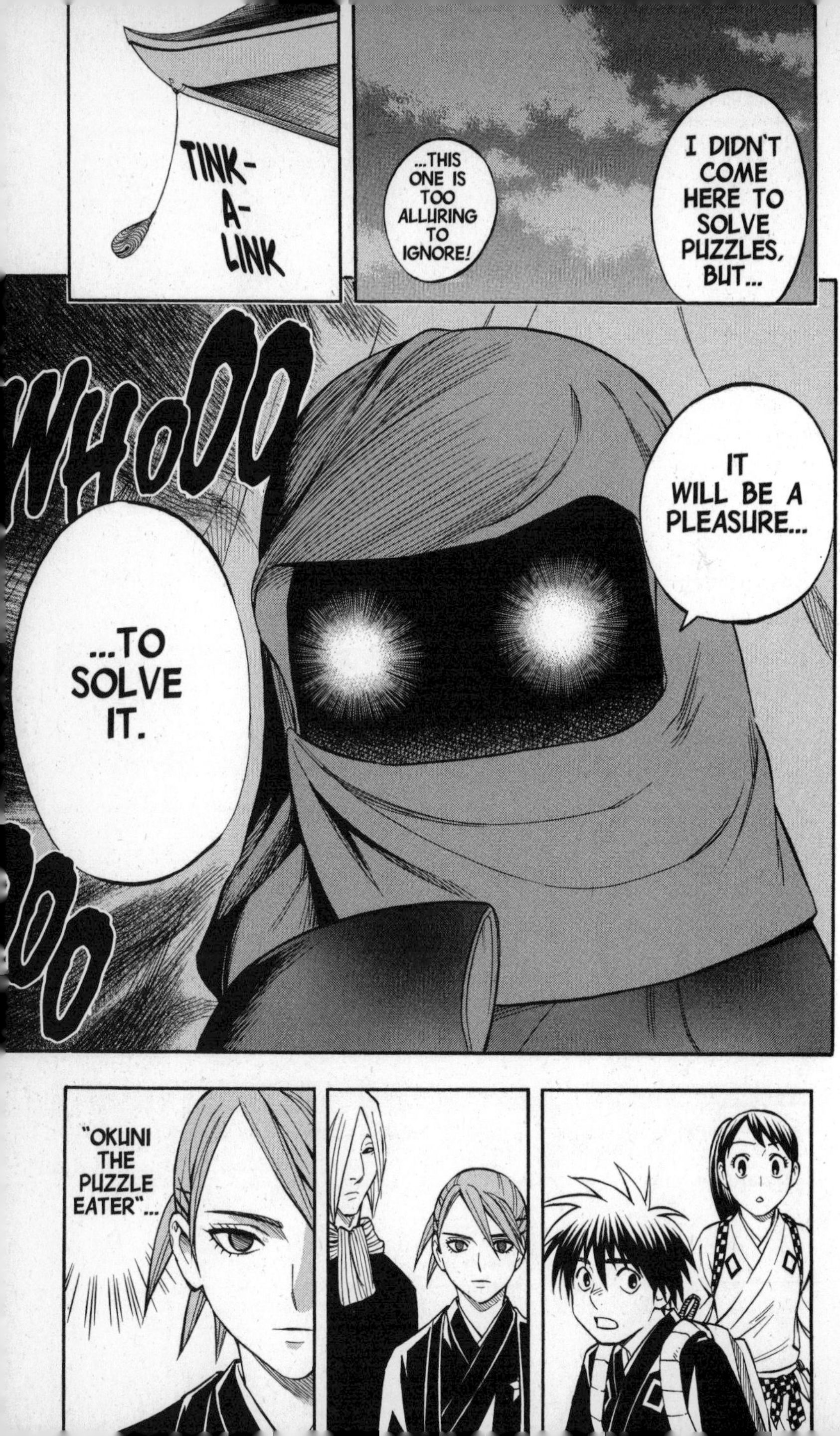
I DIDN'T COME HERE TO SOLVE PUZZLES, BUT...
...THIS ONE IS TOO ALLURING TO IGNORE!
TINK-A-LINK
IT WILL BE A PLEASURE...
...TO SOLVE IT.
WHOOOO
OOO
"OKUNI THE PUZZLE EATER"...

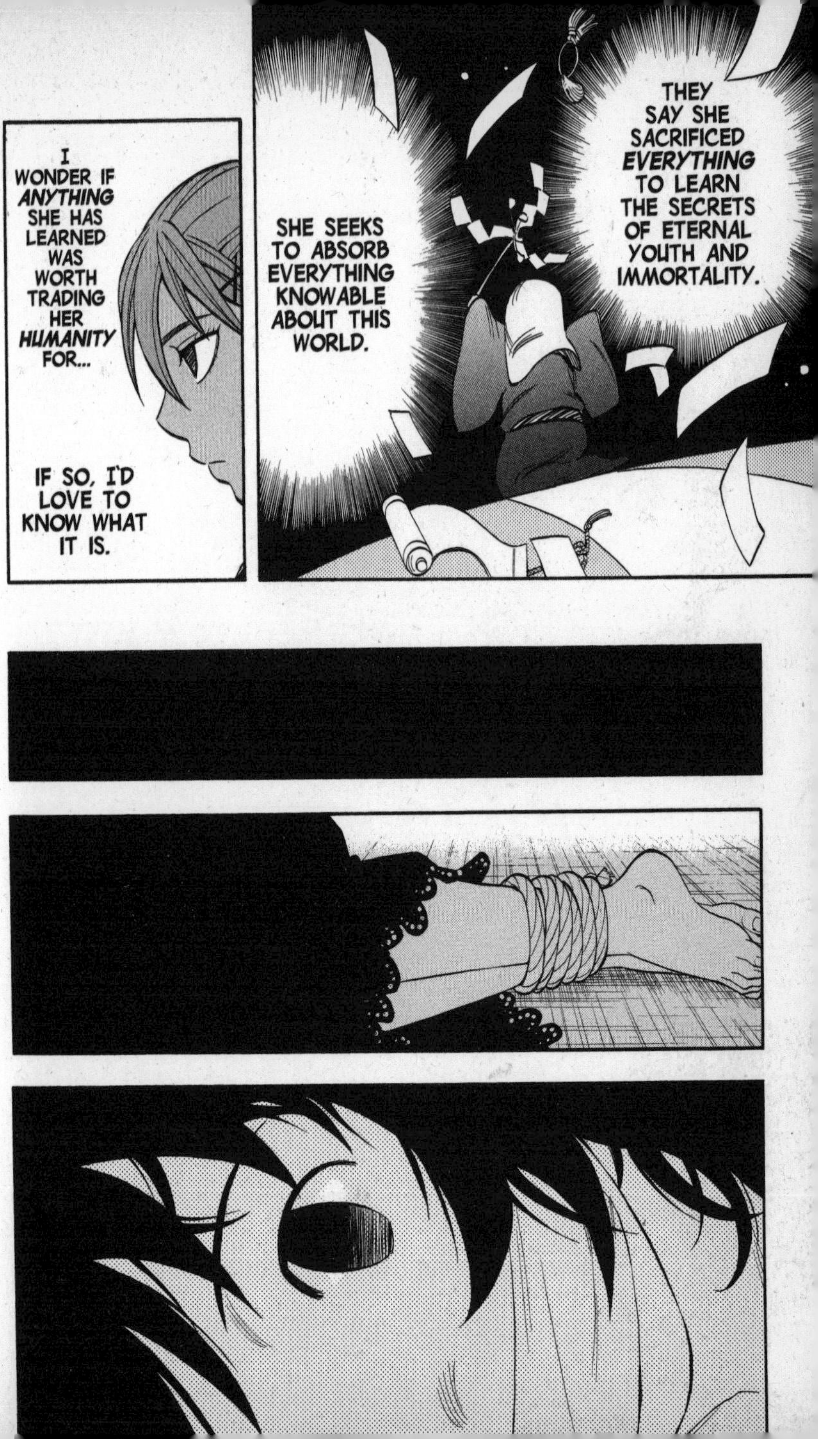
THEY SAY SHE SACRIFICED EVERYTHING TO LEARN THE SECRETS OF ETERNAL YOUTH AND IMMORTALITY.
SHE SEEKS TO ABSORB EVERYTHING KNOWABLE ABOUT THIS WORLD.
I WONDER IF ANYTHING SHE HAS LEARNED WAS WORTH TRADING HER HUMANITY FOR...
IF SO, I'D LOVE TO KNOW WHAT IT IS.

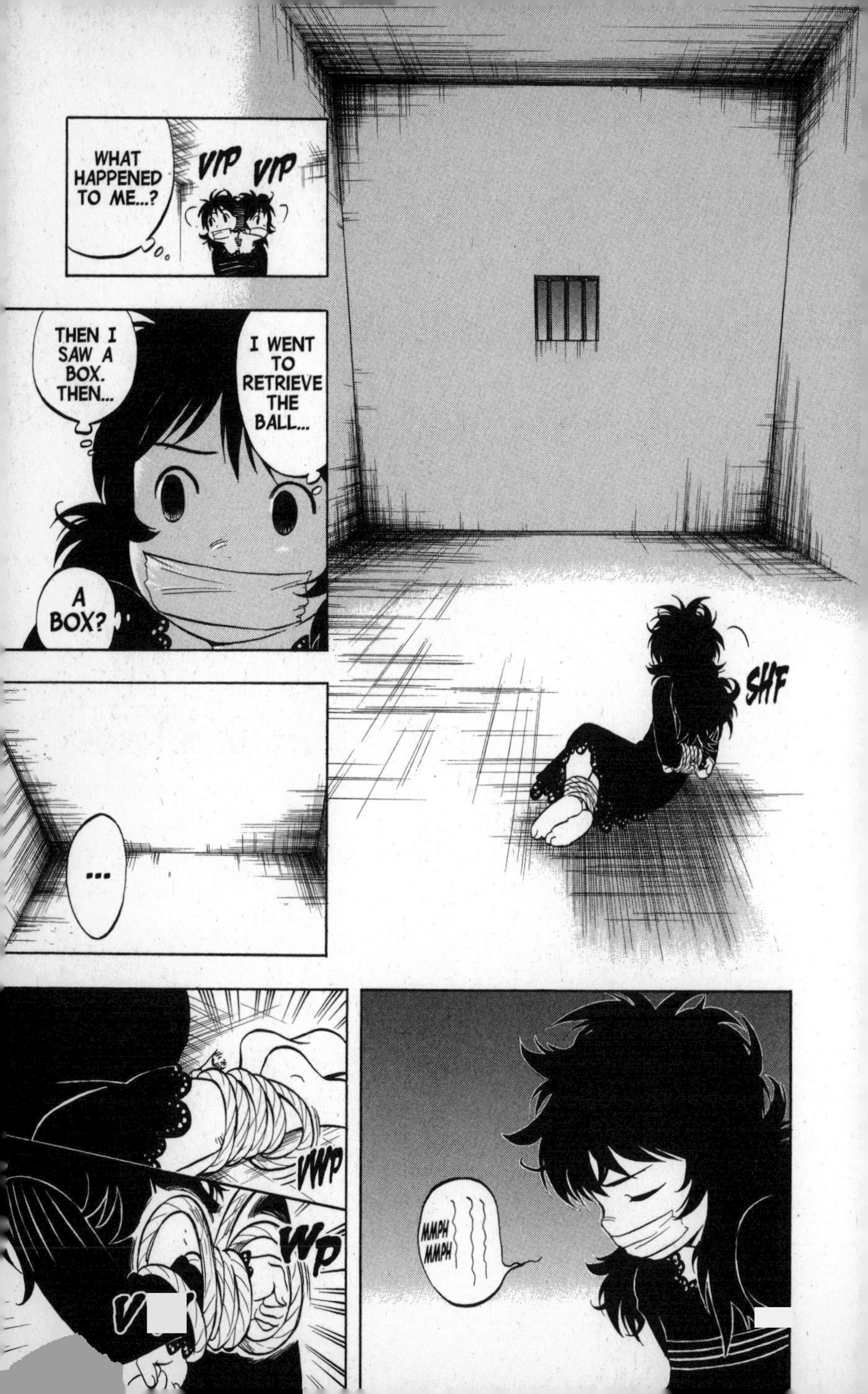
SHF
WHAT HAPPENED TO ME...?
VIP VIP
I WENT TO RETRIEVE THE BALL...
THEN I SAW A BOX. THEN...
A BOX?
...
MMPH MMPH
VWP
WP
V

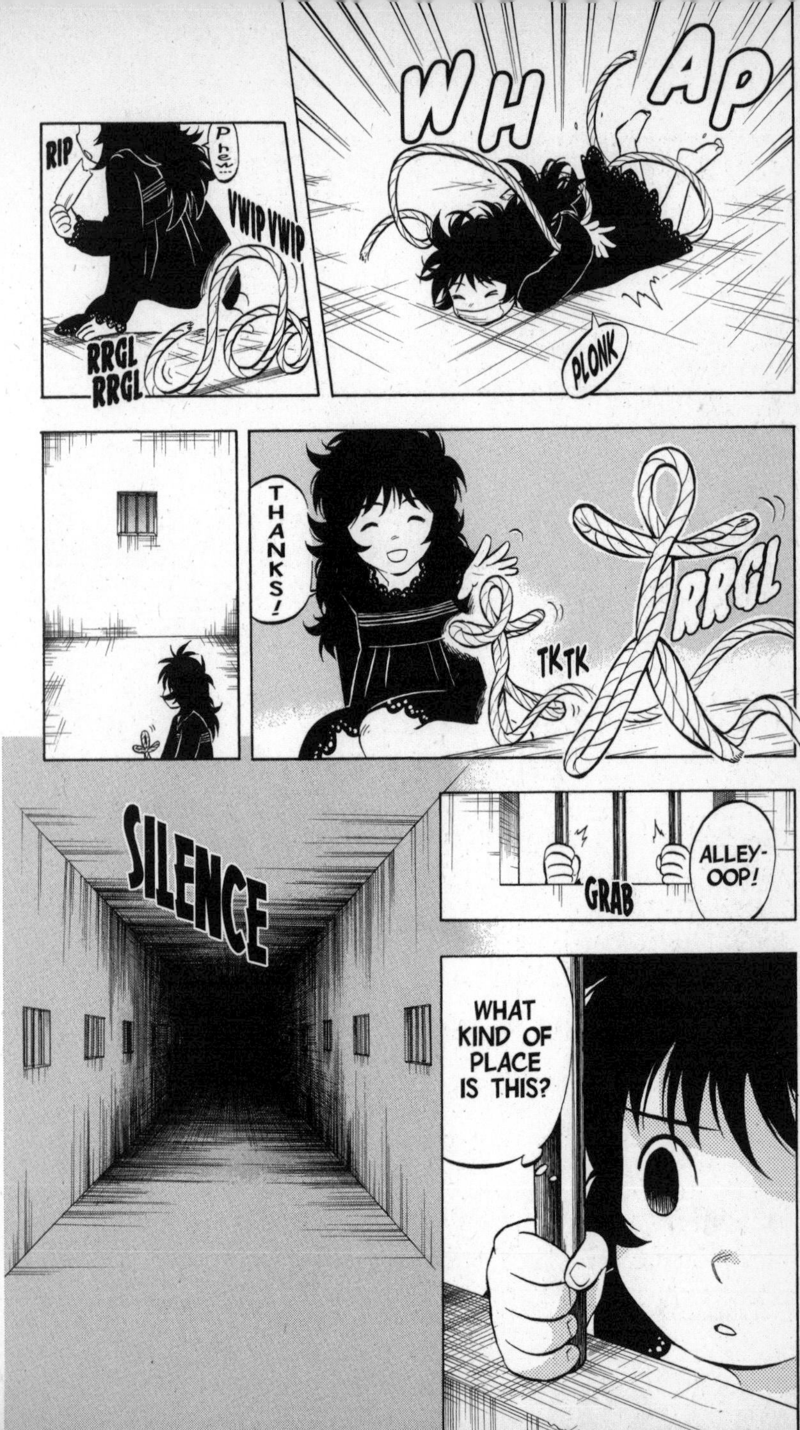
WHAP
PLONK
RIP
Phew...
VWIP VWIP
RRGL RRGL
THANKS!
RRGL
TKTK
ALLEY-OOP!
GRAB
WHAT KIND OF PLACE IS THIS?
SILENCE

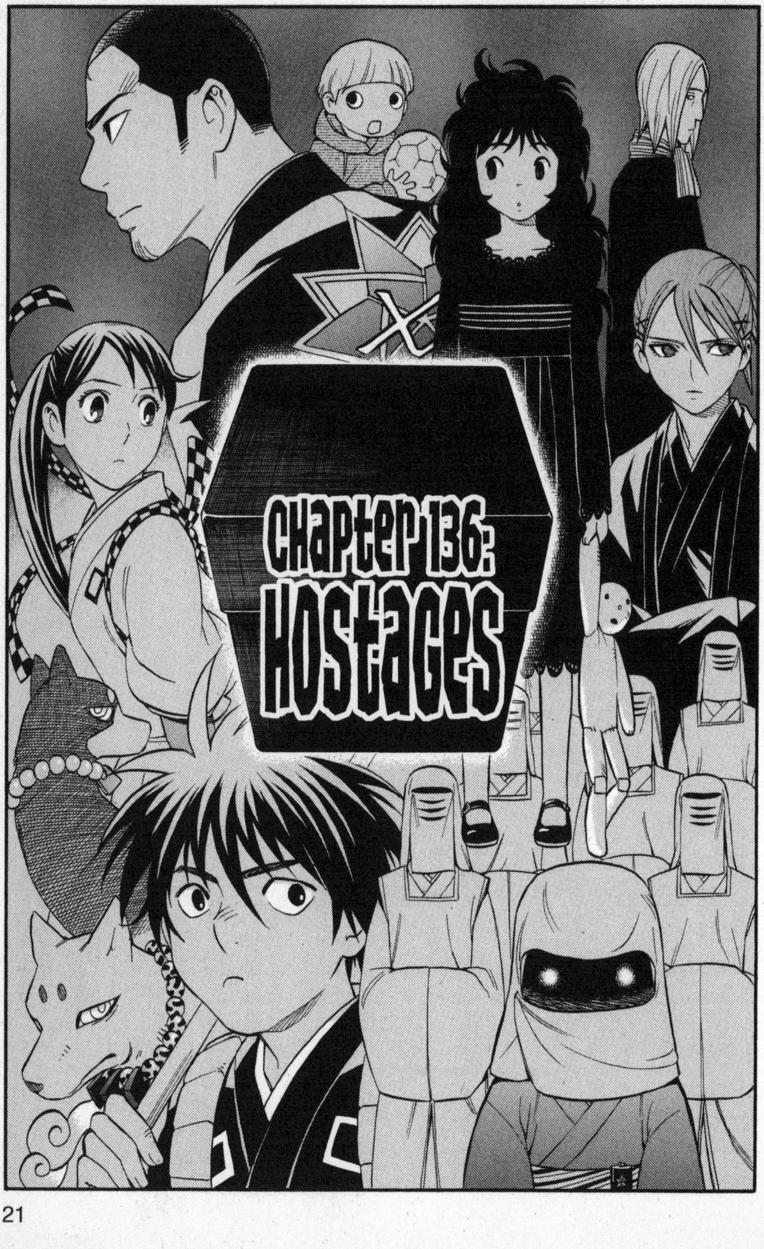
CHAPTER 136:
HOSTAGES

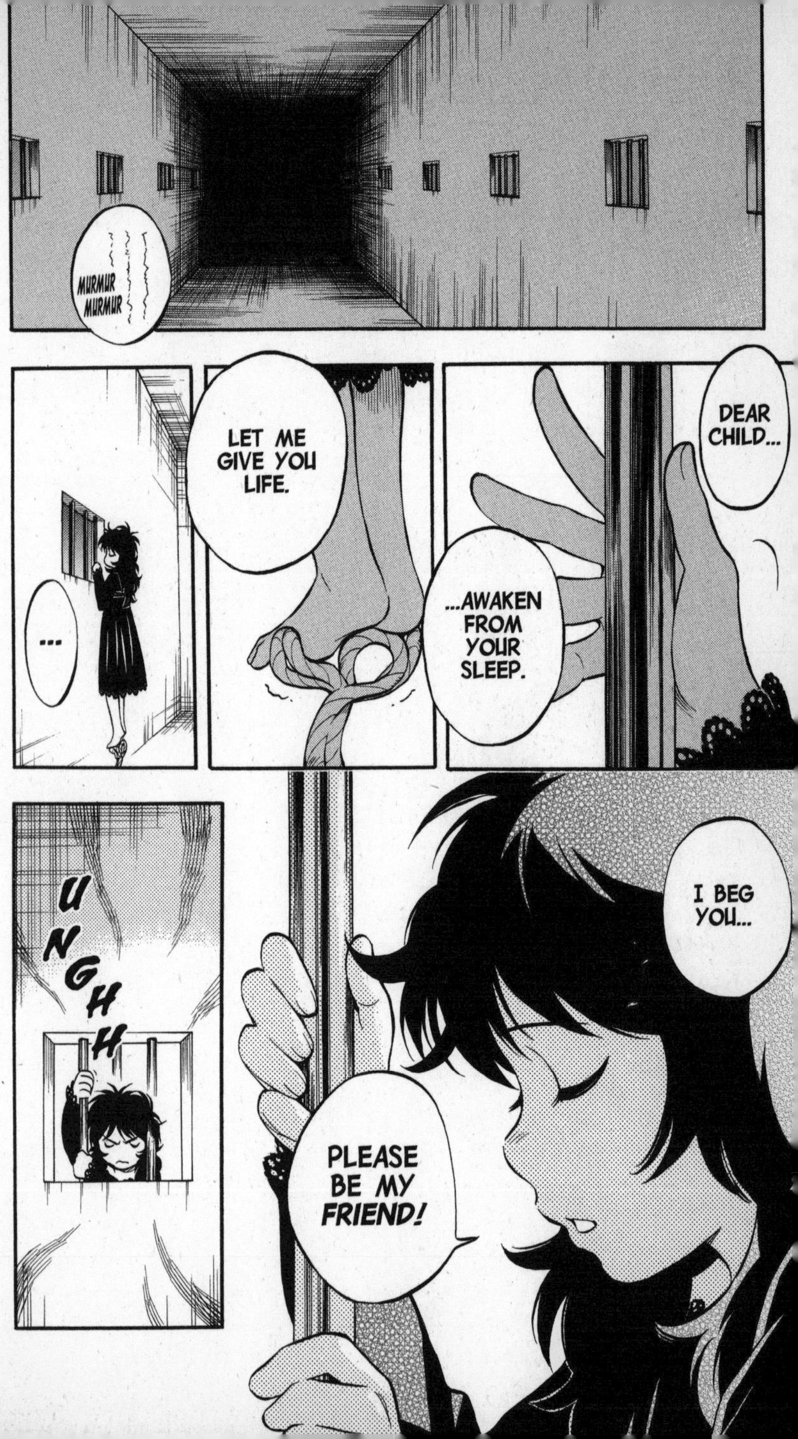
MURMUR MURMUR
DEAR CHILD...
...AWAKEN FROM YOUR SLEEP.
LET ME GIVE YOU LIFE.
...
I BEG YOU...
PLEASE BE MY FRIEND!
UNGHH

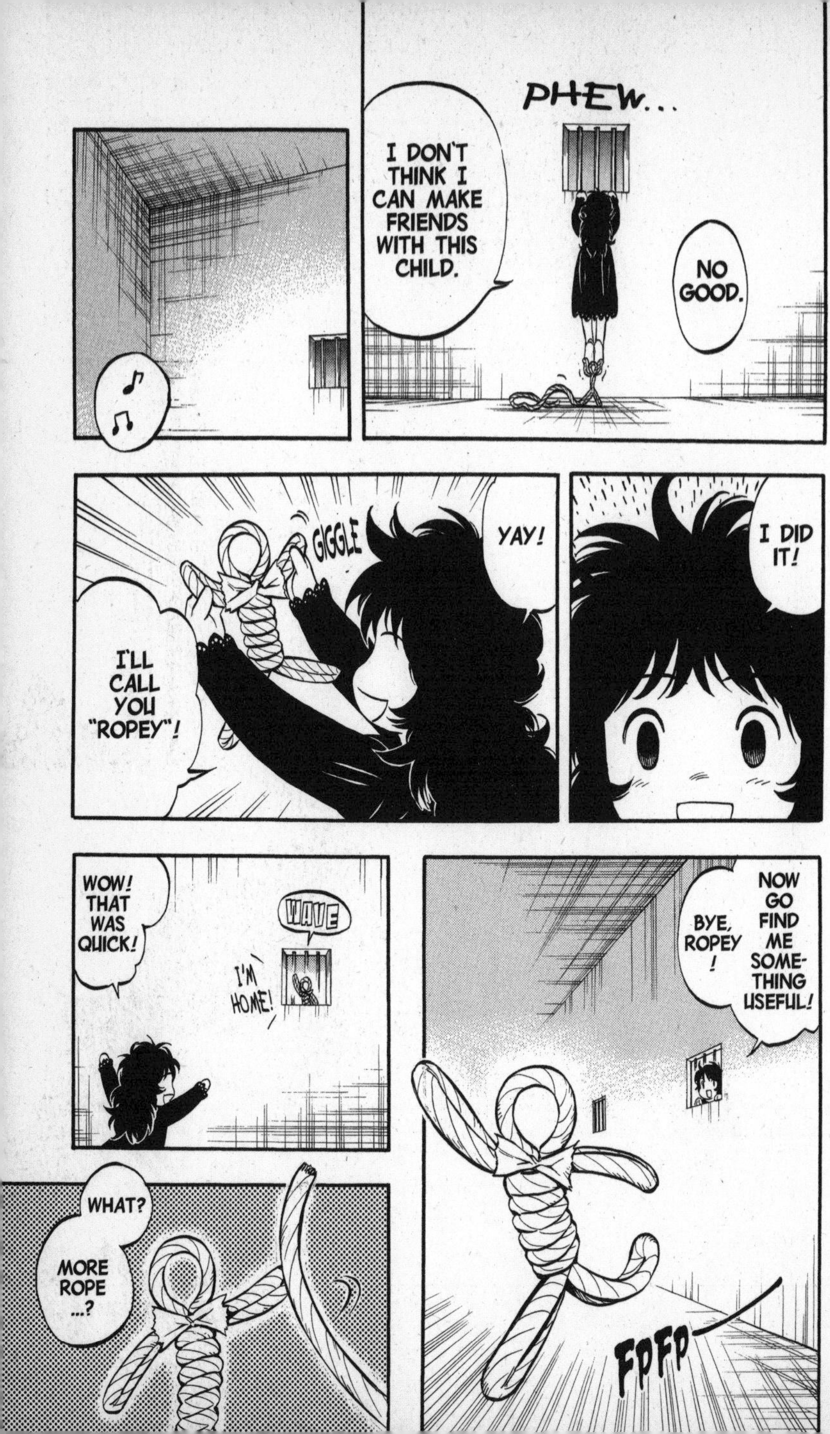
PHEW...
NO GOOD.
I DON'T THINK I CAN MAKE FRIENDS WITH THIS CHILD.
I DID IT!
YAY!
GIGGLE
I'LL CALL YOU "ROPEY"!
NOW GO FIND ME SOMETHING USEFUL!
BYE, ROPEY!
FPFP
WAVE
I'M HOME!
WOW! THAT WAS QUICK!
WHAT?
MORE ROPE ...?

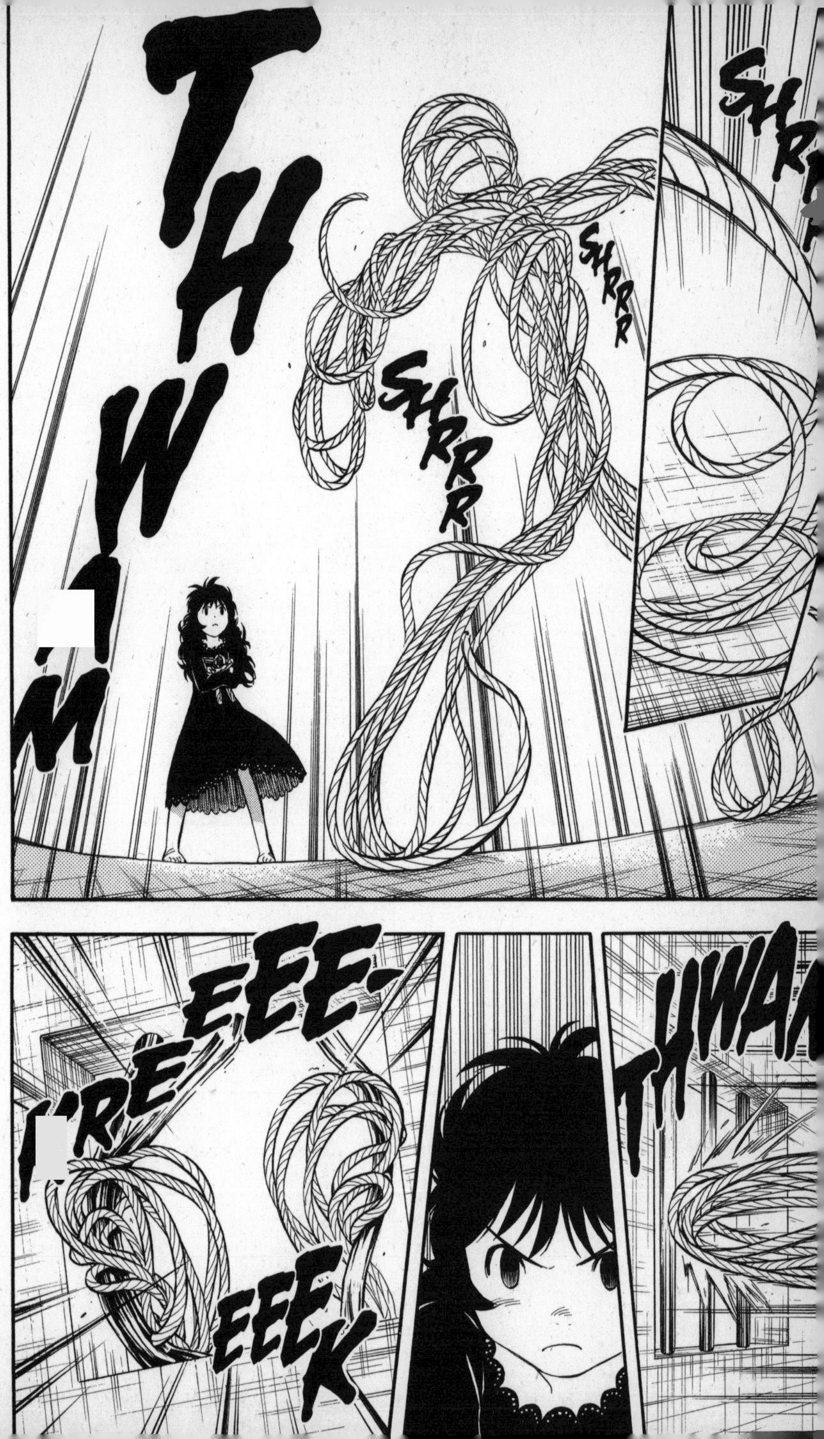
SHR
SHRRR
SHRRRR
THWUM
THWA
REEEEE-
EEEK

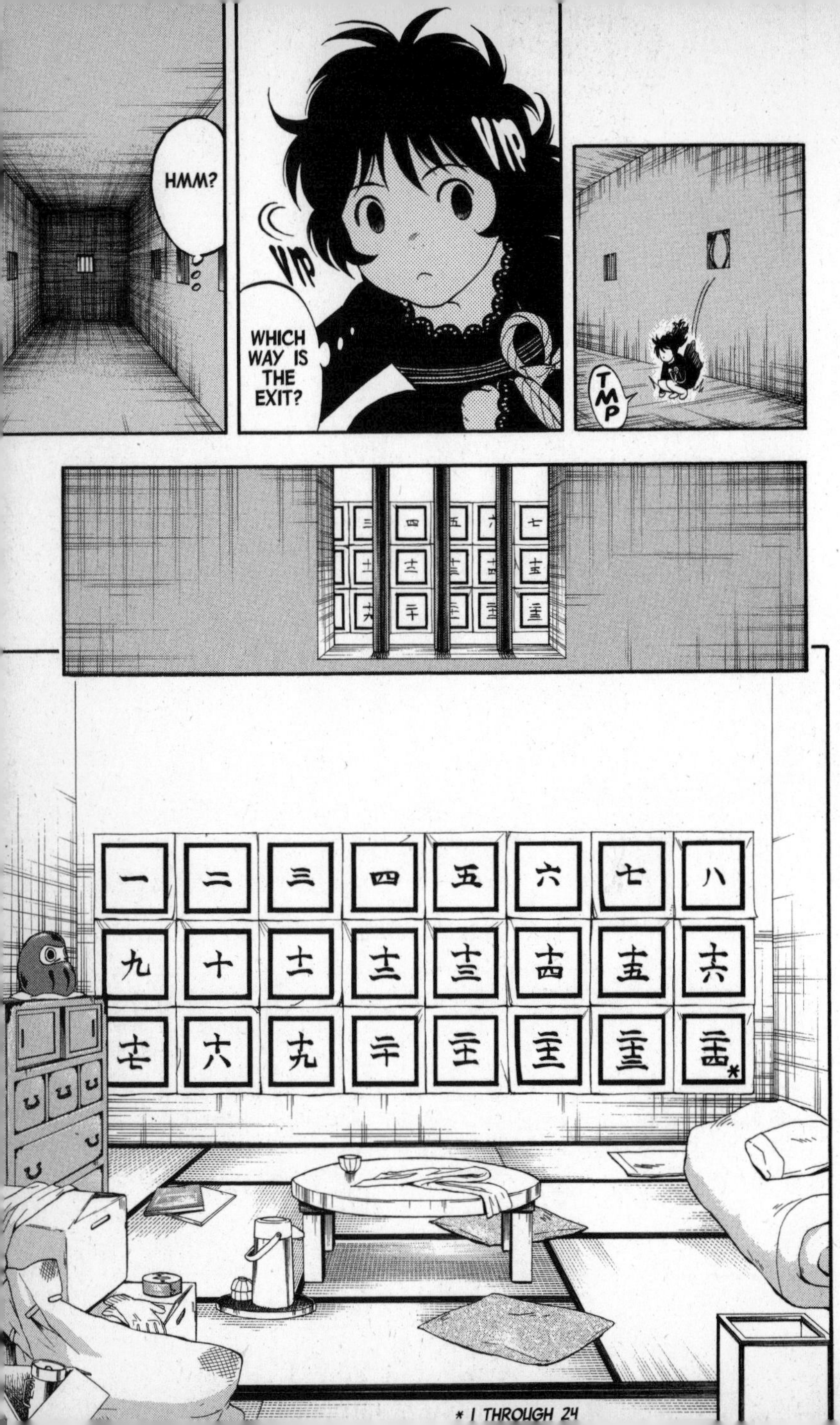
TMP
VIP
VIP
WHICH WAY IS THE EXIT?
HMM?
一 二 三 四 五 六 七 八
九 十
* I THROUGH 24

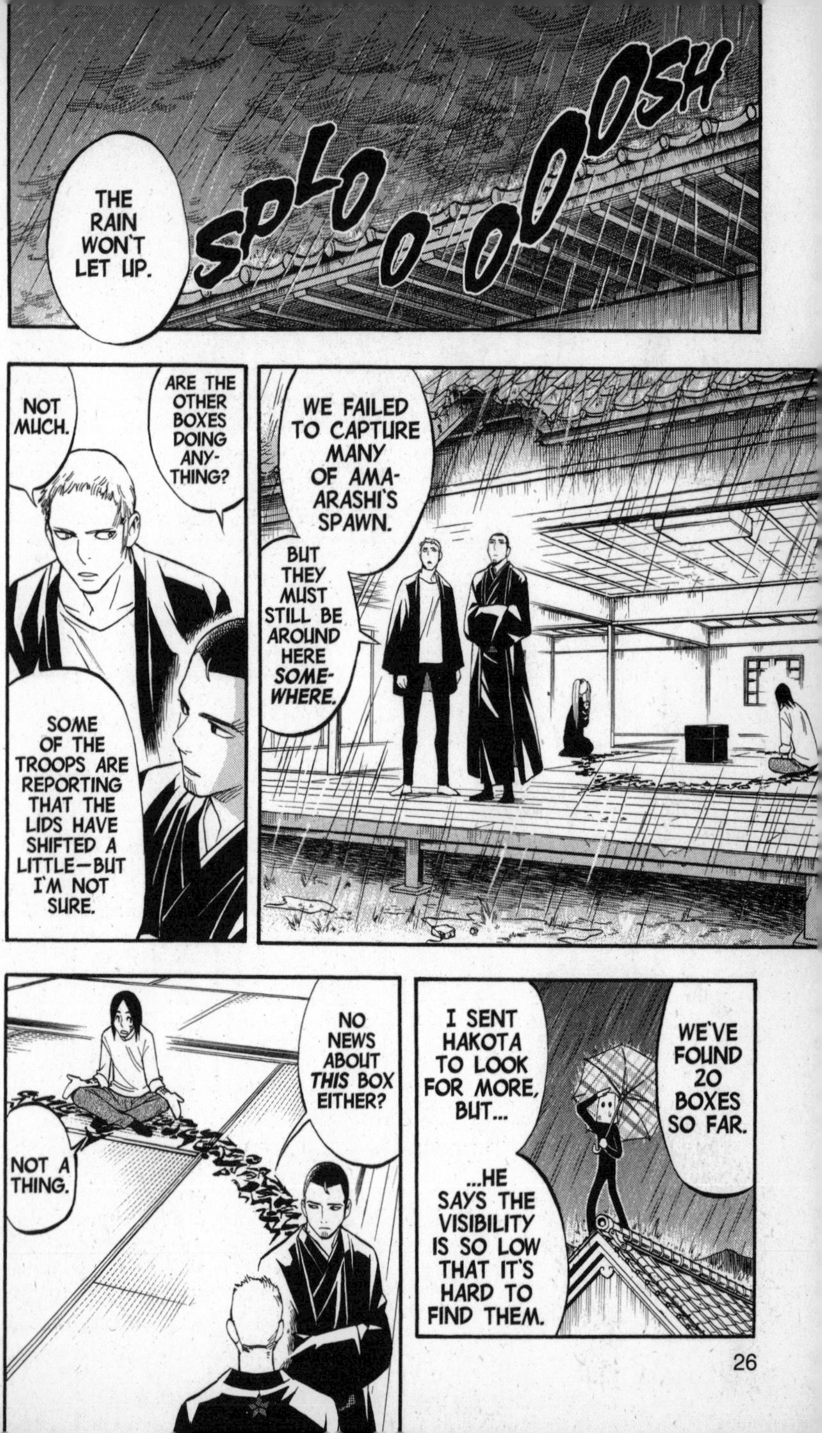
SPLOOOOOOSH
THE RAIN WON'T LET UP.
WE FAILED TO CAPTURE MANY OF AMA-ARASHI'S SPAWN.
BUT THEY MUST STILL BE AROUND HERE *SOME-WHERE.*
ARE THE OTHER BOXES DOING ANYTHING?
NOT MUCH.
SOME OF THE TROOPS ARE REPORTING THAT THE LIDS HAVE SHIFTED A LITTLE—BUT I'M NOT SURE.
WE'VE FOUND 20 BOXES SO FAR.
I SENT HAKOTA TO LOOK FOR MORE, BUT...
...HE SAYS THE VISIBILITY IS SO LOW THAT IT'S HARD TO FIND THEM.
NO NEWS ABOUT *THIS* BOX EITHER?
NOT A THING.

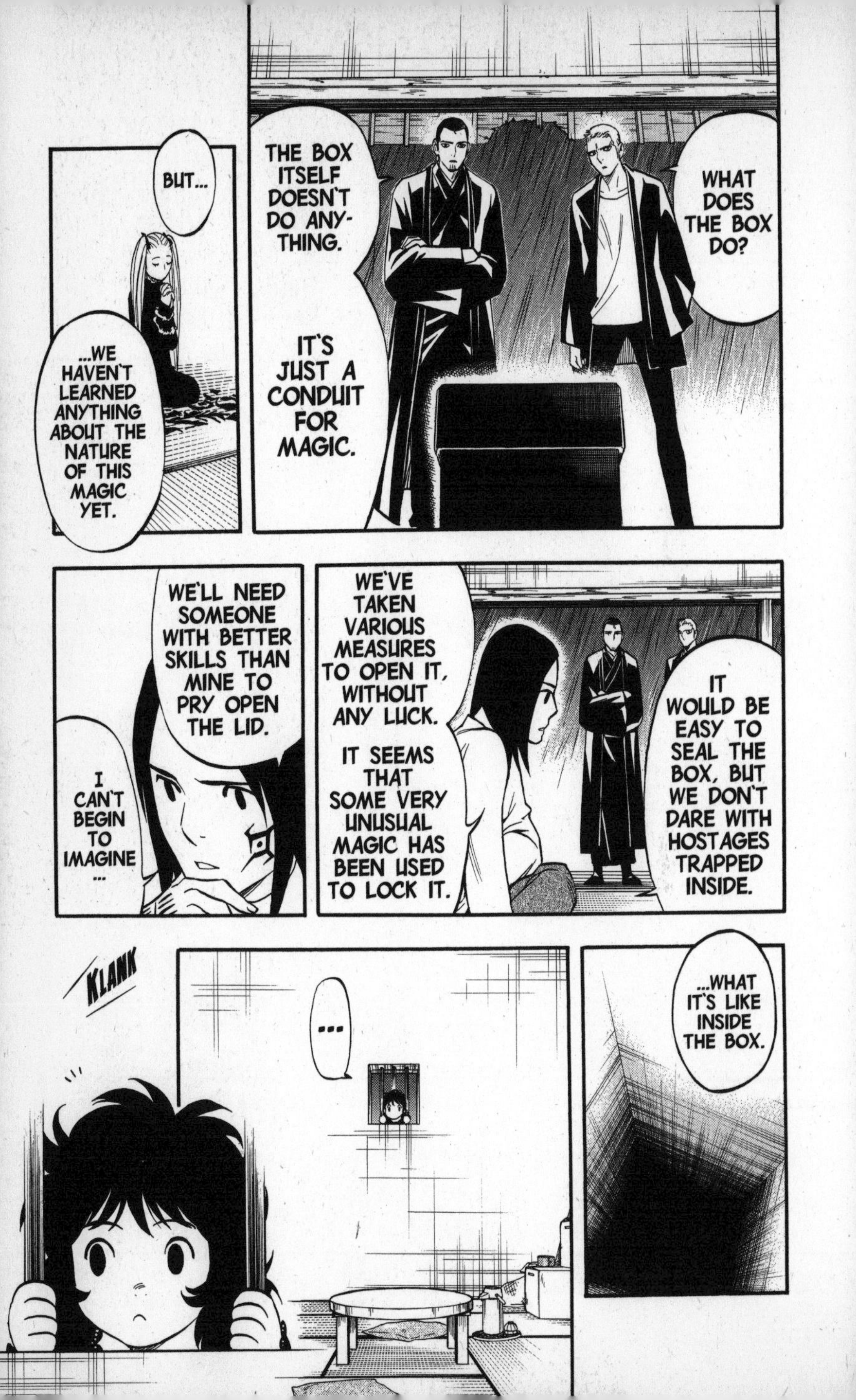
WHAT DOES THE BOX DO?
THE BOX ITSELF DOESN'T DO ANYTHING.
IT'S JUST A CONDUIT FOR MAGIC.
BUT...
...WE HAVEN'T LEARNED ANYTHING ABOUT THE NATURE OF THIS MAGIC YET.
IT WOULD BE EASY TO SEAL THE BOX, BUT WE DON'T DARE WITH HOSTAGES TRAPPED INSIDE.
WE'VE TAKEN VARIOUS MEASURES TO OPEN IT, WITHOUT ANY LUCK.
IT SEEMS THAT SOME VERY UNUSUAL MAGIC HAS BEEN USED TO LOCK IT.
WE'LL NEED SOMEONE WITH BETTER SKILLS THAN MINE TO PRY OPEN THE LID.
I CAN'T BEGIN TO IMAGINE...
...WHAT IT'S LIKE INSIDE THE BOX.
...
KLANK

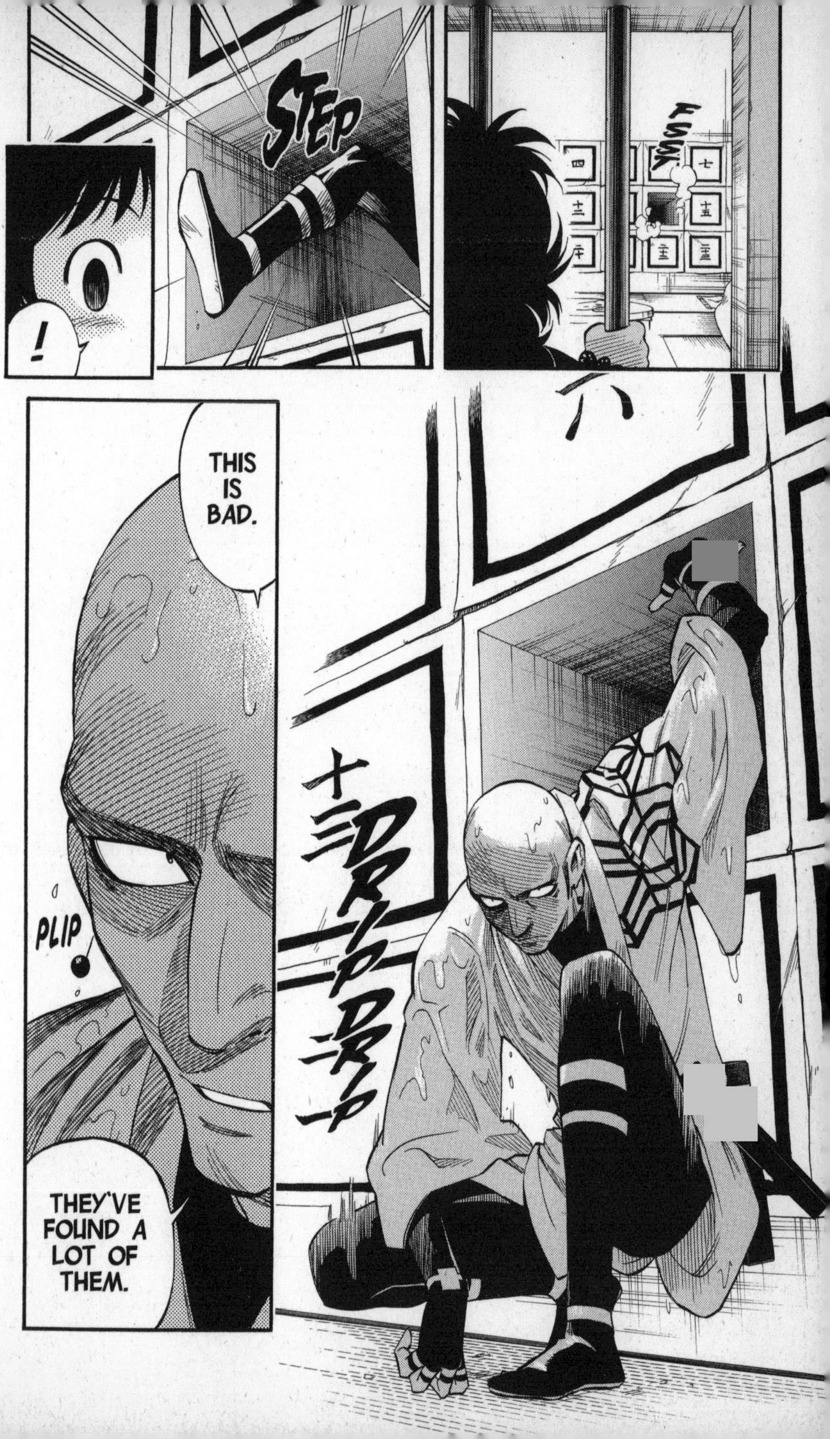
FSSSK
STEP
!
八
DRIP DRIP
THIS IS BAD.
PLIP
THEY'VE FOUND A LOT OF THEM.

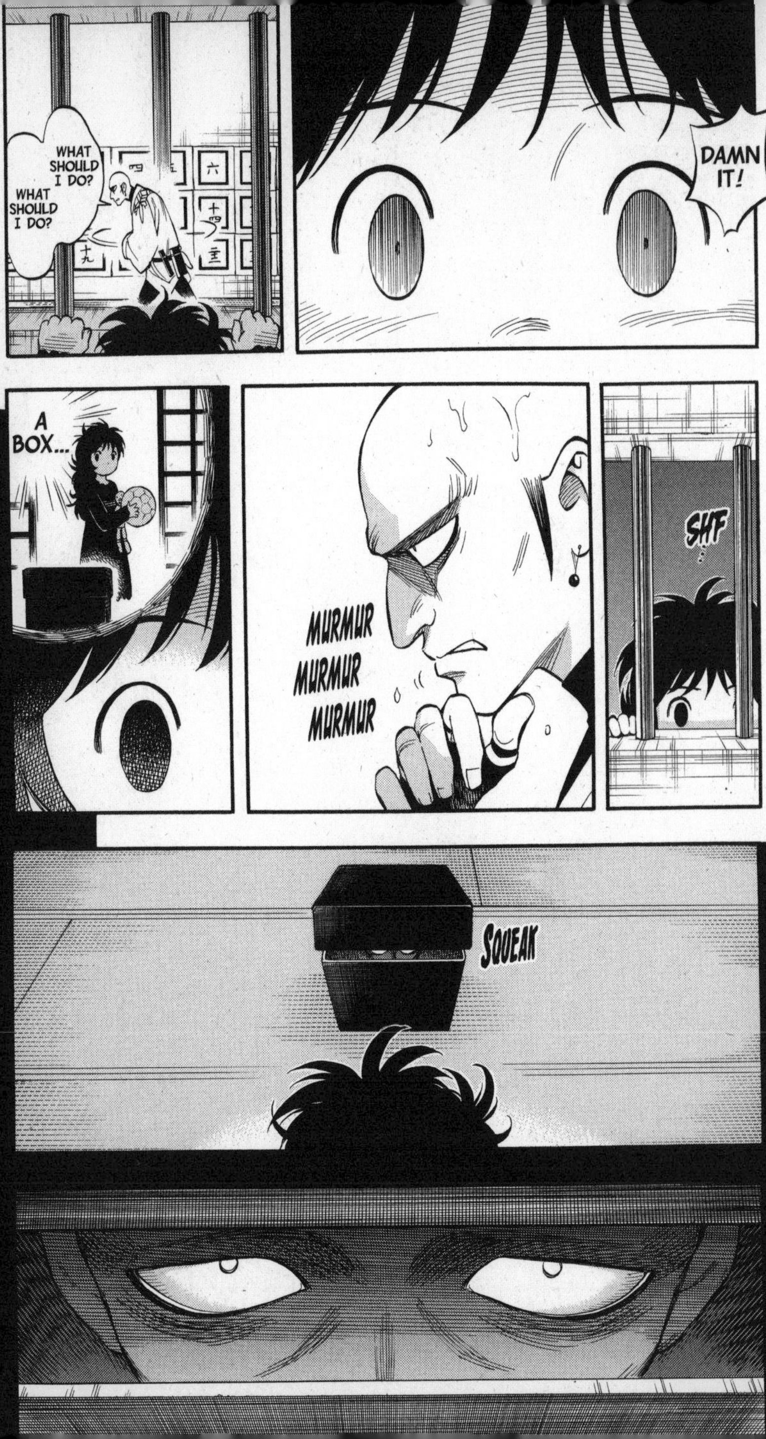
DAMN IT!
WHAT SHOULD I DO? WHAT SHOULD I DO?
SHF
MURMUR MURMUR MURMUR
A BOX...
SQUEAK

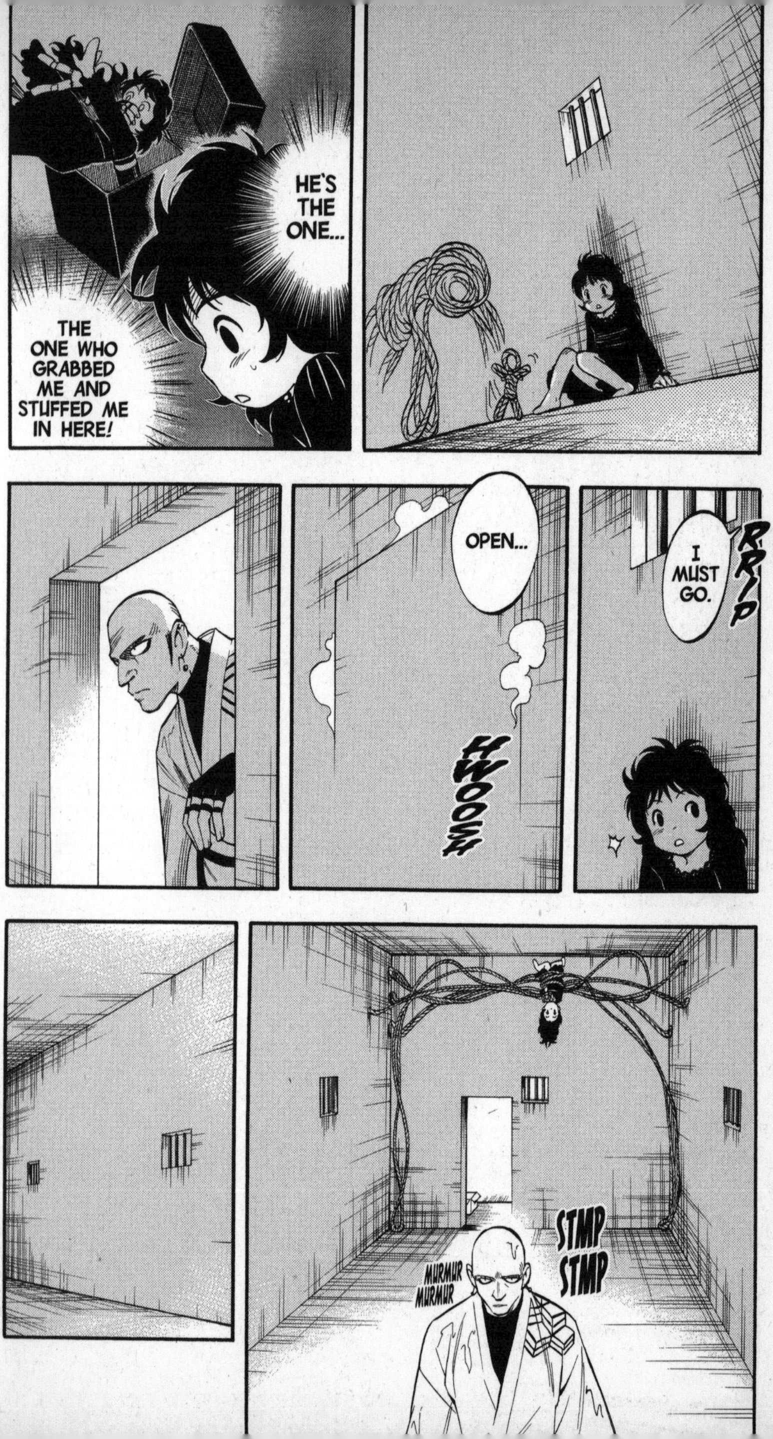
HE'S THE ONE...
THE ONE WHO GRABBED ME AND STUFFED ME IN HERE!
I MUST GO.
RRIP
OPEN...
HWOOSH
STMP STMP
MURMUR MURMUR

SHA

AAA

OO OOO

OO

OO

WH

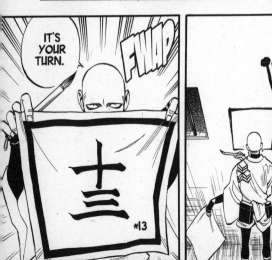

IT'S YOUR TURN.

FWAP

十三

*13

TEAR

SHF

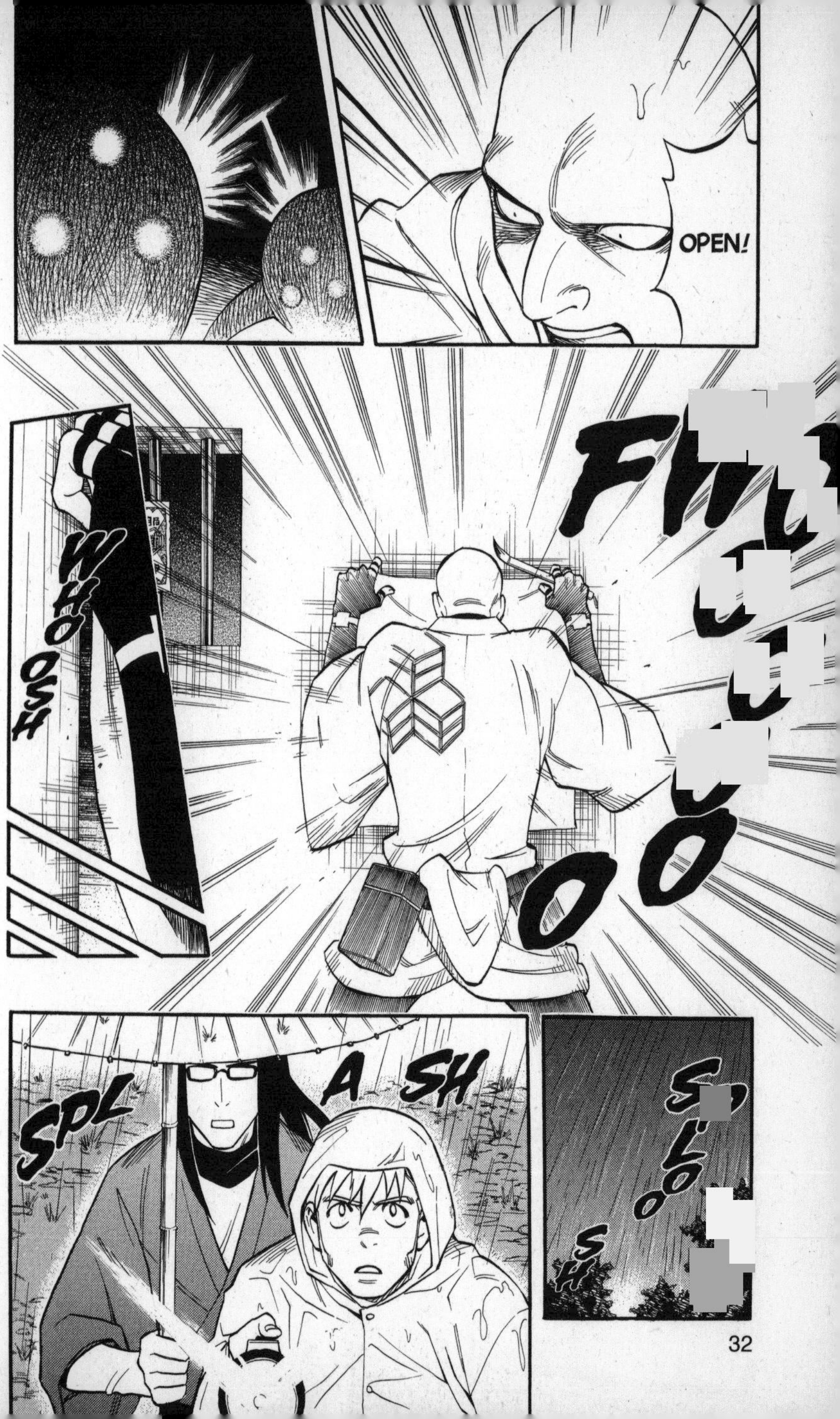
OPEN!
FW
OO
WHOOSH
SPL A SH

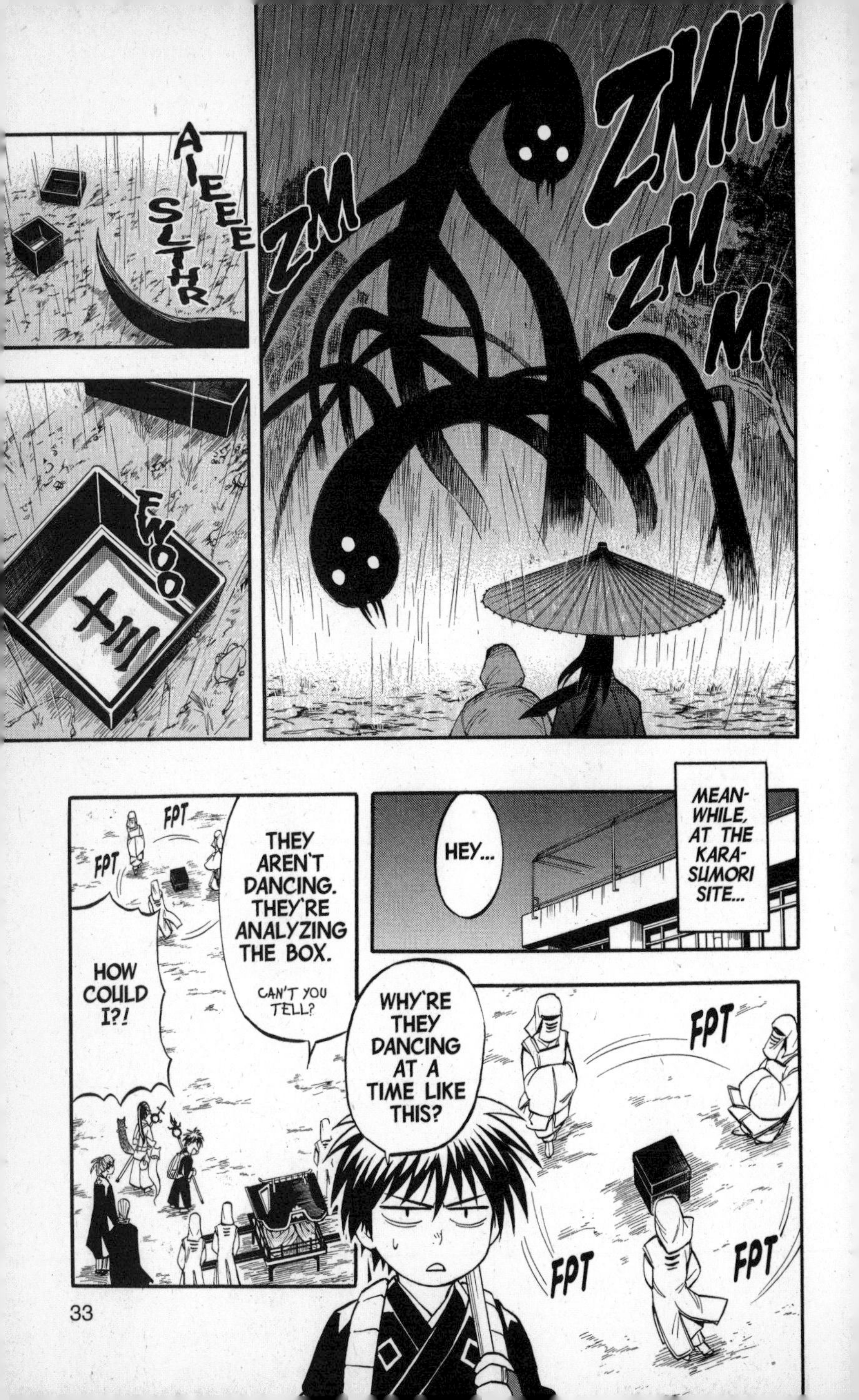
ZMMM
ZM
M
ZM
AIEEE
SLTHR
EWOO
MEAN-WHILE, AT THE KARA-SUMORI SITE...
HEY...
WHY'RE THEY DANCING AT A TIME LIKE THIS?
FPT
FPT
FPT
FPT
FPT
THEY AREN'T DANCING. THEY'RE ANALYZING THE BOX.
CAN'T YOU TELL?
HOW COULD I?!

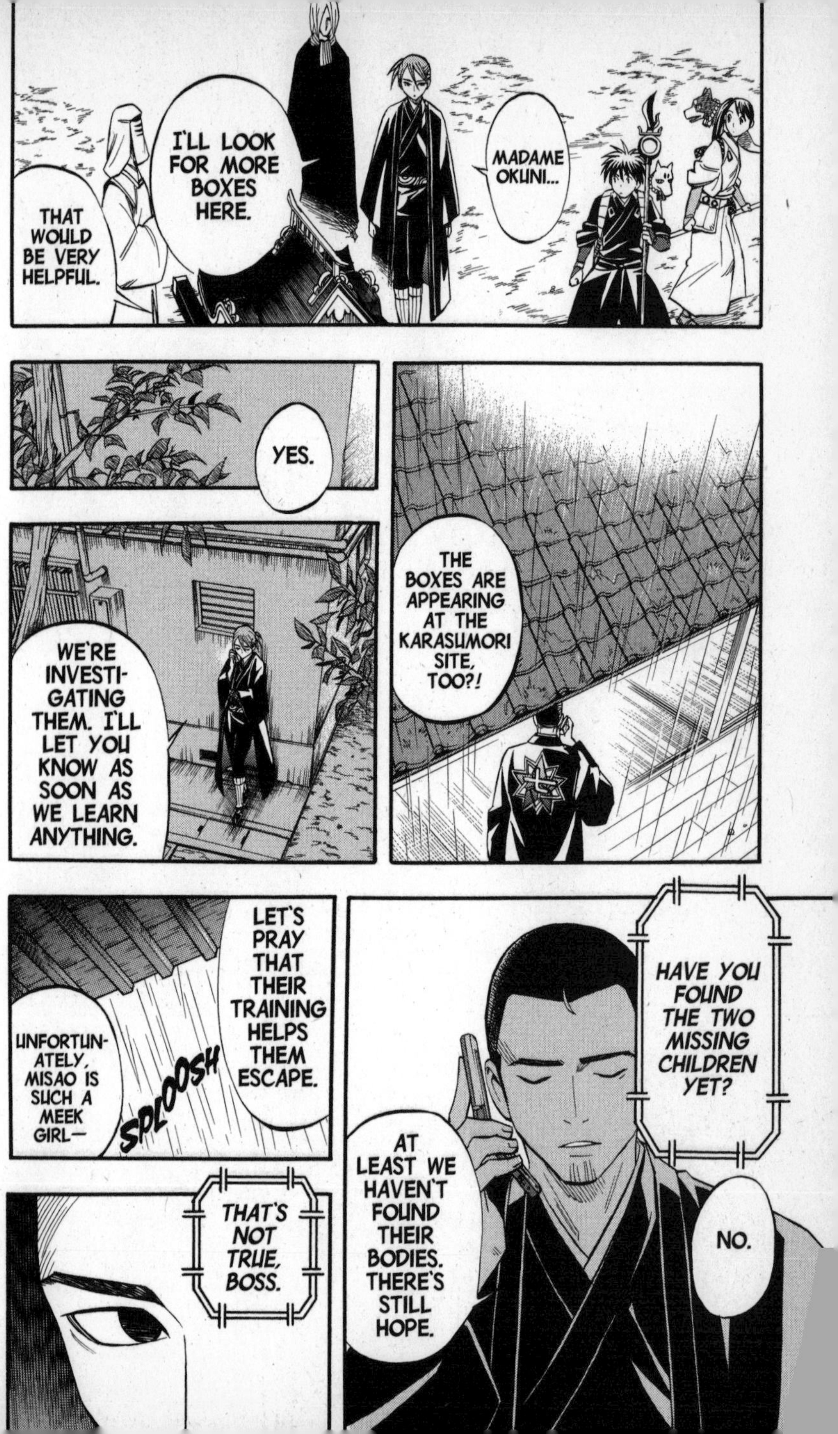
MADAME OKUNI...
I'LL LOOK FOR MORE BOXES HERE.
THAT WOULD BE VERY HELPFUL.
THE BOXES ARE APPEARING AT THE KARASUMORI SITE, TOO?!
YES.
WE'RE INVESTI-GATING THEM. I'LL LET YOU KNOW AS SOON AS WE LEARN ANYTHING.
HAVE YOU FOUND THE TWO MISSING CHILDREN YET?
NO.
AT LEAST WE HAVEN'T FOUND THEIR BODIES. THERE'S STILL HOPE.
LET'S PRAY THAT THEIR TRAINING HELPS THEM ESCAPE.
SPLOOSH
UNFORTUN-ATELY, MISAO IS SUCH A MEEK GIRL—
THAT'S NOT TRUE, BOSS.

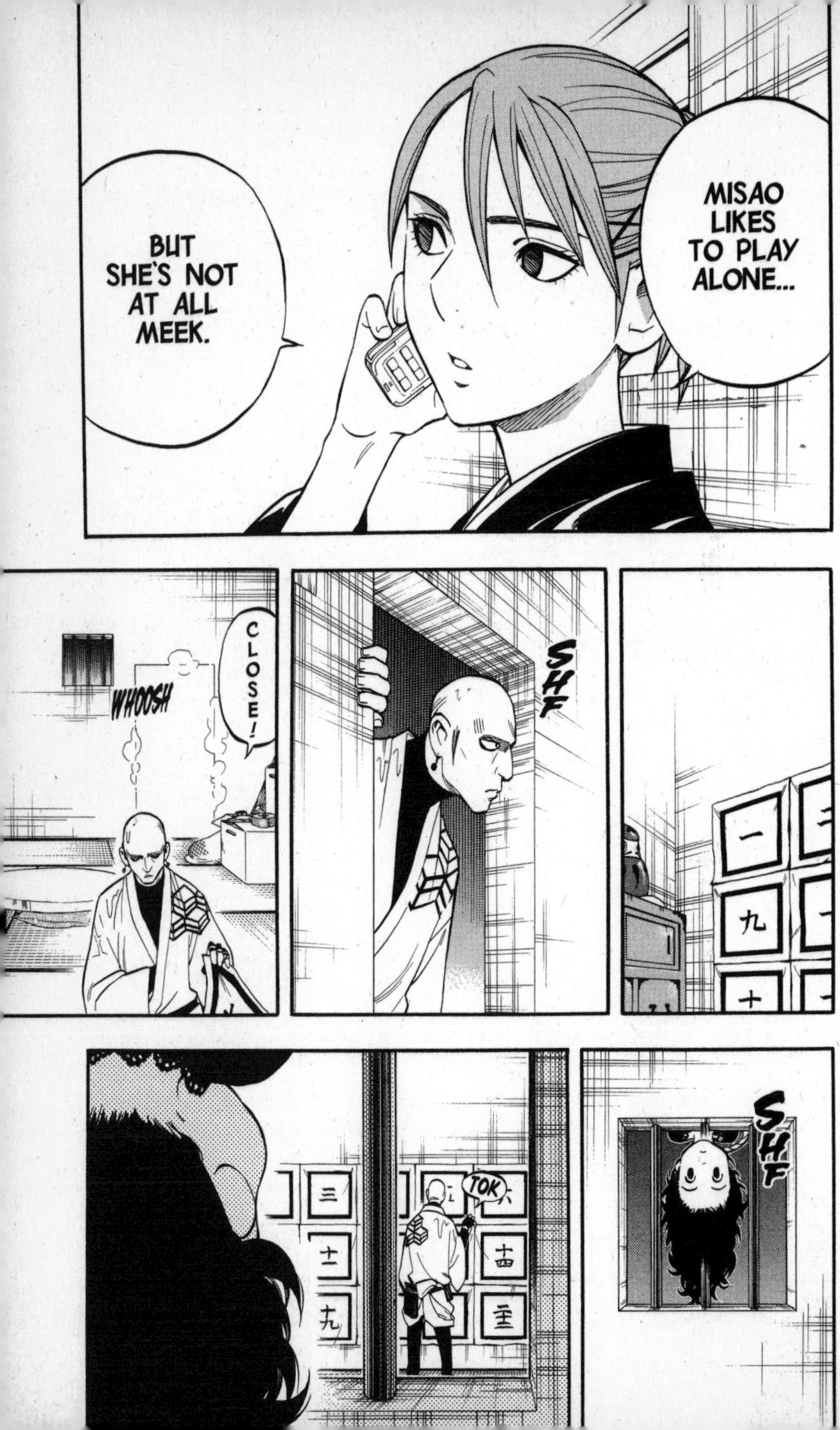
MISAO LIKES TO PLAY ALONE...
BUT SHE'S NOT AT ALL MEEK.
SHF
CLOSE!
WHOOSH
SHF
TOK

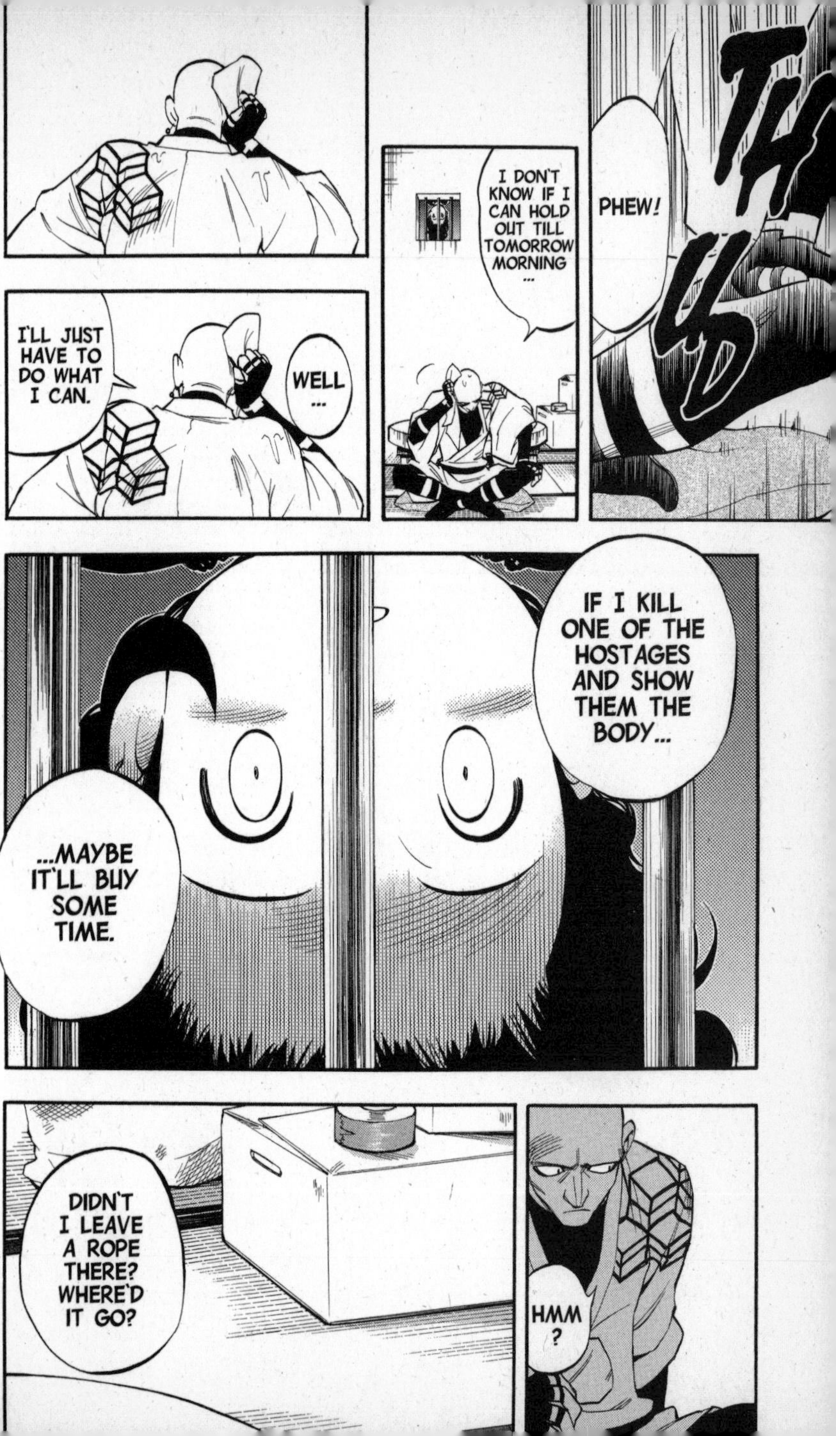
THUD
PHEW!
I DON'T KNOW IF I CAN HOLD OUT TILL TOMORROW MORNING ...
WELL ...
I'LL JUST HAVE TO DO WHAT I CAN.
IF I KILL ONE OF THE HOSTAGES AND SHOW THEM THE BODY...
...MAYBE IT'LL BUY SOME TIME.
HMM ?
DIDN'T I LEAVE A ROPE THERE? WHERE'D IT GO?

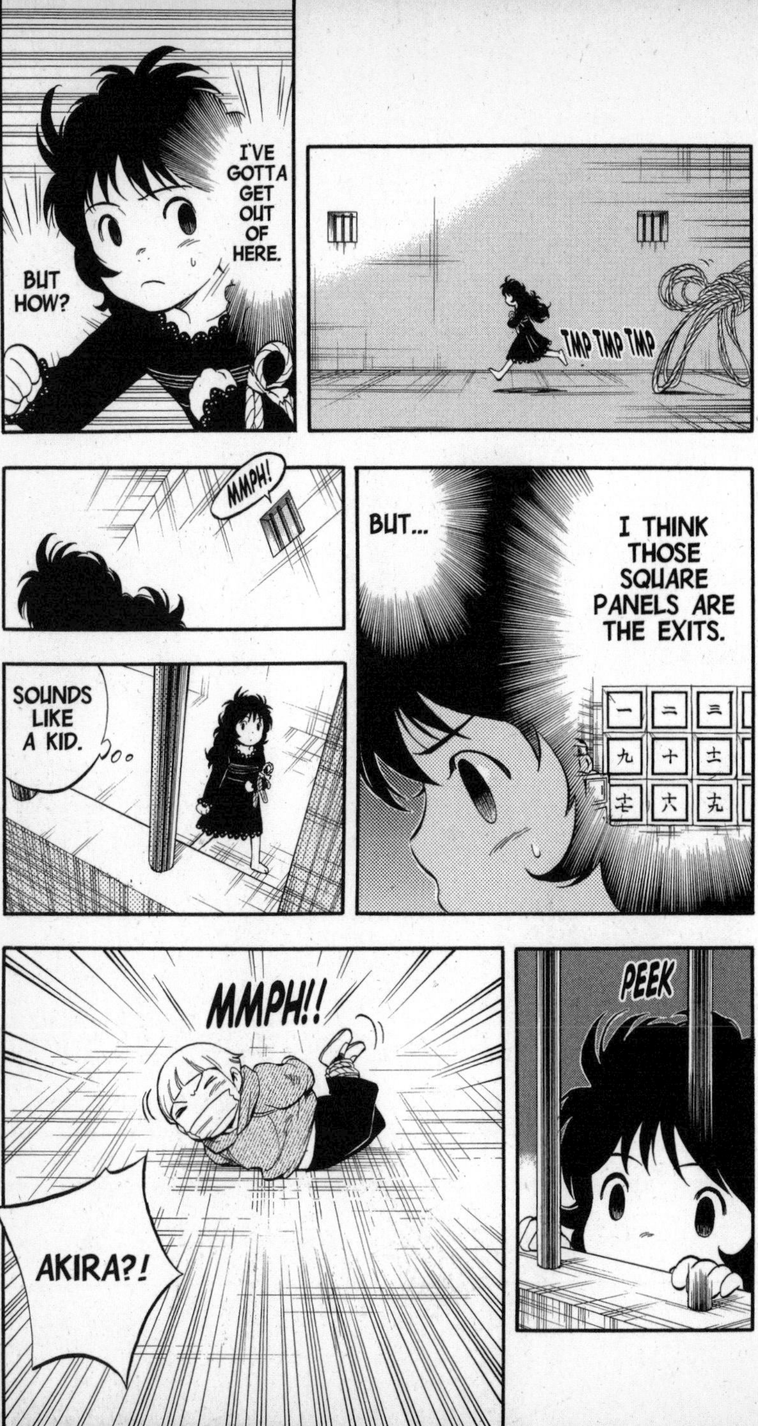
TMP TMP TMP
I'VE GOTTA GET OUT OF HERE.
BUT HOW?
BUT...
I THINK THOSE SQUARE PANELS ARE THE EXITS.
MMPH!
SOUNDS LIKE A KID.
PEEK
MMPH!!
AKIRA?!

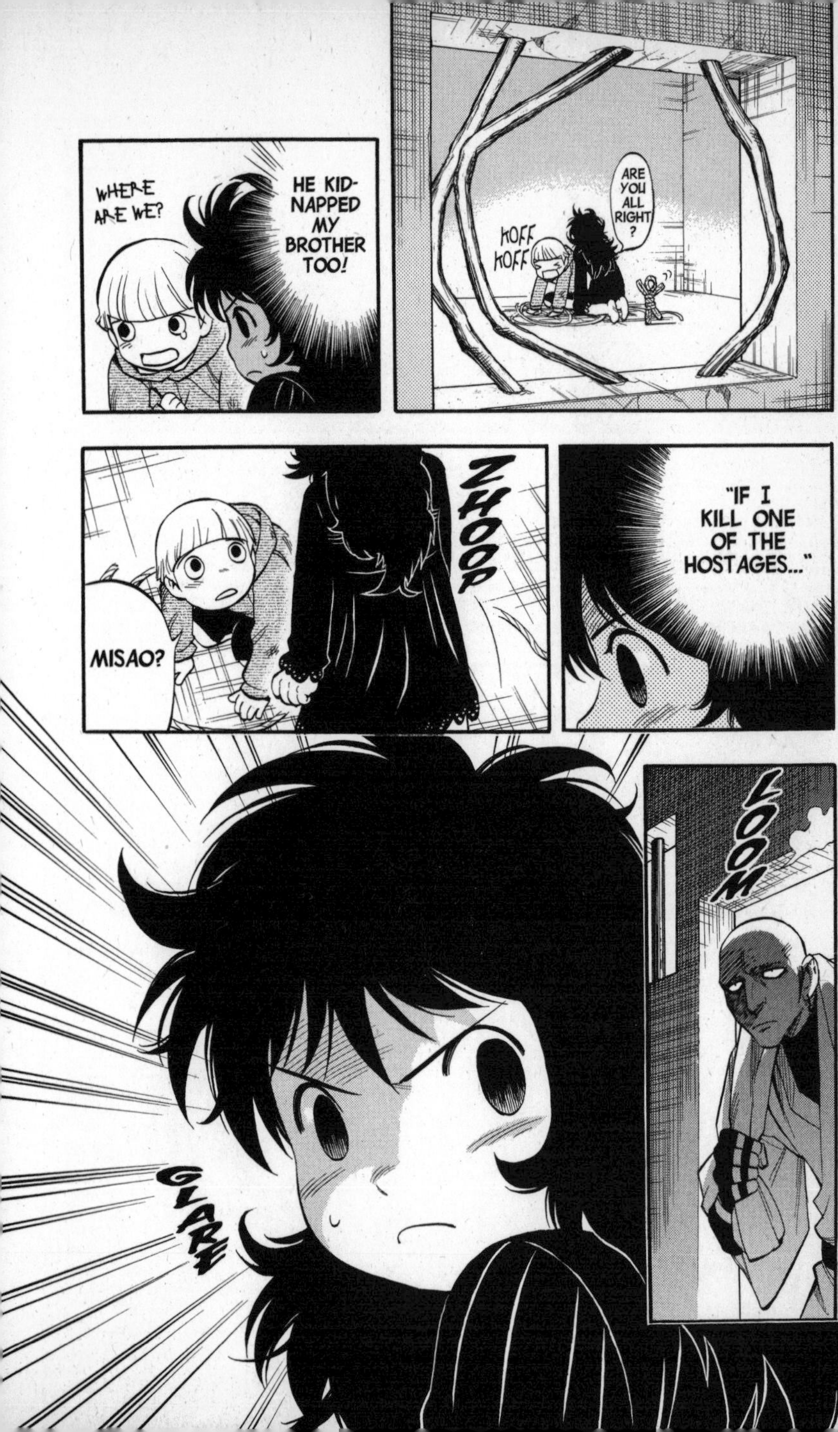
ARE YOU ALL RIGHT?
KOFF KOFF
HE KID-NAPPED MY BROTHER TOO!
WHERE ARE WE?
"IF I KILL ONE OF THE HOSTAGES..."
ZHOOP
MISAO?
LOOOM
GLARE

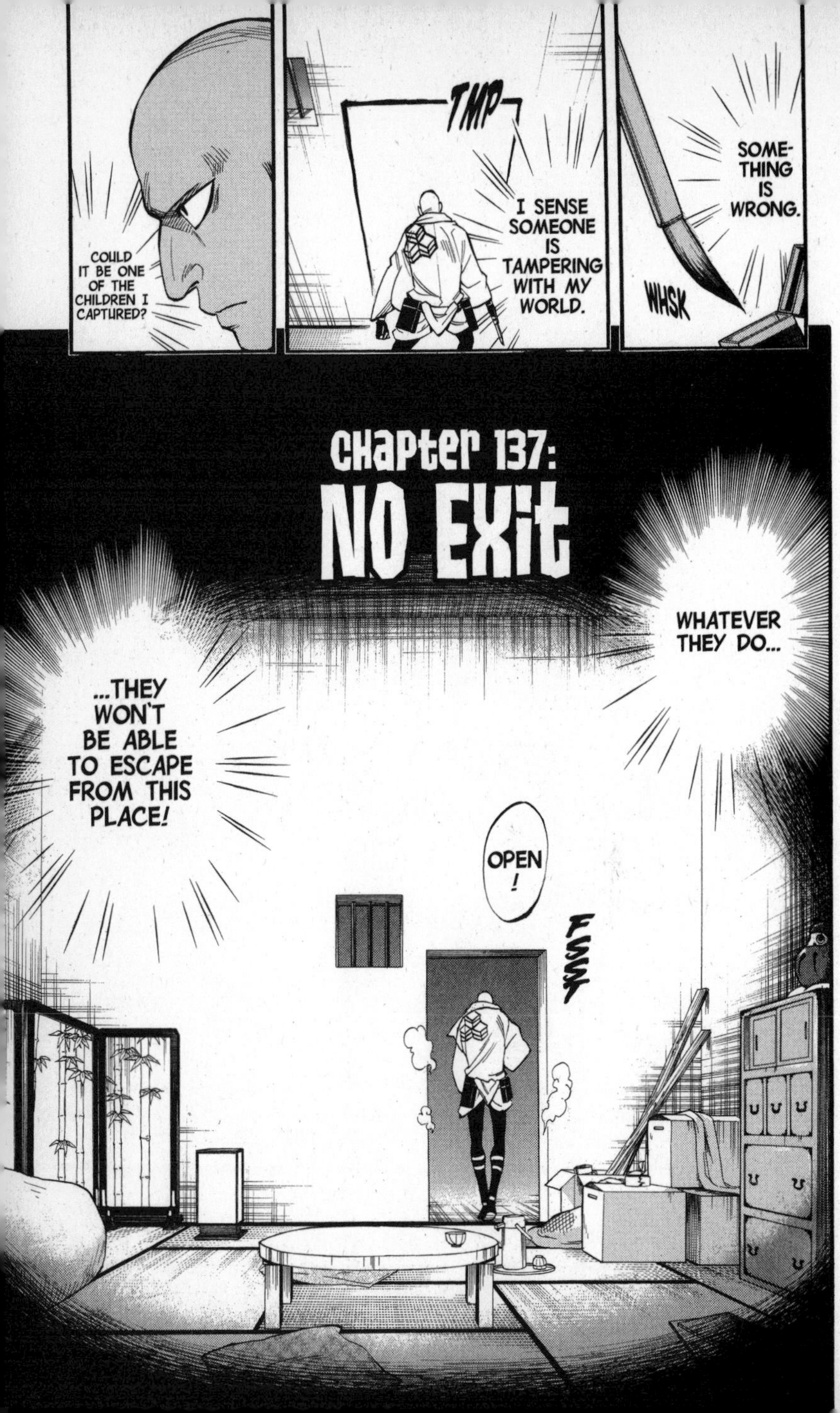
SOMETHING IS WRONG.
WHSK
TMP
I SENSE SOMEONE IS TAMPERING WITH MY WORLD.
COULD IT BE ONE OF THE CHILDREN I CAPTURED?
Chapter 137:
NO EXit
WHATEVER THEY DO...
...THEY WON'T BE ABLE TO ESCAPE FROM THIS PLACE!
OPEN!
FSSS

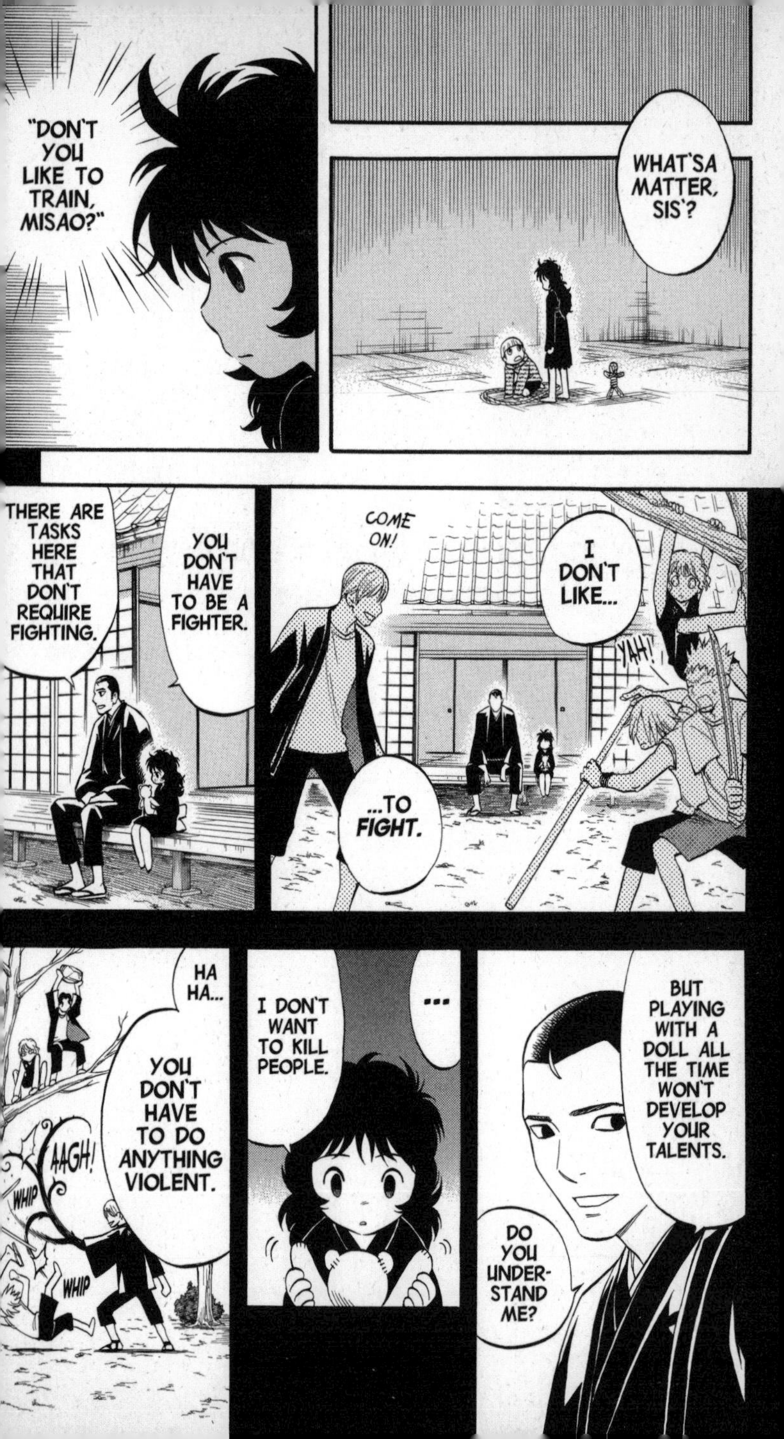
WHAT'SA MATTER, SIS'?
"DON'T YOU LIKE TO TRAIN, MISAO?"
I DON'T LIKE...
YAH!
COME ON!
...TO FIGHT.
YOU DON'T HAVE TO BE A FIGHTER.
THERE ARE TASKS HERE THAT DON'T REQUIRE FIGHTING.
BUT PLAYING WITH A DOLL ALL THE TIME WON'T DEVELOP YOUR TALENTS.
DO YOU UNDERSTAND ME?
...
I DON'T WANT TO KILL PEOPLE.
HA HA...
YOU DON'T HAVE TO DO ANYTHING VIOLENT.
AAGH!
WHIP
WHIP

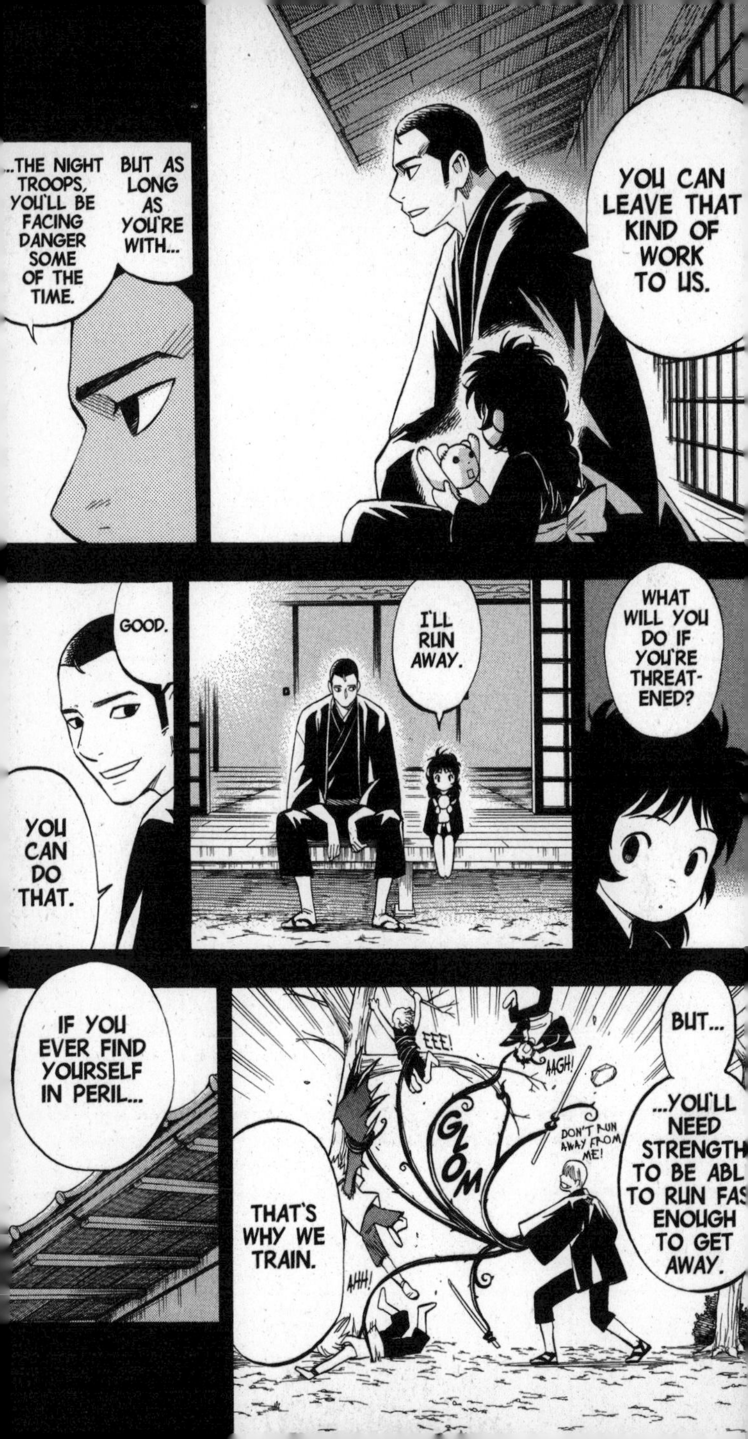
YOU CAN LEAVE THAT KIND OF WORK TO US.
BUT AS LONG AS YOU'RE WITH...
...THE NIGHT TROOPS, YOU'LL BE FACING DANGER SOME OF THE TIME.
WHAT WILL YOU DO IF YOU'RE THREAT-ENED?
I'LL RUN AWAY.
GOOD.
YOU CAN DO THAT.
BUT...
...YOU'LL NEED STRENGTH TO BE ABL TO RUN FAS ENOUGH TO GET AWAY.
EEE!
AAGH!
GLOM
DON'T RUN AWAY FROM ME!
AHH!
THAT'S WHY WE TRAIN.
IF YOU EVER FIND YOURSELF IN PERIL...

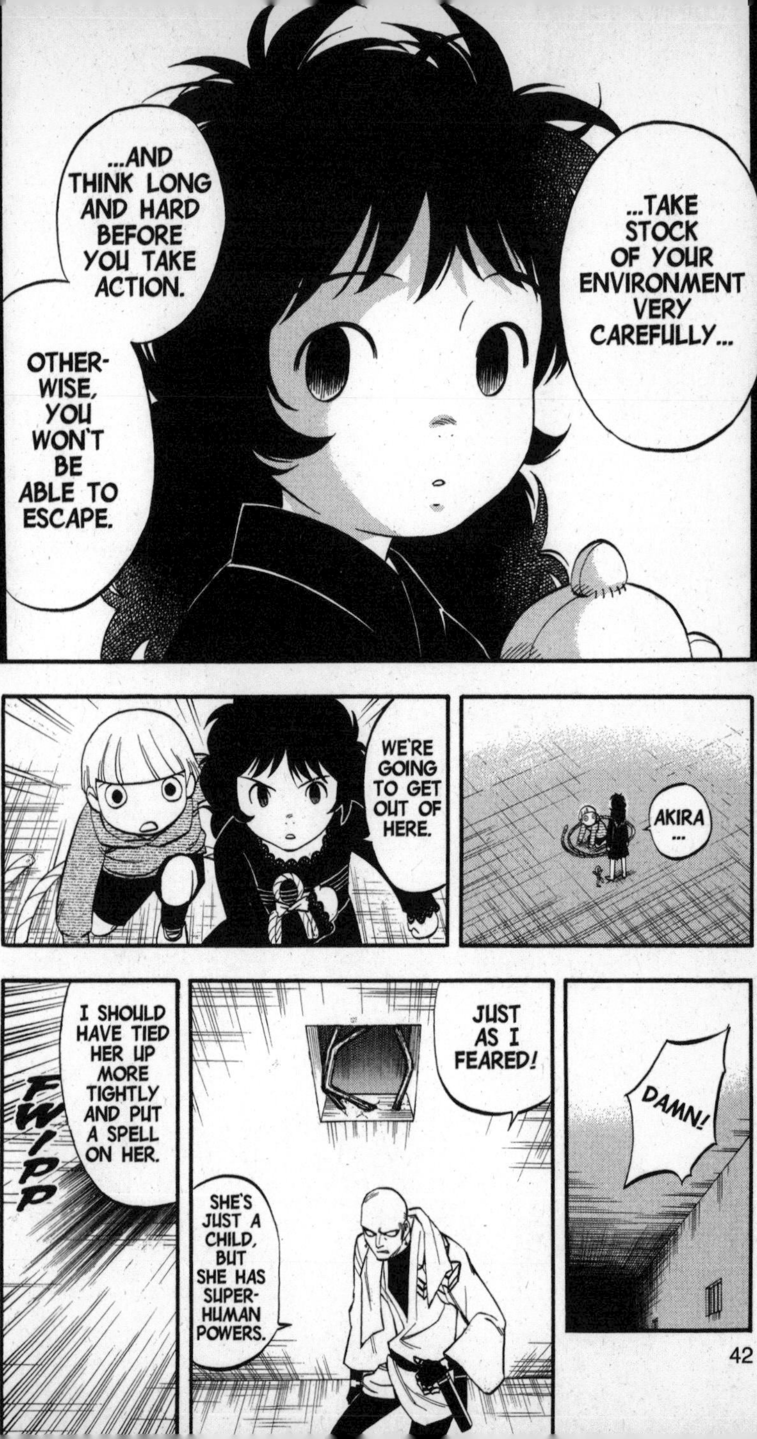
...TAKE STOCK OF YOUR ENVIRONMENT VERY CAREFULLY...
...AND THINK LONG AND HARD BEFORE YOU TAKE ACTION.
OTHER-WISE, YOU WON'T BE ABLE TO ESCAPE.
AKIRA ...
WE'RE GOING TO GET OUT OF HERE.
DAMN!
JUST AS I FEARED!
SHE'S JUST A CHILD, BUT SHE HAS SUPER-HUMAN POWERS.
I SHOULD HAVE TIED HER UP MORE TIGHTLY AND PUT A SPELL ON HER.
FWIPP

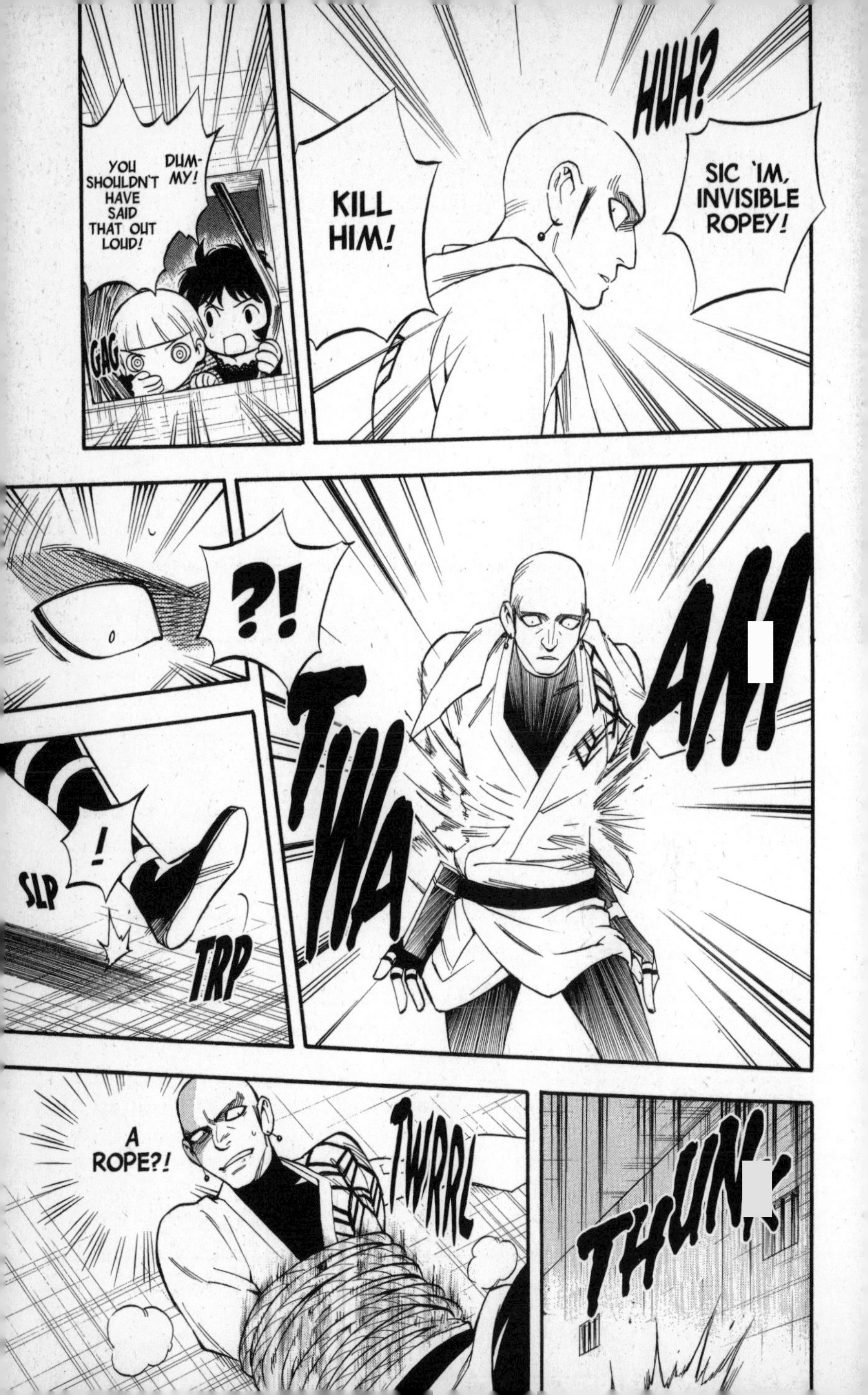
HUH?
SIC 'IM, INVISIBLE ROPEY!
KILL HIM!
DUM-MY!
YOU SHOULDN'T HAVE SAID THAT OUT LOUD!
GAG
TWA
AM
?!
!
SLP
TRP
THUN
A ROPE?!
TWRRL

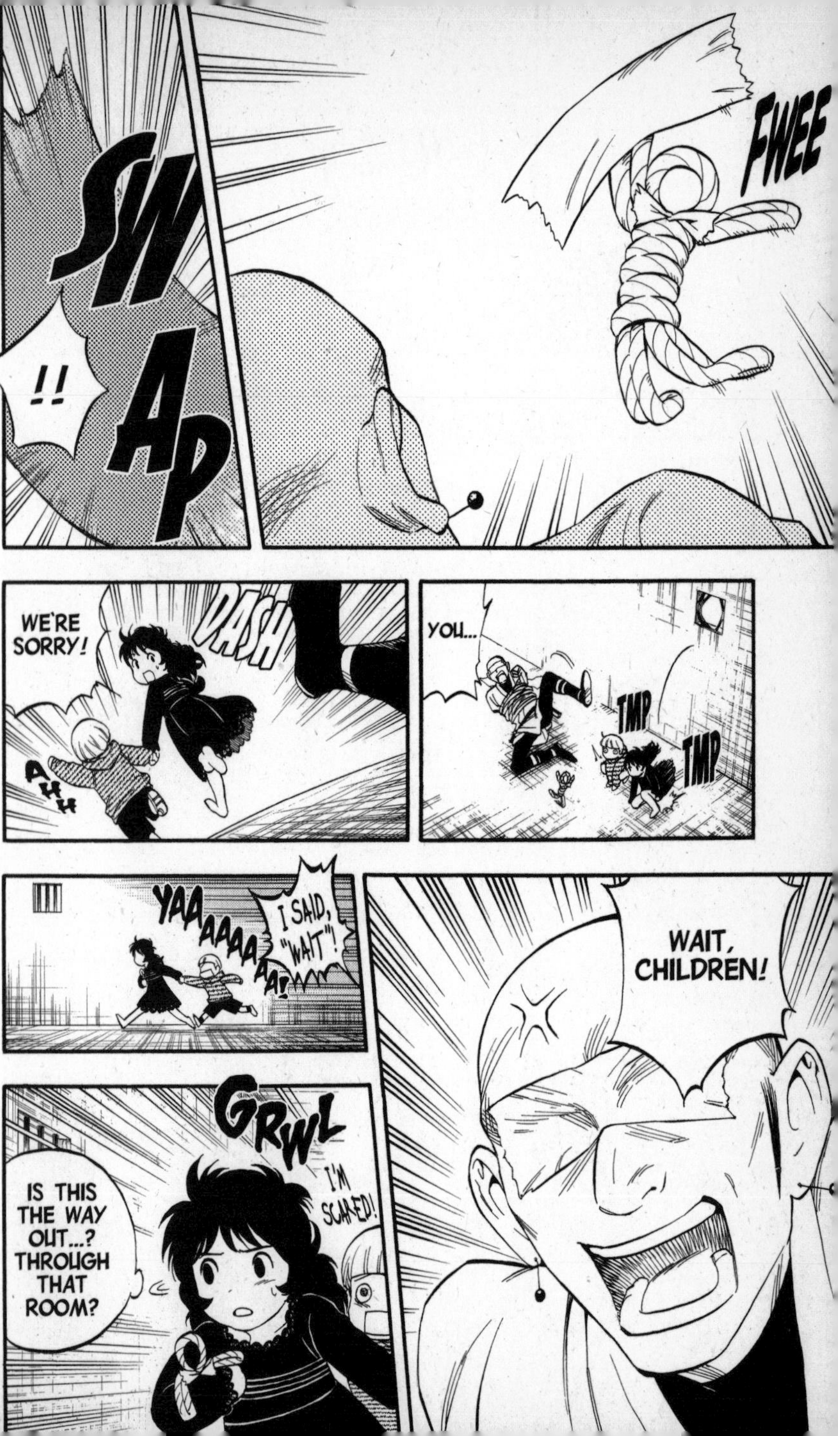
FWEE
SNAP
!!
YOU...
TMP
TMP
WE'RE SORRY!
DASH
AHH
WAIT, CHILDREN!
I SAID, "WAIT"!
YAAAAAAAAA!
GRWL
I'M SCARED!
IS THIS THE WAY OUT...? THROUGH THAT ROOM?

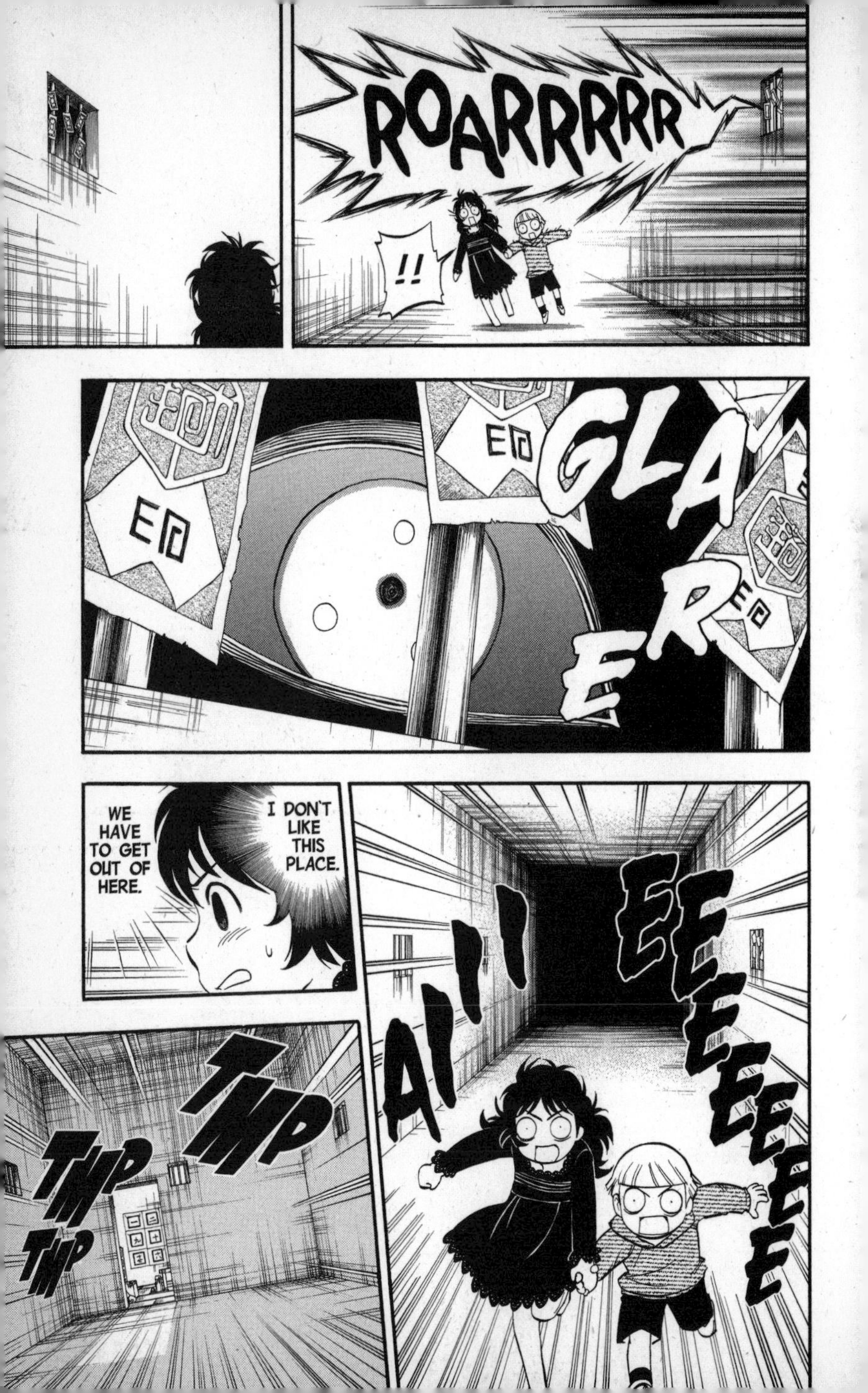
ROARRRRR
!!
GLAREE
AIIEEEEEEEEEE
I DON'T LIKE THIS PLACE.
WE HAVE TO GET OUT OF HERE.
THP
THP
THP

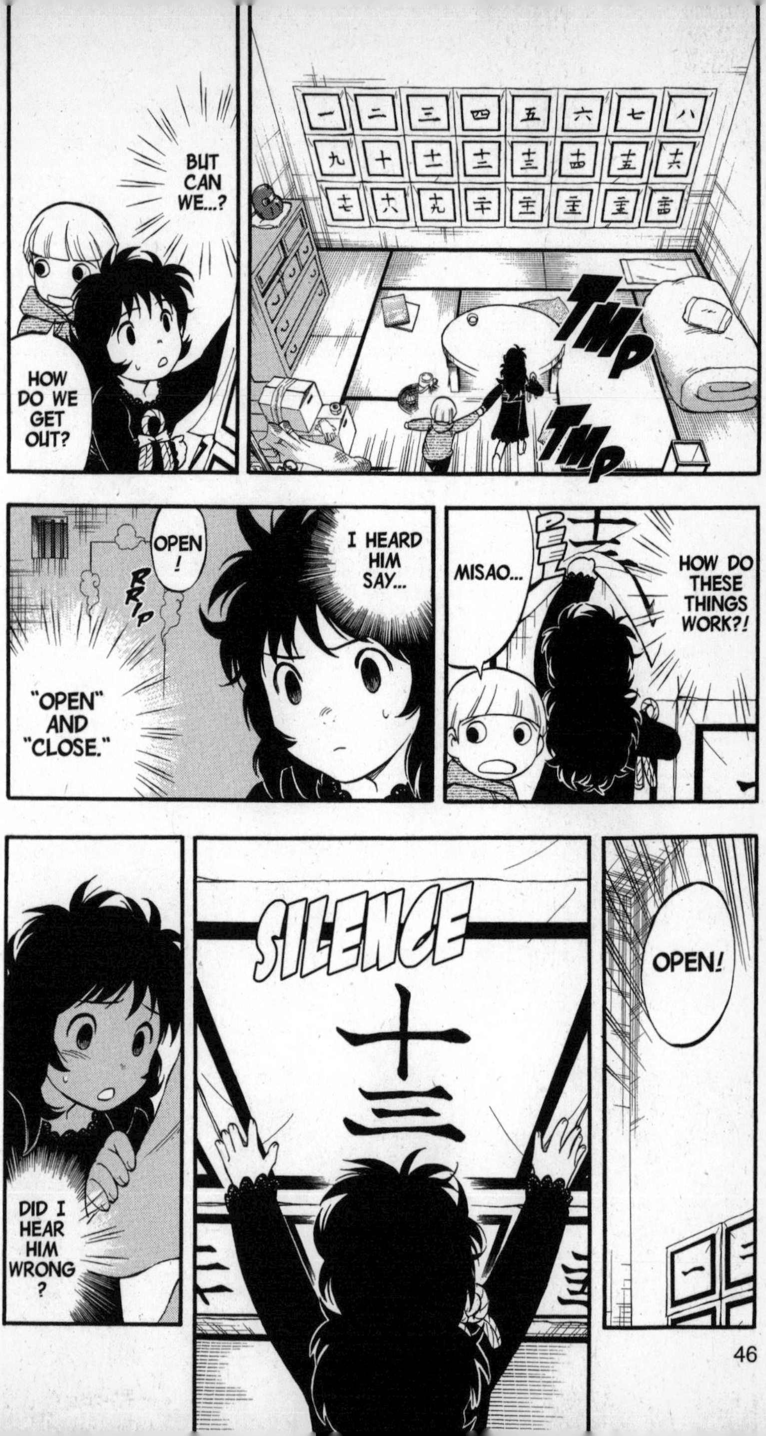
TMP
TMP
BUT CAN WE...?
HOW DO WE GET OUT?
HOW DO THESE THINGS WORK?!
PEEL
MISAO...
I HEARD HIM SAY...
"OPEN" AND "CLOSE."
OPEN!
RRIP
OPEN!
SILENCE
十三
DID I HEAR HIM WRONG?

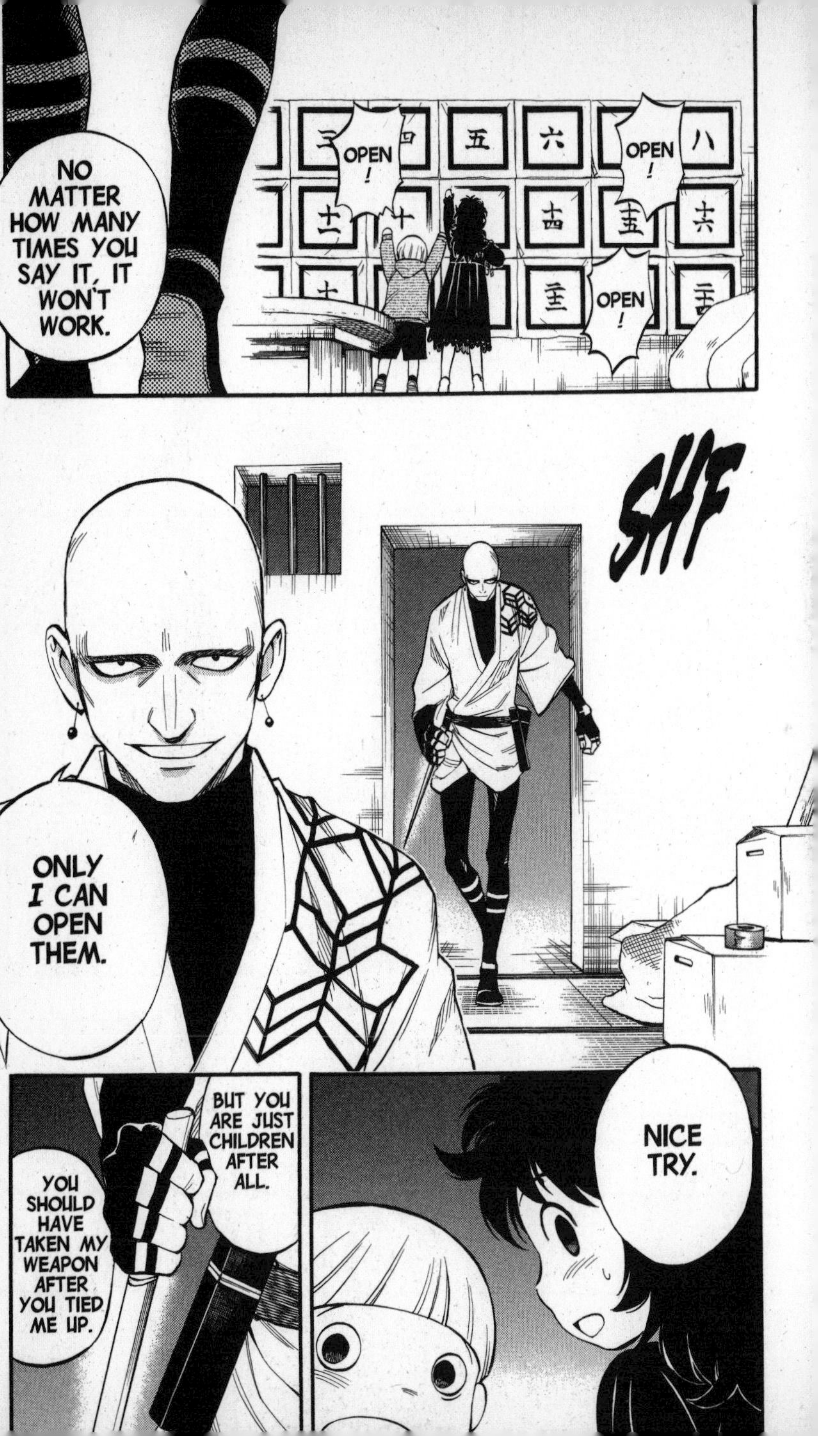
OPEN!
OPEN!
OPEN!
NO MATTER HOW MANY TIMES YOU SAY IT, IT WON'T WORK.
SHF
ONLY I CAN OPEN THEM.
NICE TRY.
BUT YOU ARE JUST CHILDREN AFTER ALL.
YOU SHOULD HAVE TAKEN MY WEAPON AFTER YOU TIED ME UP.

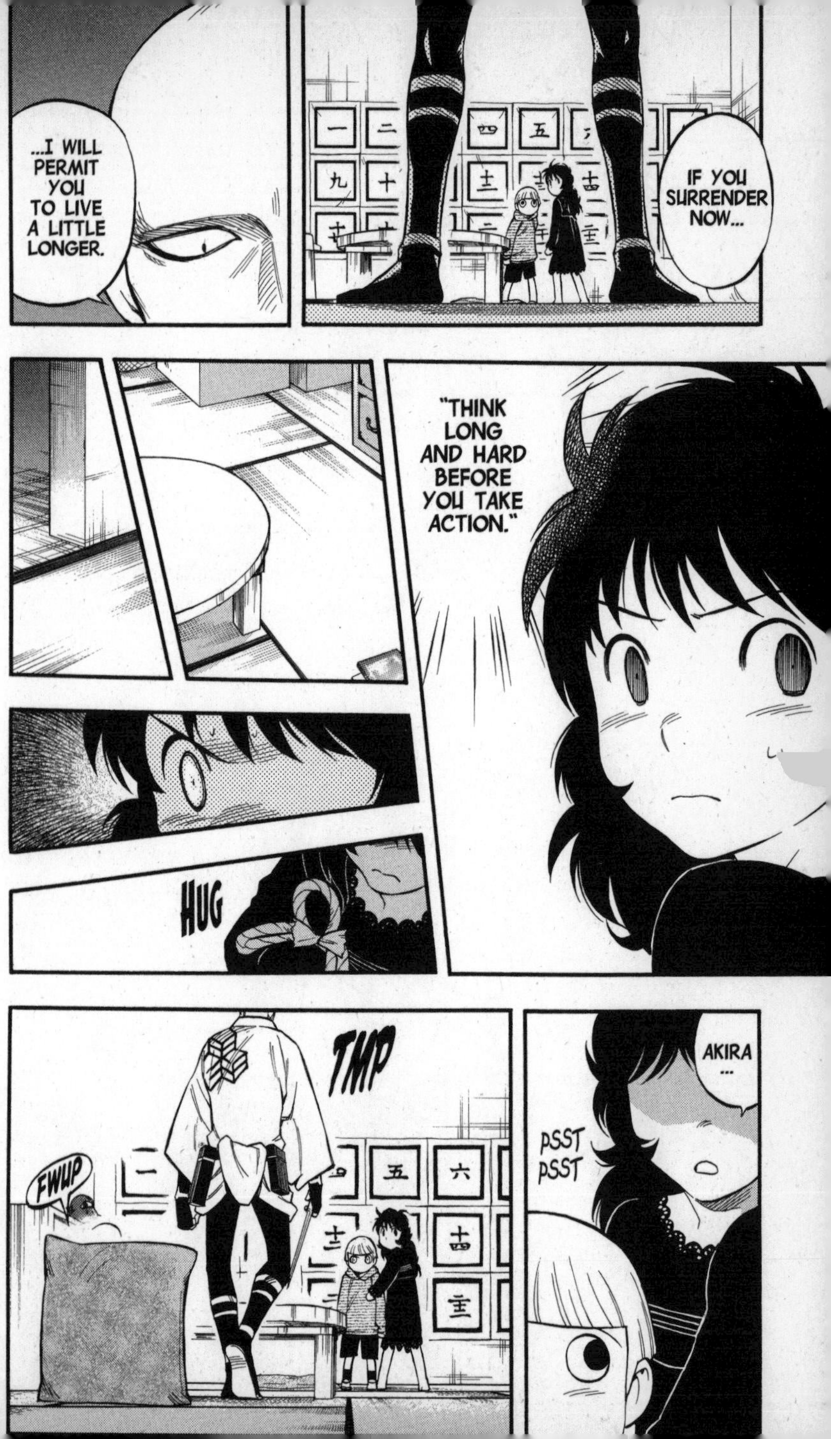
IF YOU SURRENDER NOW...
...I WILL PERMIT YOU TO LIVE A LITTLE LONGER.
"THINK LONG AND HARD BEFORE YOU TAKE ACTION."
HUG
AKIRA ...
PSST PSST
TMP
FWUP

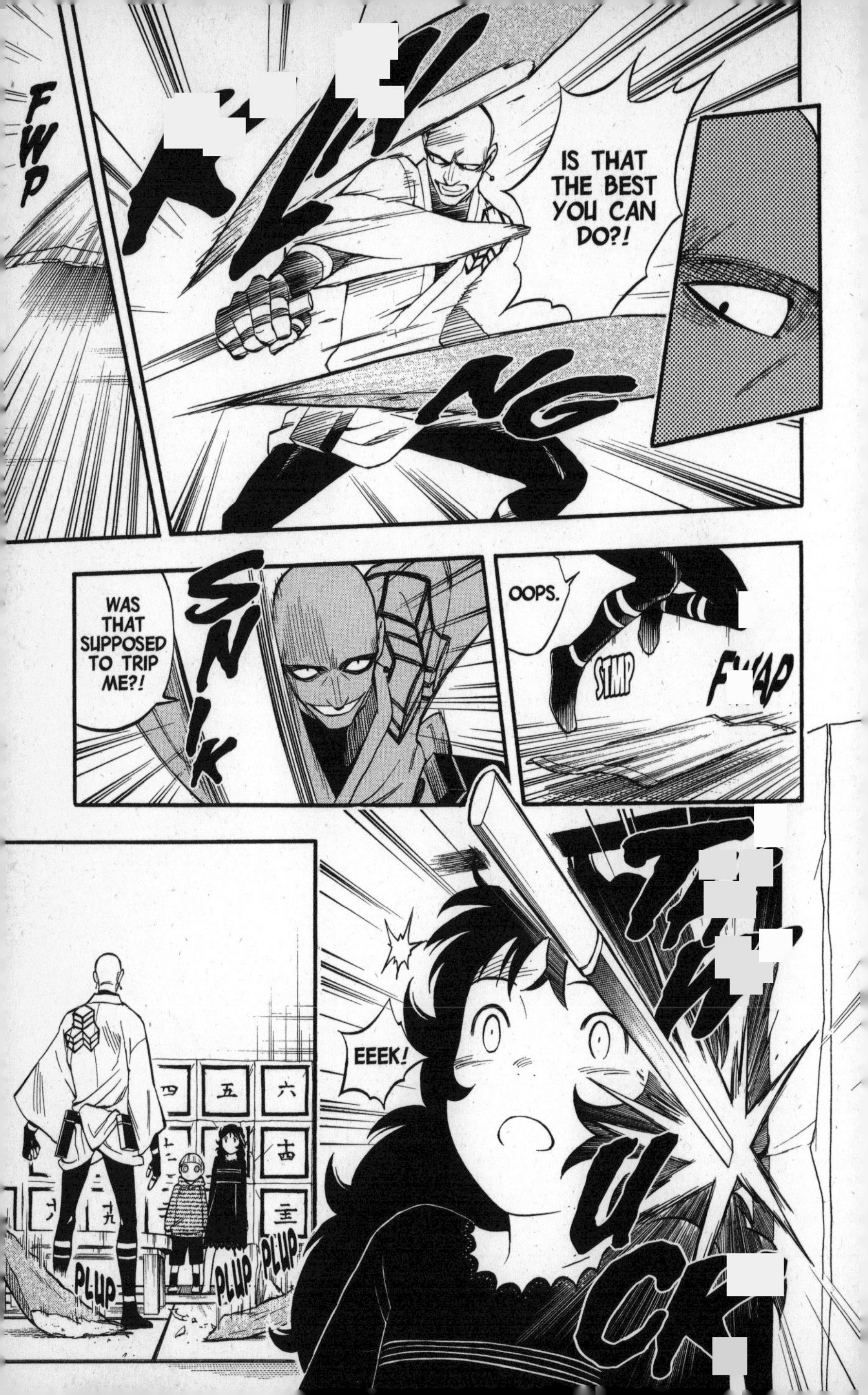
IS THAT THE BEST YOU CAN DO?!
FWP
OOPS.
STMP
WAS THAT SUPPOSED TO TRIP ME?!
SNIK
EEEK!
PLUP
PLUP
PLUP

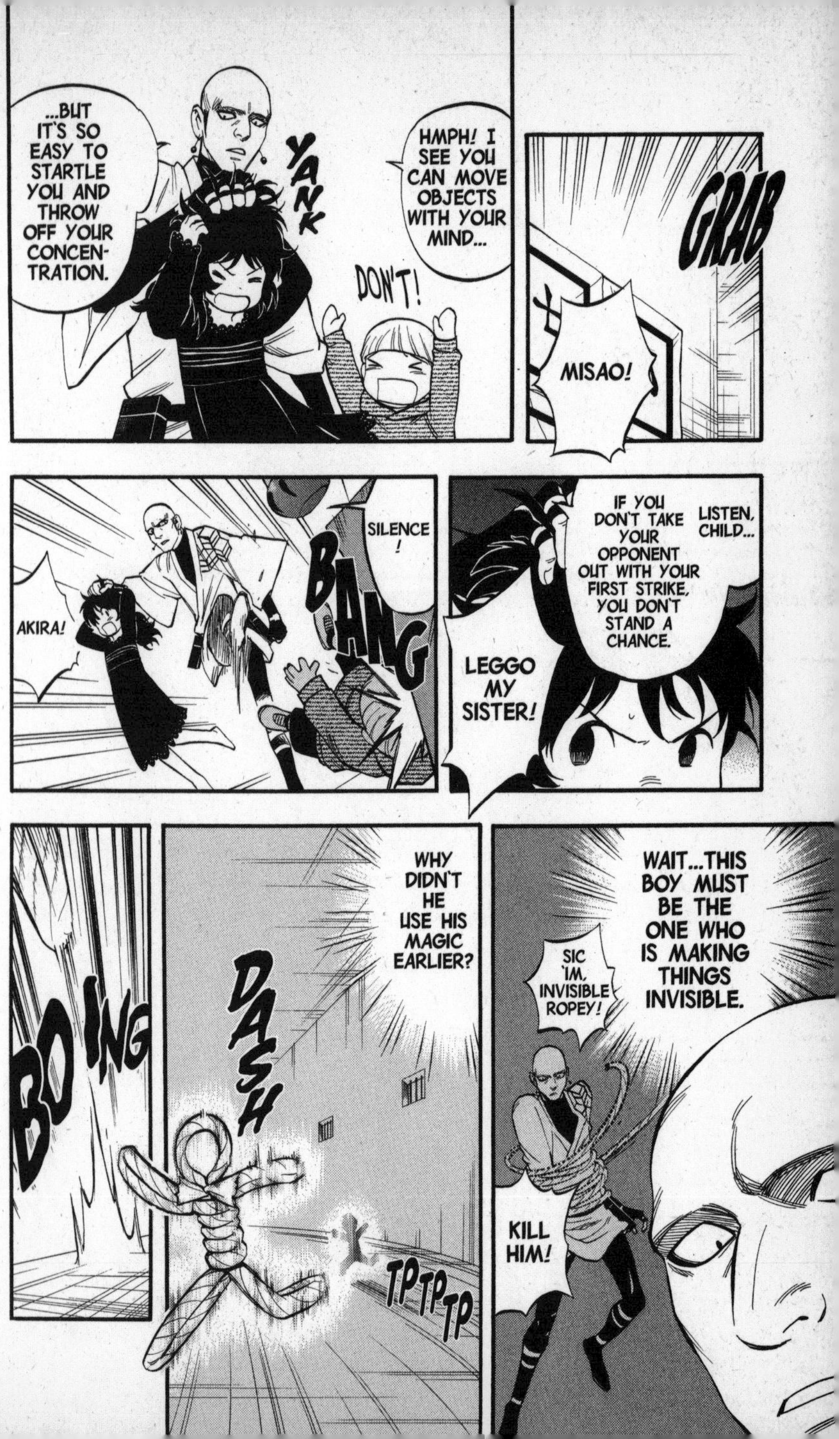
GRAB
MISAO!
HMPH! I SEE YOU CAN MOVE OBJECTS WITH YOUR MIND...
YANK
DON'T!
...BUT IT'S SO EASY TO STARTLE YOU AND THROW OFF YOUR CONCENTRATION.
LISTEN, CHILD...
IF YOU DON'T TAKE YOUR OPPONENT OUT WITH YOUR FIRST STRIKE, YOU DON'T STAND A CHANCE.
LEGGO MY SISTER!
SILENCE!
BANG
AKIRA!
WAIT...THIS BOY MUST BE THE ONE WHO IS MAKING THINGS INVISIBLE.
SIC 'IM, INVISIBLE ROPEY!
KILL HIM!
WHY DIDN'T HE USE HIS MAGIC EARLIER?
DASH
TPTPTP
BOING

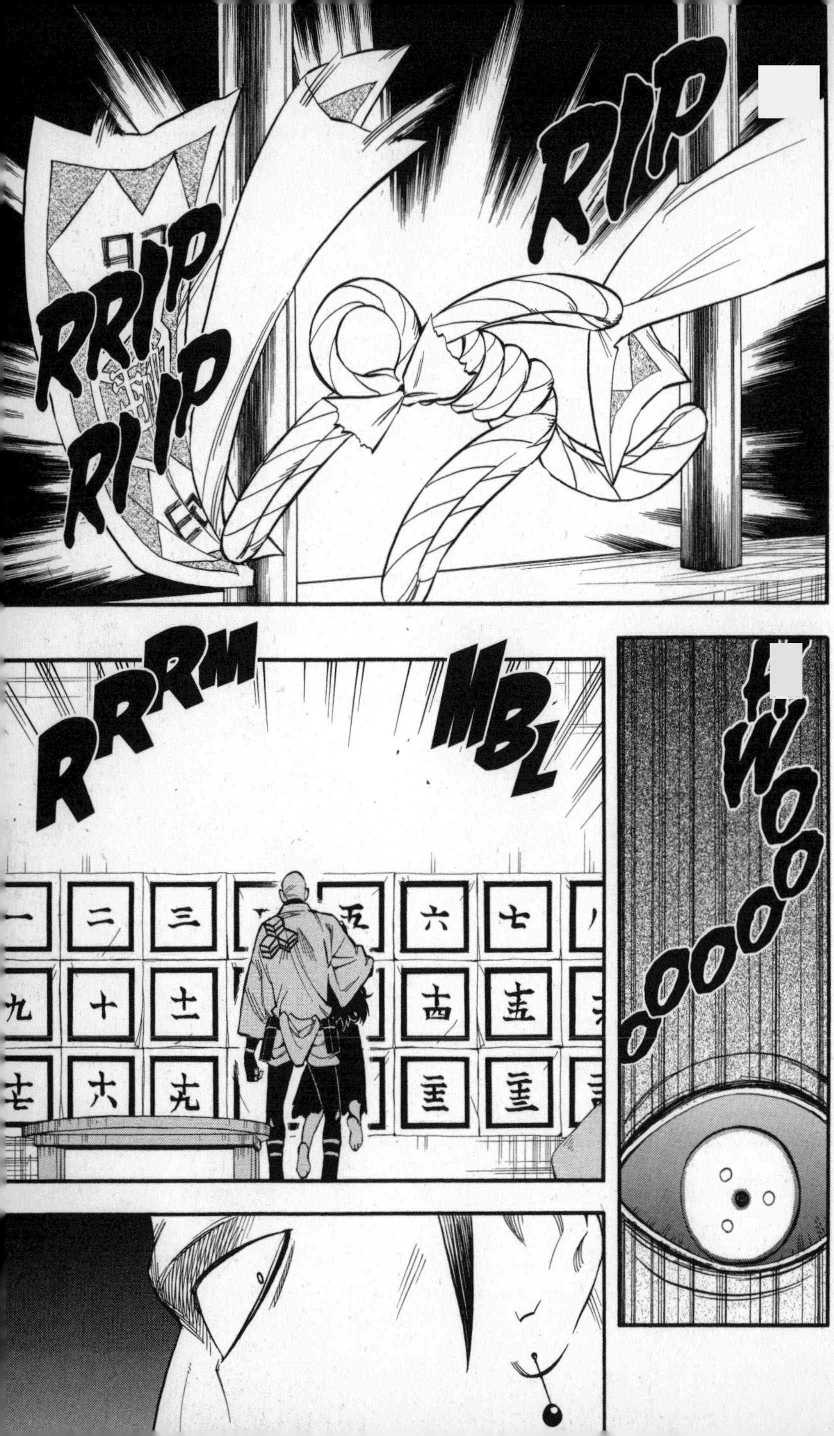
RIP
RRIP
RIIP
WOOOOOOO
RRRRM
MBL

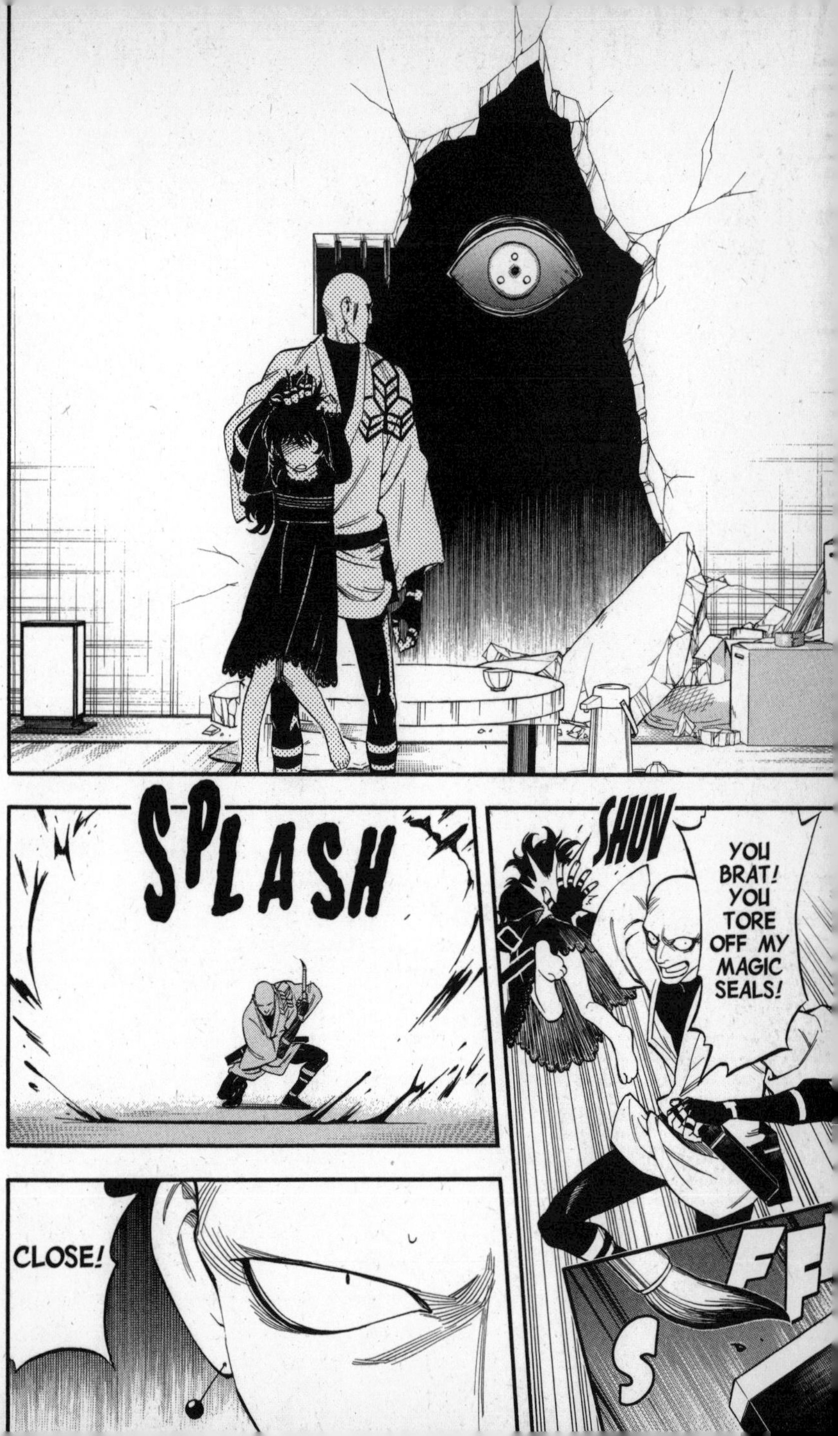
SHUV
YOU BRAT! YOU TORE OFF MY MAGIC SEALS!
SPLASH
CLOSE!

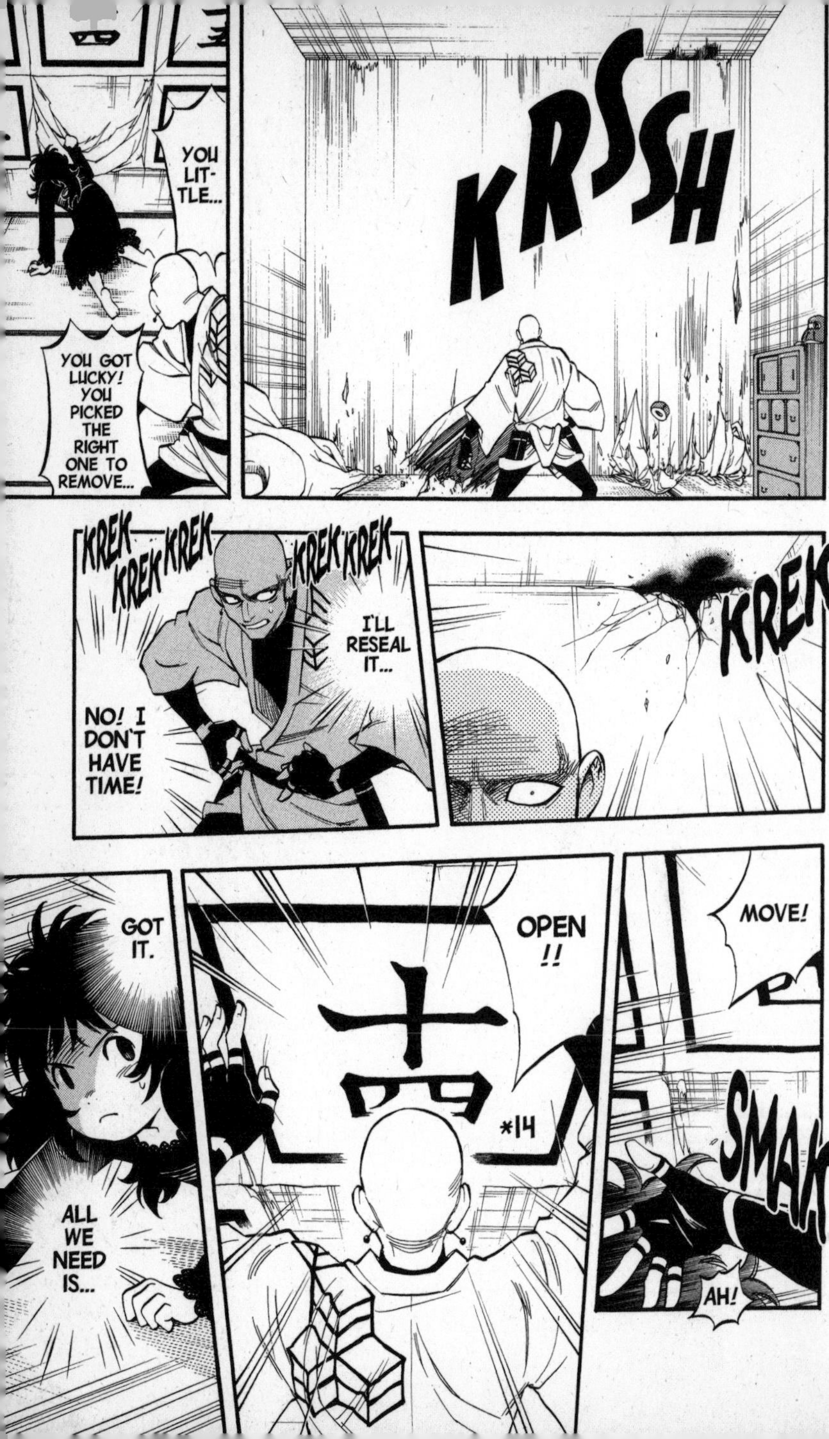
KRSSH
YOU LIT-TLE...
YOU GOT LUCKY! YOU PICKED THE RIGHT ONE TO REMOVE...
KREK
KREK KREK KREK
KREK KREK
I'LL RESEAL IT...
NO! I DON'T HAVE TIME!
MOVE!
SMAK
AH!
OPEN!!
*14
GOT IT.
ALL WE NEED IS...

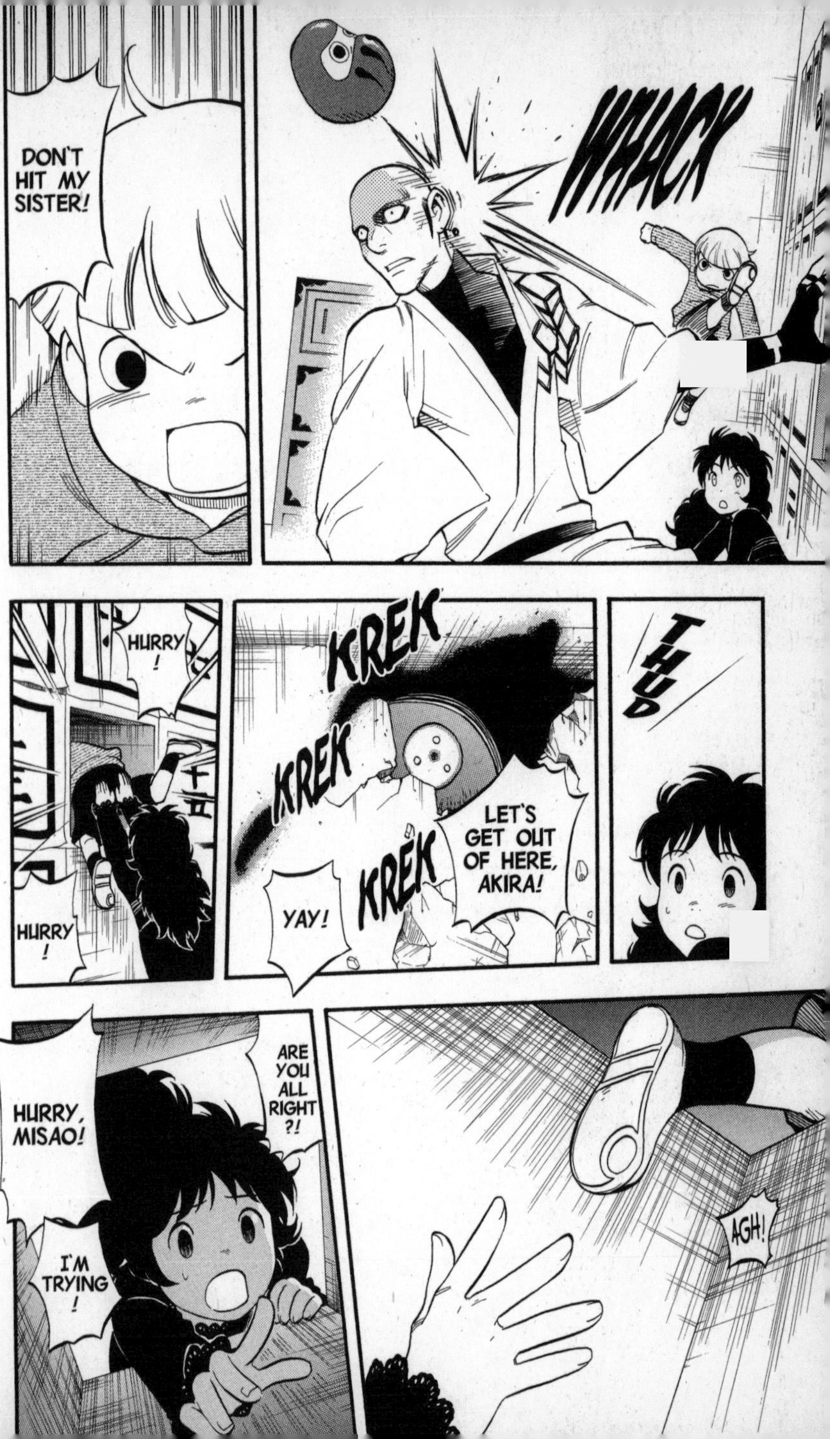
WHACK
DON'T HIT MY SISTER!
THUD
KREK
KREK
LET'S GET OUT OF HERE, AKIRA!
KREK
YAY!
HURRY!
HURRY!
AGH!
ARE YOU ALL RIGHT?!
HURRY, MISAO!
I'M TRYING!

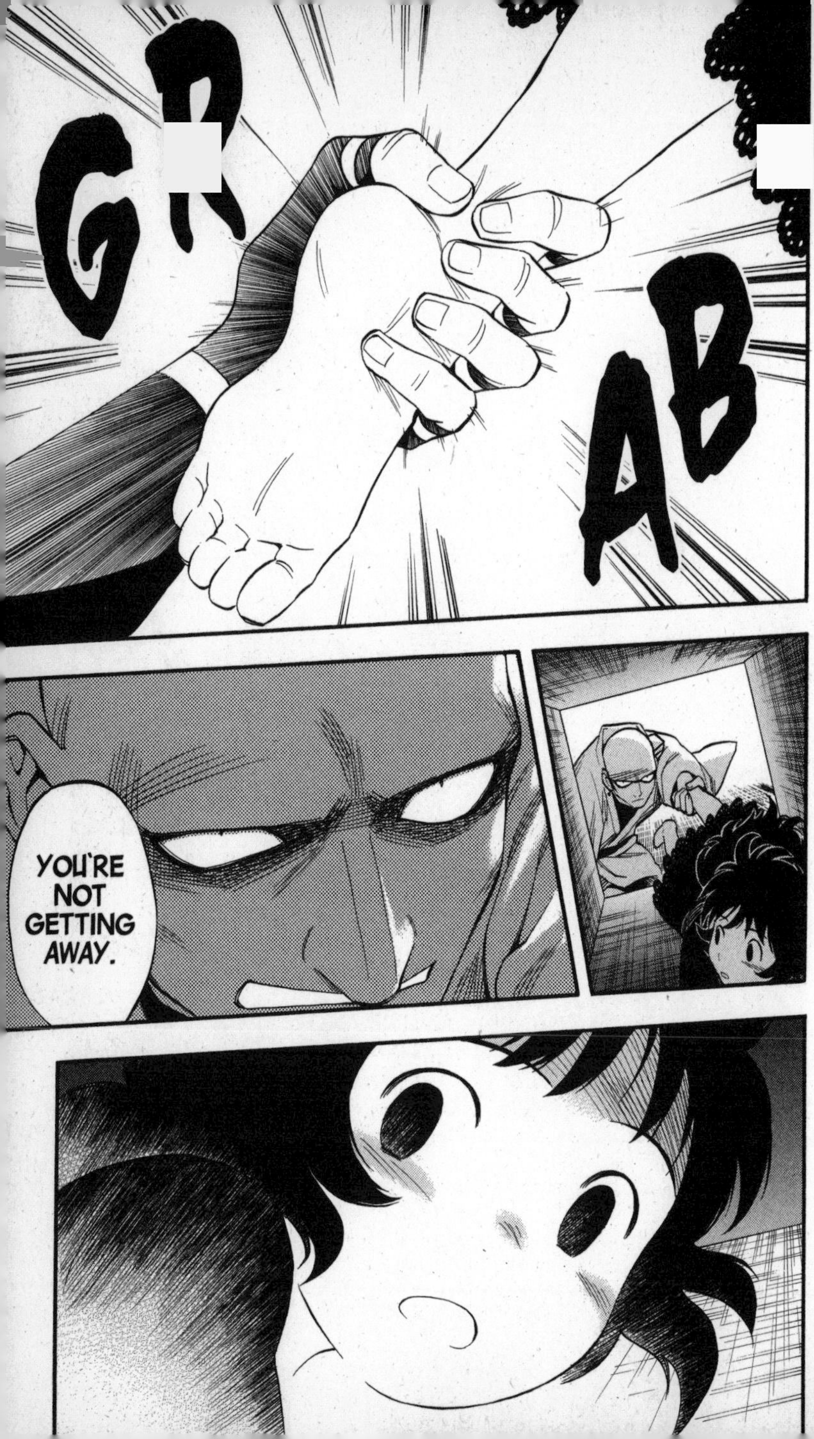
GRAB
YOU'RE NOT GETTING AWAY.

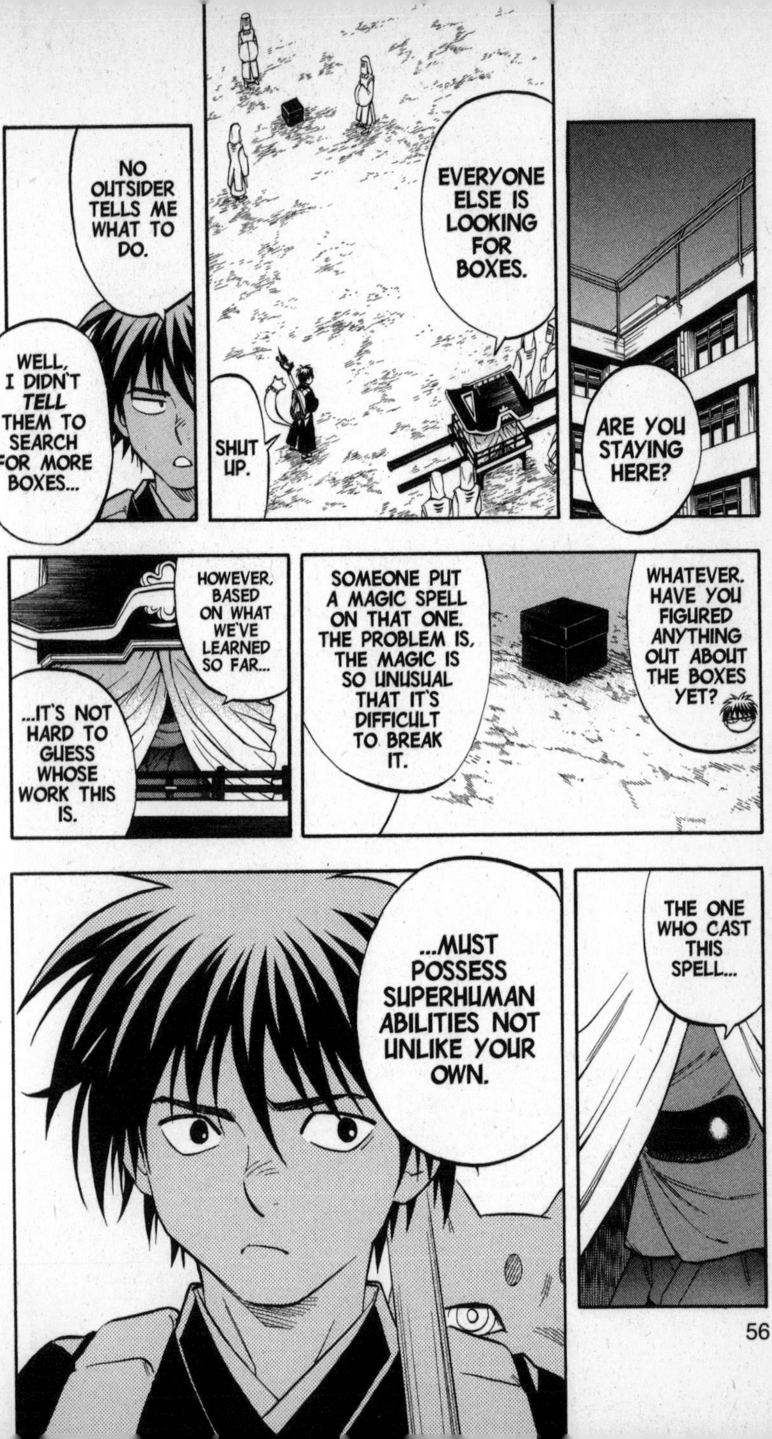
ARE YOU STAYING HERE?
EVERYONE ELSE IS LOOKING FOR BOXES.
SHUT UP.
NO OUTSIDER TELLS ME WHAT TO DO.
WELL, I DIDN'T *TELL* THEM TO SEARCH FOR MORE BOXES...
WHATEVER. HAVE YOU FIGURED ANYTHING OUT ABOUT THE BOXES YET?
SOMEONE PUT A MAGIC SPELL ON THAT ONE. THE PROBLEM IS, THE MAGIC IS SO UNUSUAL THAT IT'S DIFFICULT TO BREAK IT.
HOWEVER, BASED ON WHAT WE'VE LEARNED SO FAR...
...IT'S NOT HARD TO GUESS WHOSE WORK THIS IS.
THE ONE WHO CAST THIS SPELL...
...MUST POSSESS SUPERHUMAN ABILITIES NOT UNLIKE YOUR OWN.

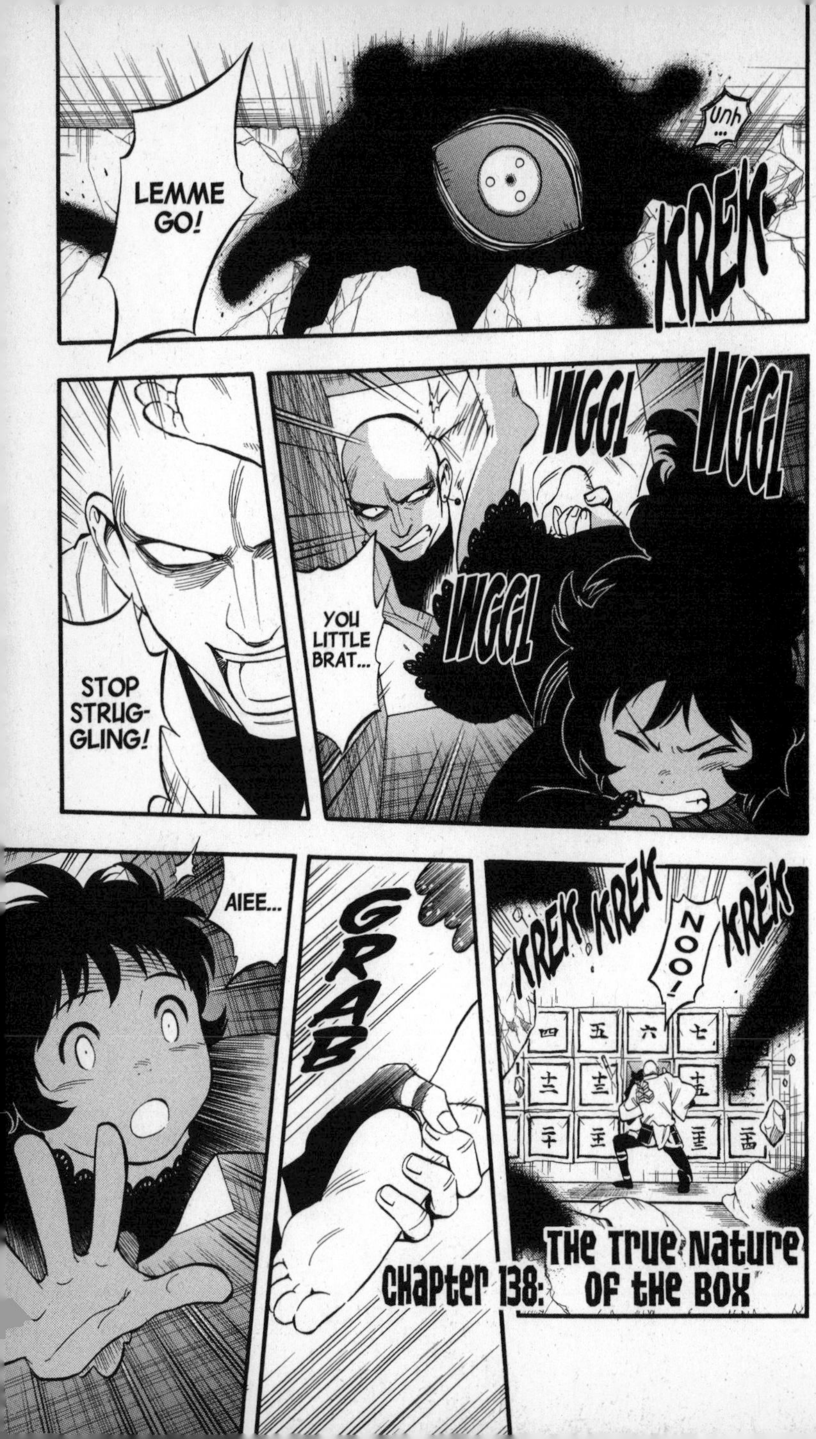
Unh...
KREK
LEMME GO!
WGGI
WGGI
YOU LITTLE BRAT...
WGGI
STOP STRUG-GLING!
KREK
NOO!
KREK
KREK
Chapter 138: The True Nature of the Box
GRAB
AIEE...

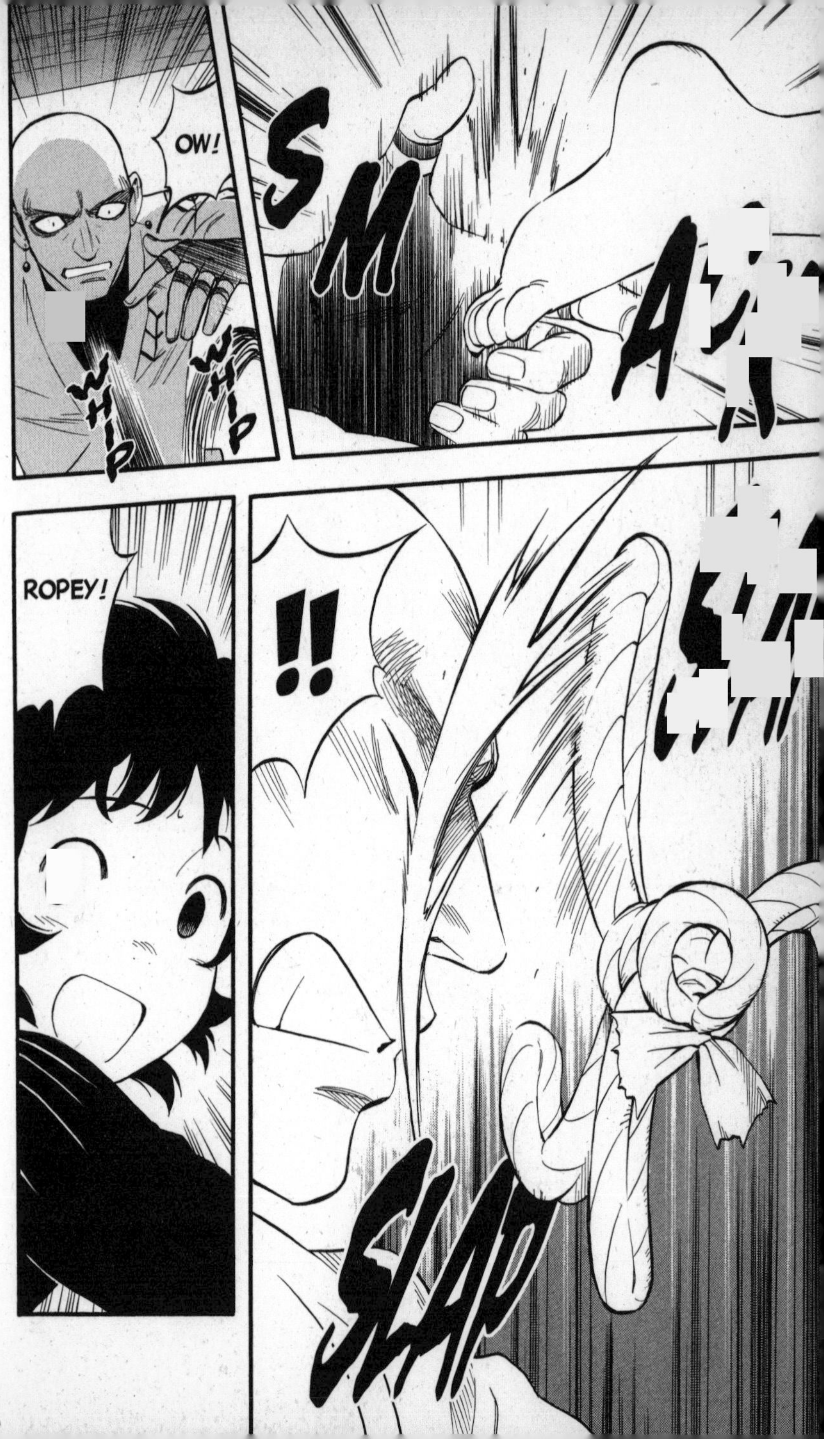
SMA
OW!
WHIP
WHIP
!!
SLAP
ROPEY!

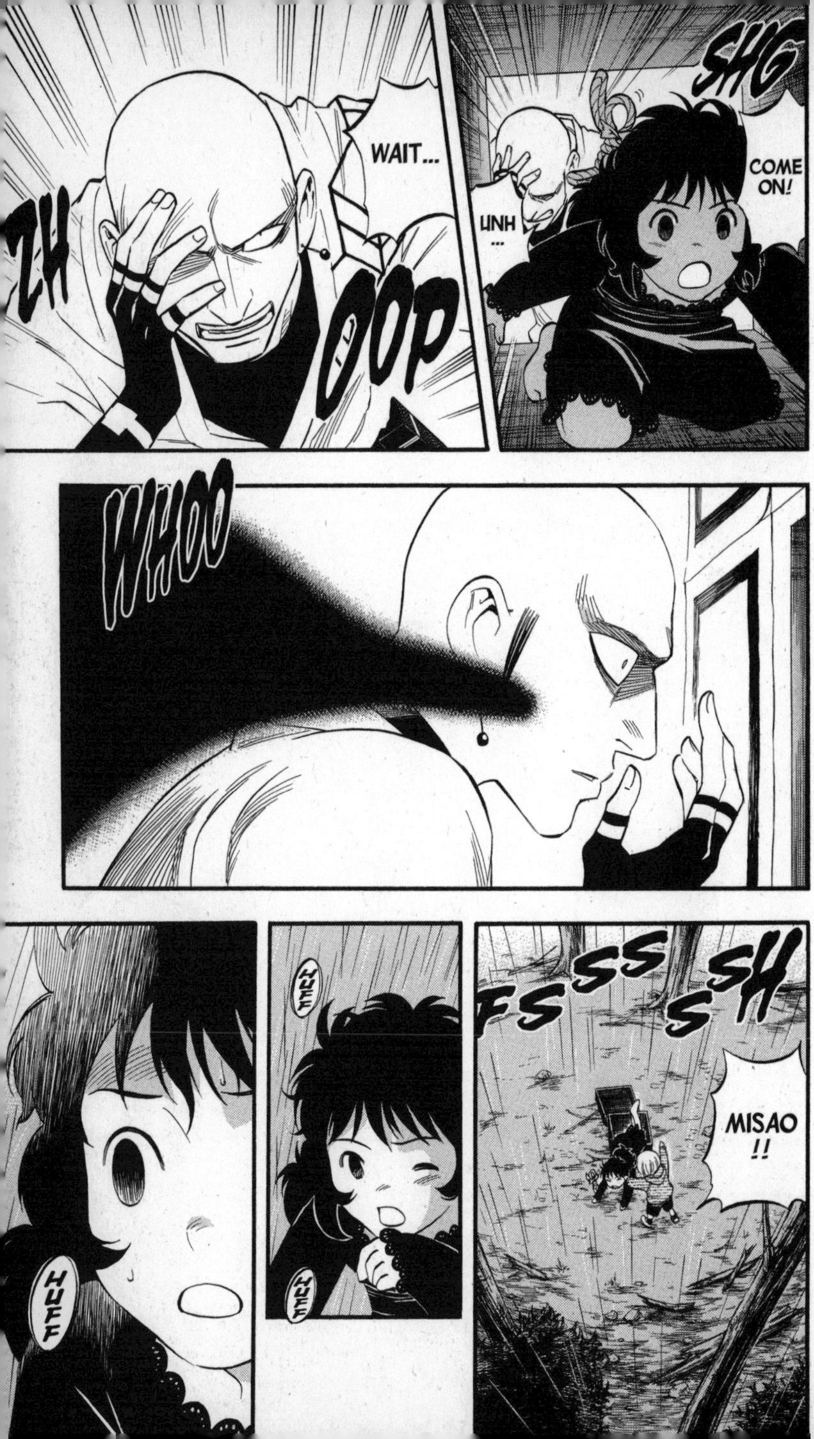
SHG
COME ON!
UNH ...
WAIT...
ZH
OOP
WHOO
FSSSSSH
MISAO !!
HUFF
HUFF
HUFF

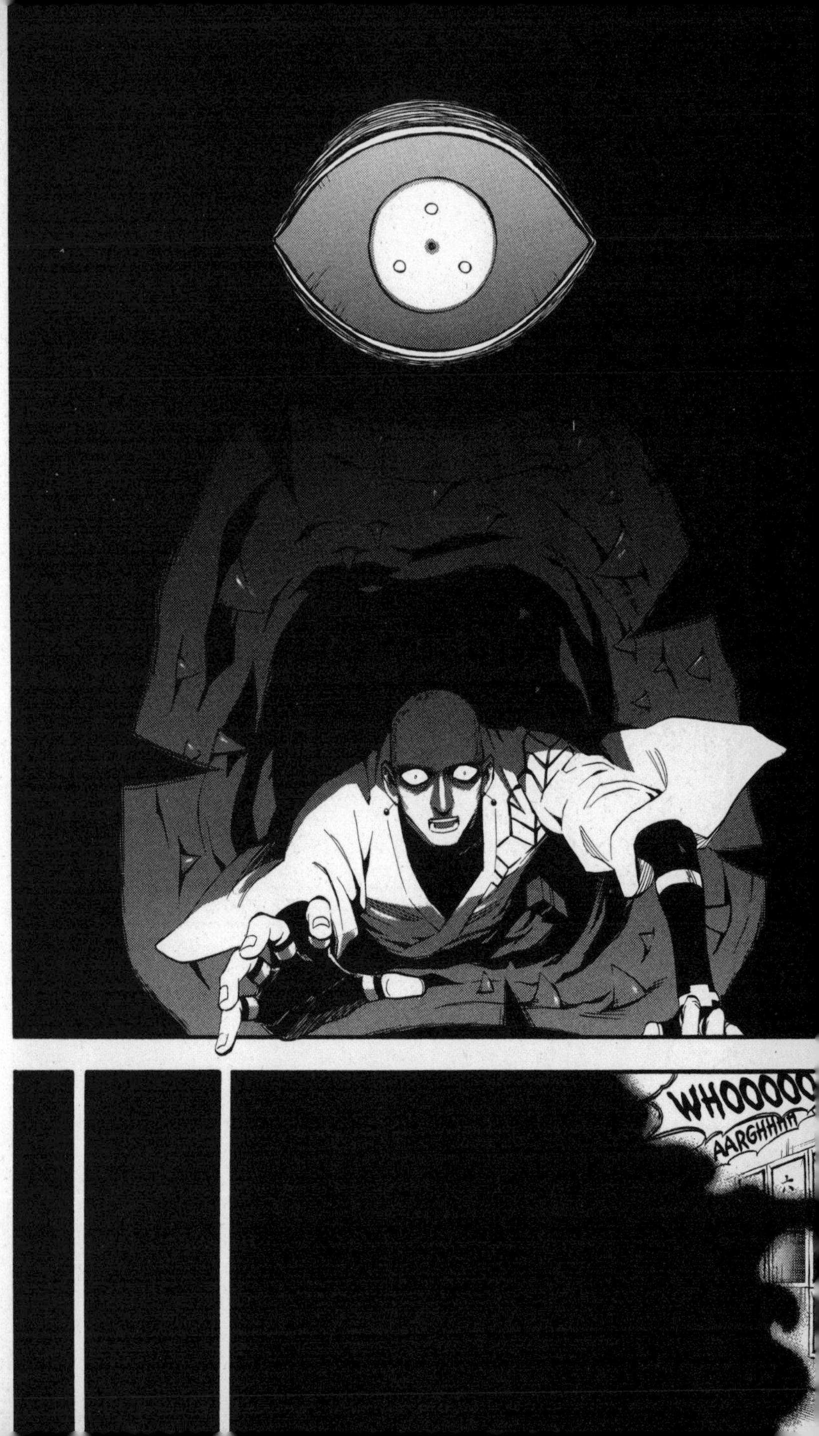
WHOOOOO
AARGHHHH
六

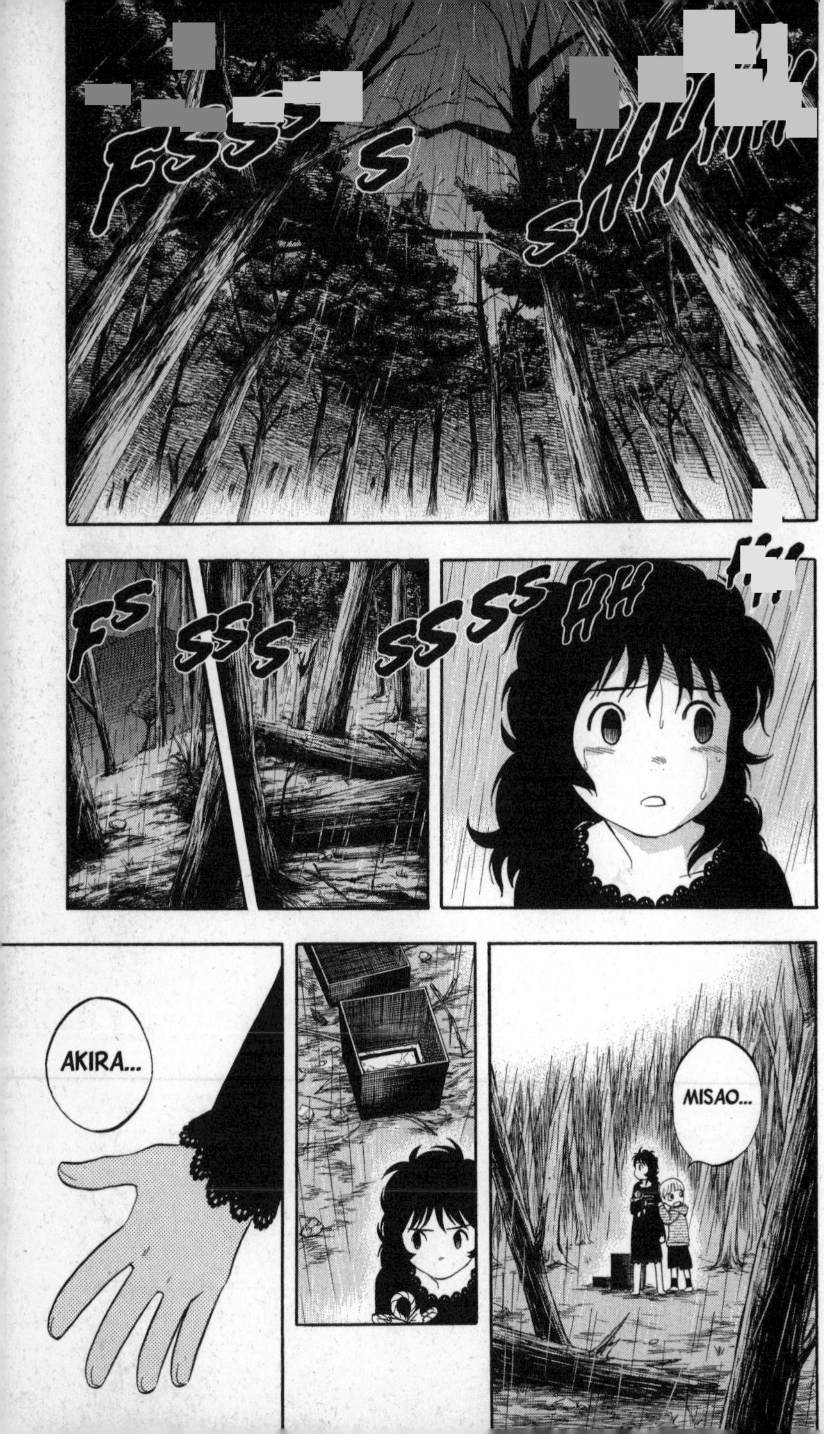
SHH
FSSS S
SSSSSHH
FS SSS
MISAO...
AKIRA...

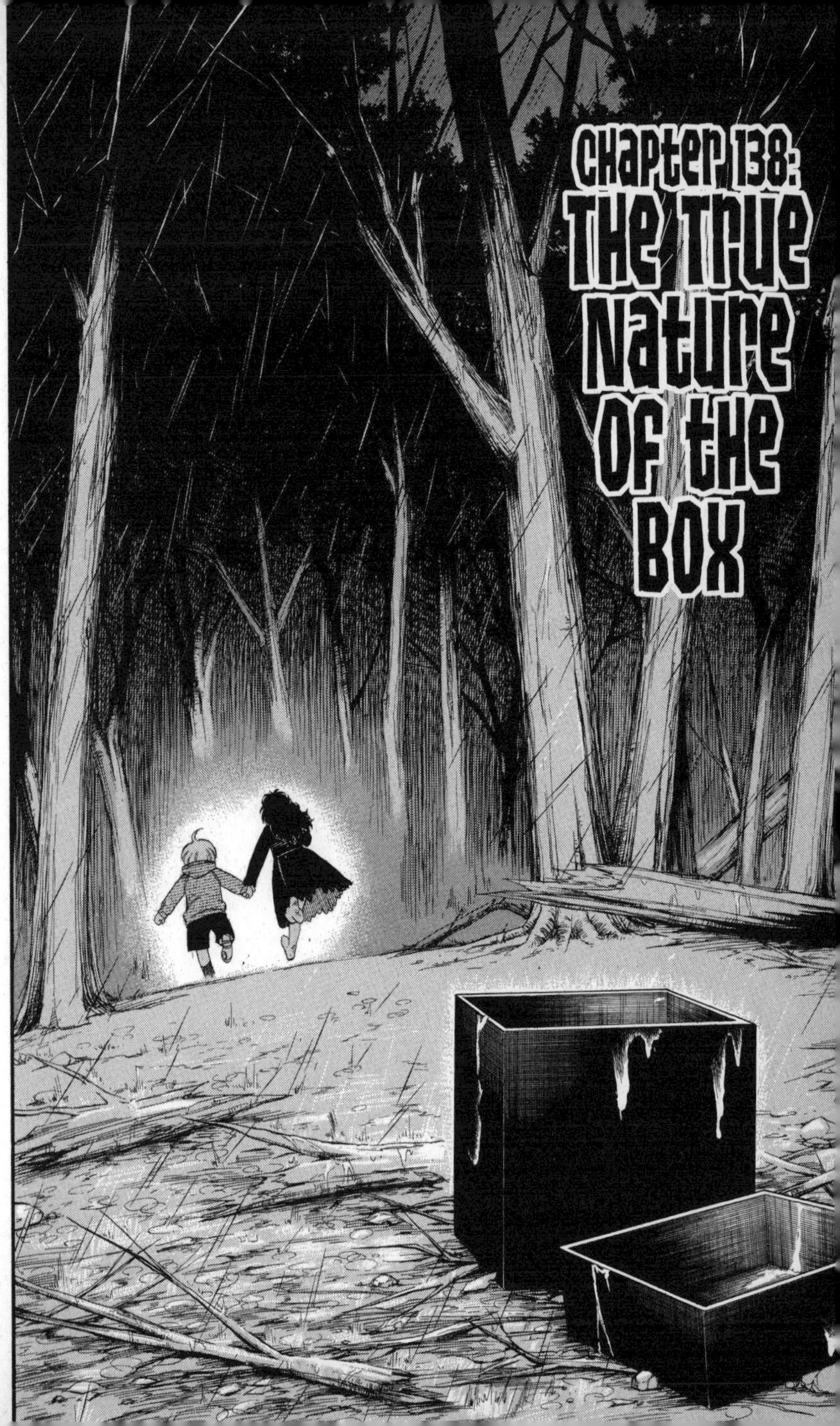
Chapter 138:
The True Nature of the Box

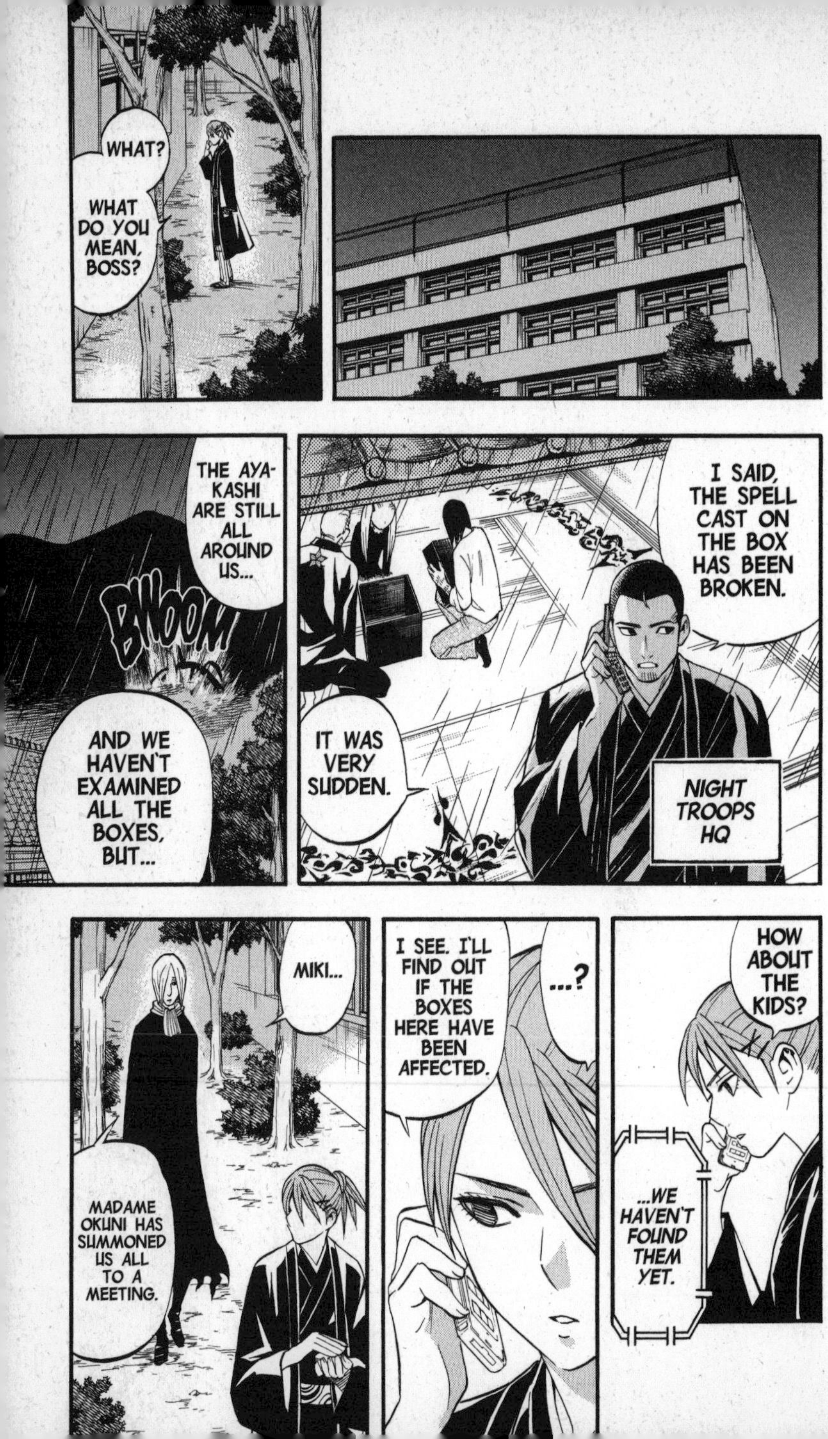
WHAT?
WHAT DO YOU MEAN, BOSS?
NIGHT TROOPS HQ
I SAID, THE SPELL CAST ON THE BOX HAS BEEN BROKEN.
IT WAS VERY SUDDEN.
THE AYA-KASHI ARE STILL ALL AROUND US...
BWOOM
AND WE HAVEN'T EXAMINED ALL THE BOXES, BUT...
HOW ABOUT THE KIDS?
...WE HAVEN'T FOUND THEM YET.
...?
I SEE. I'LL FIND OUT IF THE BOXES HERE HAVE BEEN AFFECTED.
MIKI...
MADAME OKUNI HAS SUMMONED US ALL TO A MEETING.

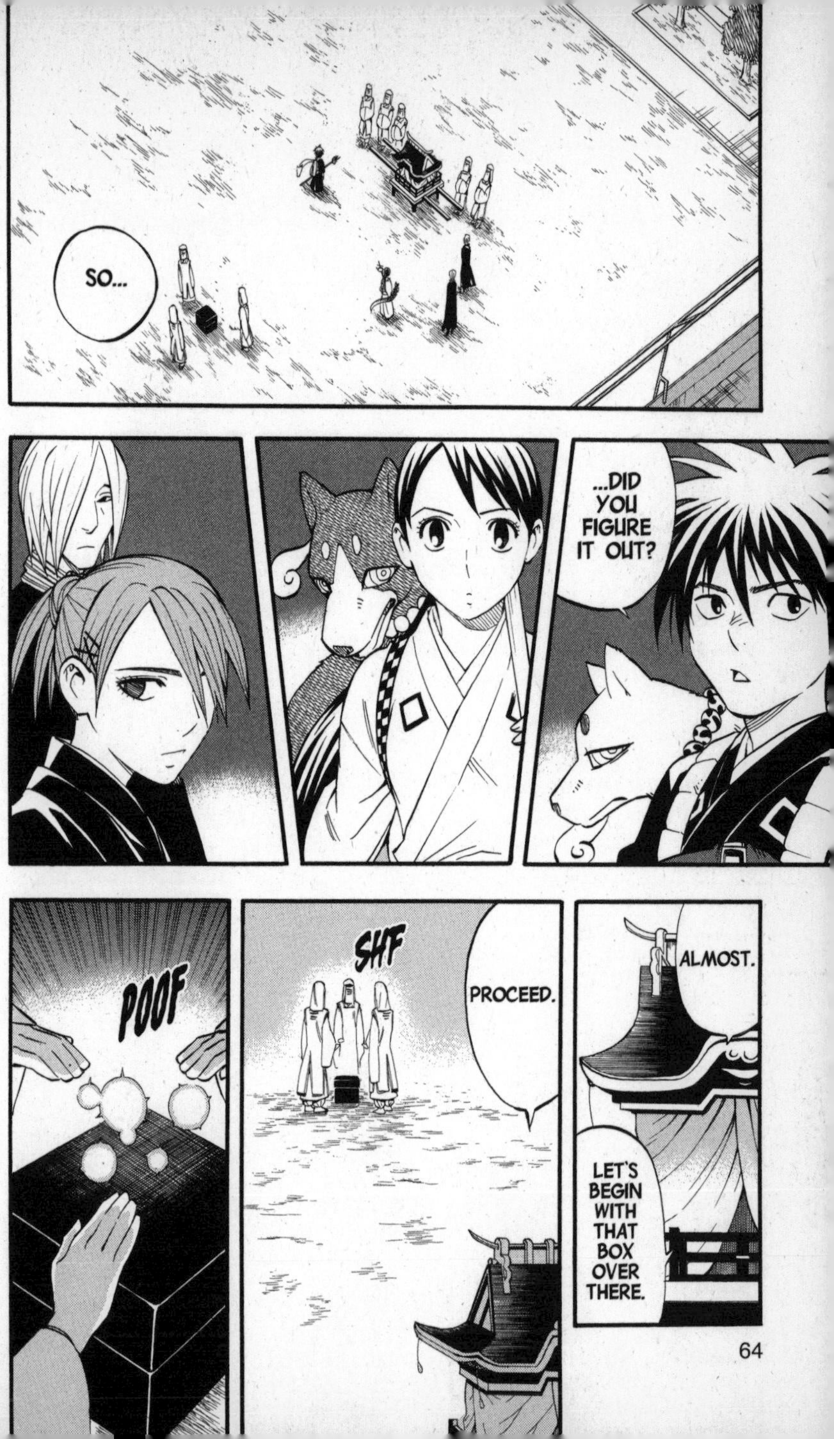
SO...
...DID YOU FIGURE IT OUT?
ALMOST.
LET'S BEGIN WITH THAT BOX OVER THERE.
PROCEED.
SHF
POOF

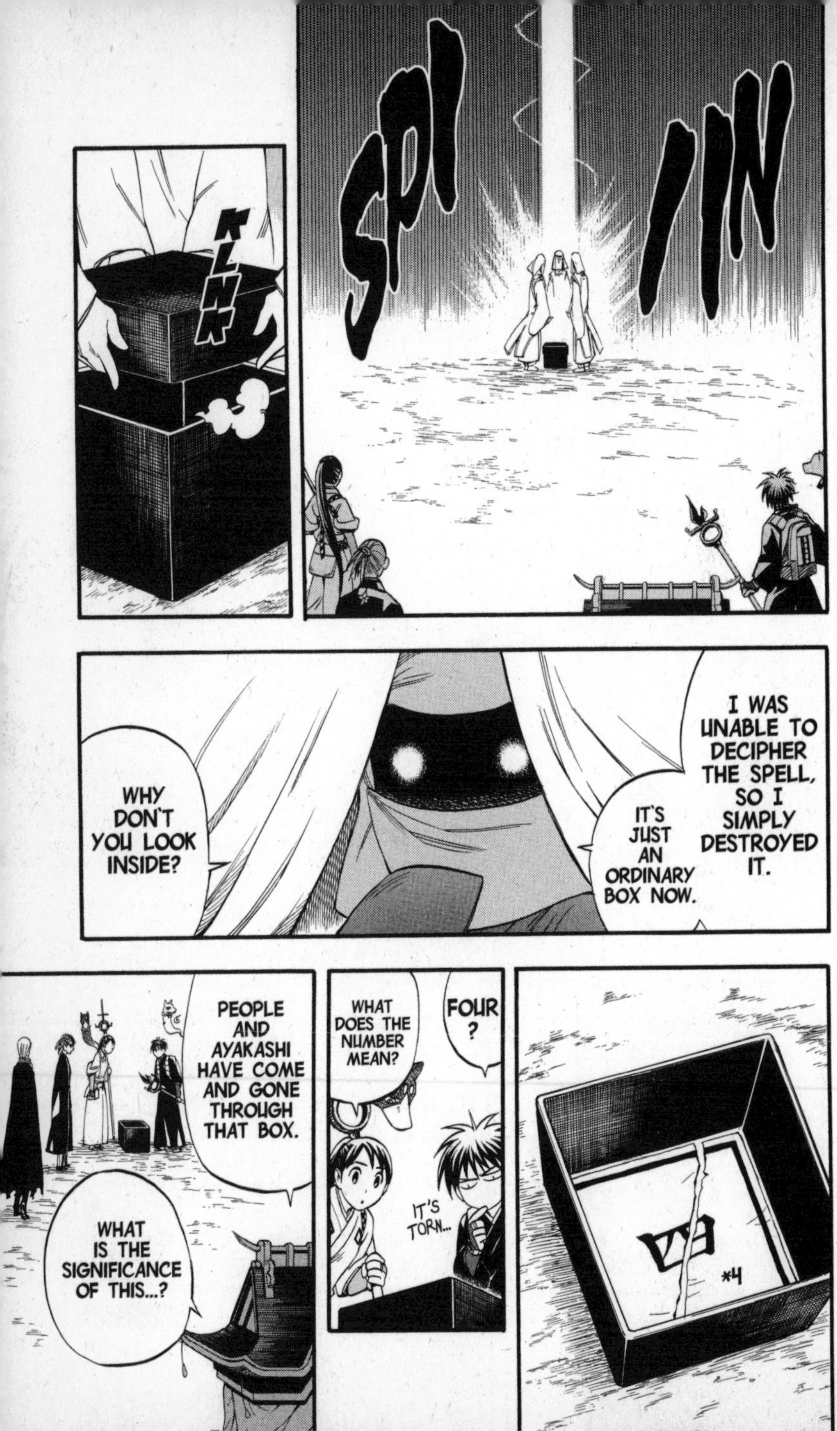
SPIIIN
KLNK
I WAS UNABLE TO DECIPHER THE SPELL, SO I SIMPLY DESTROYED IT.
IT'S JUST AN ORDINARY BOX NOW.
WHY DON'T YOU LOOK INSIDE?
四
*4
FOUR?
WHAT DOES THE NUMBER MEAN?
IT'S TORN...
PEOPLE AND AYAKASHI HAVE COME AND GONE THROUGH THAT BOX.
WHAT IS THE SIGNIFICANCE OF THIS...?

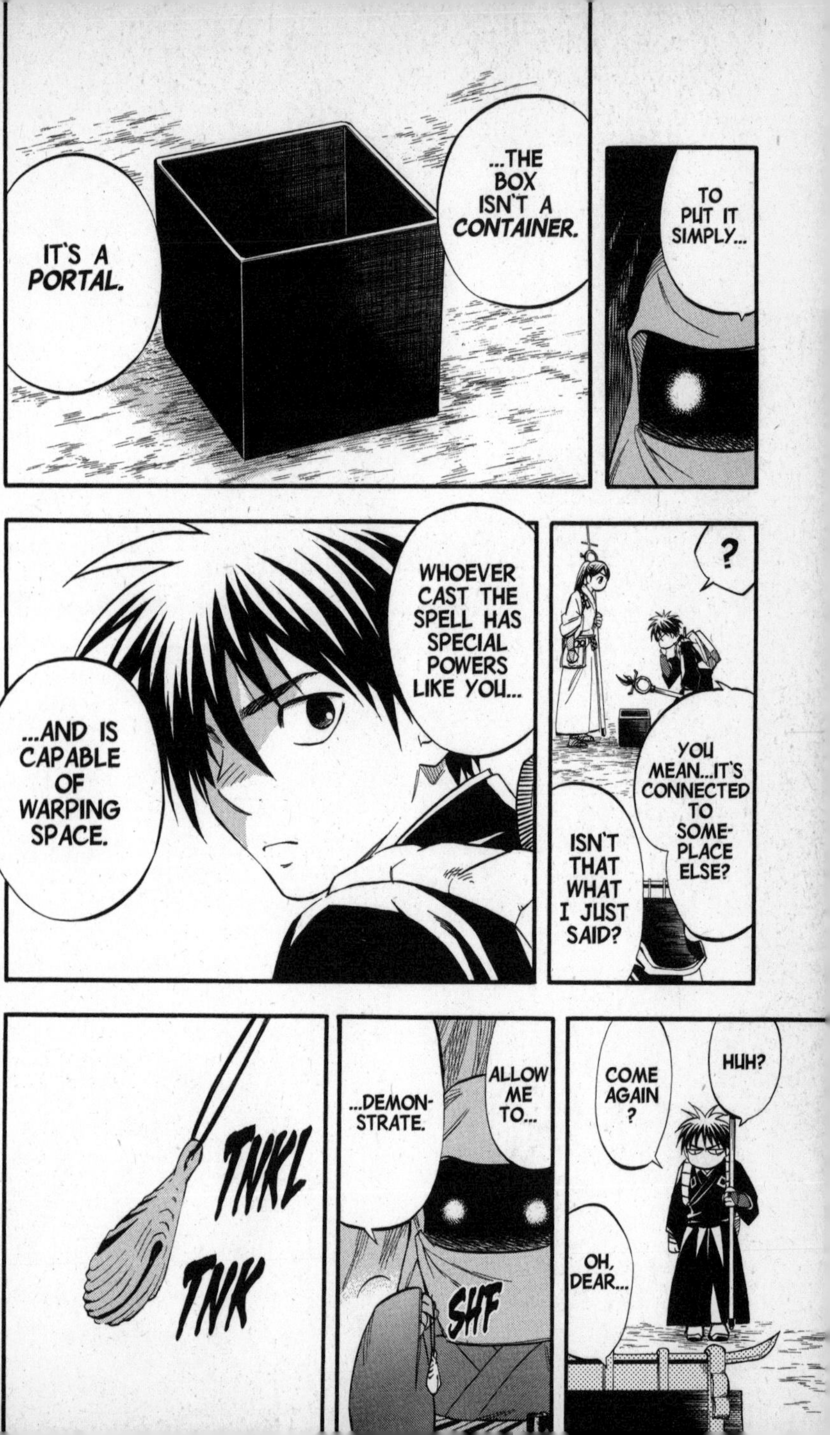
TO PUT IT SIMPLY...
...THE BOX ISN'T A CONTAINER.
IT'S A PORTAL.
?
YOU MEAN...IT'S CONNECTED TO SOME-PLACE ELSE?
ISN'T THAT WHAT I JUST SAID?
WHOEVER CAST THE SPELL HAS SPECIAL POWERS LIKE YOU...
...AND IS CAPABLE OF WARPING SPACE.
HUH?
COME AGAIN?
OH, DEAR...
ALLOW ME TO...
...DEMON-STRATE.
SHF
TNKL
TNK

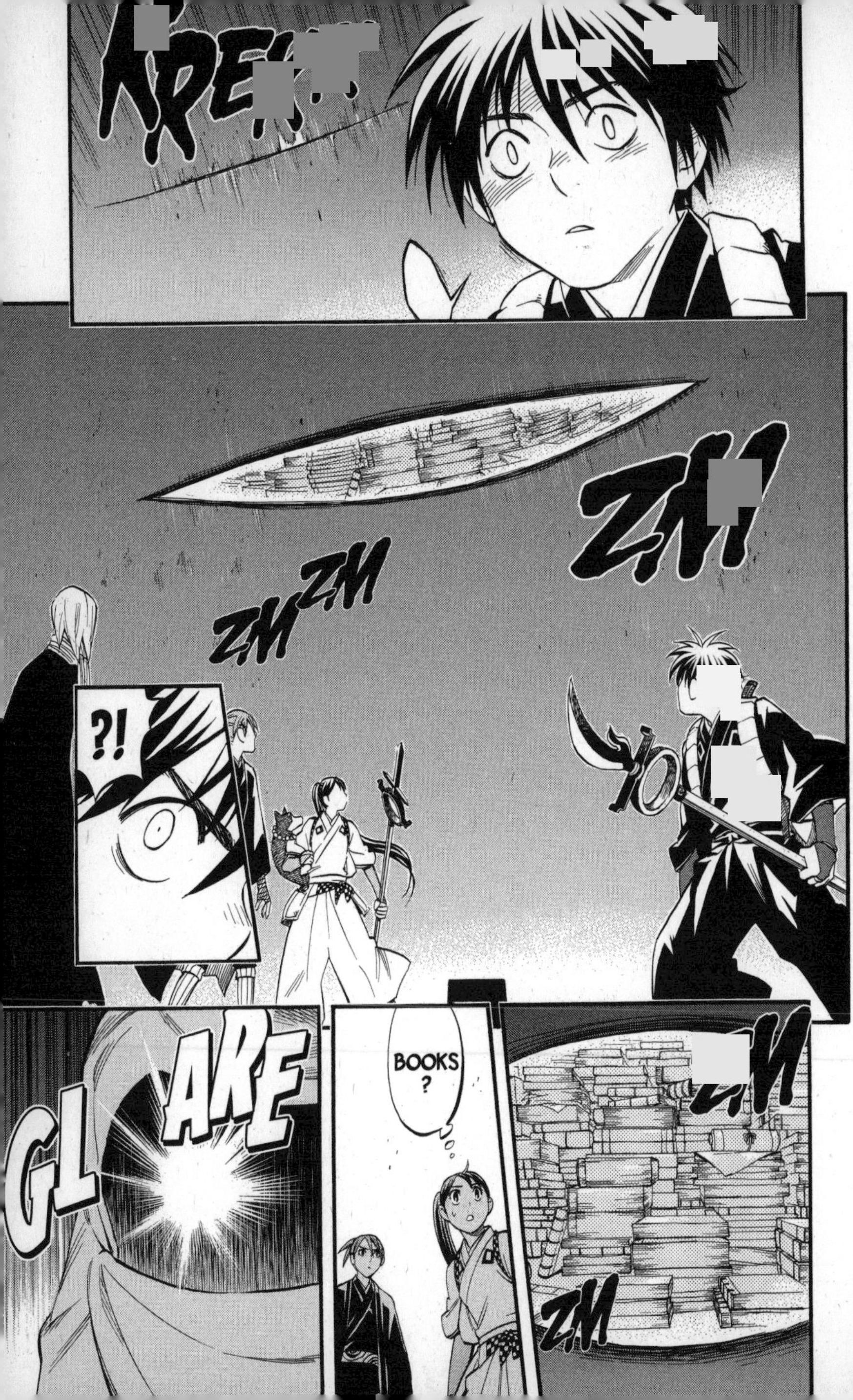
ZM ZM
?!
BOOKS ?
ZM

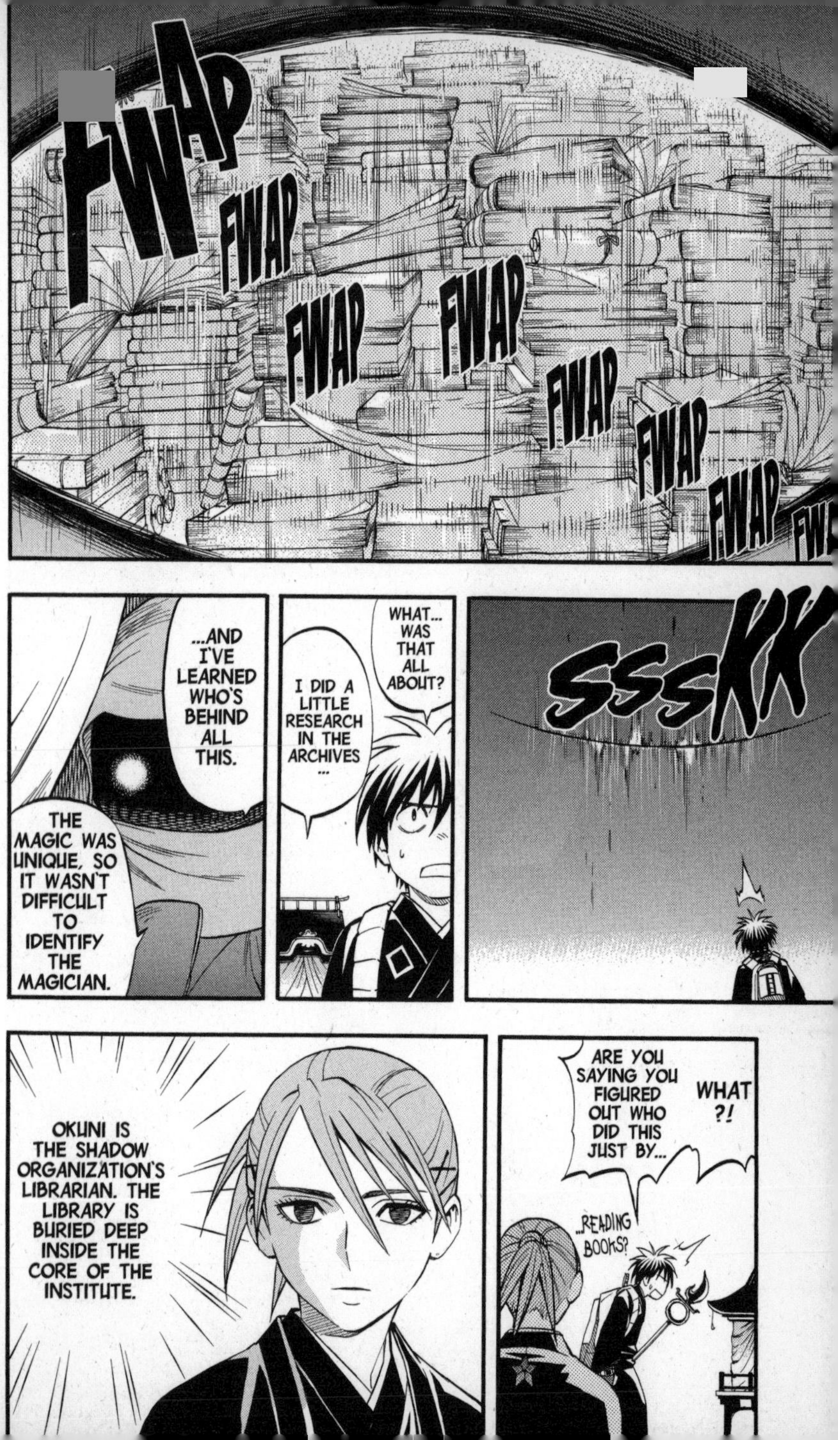
FWAP
FWAP
FWAP
FWAP
FWAP
FWAP
FWAP
SSSKK
WHAT... WAS THAT ALL ABOUT?
I DID A LITTLE RESEARCH IN THE ARCHIVES...
...AND I'VE LEARNED WHO'S BEHIND ALL THIS.
THE MAGIC WAS UNIQUE, SO IT WASN'T DIFFICULT TO IDENTIFY THE MAGICIAN.
WHAT?!
ARE YOU SAYING YOU FIGURED OUT WHO DID THIS JUST BY...
...READING BOOKS?
OKUNI IS THE SHADOW ORGANIZATION'S LIBRARIAN. THE LIBRARY IS BURIED DEEP INSIDE THE CORE OF THE INSTITUTE.

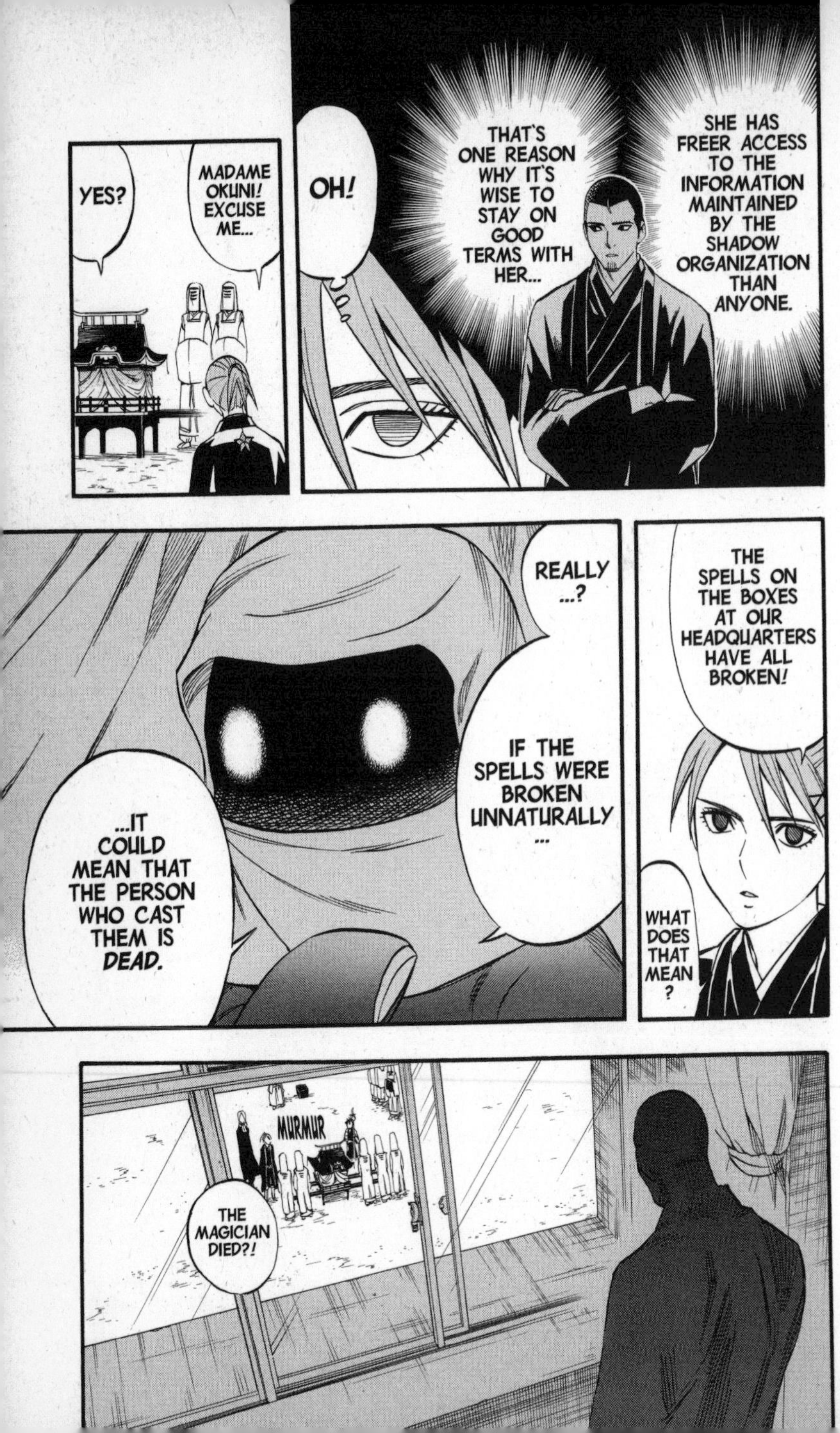
SHE HAS FREER ACCESS TO THE INFORMATION MAINTAINED BY THE SHADOW ORGANIZATION THAN ANYONE.
THAT'S ONE REASON WHY IT'S WISE TO STAY ON GOOD TERMS WITH HER...
OH!
MADAME OKUNI! EXCUSE ME...
YES?
THE SPELLS ON THE BOXES AT OUR HEADQUARTERS HAVE ALL BROKEN!
WHAT DOES THAT MEAN?
REALLY ...?
IF THE SPELLS WERE BROKEN UNNATURALLY ...
...IT COULD MEAN THAT THE PERSON WHO CAST THEM IS *DEAD.*
MURMUR
THE MAGICIAN DIED?!

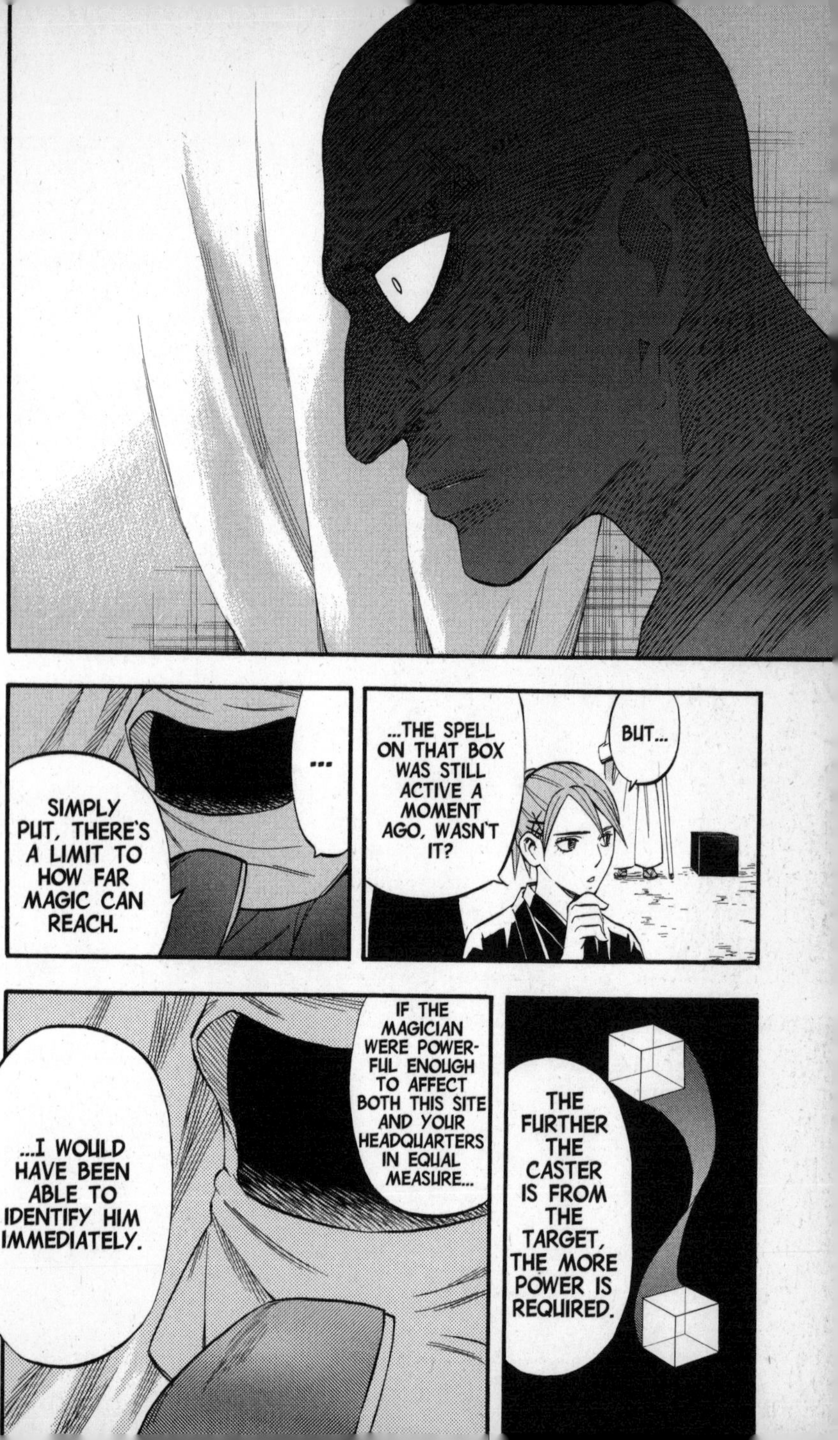
BUT...
...THE SPELL ON THAT BOX WAS STILL ACTIVE A MOMENT AGO, WASN'T IT?
...
SIMPLY PUT, THERE'S A LIMIT TO HOW FAR MAGIC CAN REACH.
THE FURTHER THE CASTER IS FROM THE TARGET, THE MORE POWER IS REQUIRED.
IF THE MAGICIAN WERE POWER-FUL ENOUGH TO AFFECT BOTH THIS SITE AND YOUR HEADQUARTERS IN EQUAL MEASURE...
...I WOULD HAVE BEEN ABLE TO IDENTIFY HIM IMMEDIATELY.

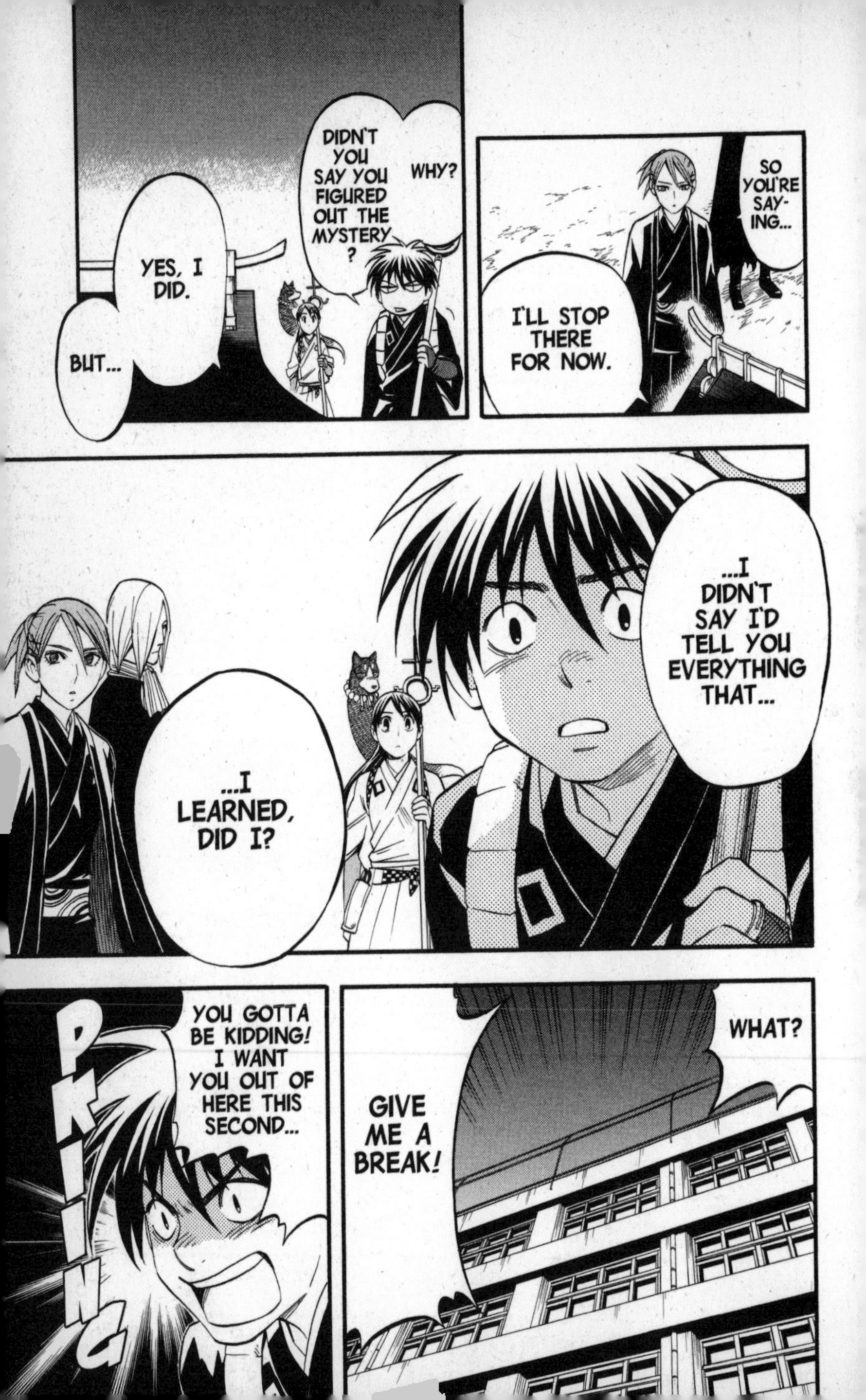
SO YOU'RE SAYING...
I'LL STOP THERE FOR NOW.
WHY?
DIDN'T YOU SAY YOU FIGURED OUT THE MYSTERY?
YES, I DID.
BUT...
...I DIDN'T SAY I'D TELL YOU EVERYTHING THAT...
...I LEARNED, DID I?
WHAT?
GIVE ME A BREAK!
YOU GOTTA BE KIDDING! I WANT YOU OUT OF HERE THIS SECOND...
PKIING

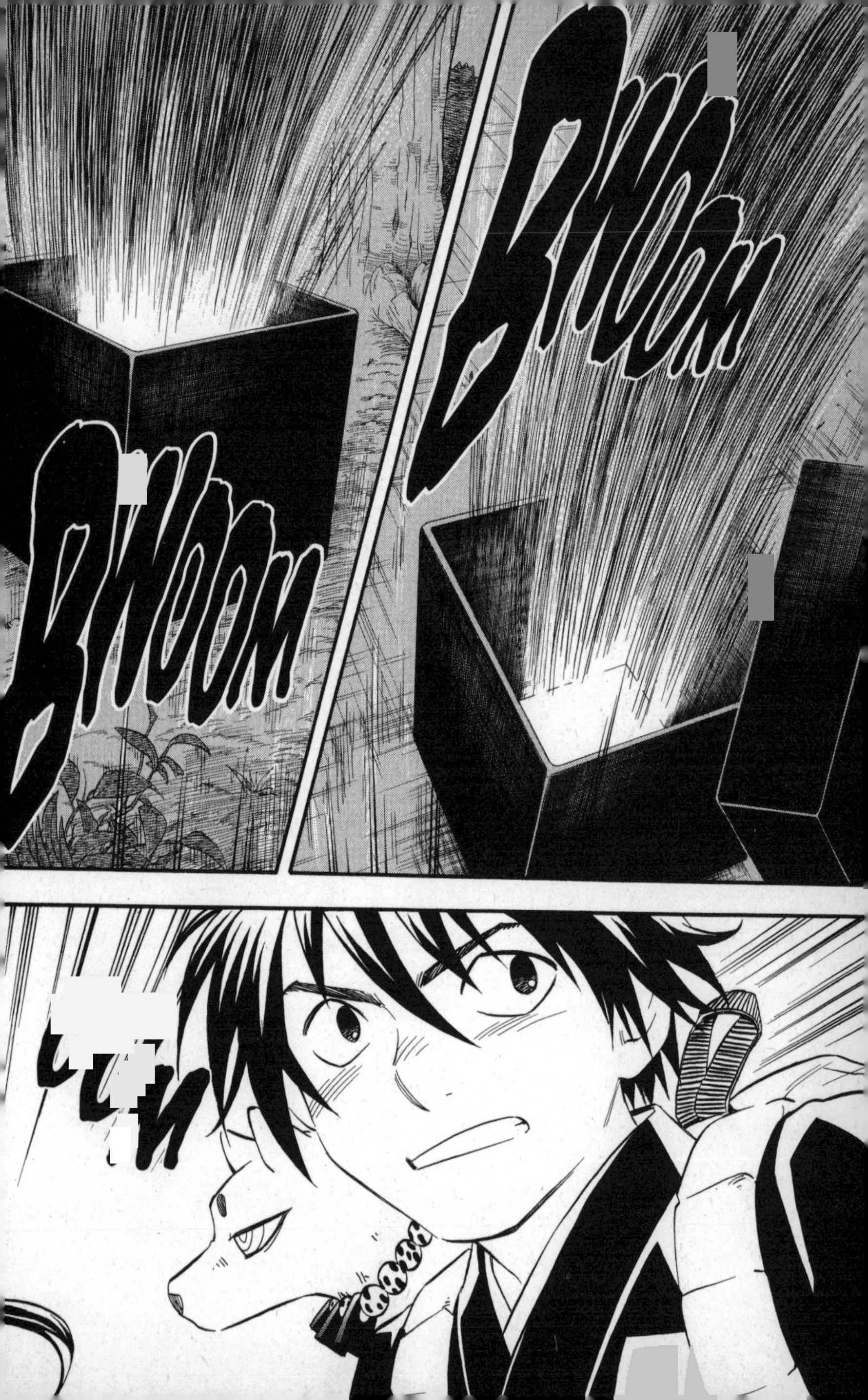
SHOOM
SHOOM

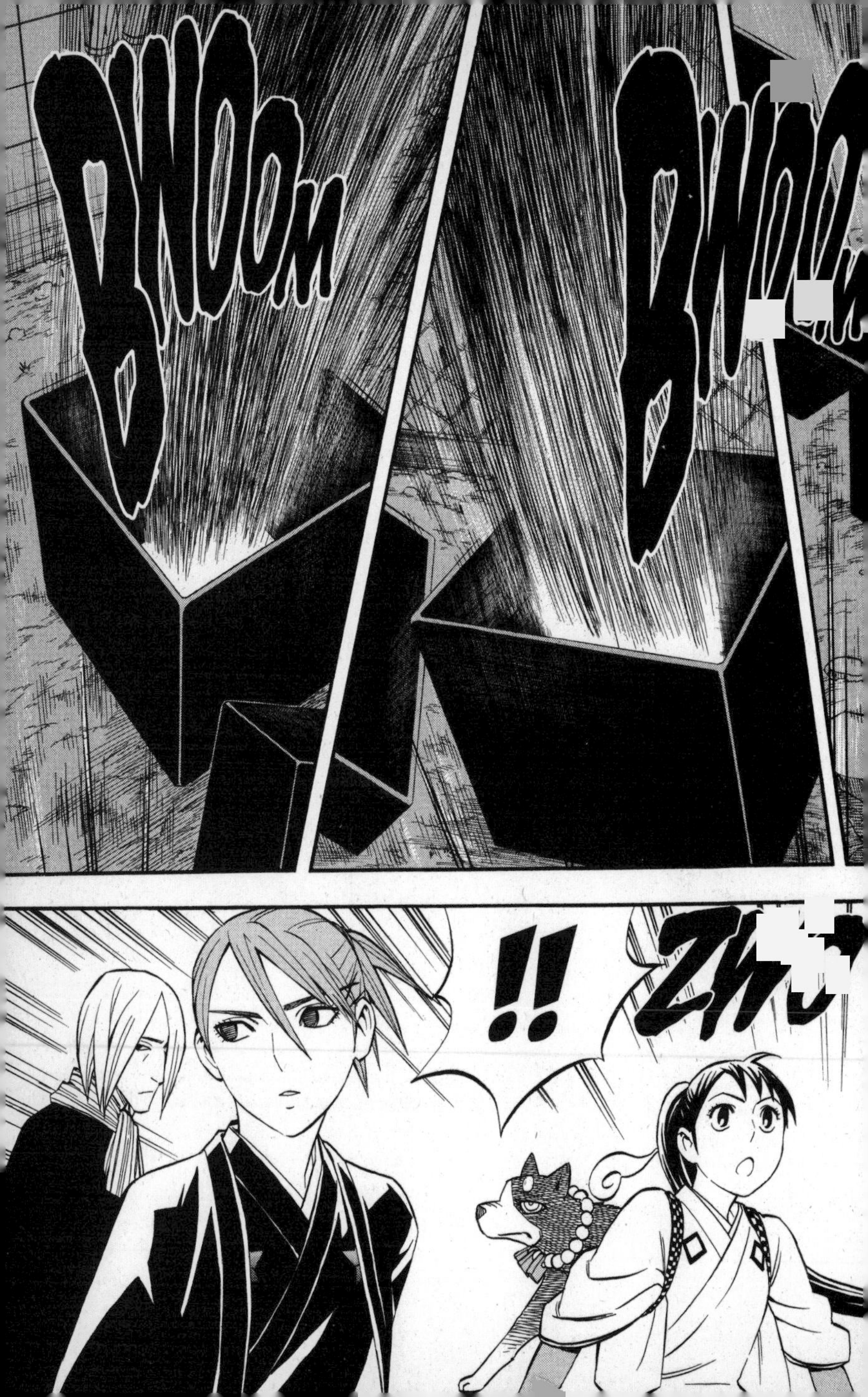
BWOOM
!!

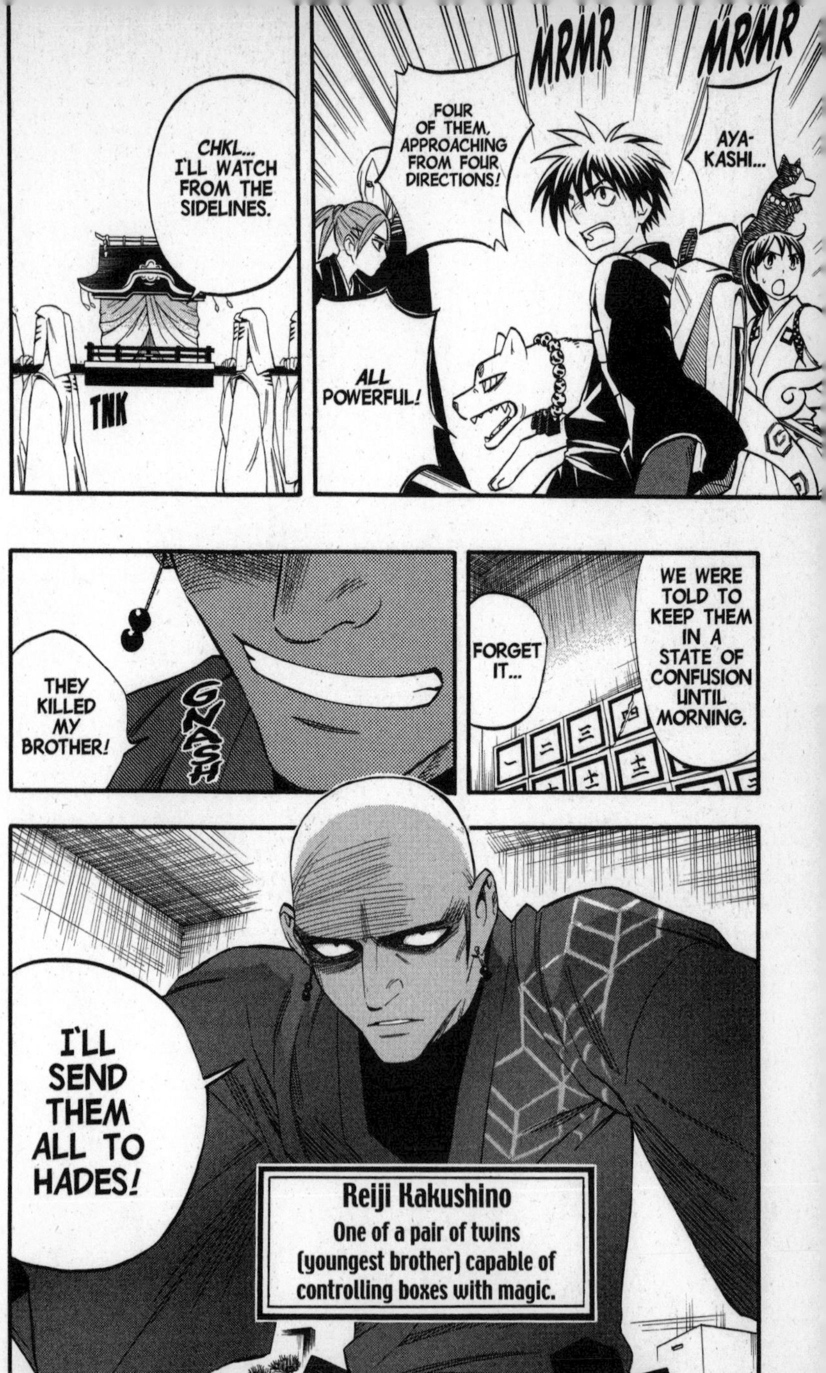
MRMR
MRMR
AYA-KASHI...
FOUR OF THEM, APPROACHING FROM FOUR DIRECTIONS!
ALL POWERFUL!
CHKL... I'LL WATCH FROM THE SIDELINES.
TNK
WE WERE TOLD TO KEEP THEM IN A STATE OF CONFUSION UNTIL MORNING.
FORGET IT...
THEY KILLED MY BROTHER!
GNASH
I'LL SEND THEM ALL TO HADES!
Reiji Kakushino
One of a pair of twins (youngest brother) capable of controlling boxes with magic.

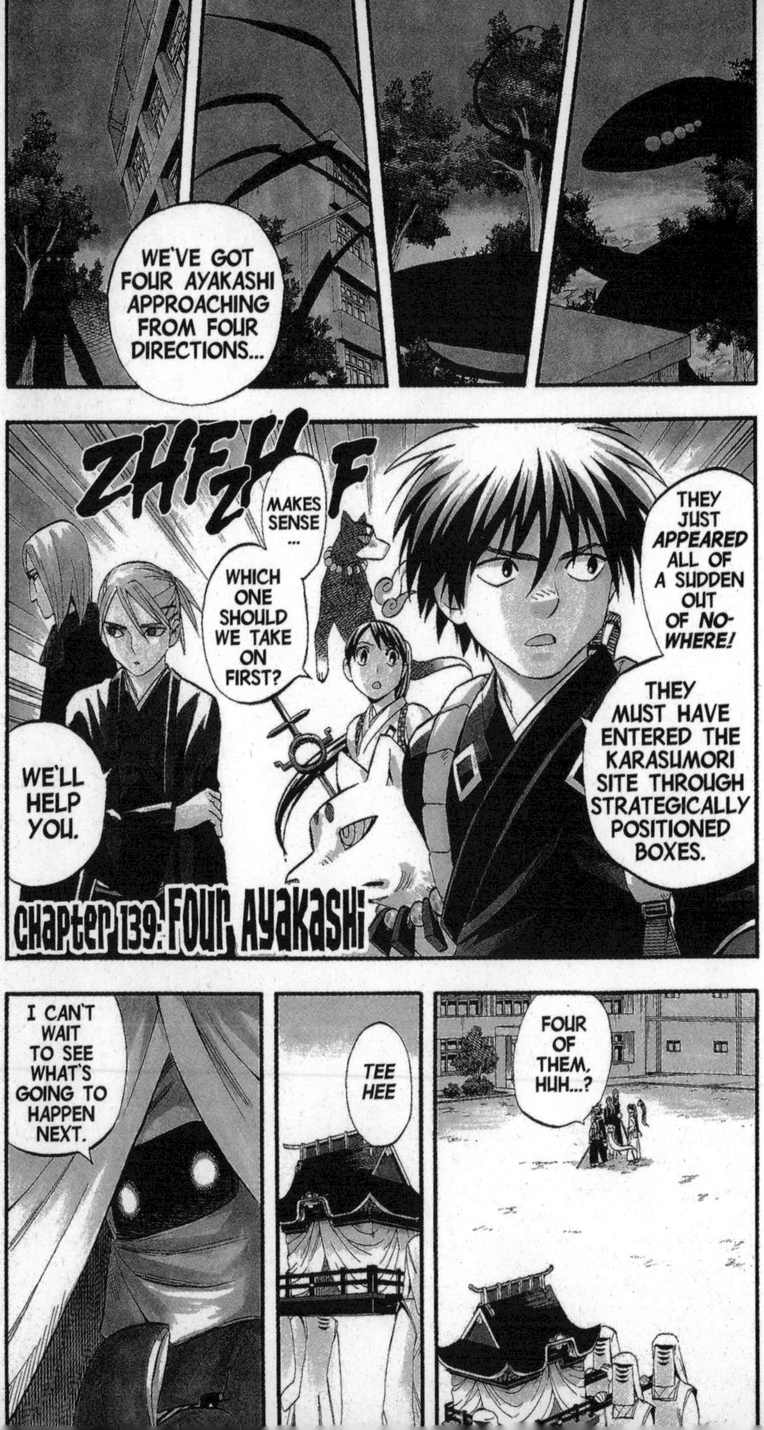
WE'VE GOT FOUR AYAKASHI APPROACHING FROM FOUR DIRECTIONS...
THEY JUST APPEARED ALL OF A SUDDEN OUT OF NO-WHERE!
THEY MUST HAVE ENTERED THE KARASUMORI SITE THROUGH STRATEGICALLY POSITIONED BOXES.
MAKES SENSE...
WHICH ONE SHOULD WE TAKE ON FIRST?
ZHFZHF
WE'LL HELP YOU.
Chapter 139: Four Ayakashi
FOUR OF THEM, HUH...?
TEE HEE
I CAN'T WAIT TO SEE WHAT'S GOING TO HAPPEN NEXT.

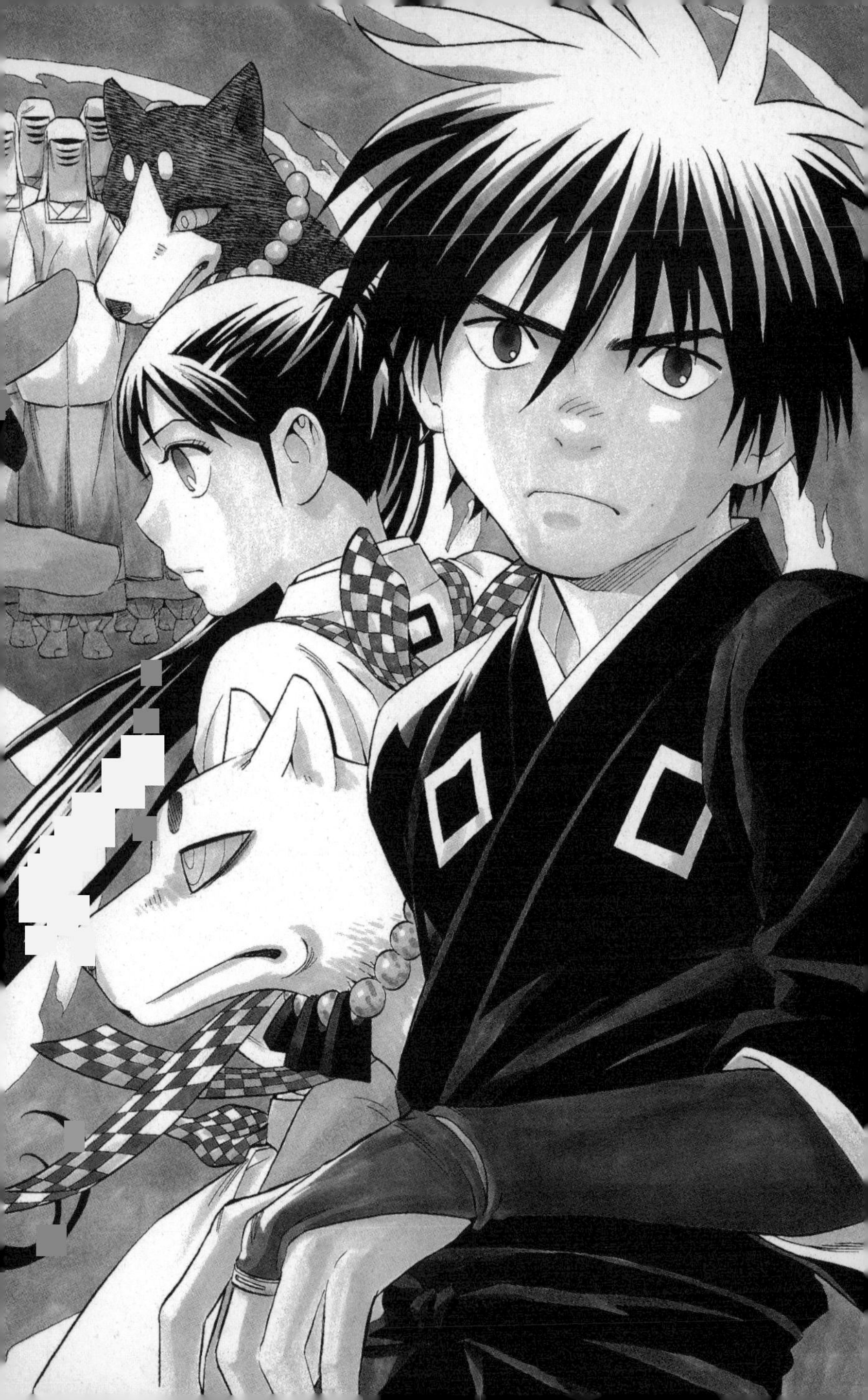

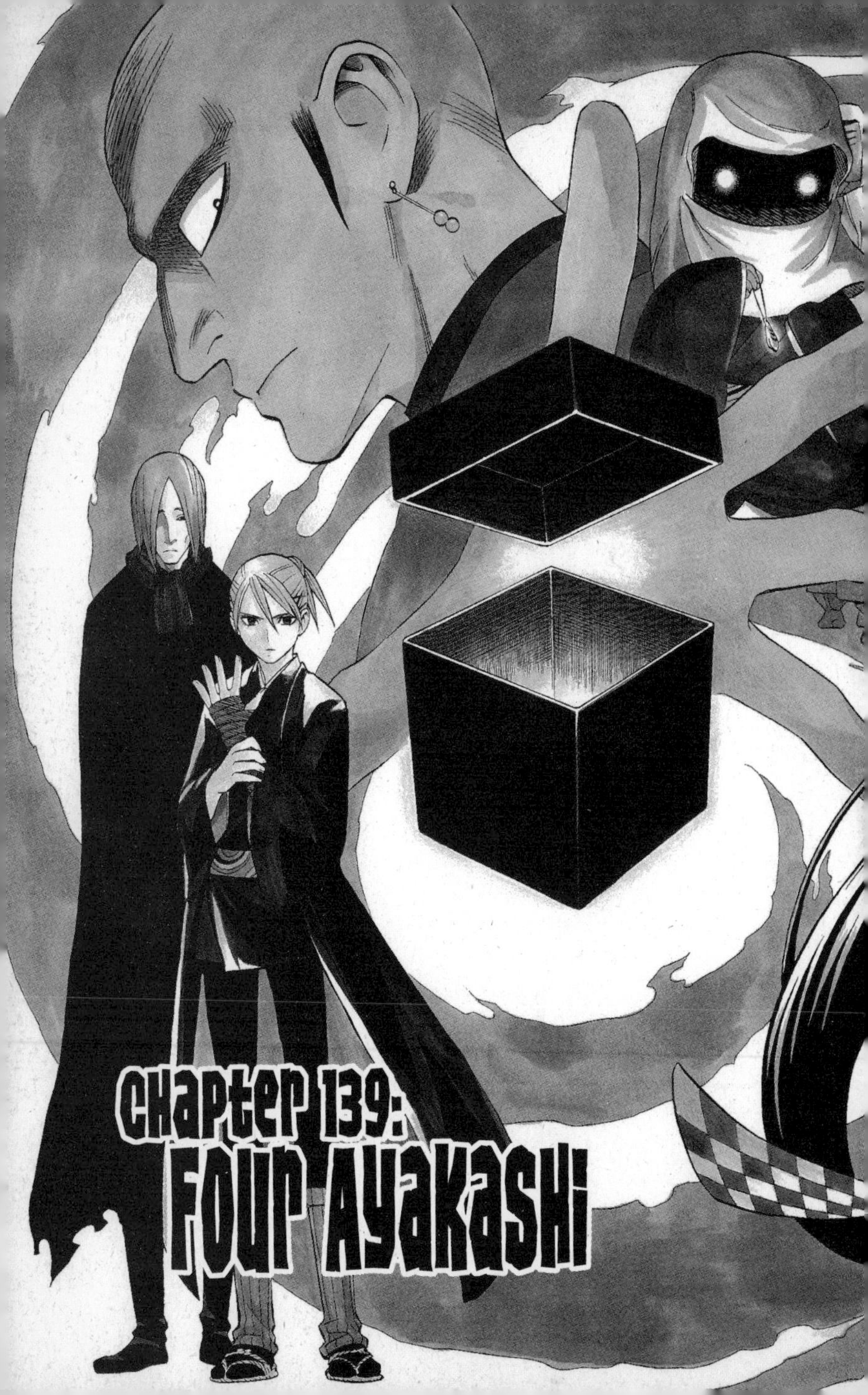
Chapter 139:
Four Ayakashi

結界師

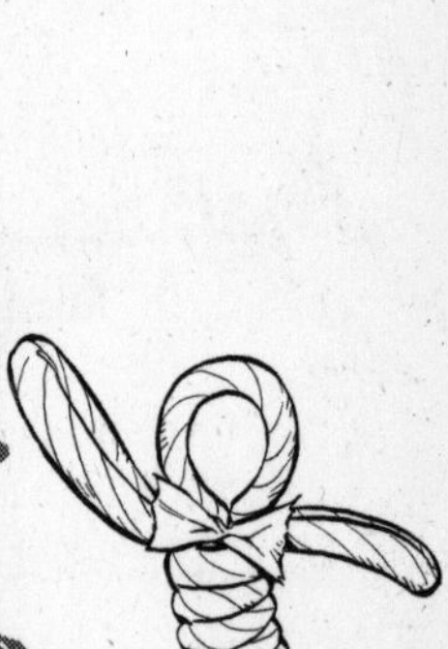

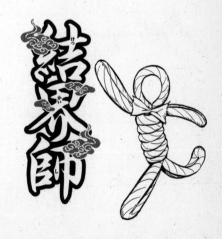

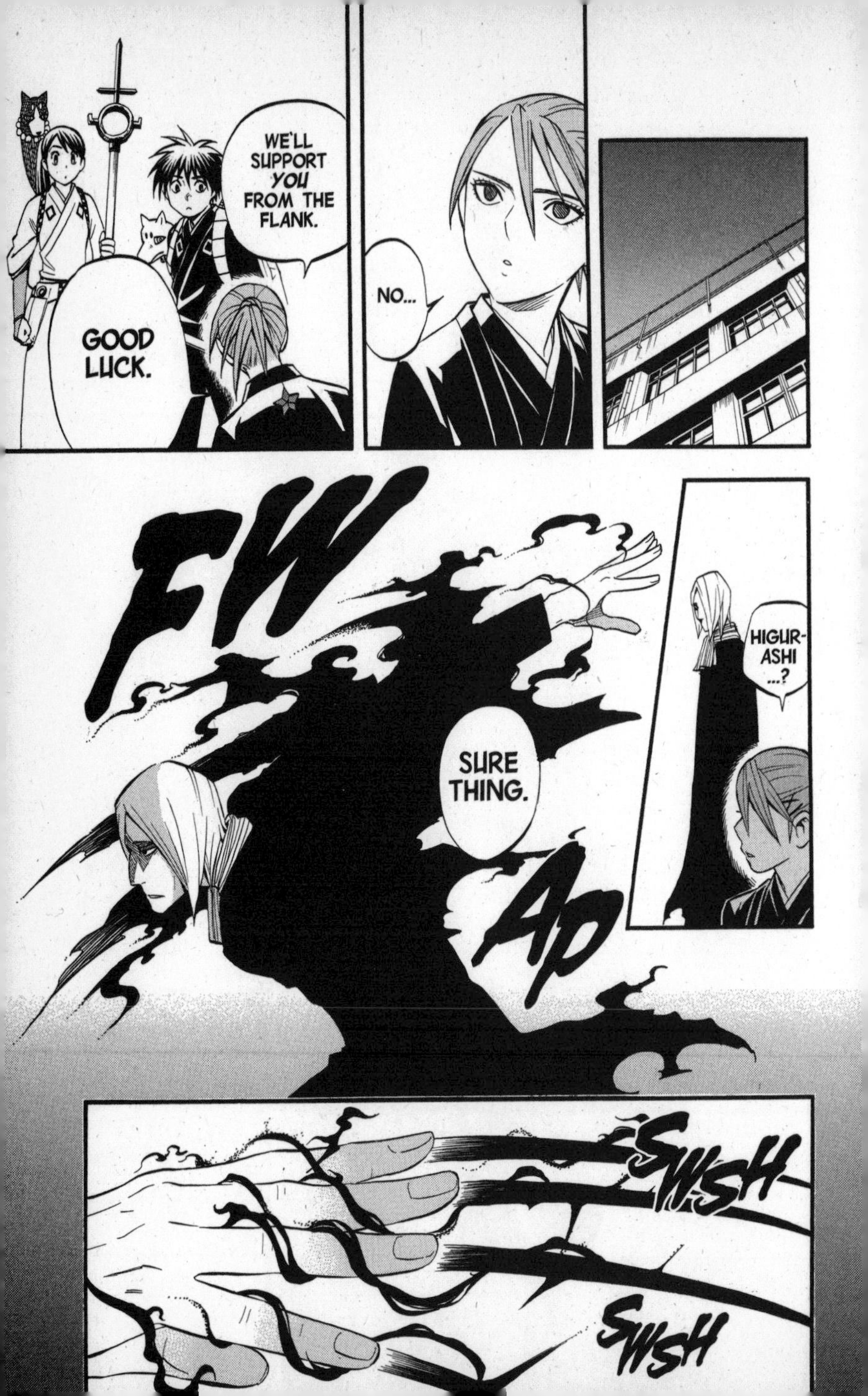
NO...
WE'LL SUPPORT *YOU* FROM THE FLANK.
GOOD LUCK.
HIGURASHI...?
FWAP
SURE THING.
SWSH
SWSH

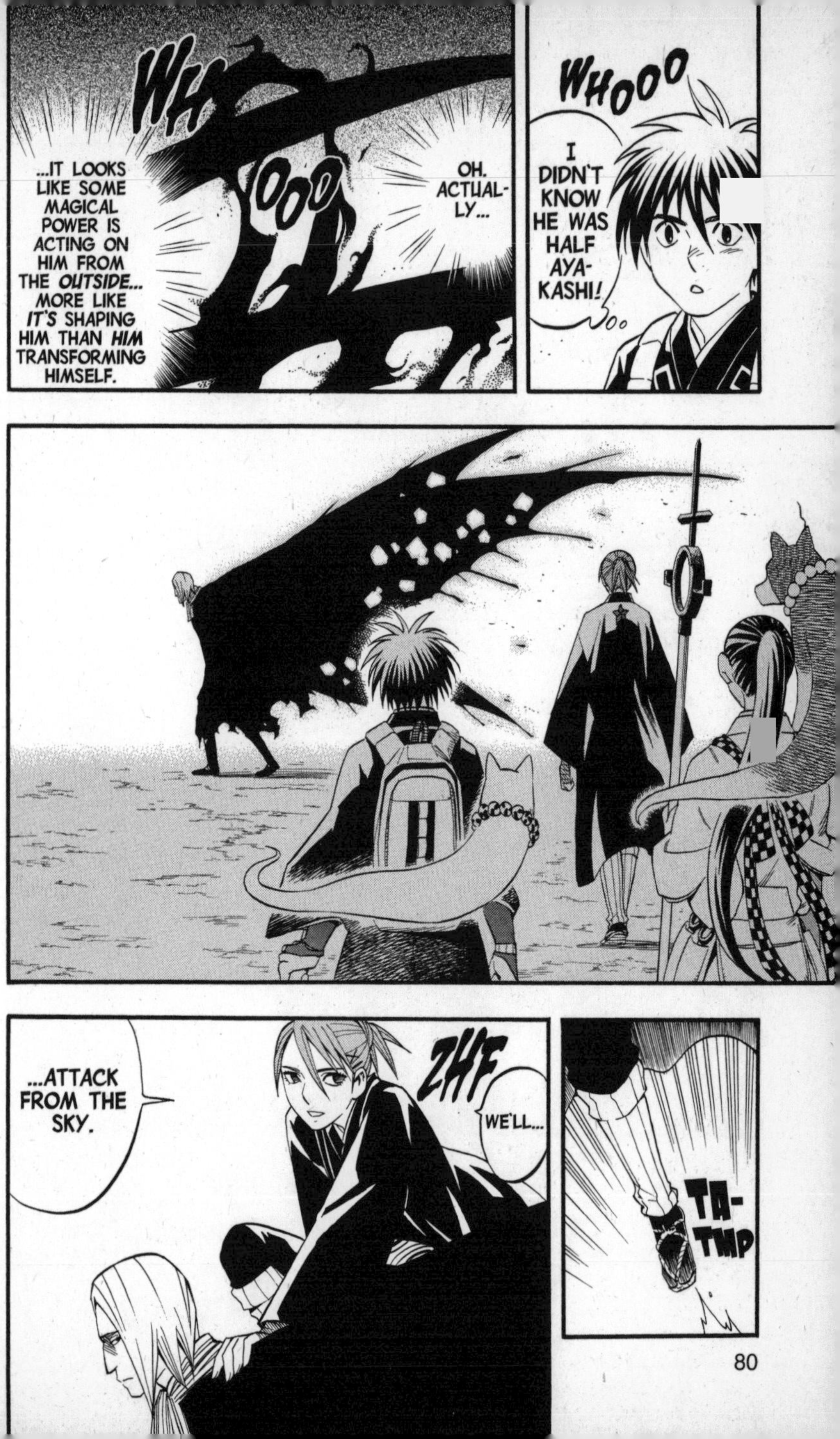
WHOOO
I DIDN'T KNOW HE WAS HALF AYA-KASHI!
WHOOO
OH. ACTUAL-LY...
...IT LOOKS LIKE SOME MAGICAL POWER IS ACTING ON HIM FROM THE *OUTSIDE*... MORE LIKE *IT'S* SHAPING HIM THAN *HIM* TRANSFORMING HIMSELF.
TA-TMP
ZHF
WE'LL...
...ATTACK FROM THE SKY.

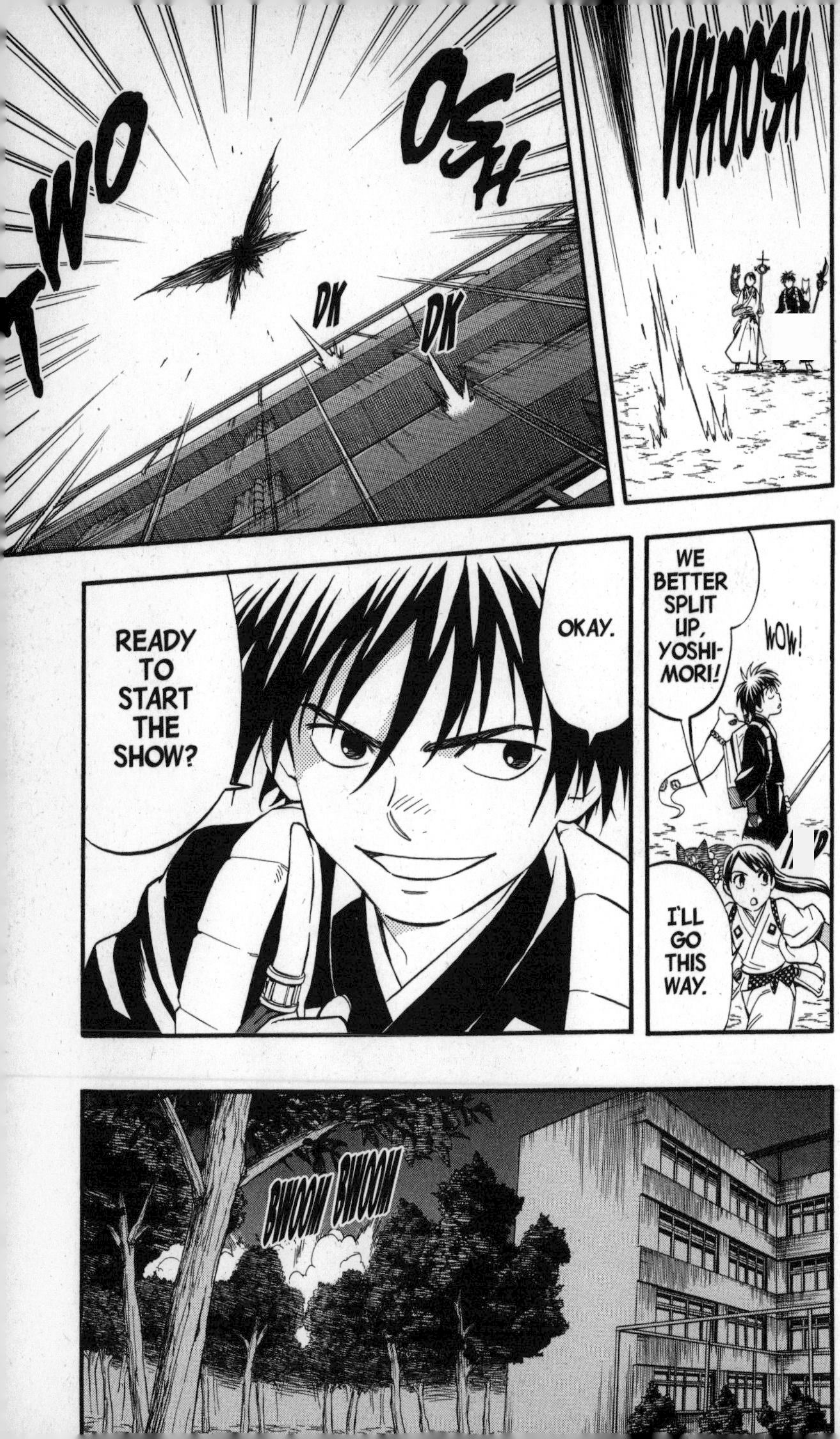
WHOOSH
TWOOSH
DK
DK
WE BETTER SPLIT UP, YOSHIMORI!
WOW!
I'LL GO THIS WAY.
OKAY.
READY TO START THE SHOW?
BWOOM BWOOM

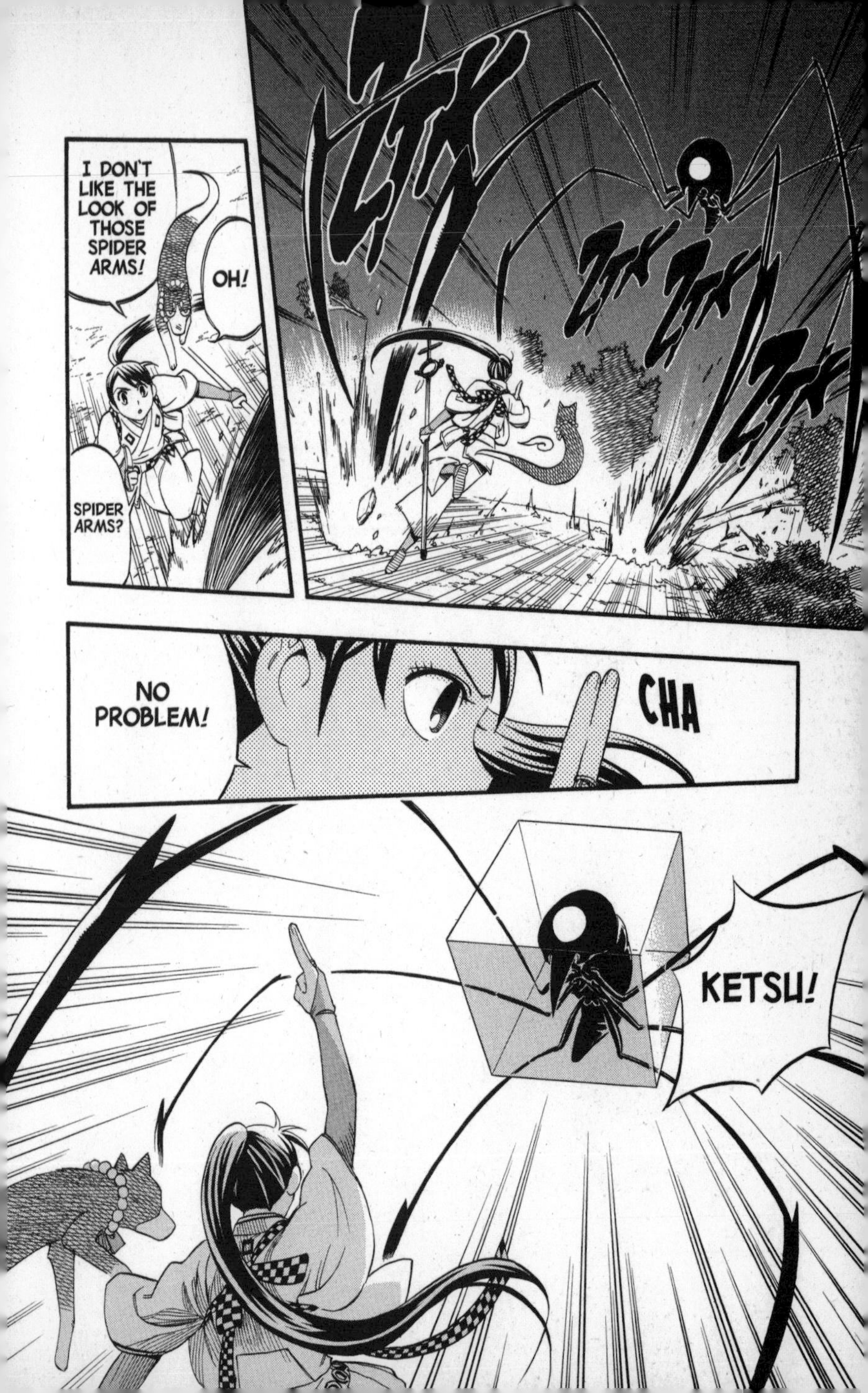
I DON'T LIKE THE LOOK OF THOSE SPIDER ARMS!
OH!
SPIDER ARMS?
NO PROBLEM!
CHA
KETSU!

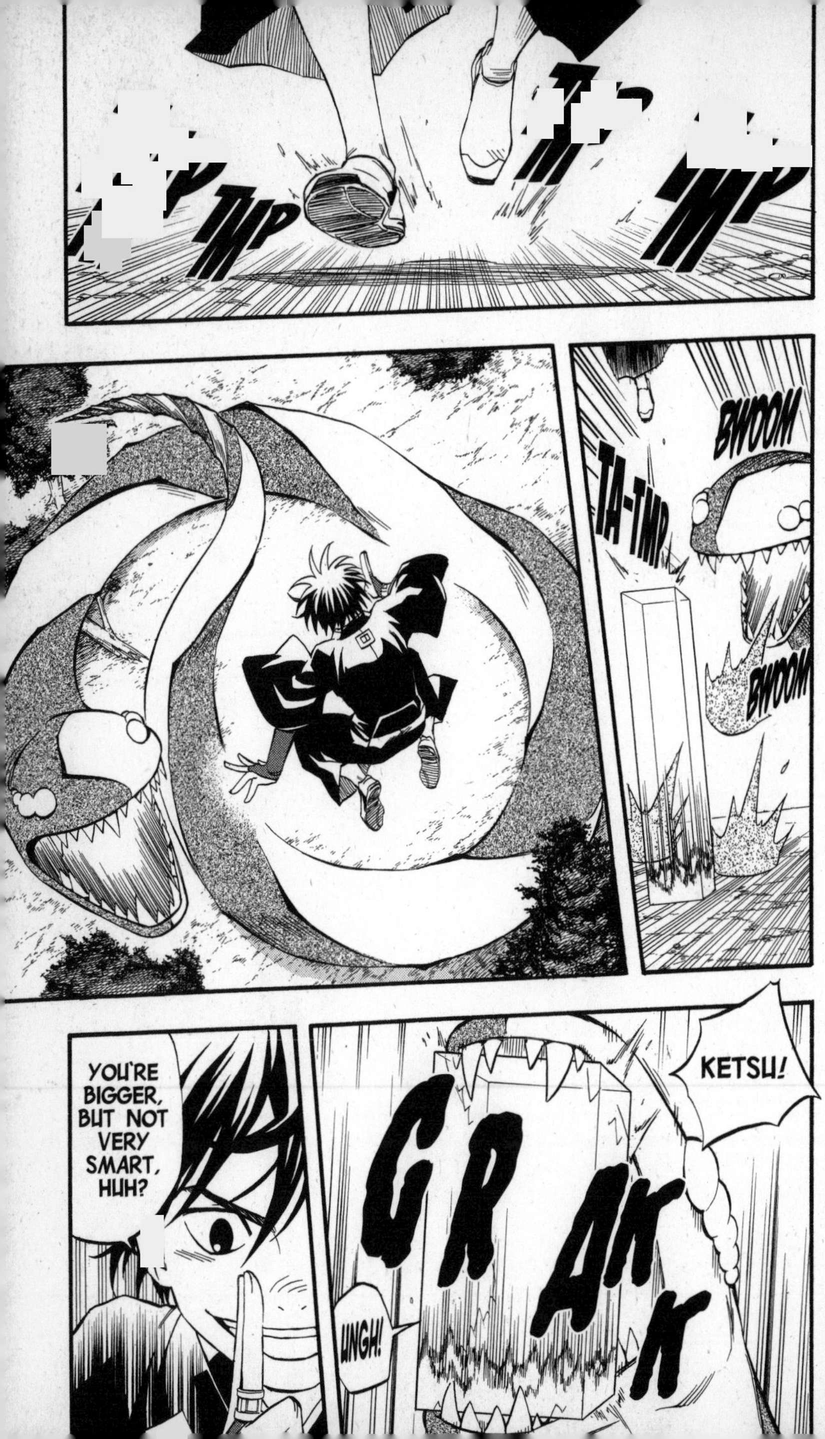
TMP
TMP
BWOOM
TA-TMP
BWOOM
KETSU!
CRAAK
UNGH!
YOU'RE BIGGER, BUT NOT VERY SMART, HUH?

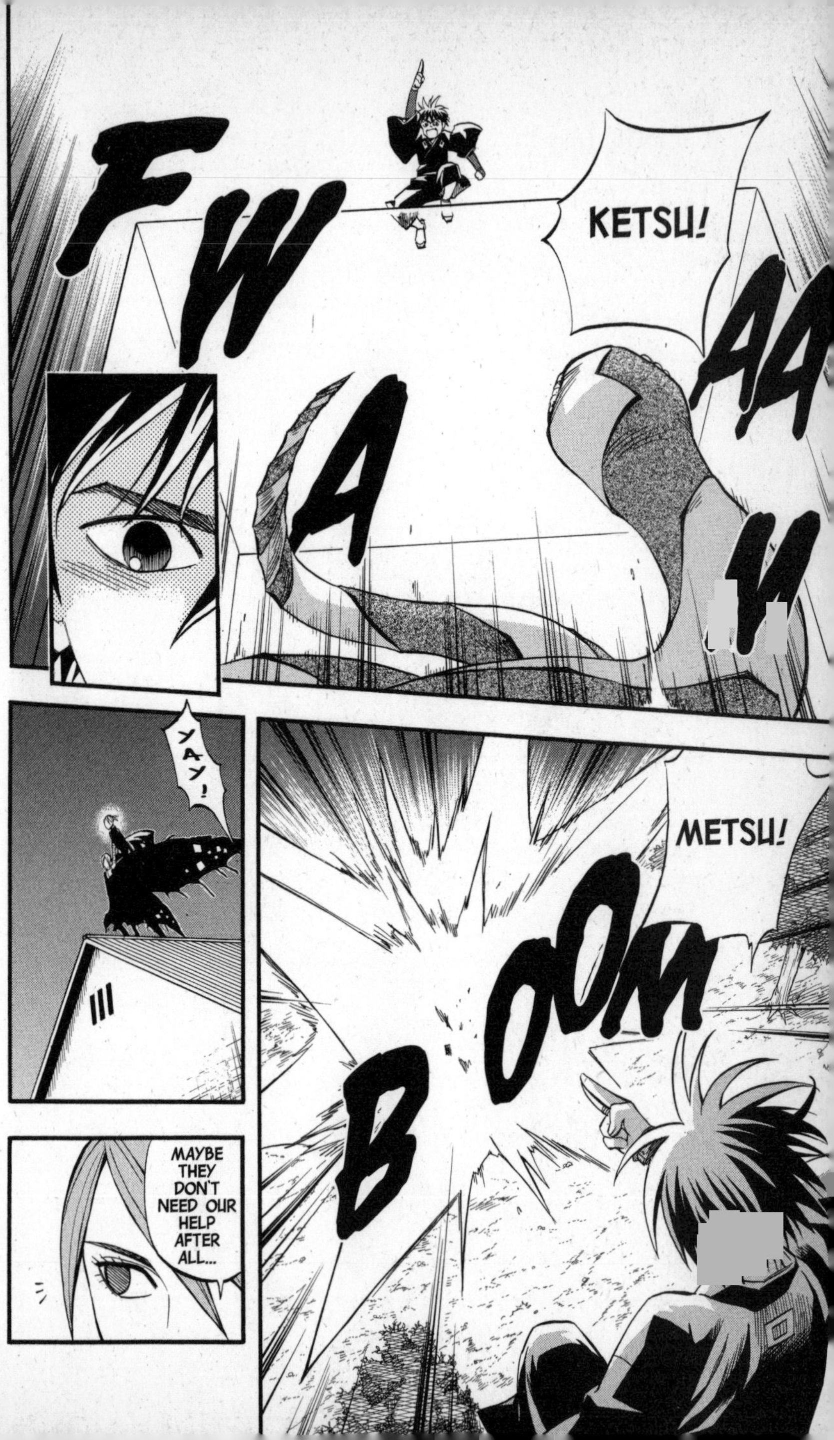
KETSU!
FWAAAN
YAY!
METSU!
BOOM
MAYBE THEY DON'T NEED OUR HELP AFTER ALL...

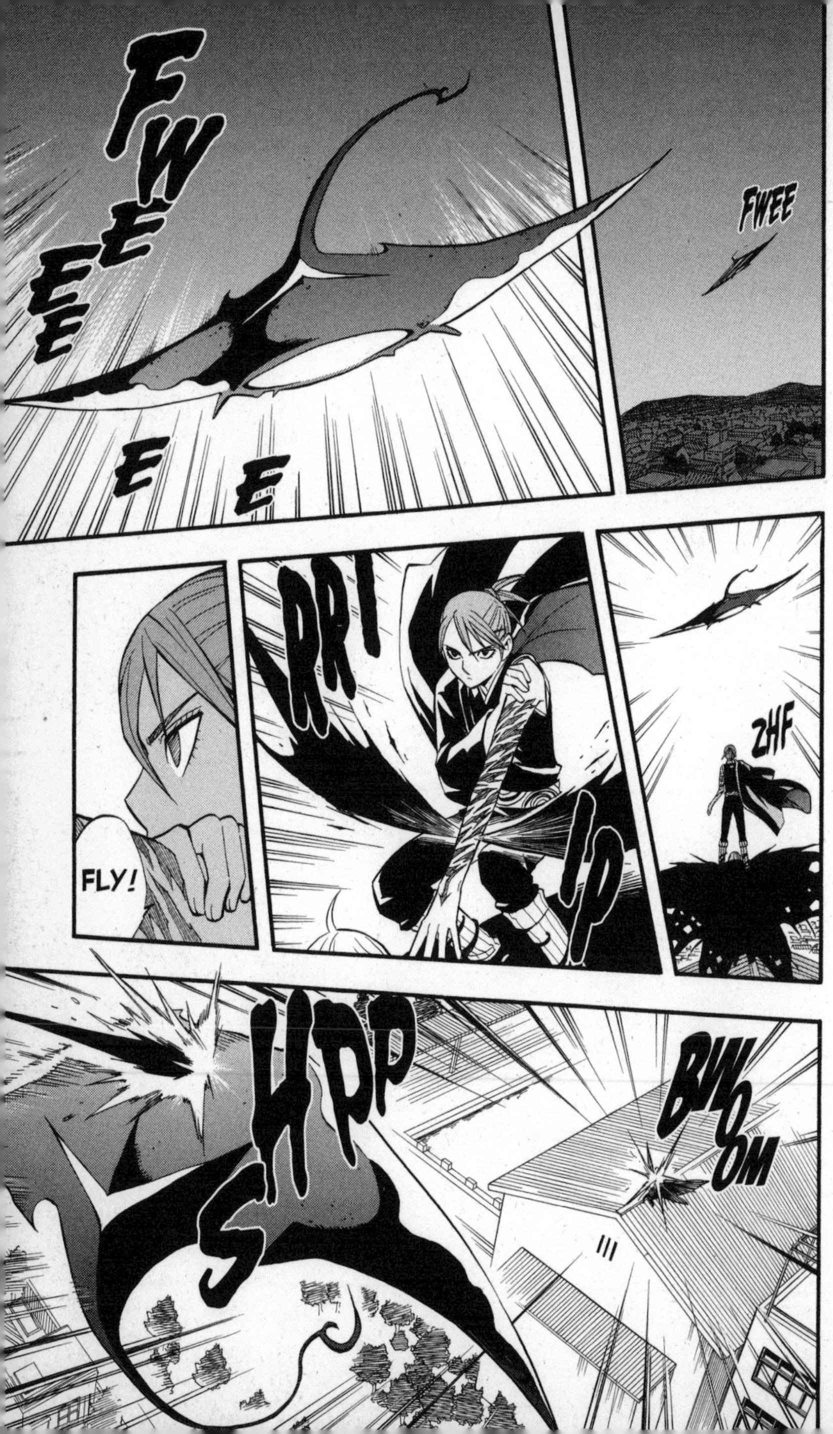
FWEE
FWEEEEE
E
E
ZHF
RRIP
FLY!
BWOOM
SHPP

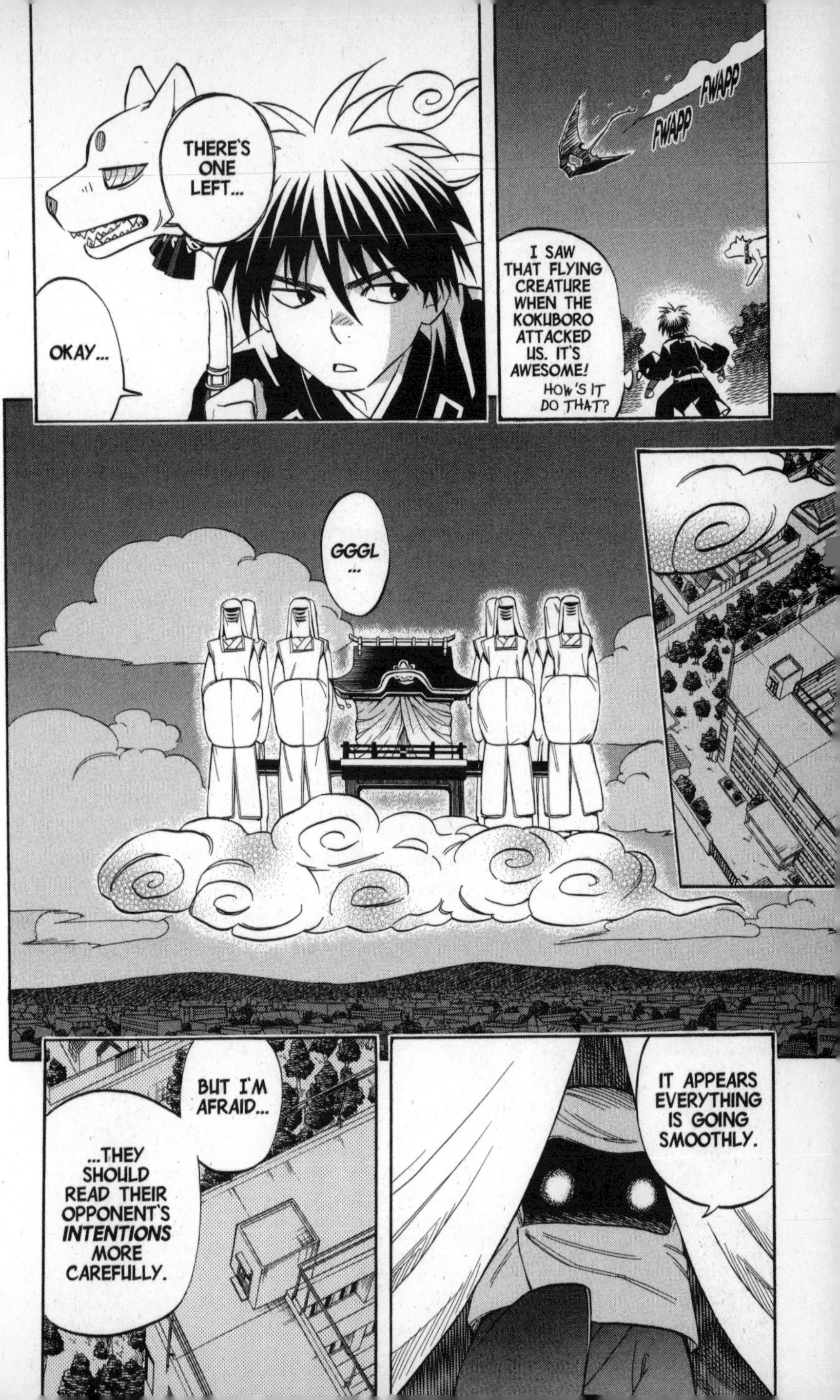
FWAPP
FWAPP
I SAW THAT FLYING CREATURE WHEN THE KOKUBORO ATTACKED US. IT'S AWESOME!
HOW'S IT DO THAT?
THERE'S ONE LEFT...
OKAY...
GGGL...
IT APPEARS EVERYTHING IS GOING SMOOTHLY.
BUT I'M AFRAID...
...THEY SHOULD READ THEIR OPPONENT'S *INTENTIONS* MORE CAREFULLY.

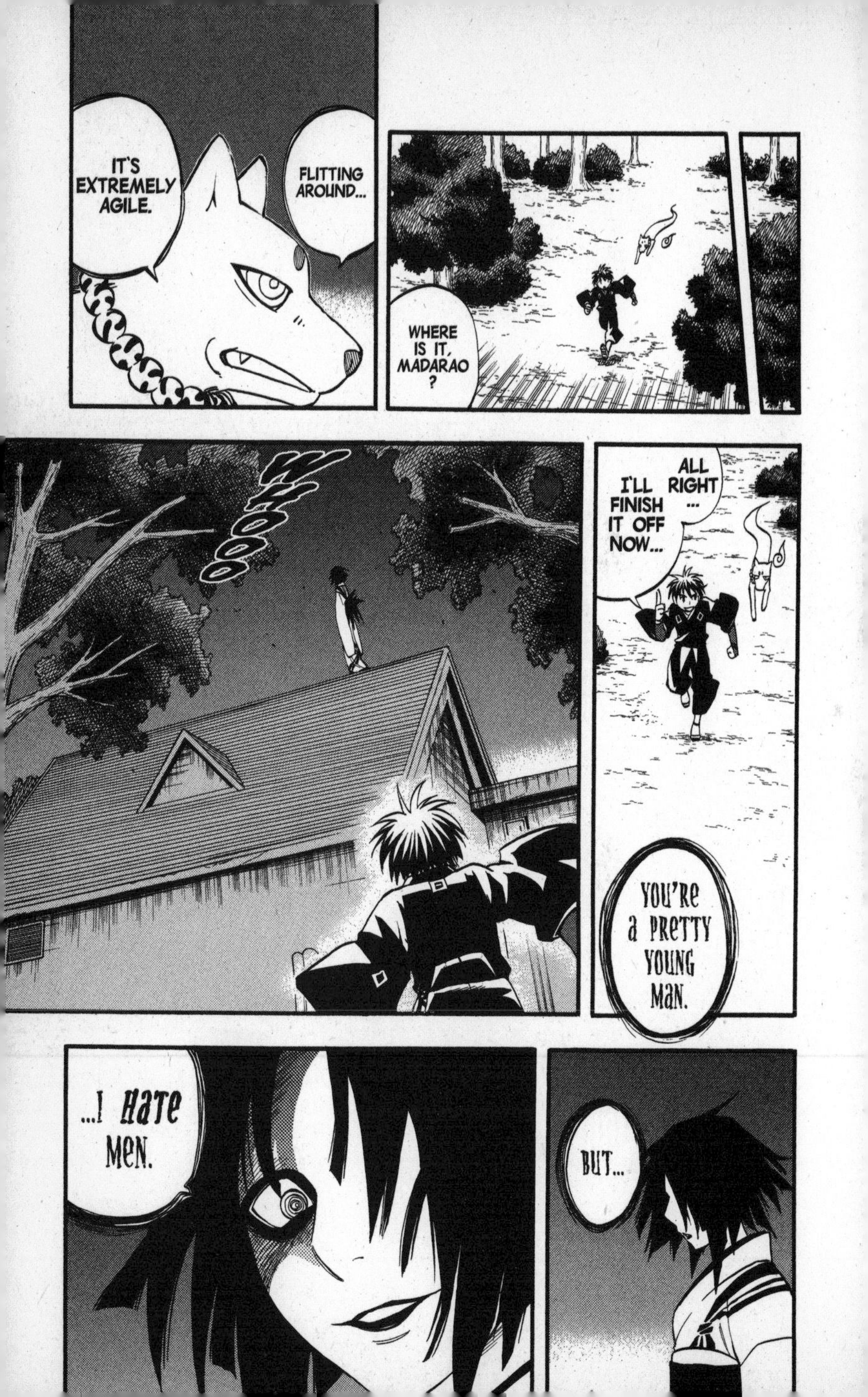
WHERE IS IT, MADARAO?
FLITTING AROUND...
IT'S EXTREMELY AGILE.
ALL RIGHT... I'LL FINISH IT OFF NOW...
YOU'RE A PRETTY YOUNG MAN.
WHOOOO
BUT...
...I HATE MEN.

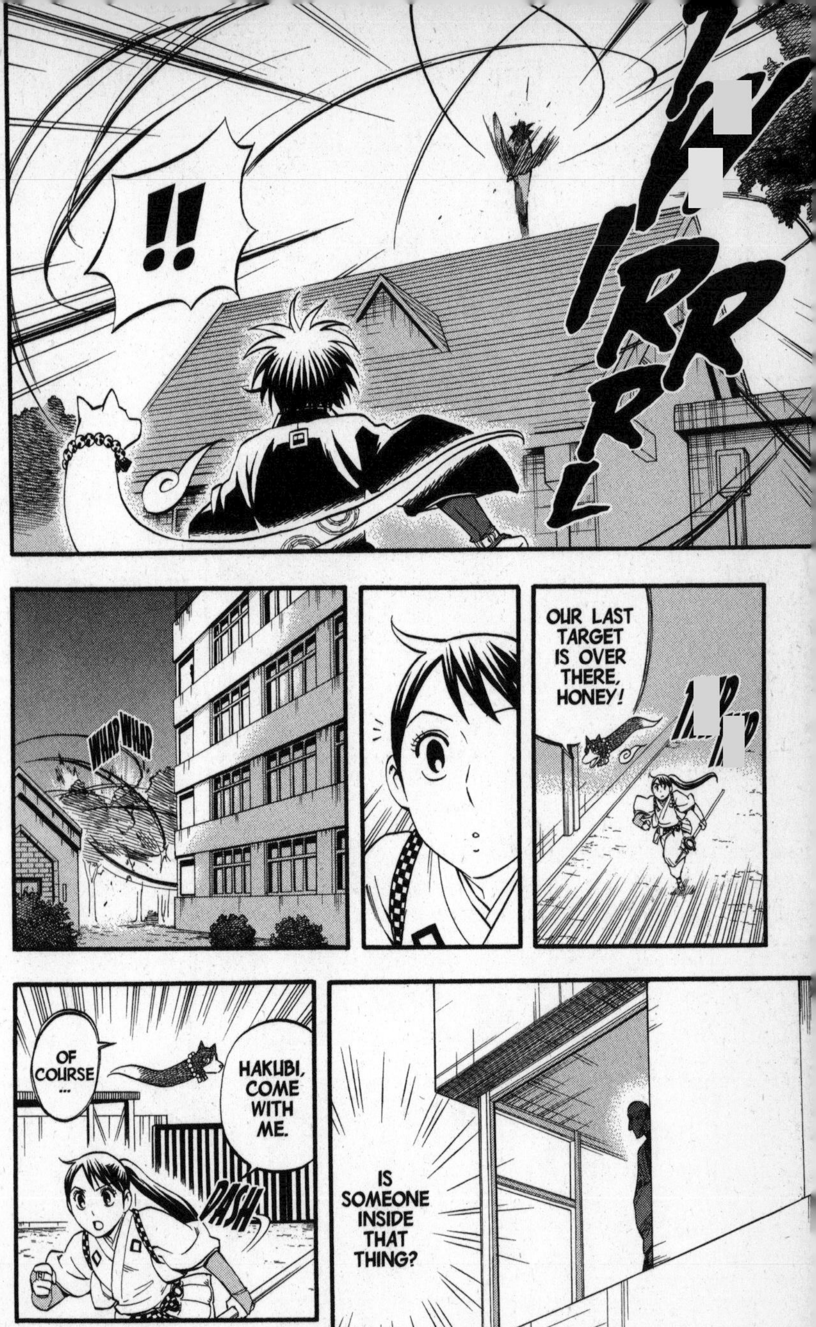

IRRRL
!!
OUR LAST TARGET IS OVER THERE, HONEY!
WHAP WHAP
IS SOMEONE INSIDE THAT THING?
HAKUBI, COME WITH ME.
OF COURSE ...
DASH

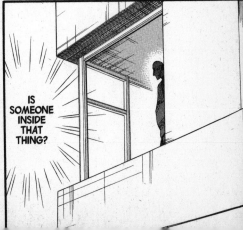

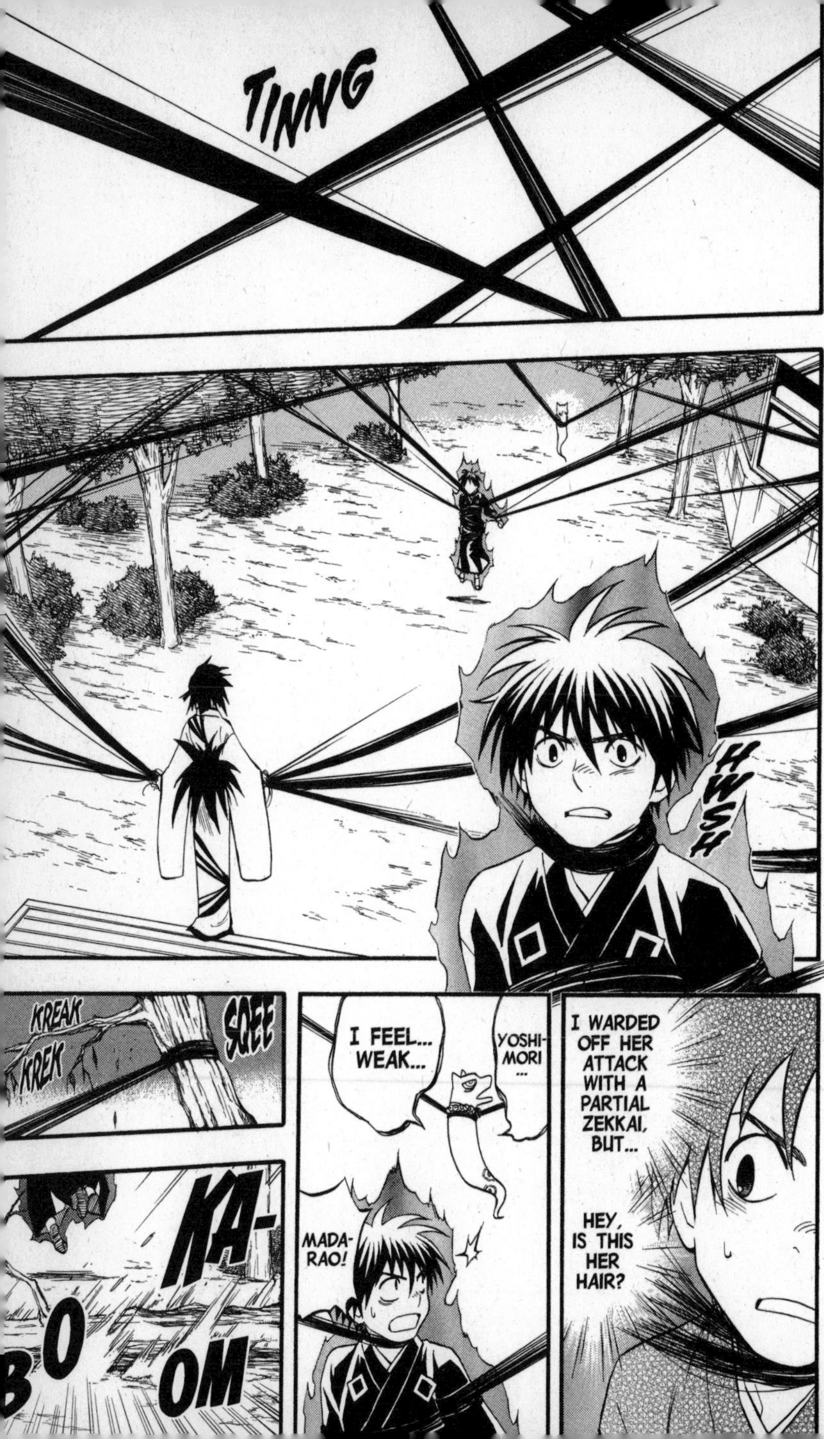
TINNG
HWSH
I WARDED OFF HER ATTACK WITH A PARTIAL ZEKKAI, BUT...
HEY, IS THIS HER HAIR?
YOSHI-MORI...
I FEEL... WEAK...
MADA-RAO!
SQEE
KREAK
KREK
KA-BOOM

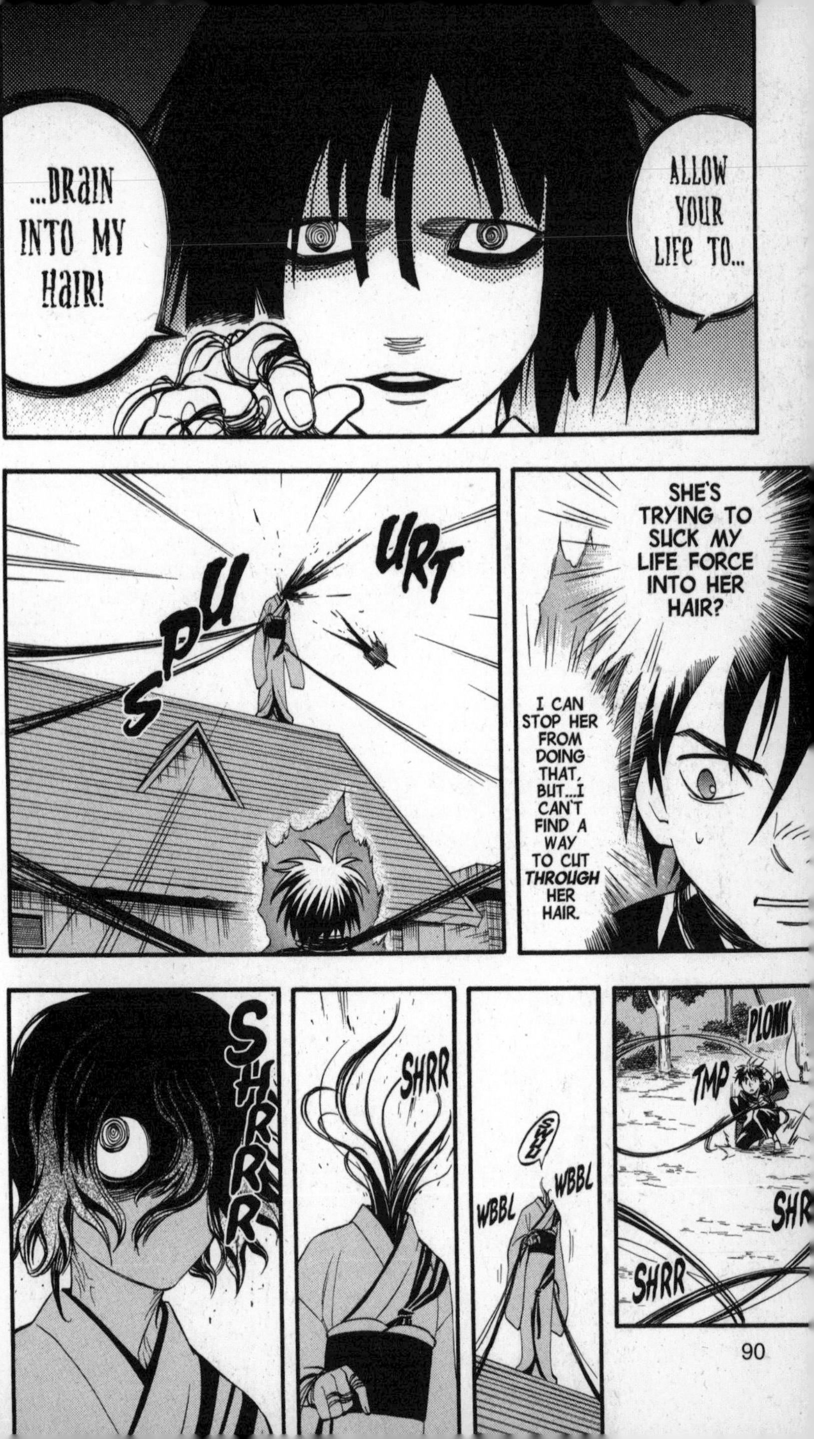
ALLOW YOUR LIFE TO...
...DRAIN INTO MY HAIR!
SHE'S TRYING TO SUCK MY LIFE FORCE INTO HER HAIR?
I CAN STOP HER FROM DOING THAT, BUT...I CAN'T FIND A WAY TO CUT *THROUGH* HER HAIR.
SPURT
PLONK
TMP
SHR
SHRR
SWU
WBBL
WBBL
SHRR
SHRRRR

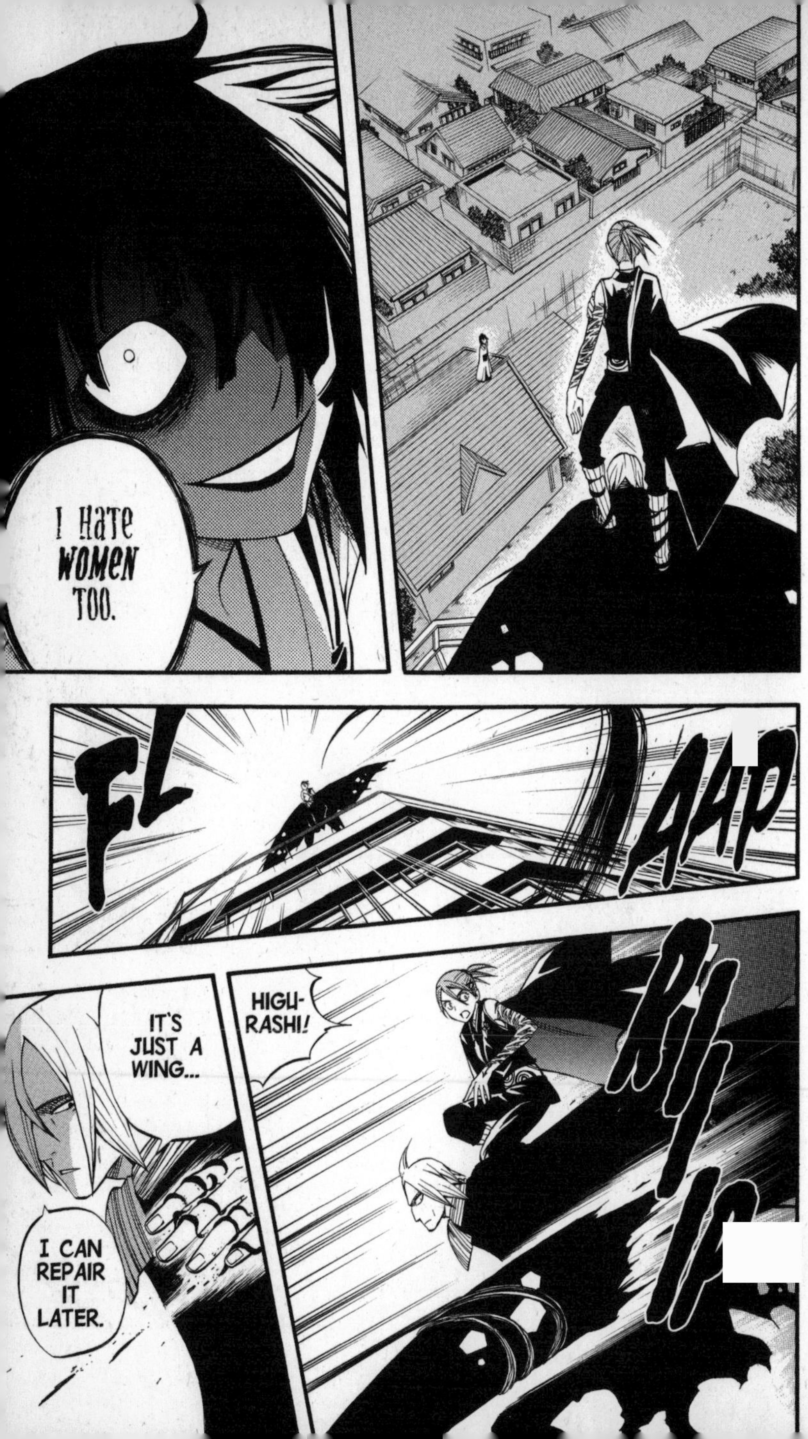
I HATE WOMEN TOO.
FL
AAP
HIGU-RASHI!
IT'S JUST A WING...
I CAN REPAIR IT LATER.

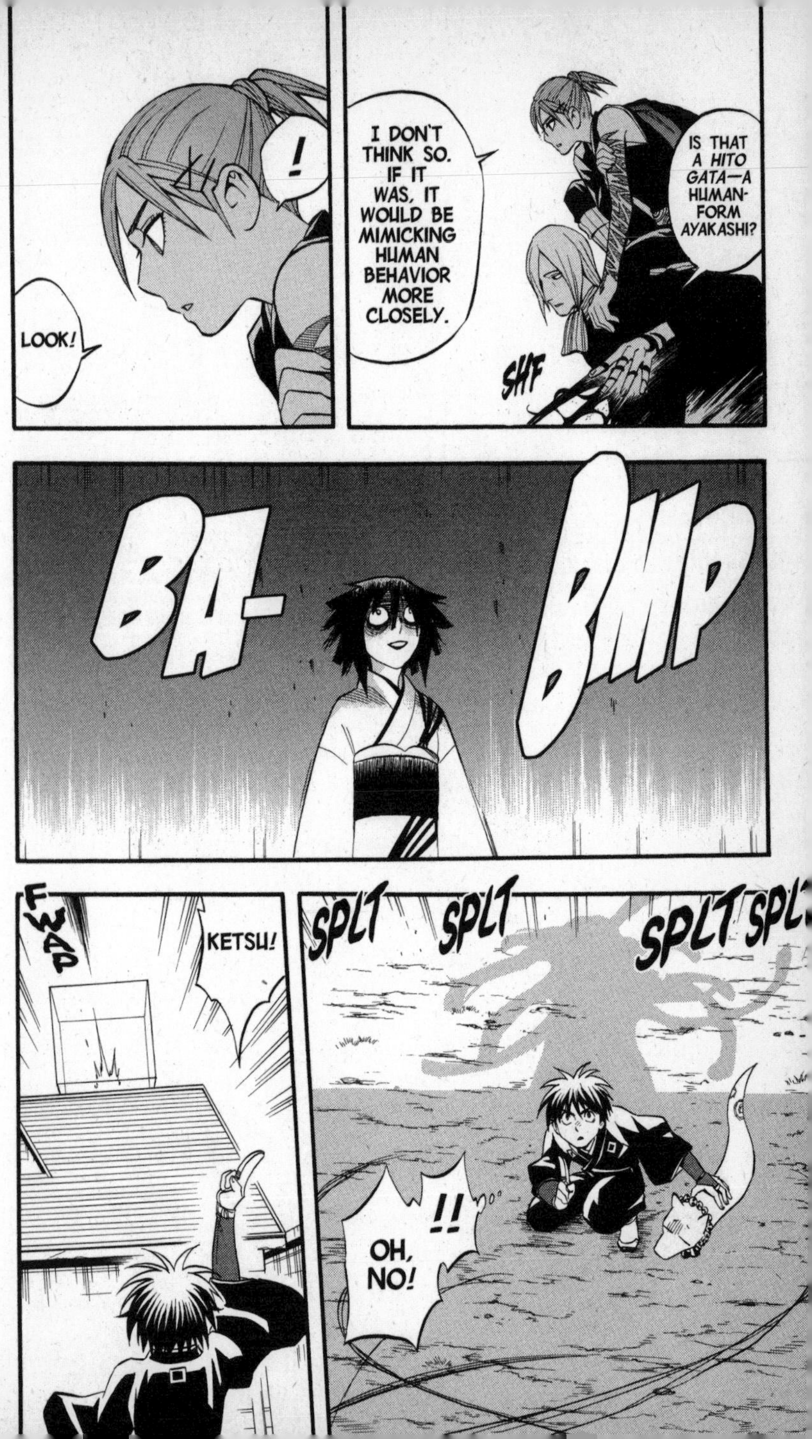
IS THAT A HITO GATA—A HUMAN-FORM AYAKASHI?
SHF
I DON'T THINK SO. IF IT WAS, IT WOULD BE MIMICKING HUMAN BEHAVIOR MORE CLOSELY.
!
LOOK!
BA-
BMP
SPLT SPLT SPLT SPLT
!!
OH, NO!
KETSU!
FWAP

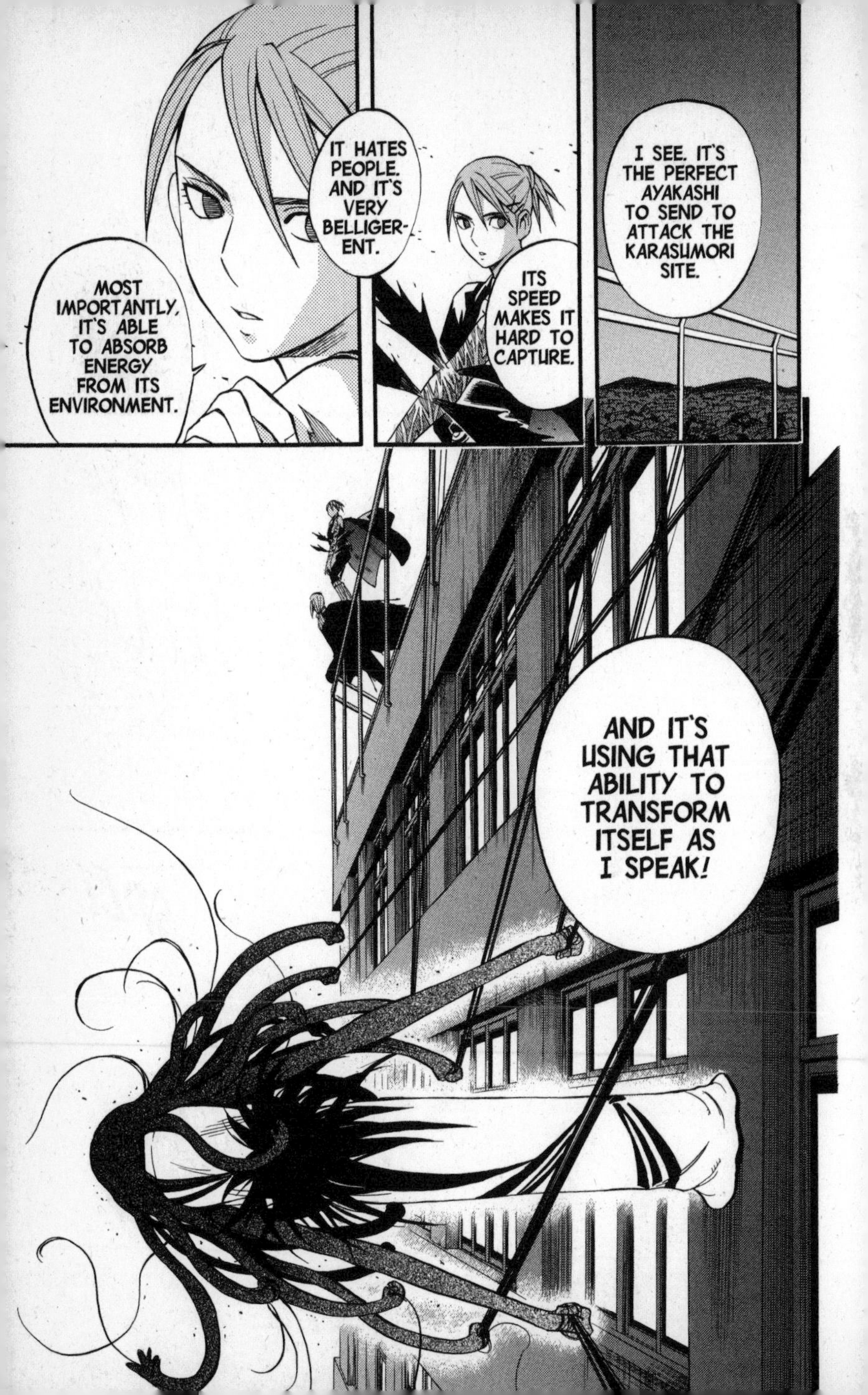
I SEE. IT'S THE PERFECT AYAKASHI TO SEND TO ATTACK THE KARASUMORI SITE.
IT HATES PEOPLE. AND IT'S VERY BELLIGER-ENT.
ITS SPEED MAKES IT HARD TO CAPTURE.
MOST IMPORTANTLY, IT'S ABLE TO ABSORB ENERGY FROM ITS ENVIRONMENT.
AND IT'S USING THAT ABILITY TO TRANSFORM ITSELF AS I SPEAK!

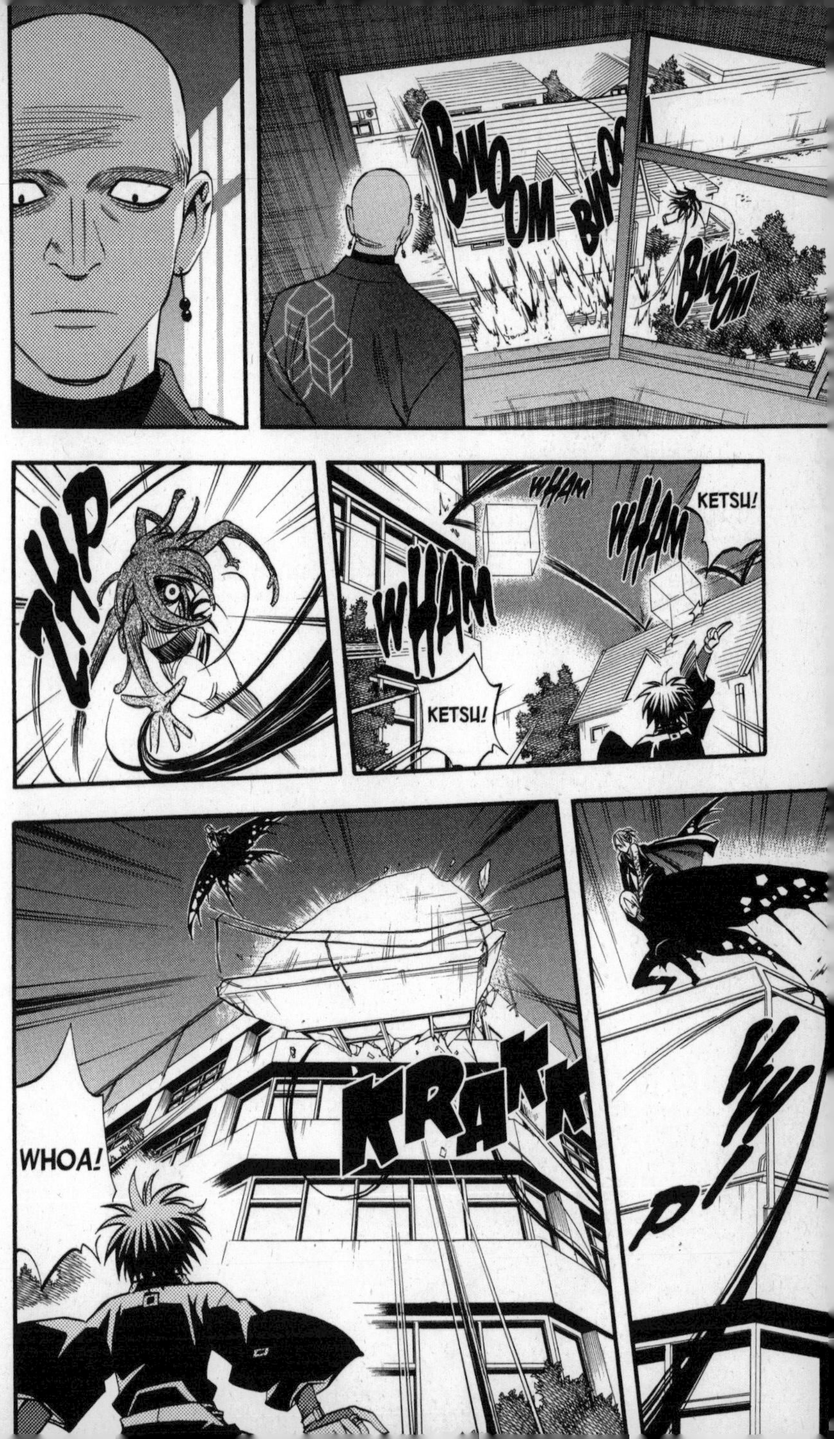

BWOOOM
BWOOOM
BWOOOM
KETSU!
WHAM
WHAM
WHAM
KETSU!
ZHP
WHIP!
KRAKK
WHOA!

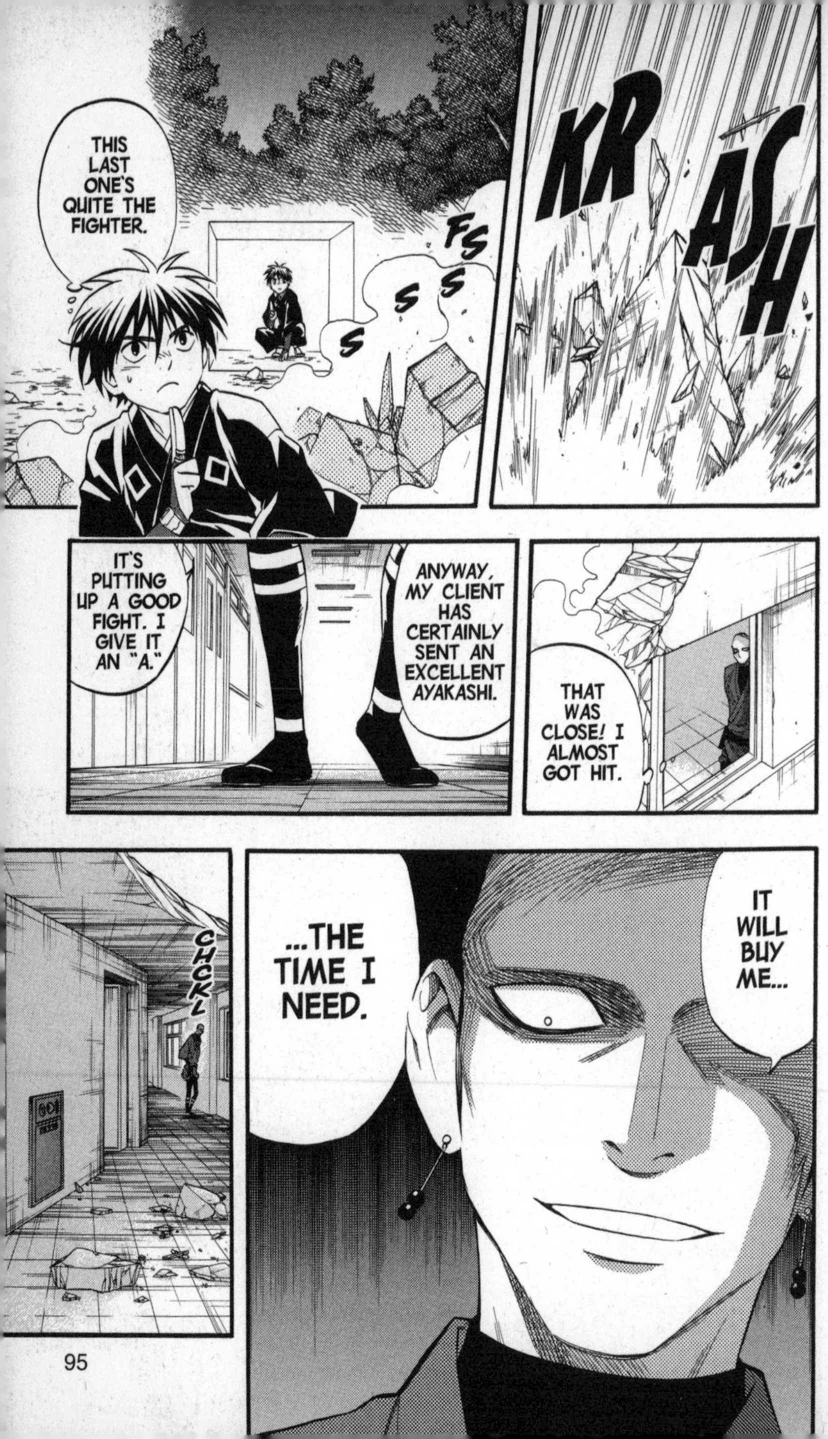
KRASH
FSSSSS
THIS LAST ONE'S QUITE THE FIGHTER.
THAT WAS CLOSE! I ALMOST GOT HIT.
ANYWAY, MY CLIENT HAS CERTAINLY SENT AN EXCELLENT AYAKASHI.
IT'S PUTTING UP A GOOD FIGHT. I GIVE IT AN "A."
IT WILL BUY ME...
...THE TIME I NEED.
CHCKL

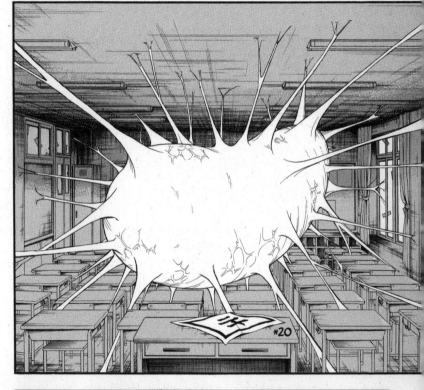

*20

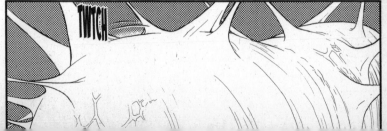

TWITCH

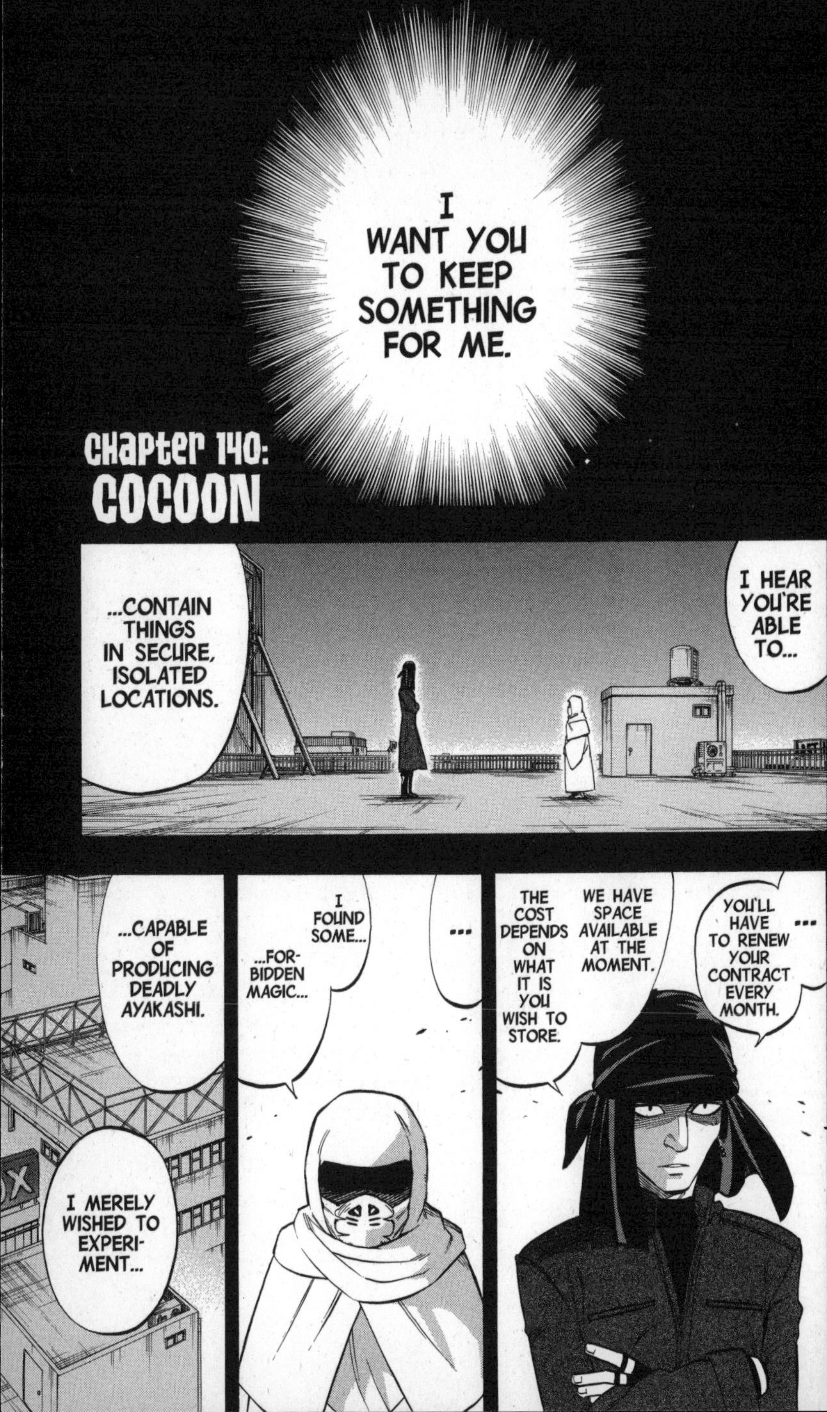
I WANT YOU TO KEEP SOMETHING FOR ME.
Chapter 140: COCOON
I HEAR YOU'RE ABLE TO...
...CONTAIN THINGS IN SECURE, ISOLATED LOCATIONS.
...
YOU'LL HAVE TO RENEW YOUR CONTRACT EVERY MONTH.
WE HAVE SPACE AVAILABLE AT THE MOMENT.
THE COST DEPENDS ON WHAT IT IS YOU WISH TO STORE.
...
I FOUND SOME...
...FOR-BIDDEN MAGIC...
...CAPABLE OF PRODUCING DEADLY AYAKASHI.
I MERELY WISHED TO EXPERI-MENT...

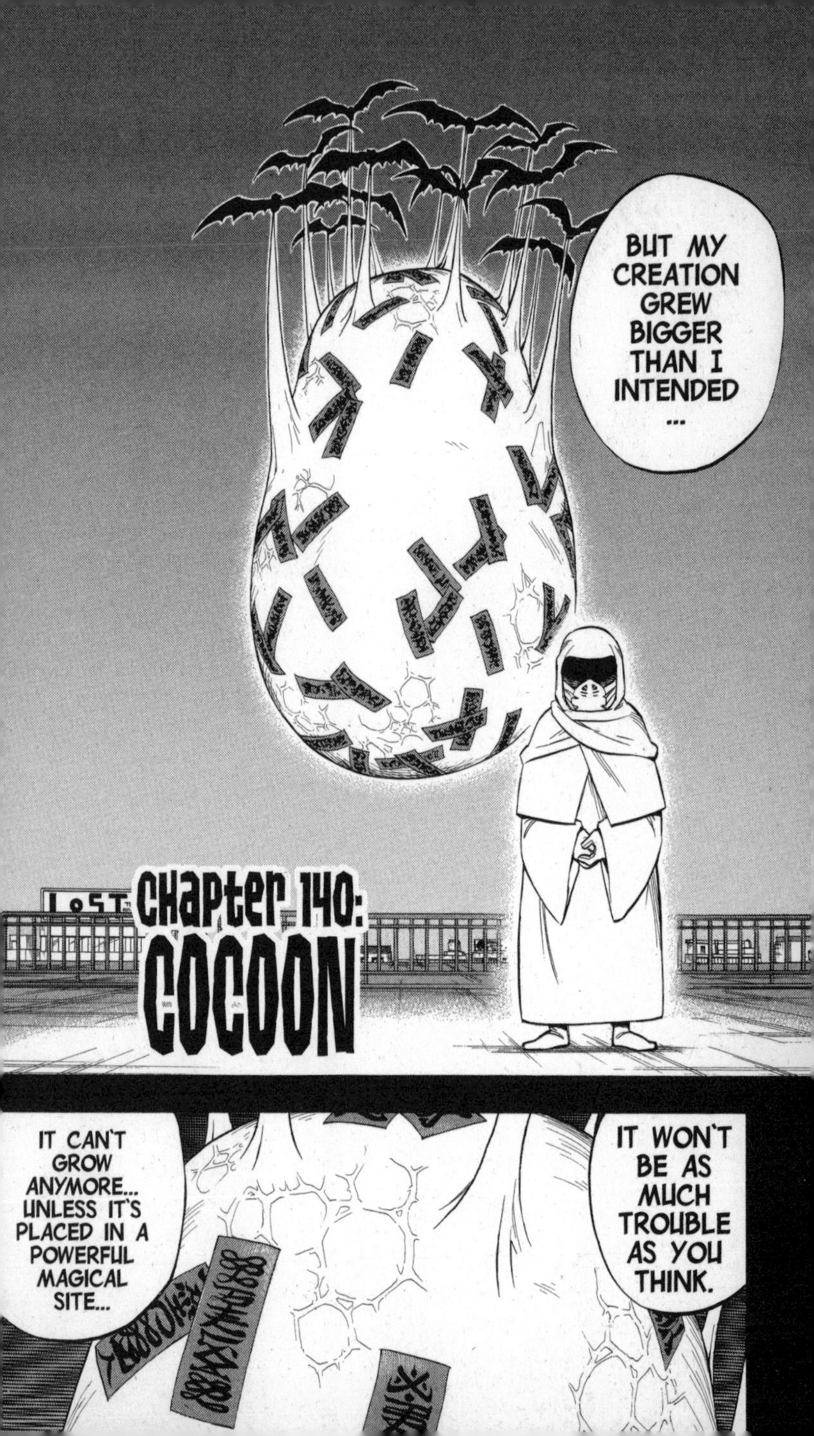
BUT MY CREATION GREW BIGGER THAN I INTENDED ...
CHAPTER 140: COCOON
LOST
IT WON'T BE AS MUCH TROUBLE AS YOU THINK.
IT CAN'T GROW ANYMORE... UNLESS IT'S PLACED IN A POWERFUL MAGICAL SITE...

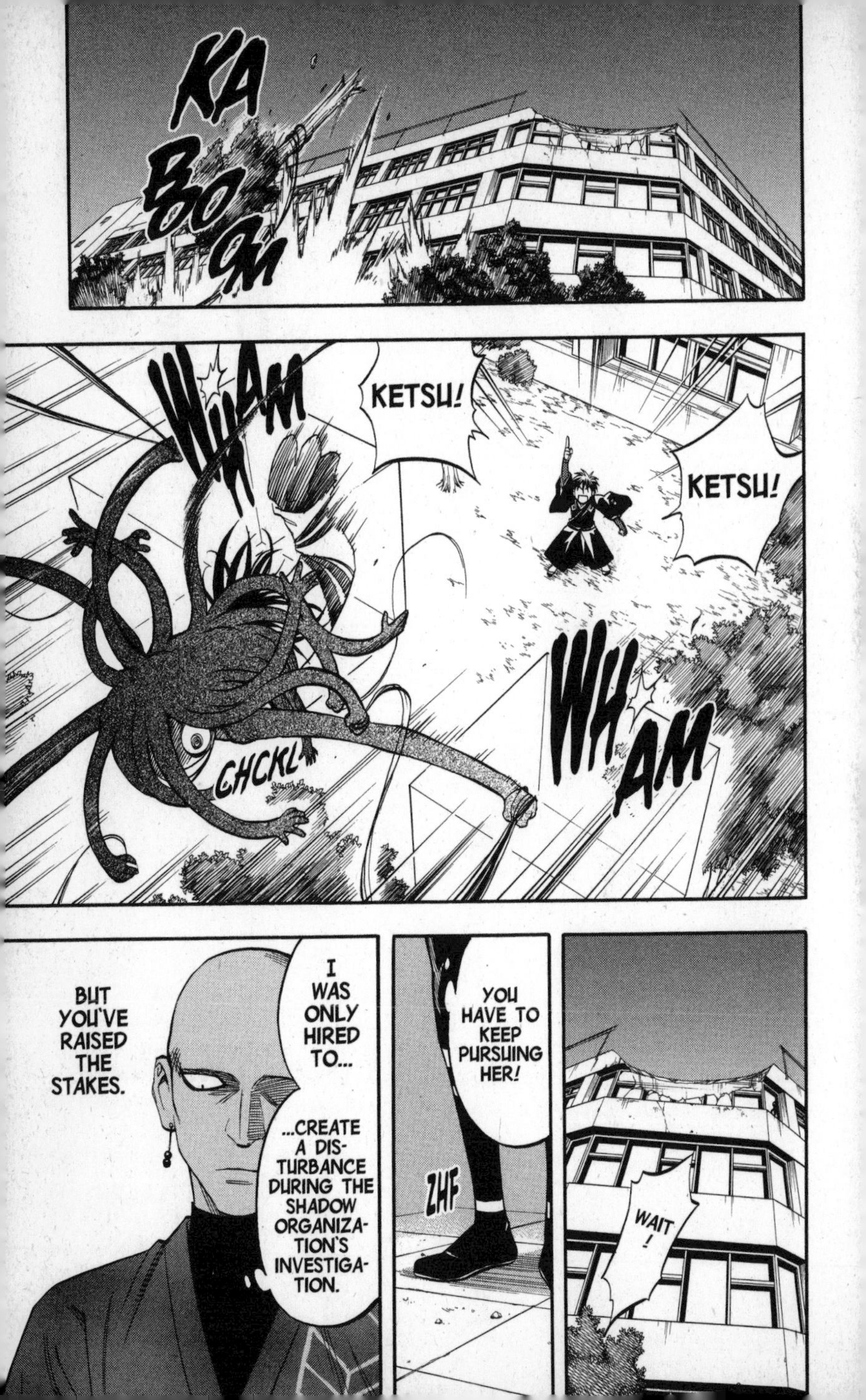
KABOOM
KETSU!
KETSU!
WHAM
WHAM
CHCKL
WAIT!
YOU HAVE TO KEEP PURSUING HER!
ZHF
I WAS ONLY HIRED TO...
...CREATE A DISTURBANCE DURING THE SHADOW ORGANIZATION'S INVESTIGATION.
BUT YOU'VE RAISED THE STAKES.

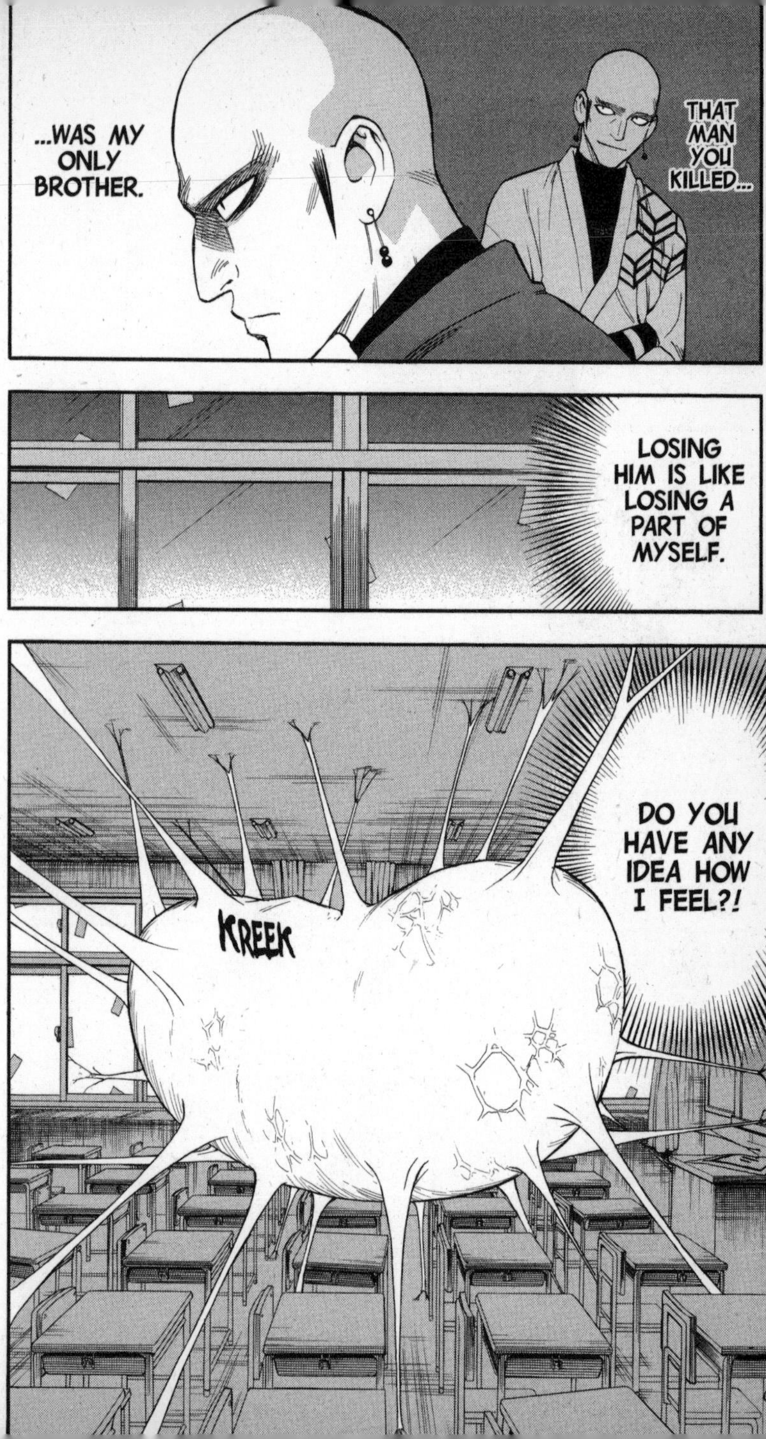
THAT MAN YOU KILLED...
...WAS MY ONLY BROTHER.
LOSING HIM IS LIKE LOSING A PART OF MYSELF.
DO YOU HAVE ANY IDEA HOW I FEEL?!
KREEK

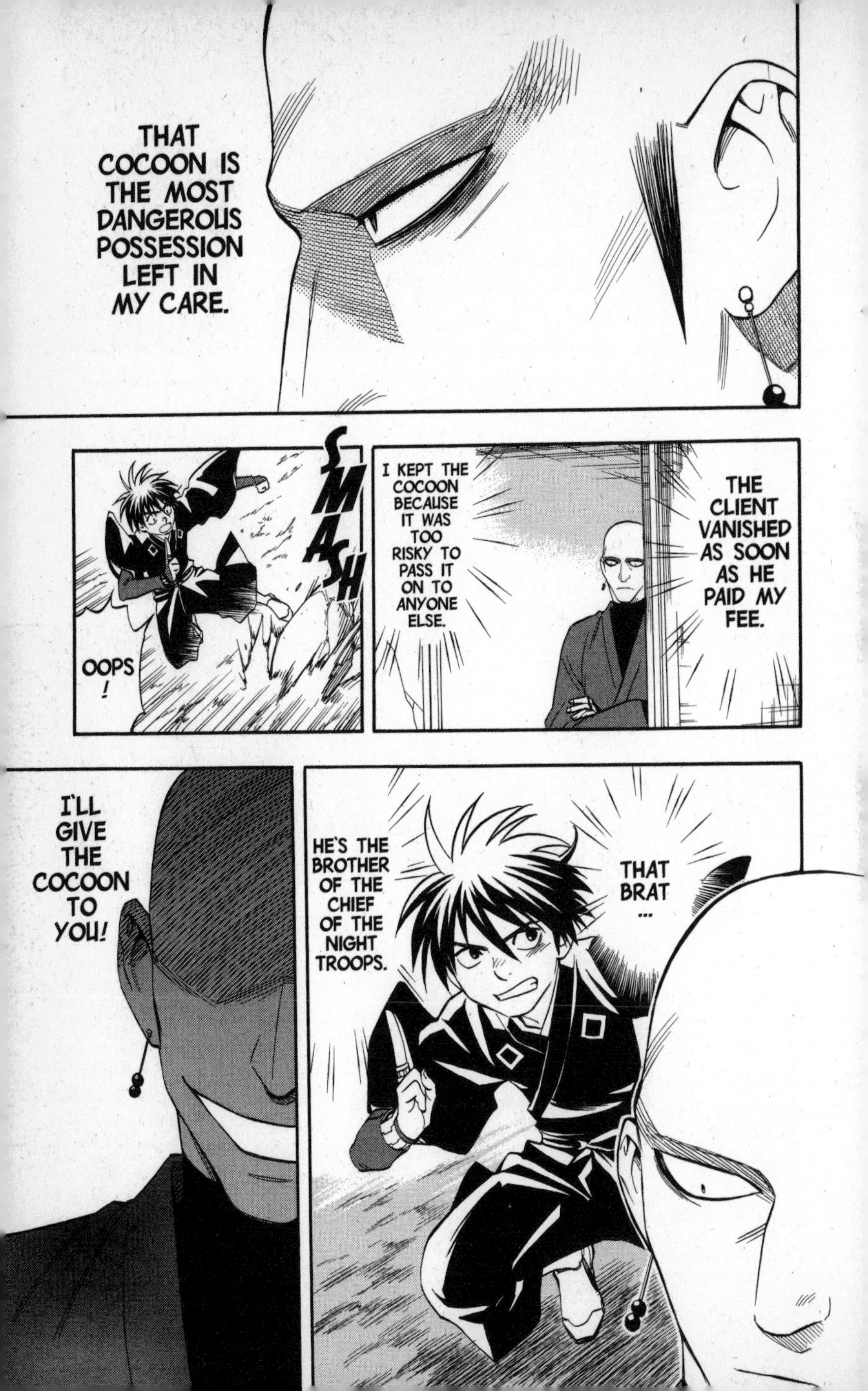
THAT COCOON IS THE MOST DANGEROUS POSSESSION LEFT IN MY CARE.
THE CLIENT VANISHED AS SOON AS HE PAID MY FEE.
I KEPT THE COCOON BECAUSE IT WAS TOO RISKY TO PASS IT ON TO ANYONE ELSE.
SMASH
OOPS!
THAT BRAT...
HE'S THE BROTHER OF THE CHIEF OF THE NIGHT TROOPS.
I'LL GIVE THE COCOON TO YOU!

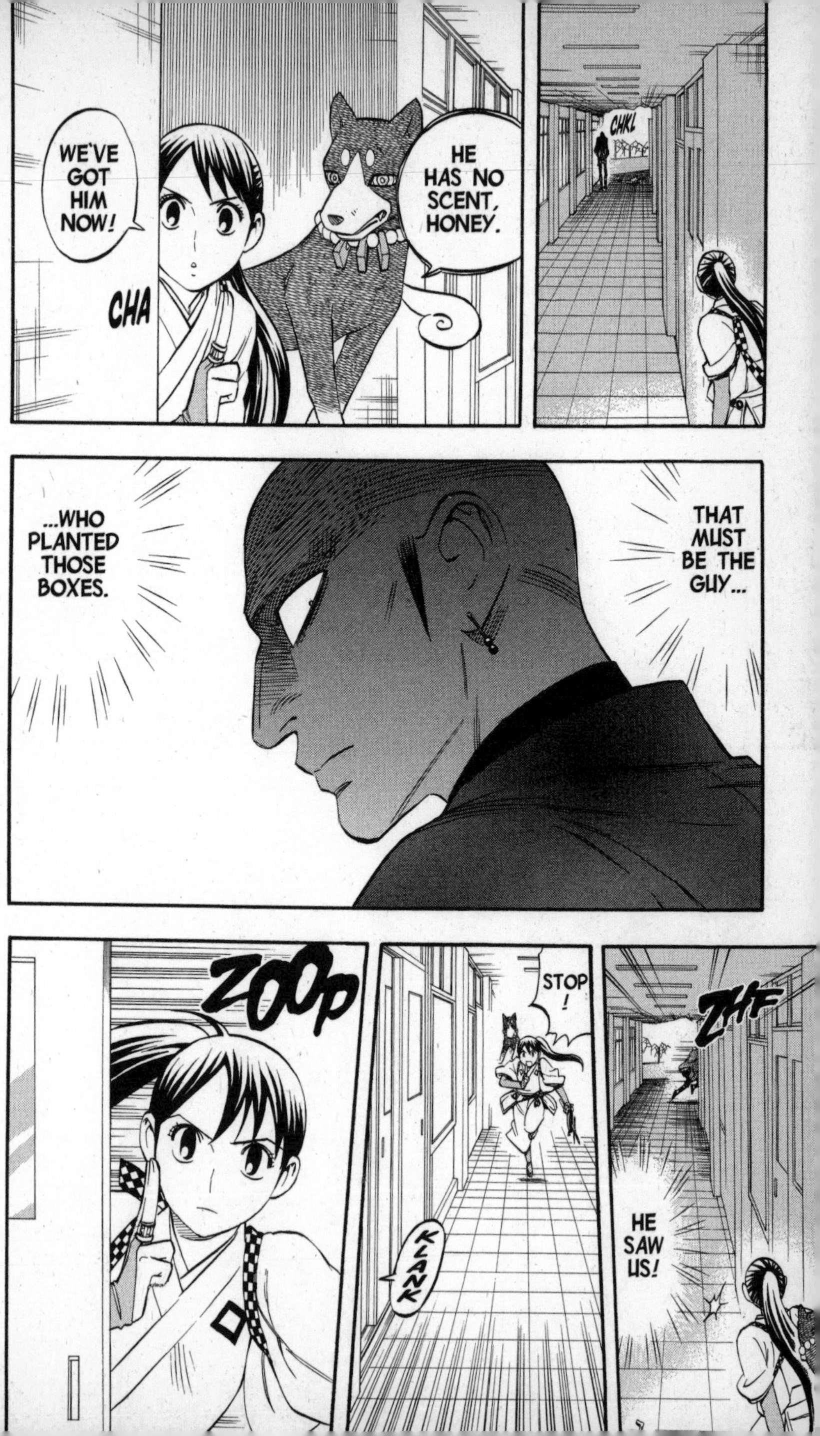
CHKL
HE HAS NO SCENT, HONEY.
WE'VE GOT HIM NOW!
CHA
THAT MUST BE THE GUY...
...WHO PLANTED THOSE BOXES.
ZHF
HE SAW US!
STOP!
KLANK
ZOOP

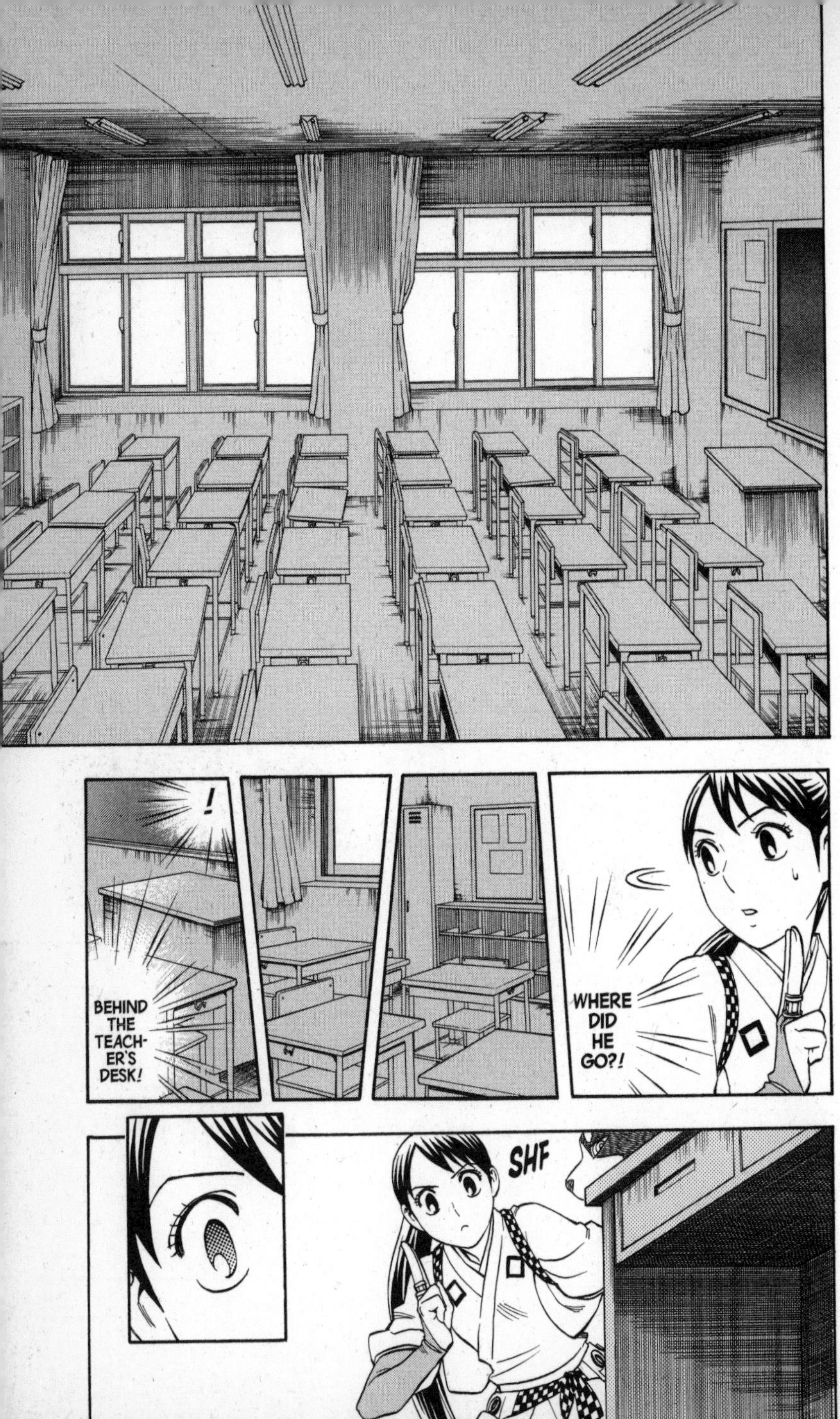
WHERE DID HE GO?!
!
BEHIND THE TEACHER'S DESK!
SHF

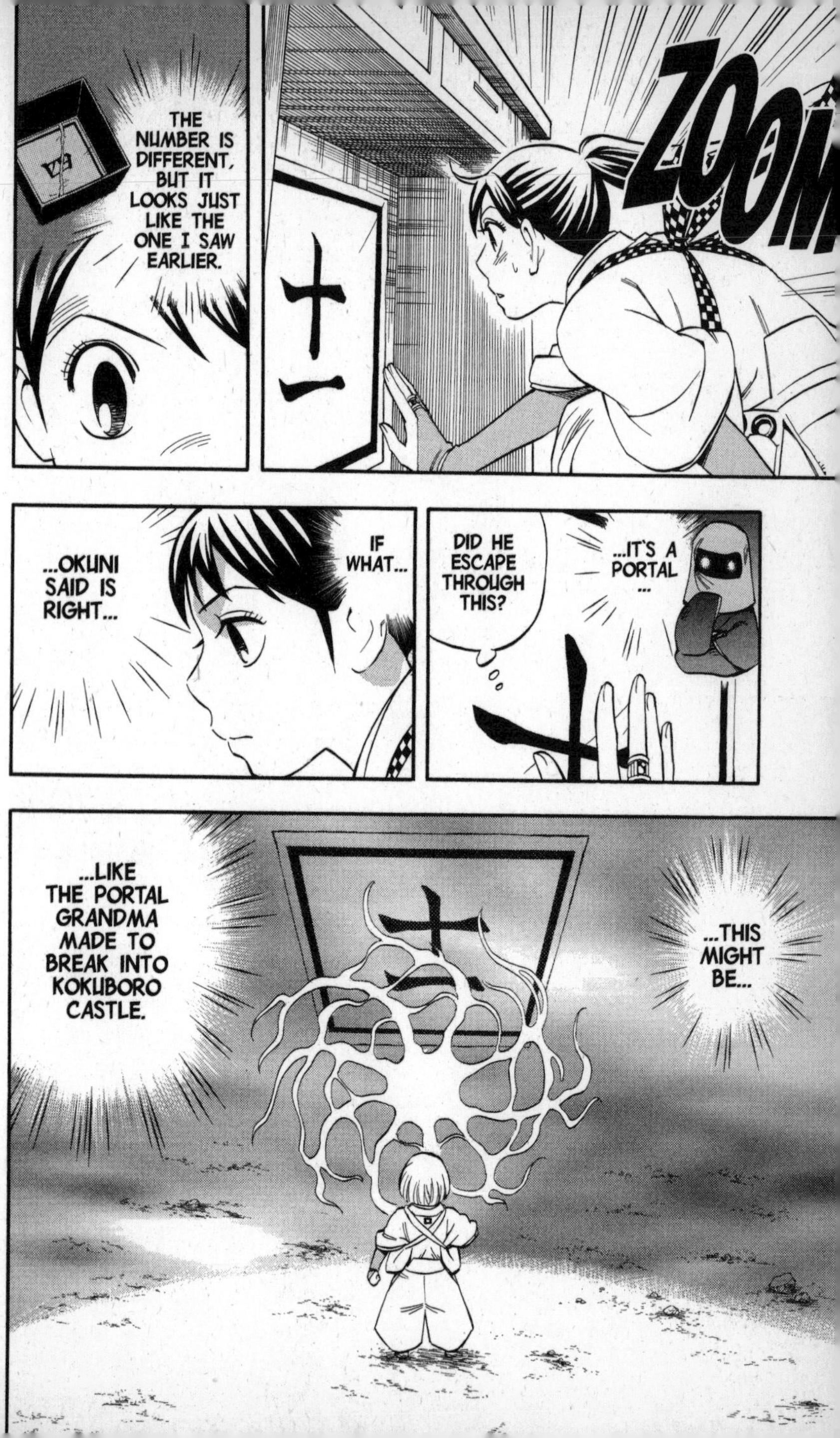
ZOOM
THE NUMBER IS DIFFERENT, BUT IT LOOKS JUST LIKE THE ONE I SAW EARLIER.
...IT'S A PORTAL ...
DID HE ESCAPE THROUGH THIS?
IF WHAT...
...OKUNI SAID IS RIGHT...
...THIS MIGHT BE...
...LIKE THE PORTAL GRANDMA MADE TO BREAK INTO KOKUBORO CASTLE.

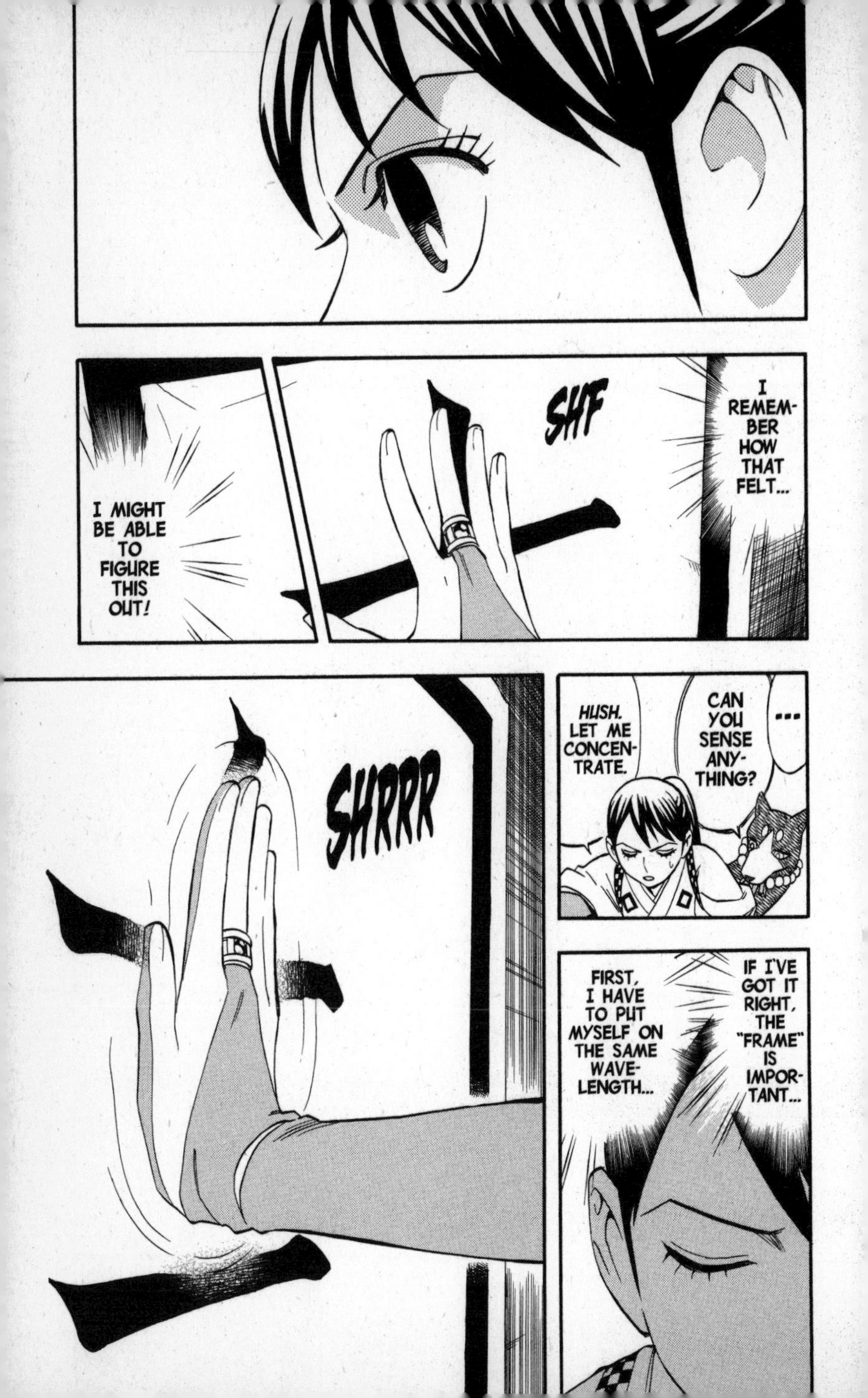
I REMEMBER HOW THAT FELT...
SHF
I MIGHT BE ABLE TO FIGURE THIS OUT!
...
CAN YOU SENSE ANYTHING?
HUSH. LET ME CONCENTRATE.
IF I'VE GOT IT RIGHT, THE "FRAME" IS IMPORTANT...
FIRST, I HAVE TO PUT MYSELF ON THE SAME WAVELENGTH...
SHRRR

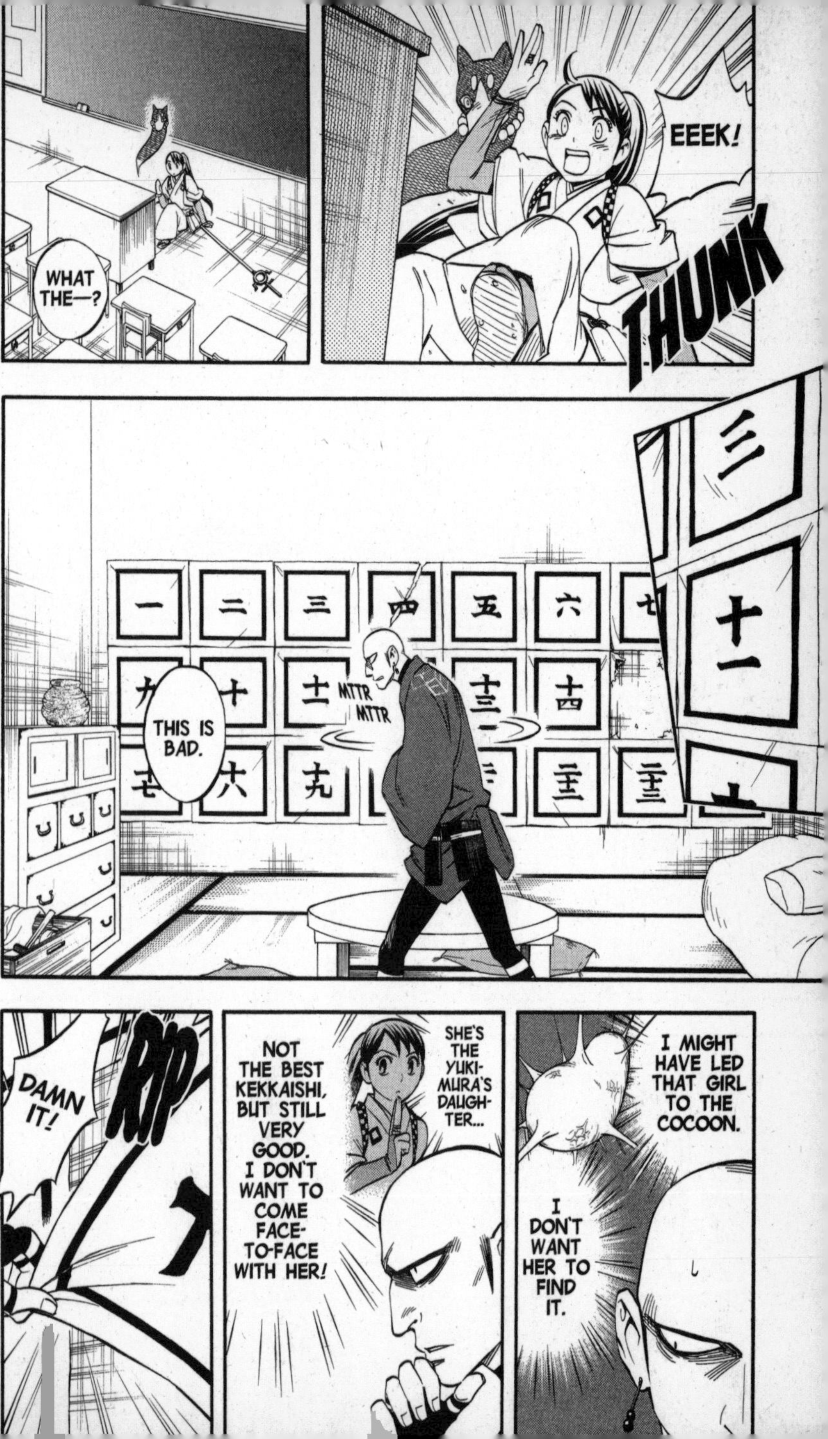
EEEK!
THUNK
WHAT THE—?
MTTR MTTR
THIS IS BAD.
I MIGHT HAVE LED THAT GIRL TO THE COCOON.
I DON'T WANT HER TO FIND IT.
SHE'S THE YUKIMURA'S DAUGHTER...
NOT THE BEST KEKKAISHI, BUT STILL VERY GOOD. I DON'T WANT TO COME FACE-TO-FACE WITH HER!
RIP
DAMN IT!

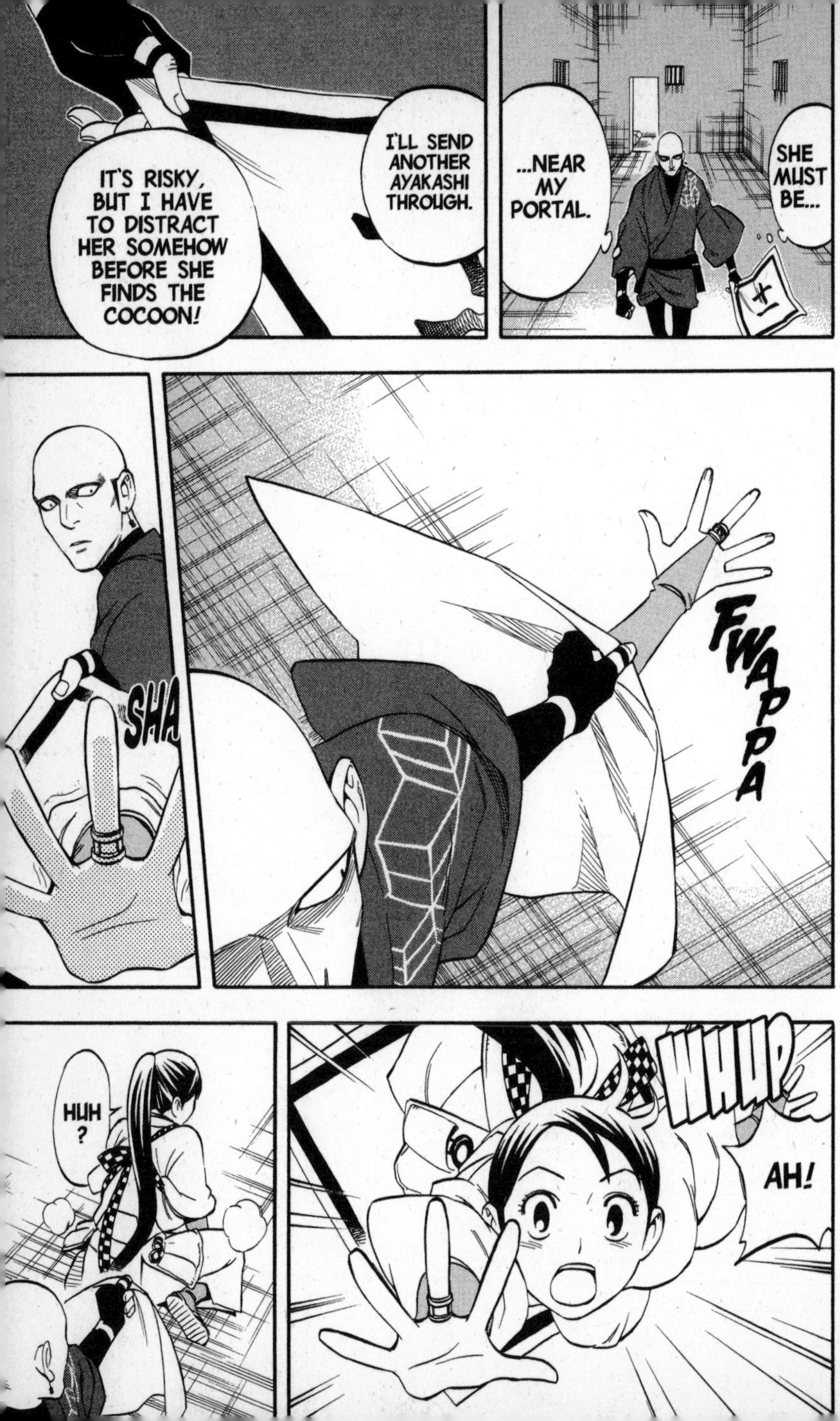
SHE MUST BE...
...NEAR MY PORTAL.
I'LL SEND ANOTHER AYAKASHI THROUGH.
IT'S RISKY, BUT I HAVE TO DISTRACT HER SOMEHOW BEFORE SHE FINDS THE COCOON!
FWAPPA
SHA
WHUP
AH!
HUH?

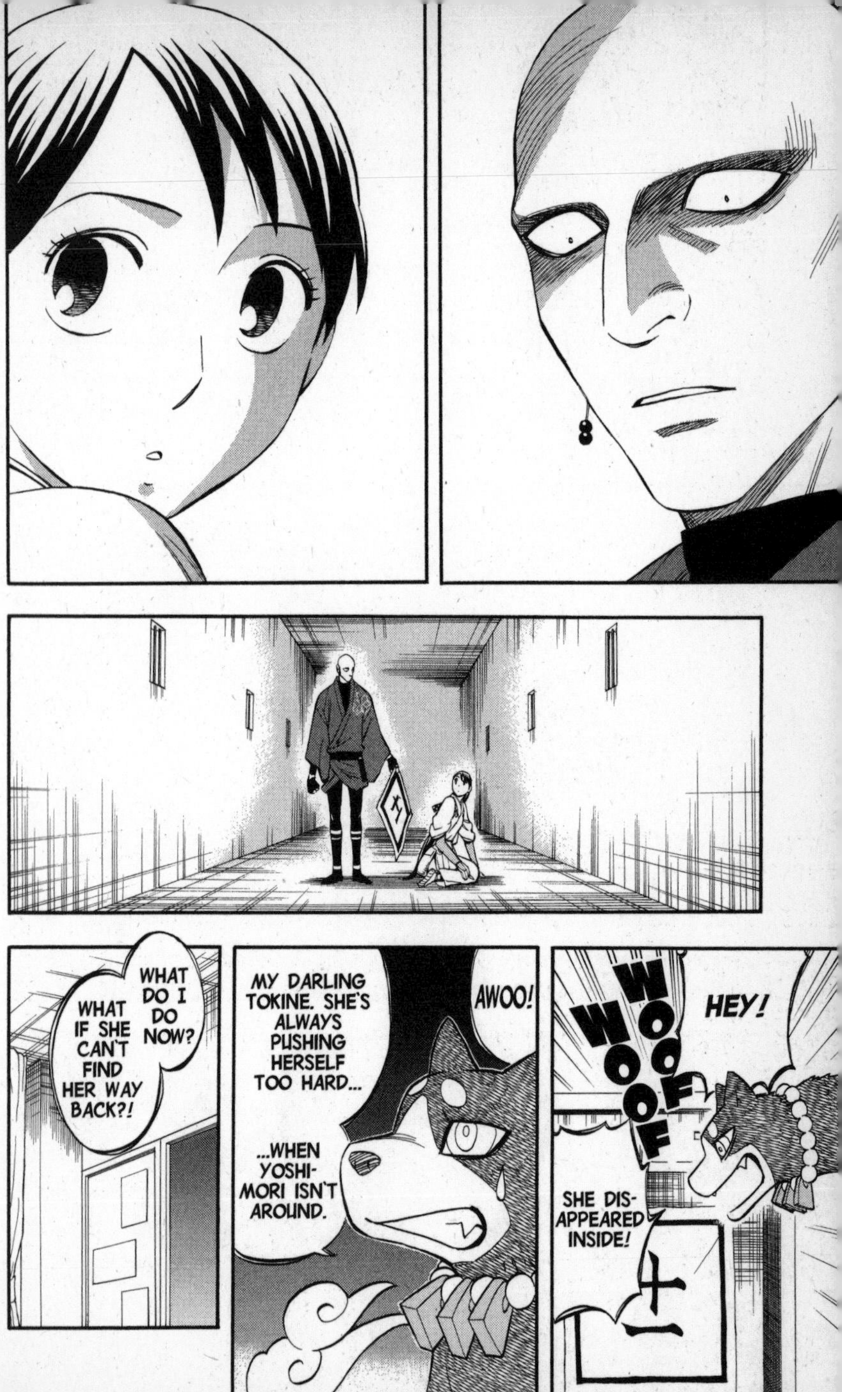
HEY!
WOOF WOOF
SHE DIS-APPEARED INSIDE!
AWOO!
MY DARLING TOKINE. SHE'S ALWAYS PUSHING HERSELF TOO HARD...
...WHEN YOSHIMORI ISN'T AROUND.
WHAT DO I DO NOW?
WHAT IF SHE CAN'T FIND HER WAY BACK?!

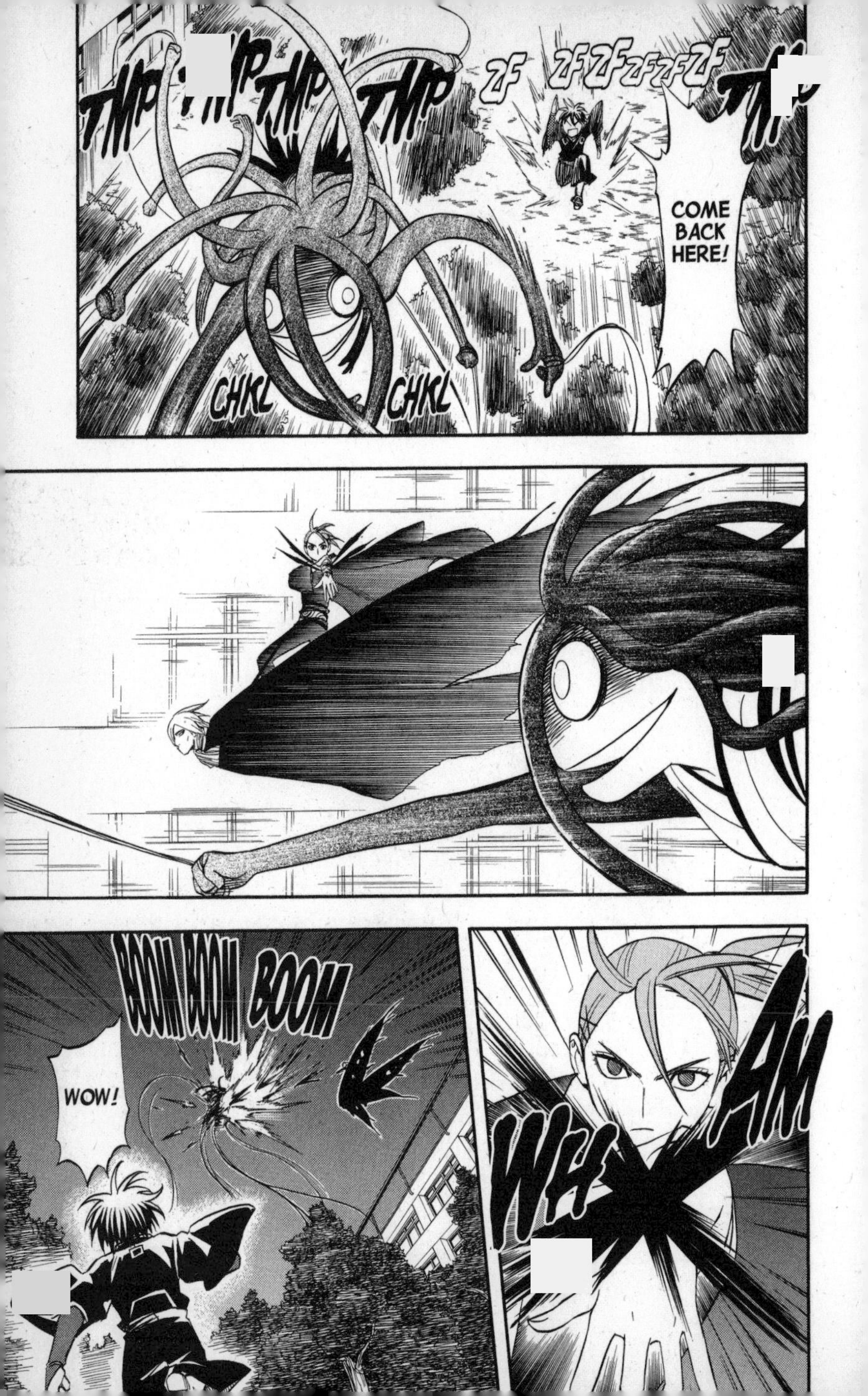
TMP
COME BACK HERE!
ZF ZF ZF ZF ZF ZF
ZF
TMP TMP TMP TMP
CHKL
CHKL
WH AM
BOOM BOOM BOOM
WOW!

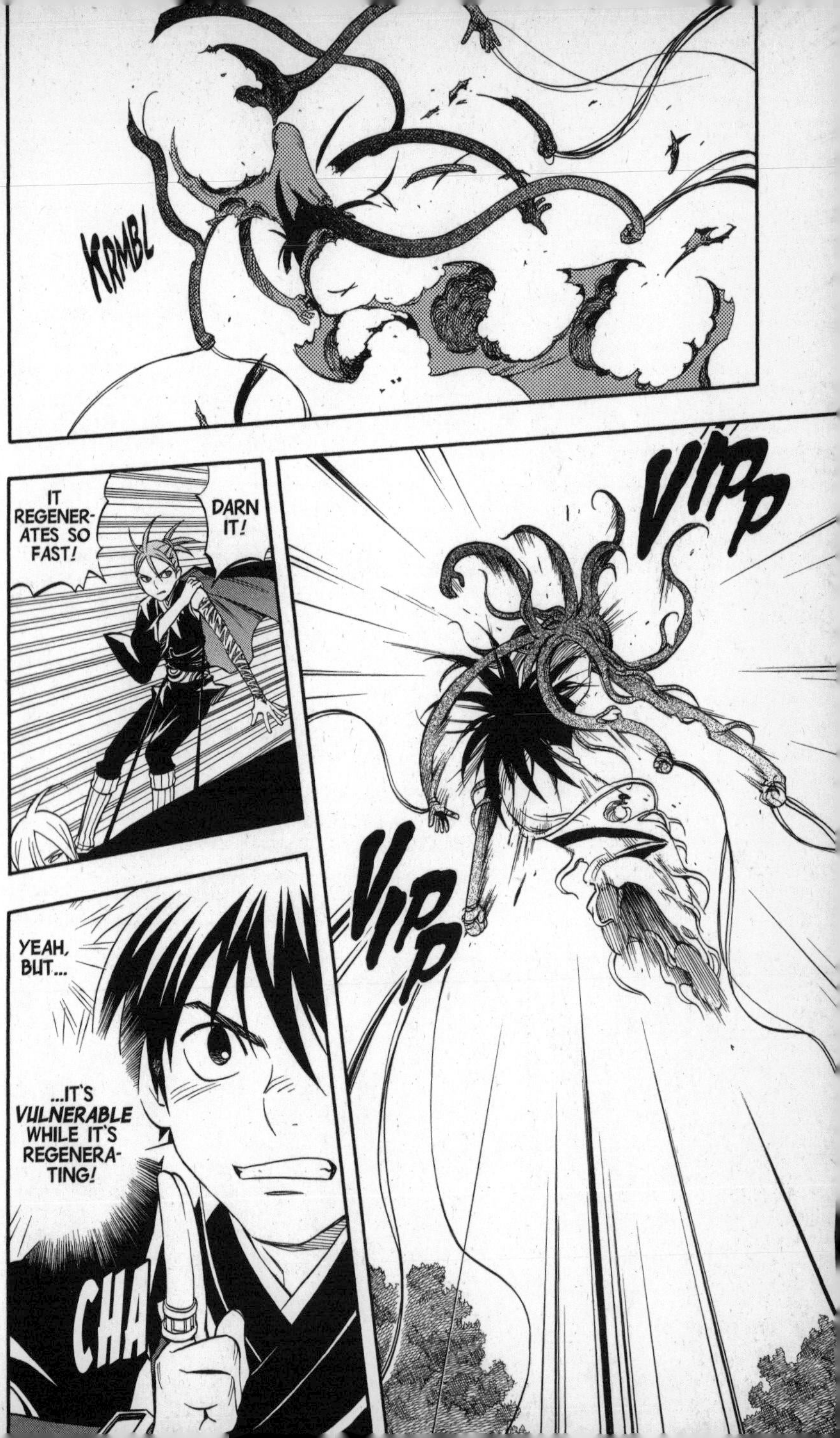
KRMBL
VIPP
VIPP
DARN IT!
IT REGENERATES SO FAST!
YEAH, BUT...
...IT'S *VULNERABLE* WHILE IT'S REGENERATING!
CHA

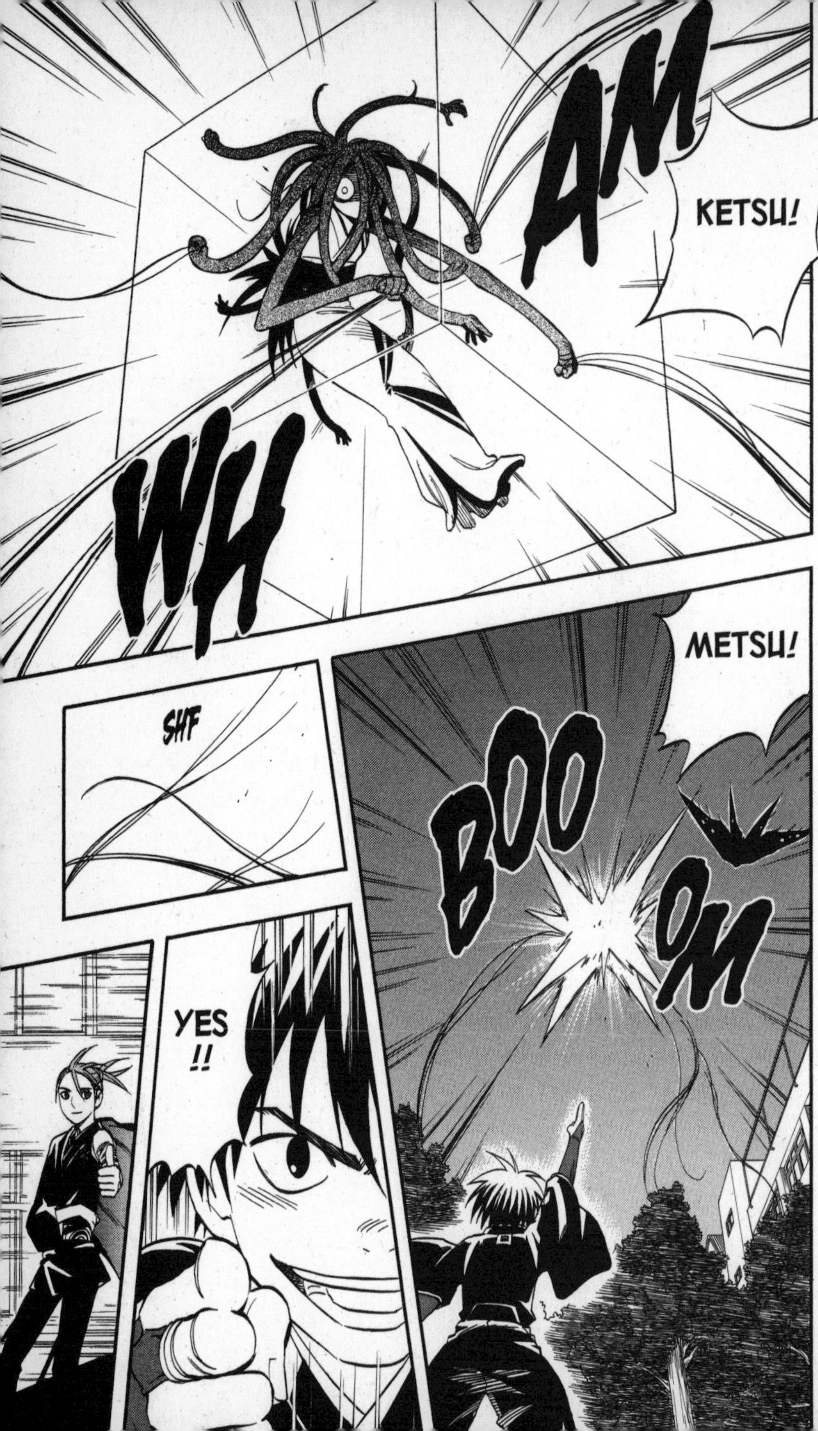
KETSU!
WH
AM
METSU!
BOO
OM
SHF
YES !!

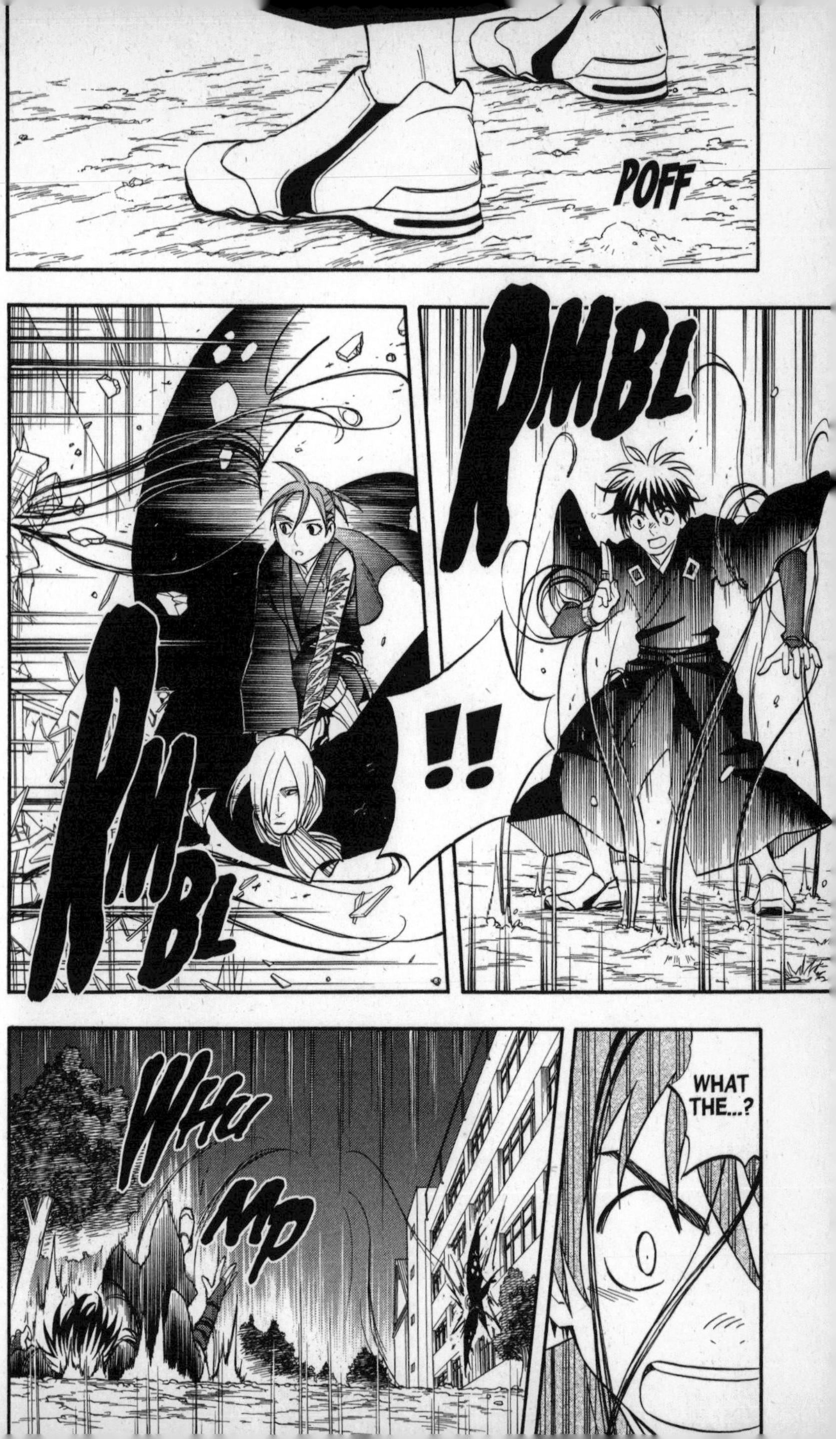
POFF
RMBL
!!
RMBL
WHAT THE...?
WHUMP

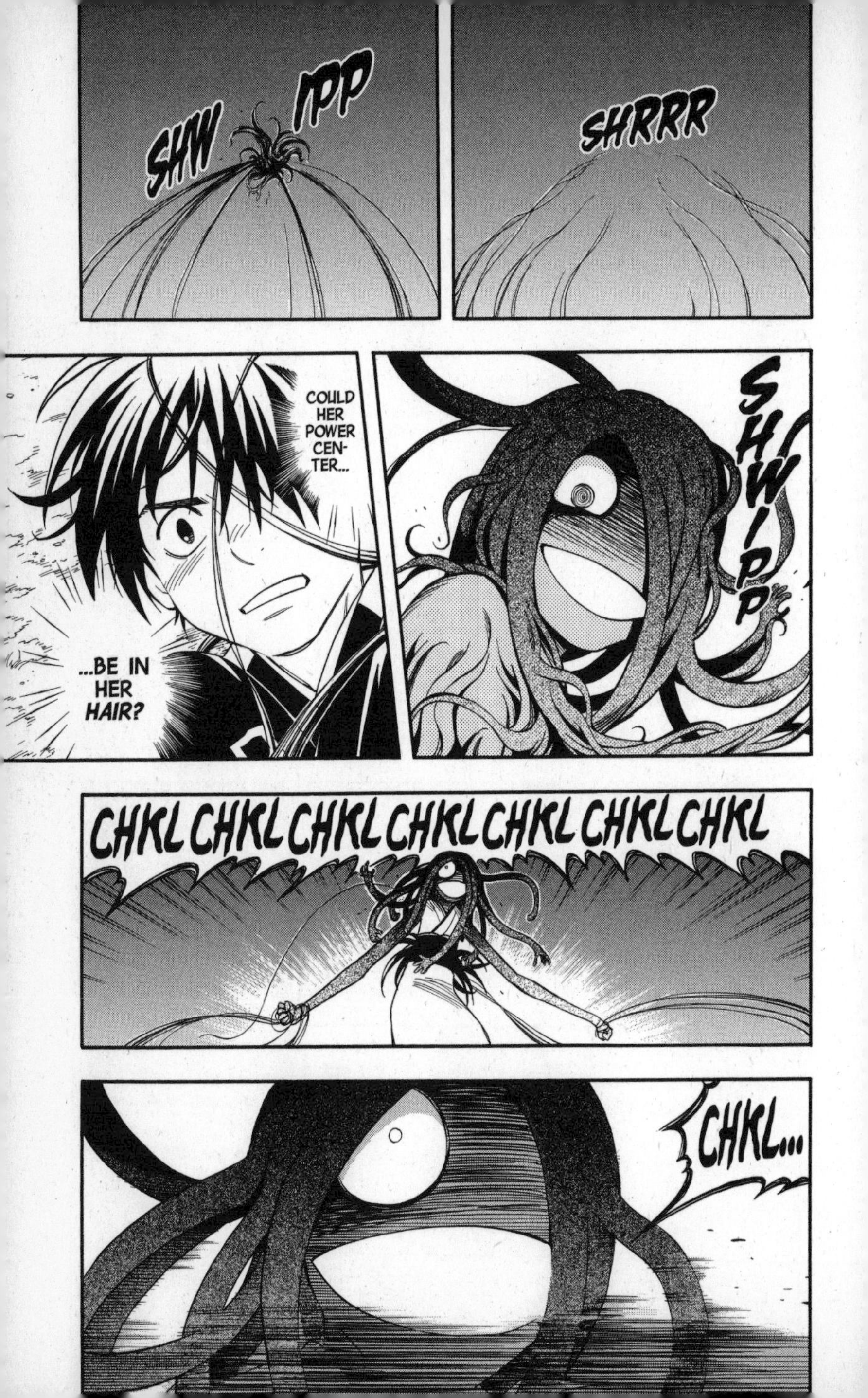
SHRRR
SHW IPP
SHWIPP
COULD HER POWER CEN-TER...
...BE IN HER HAIR?
CHKL CHKL CHKL CHKL CHKL CHKL CHKL
CHKL...

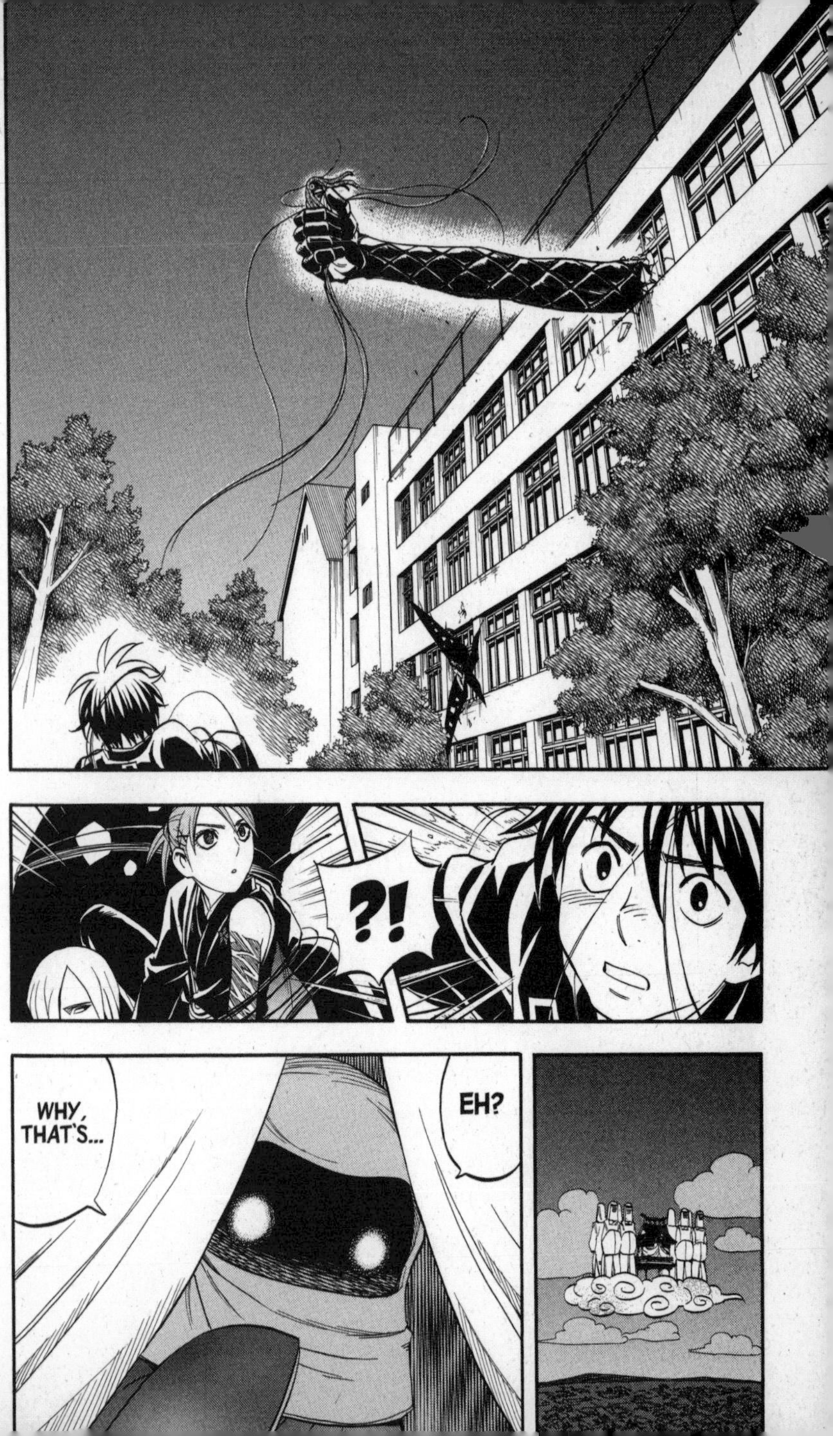
?!
EH?
WHY, THAT'S...

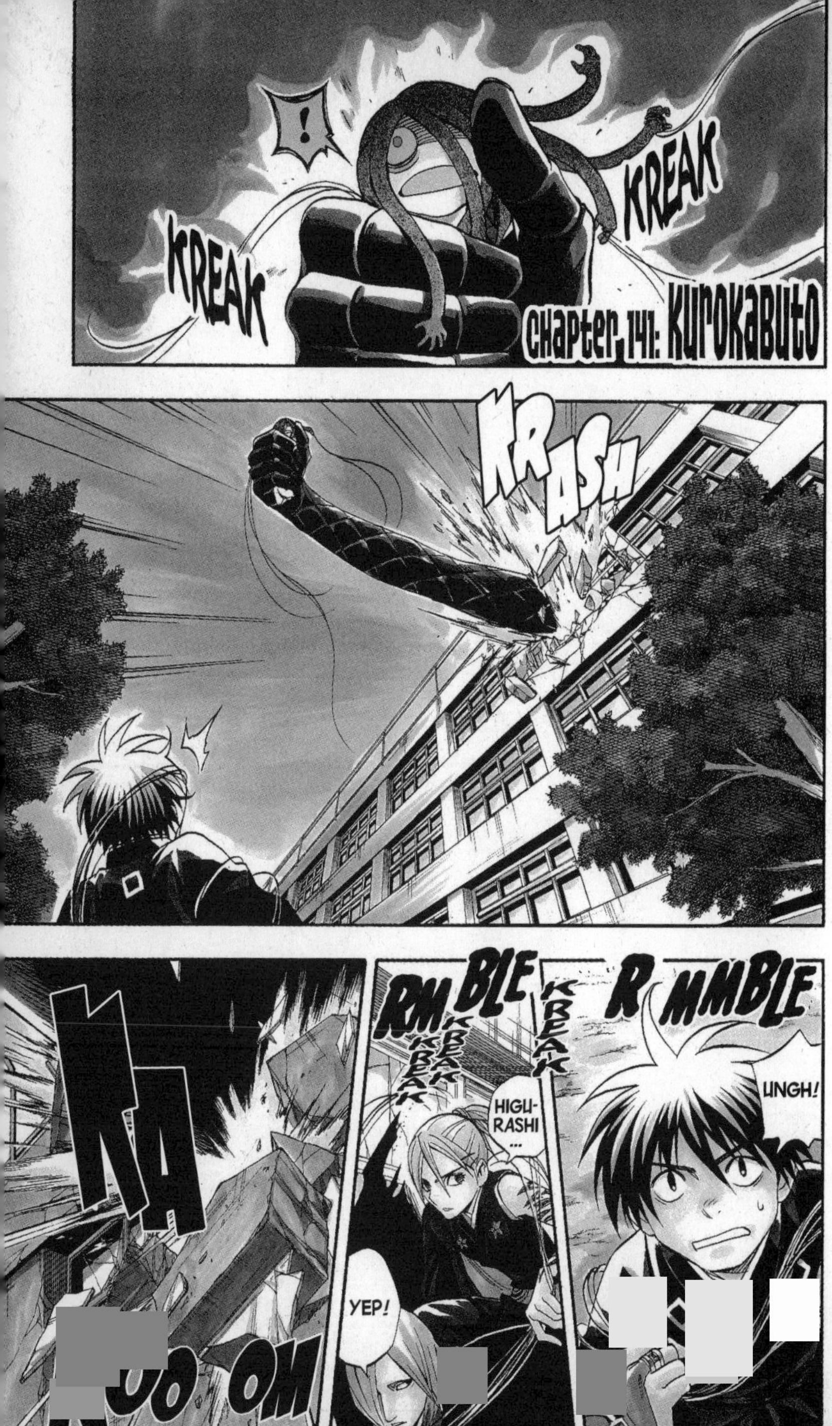
!
KREAK
KREAK
Chapter 141: Kurokabuto
KRASH
RUMMBLE
UNGH!
KREAK
RUMBLE
KREAK KREAK
HIGU-RASHI...
YEP!
KA

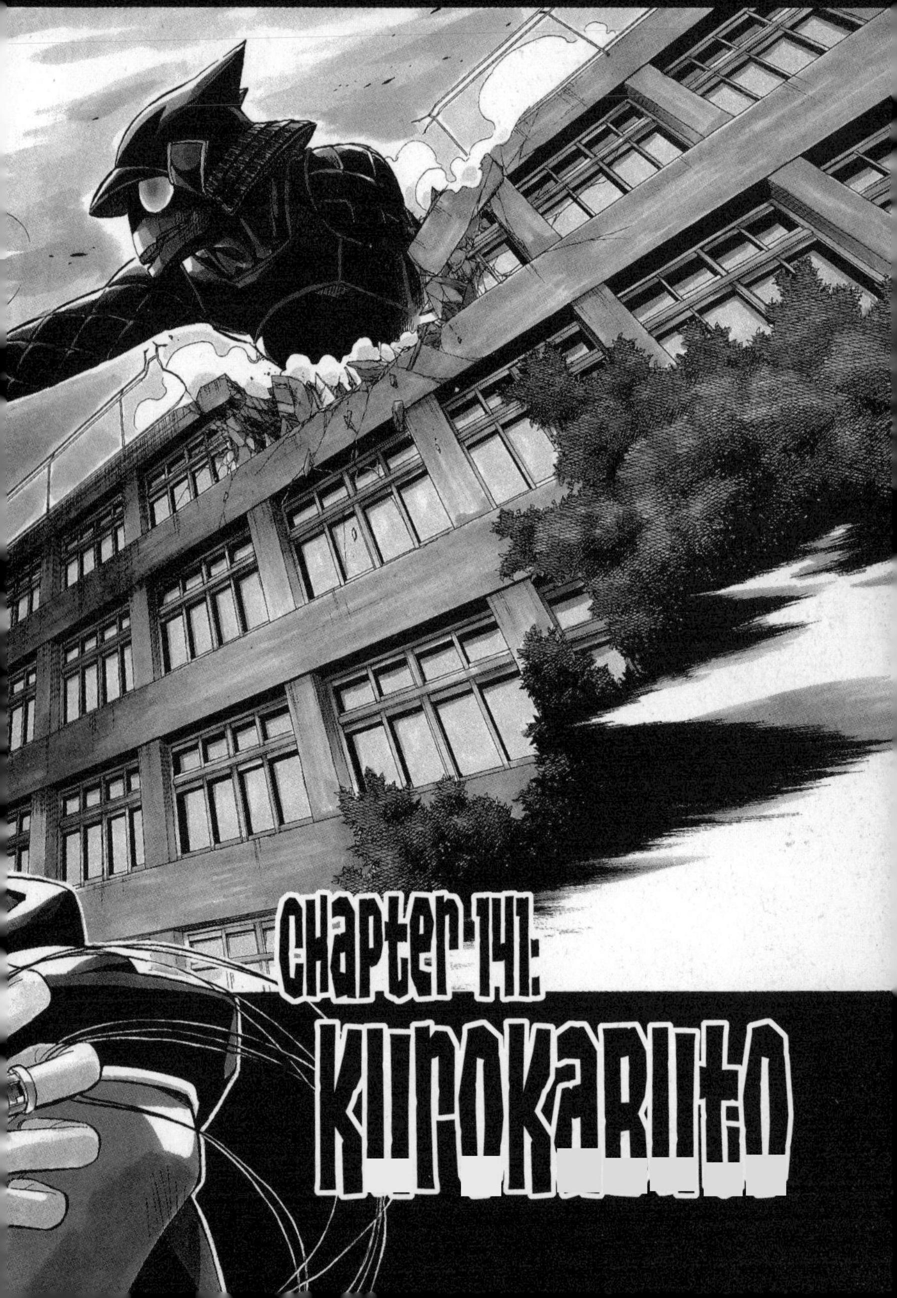
CHAPTER 141:
KUROKARUTO

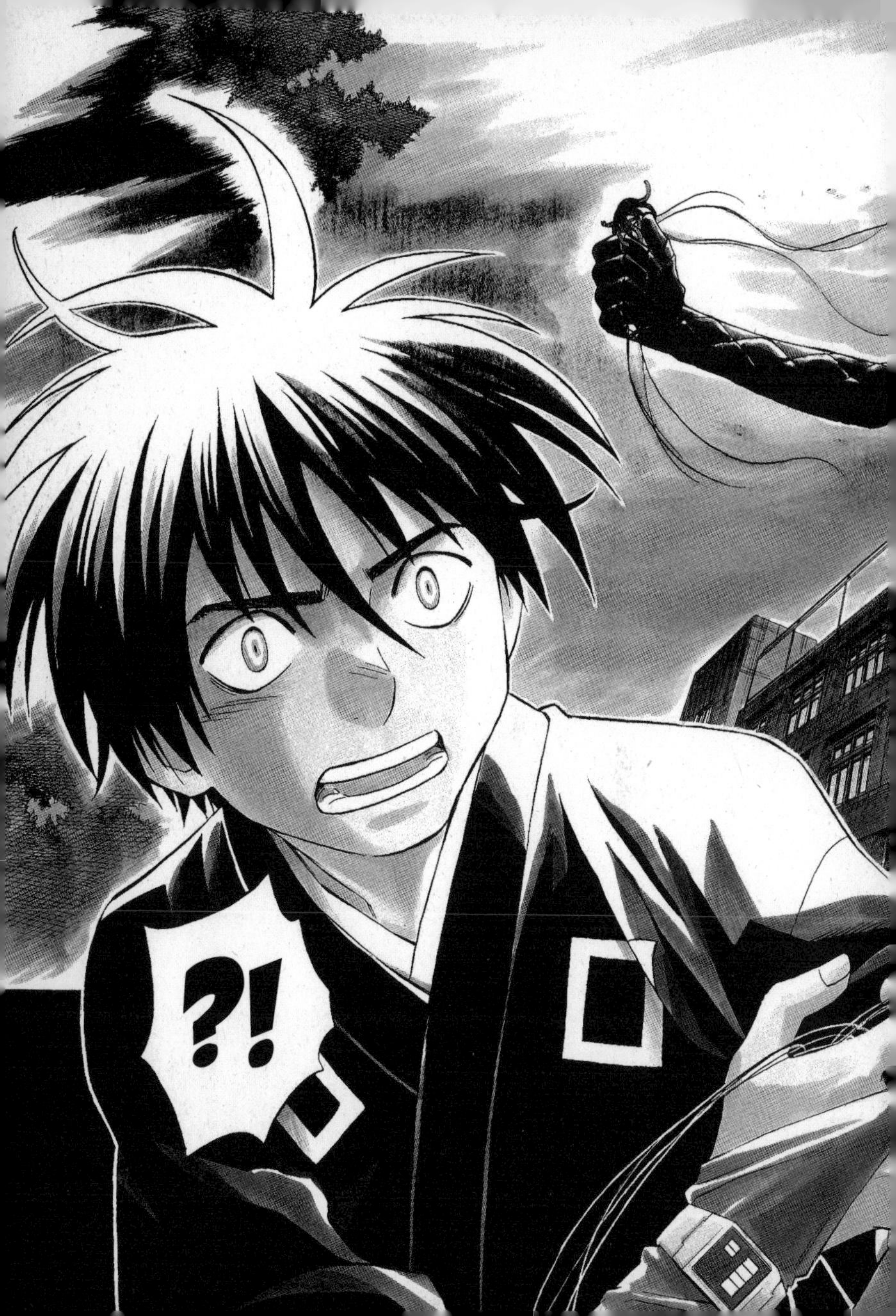
?!

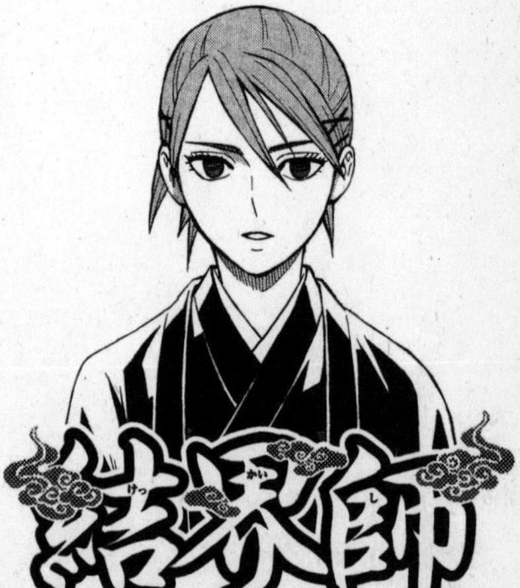
結界師

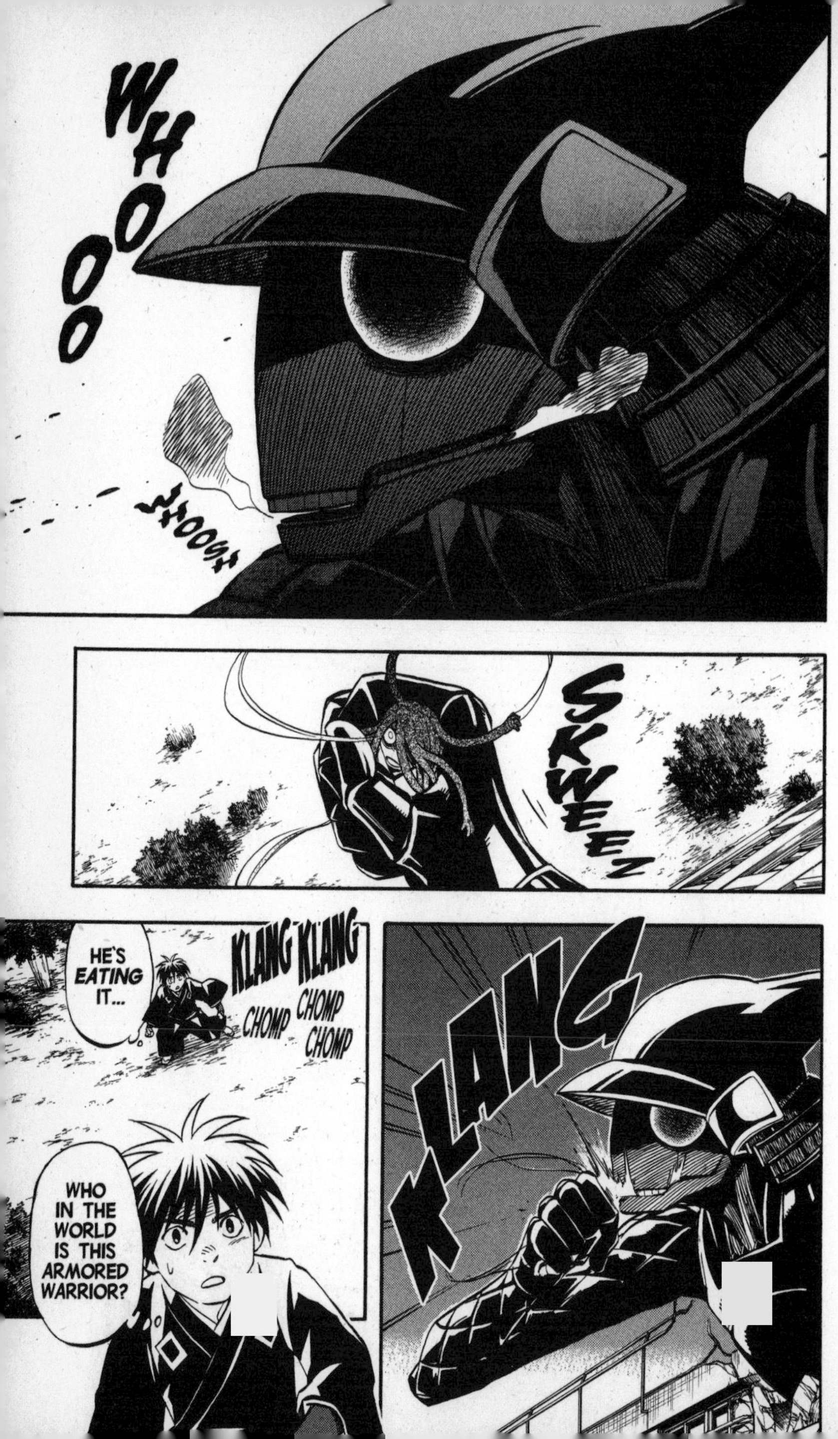
WHOOOOO
WHOOSH
SKWEEZ
KLANG
HE'S EATING IT...
KLANG KLANG
CHOMP CHOMP CHOMP
WHO IN THE WORLD IS THIS ARMORED WARRIOR?

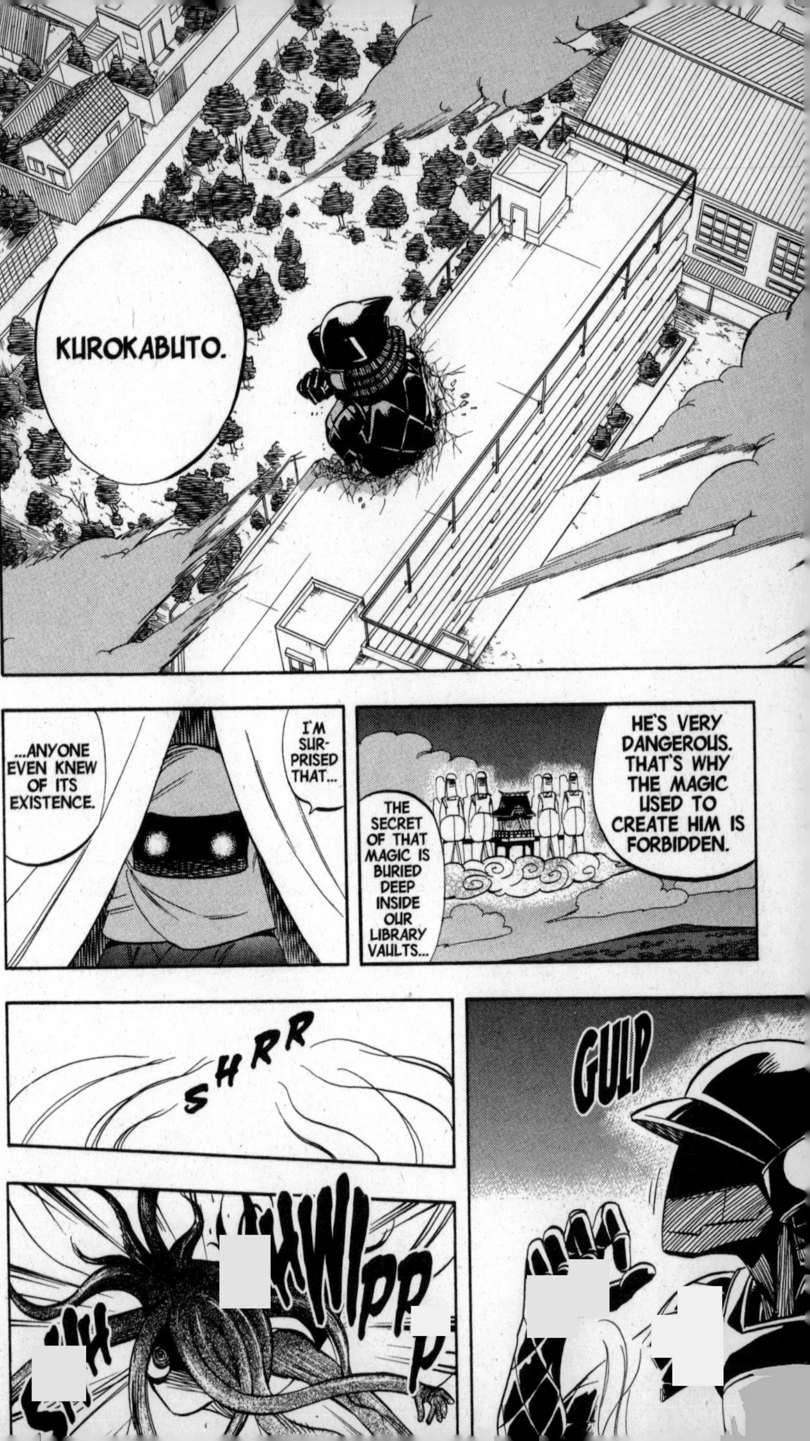
KUROKABUTO.
HE'S VERY DANGEROUS. THAT'S WHY THE MAGIC USED TO CREATE HIM IS FORBIDDEN.
THE SECRET OF THAT MAGIC IS BURIED DEEP INSIDE OUR LIBRARY VAULTS...
I'M SURPRISED THAT...
...ANYONE EVEN KNEW OF ITS EXISTENCE.
GULP
SHRR

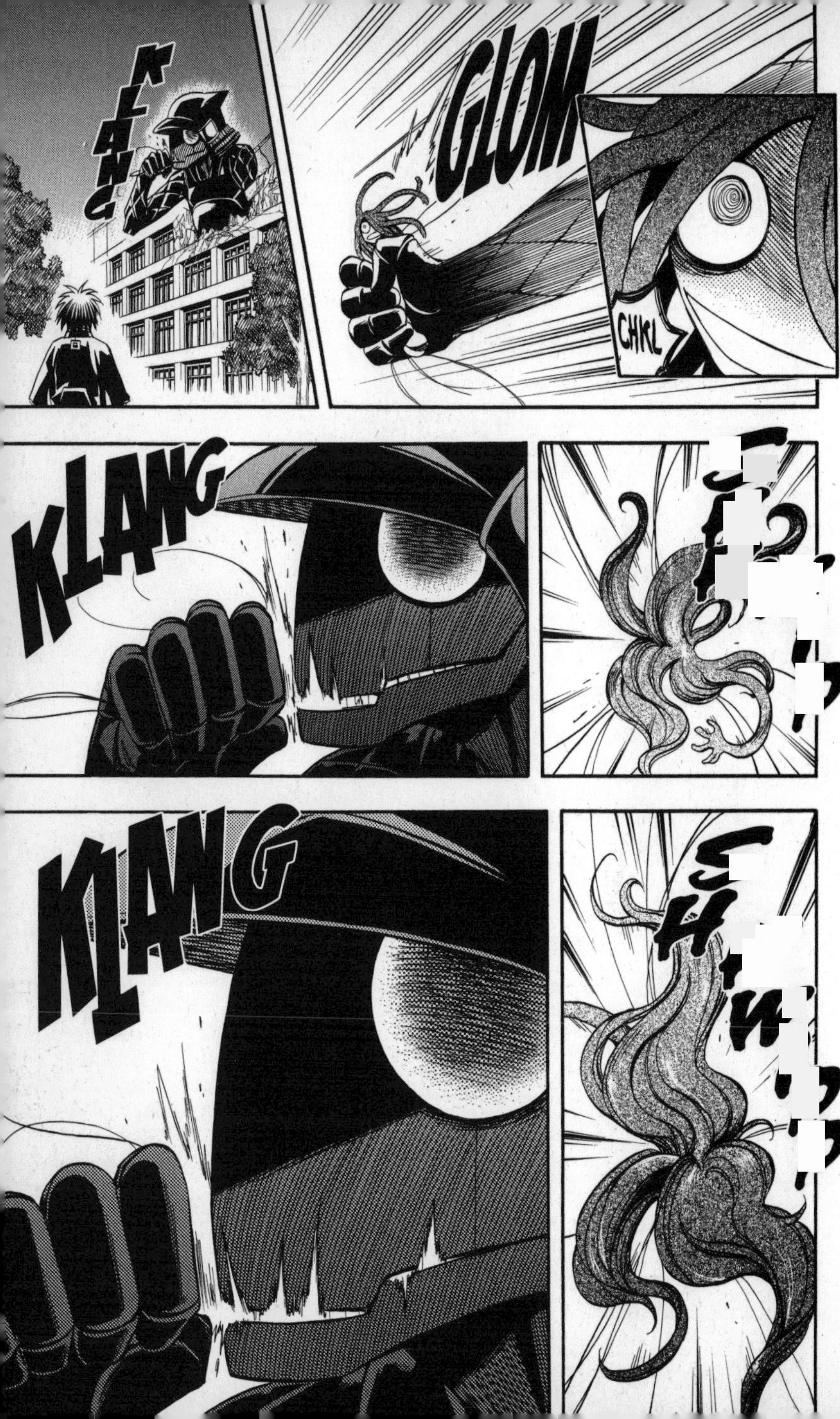
GLOM
CHKL
KLANG
KLANG
KLANG

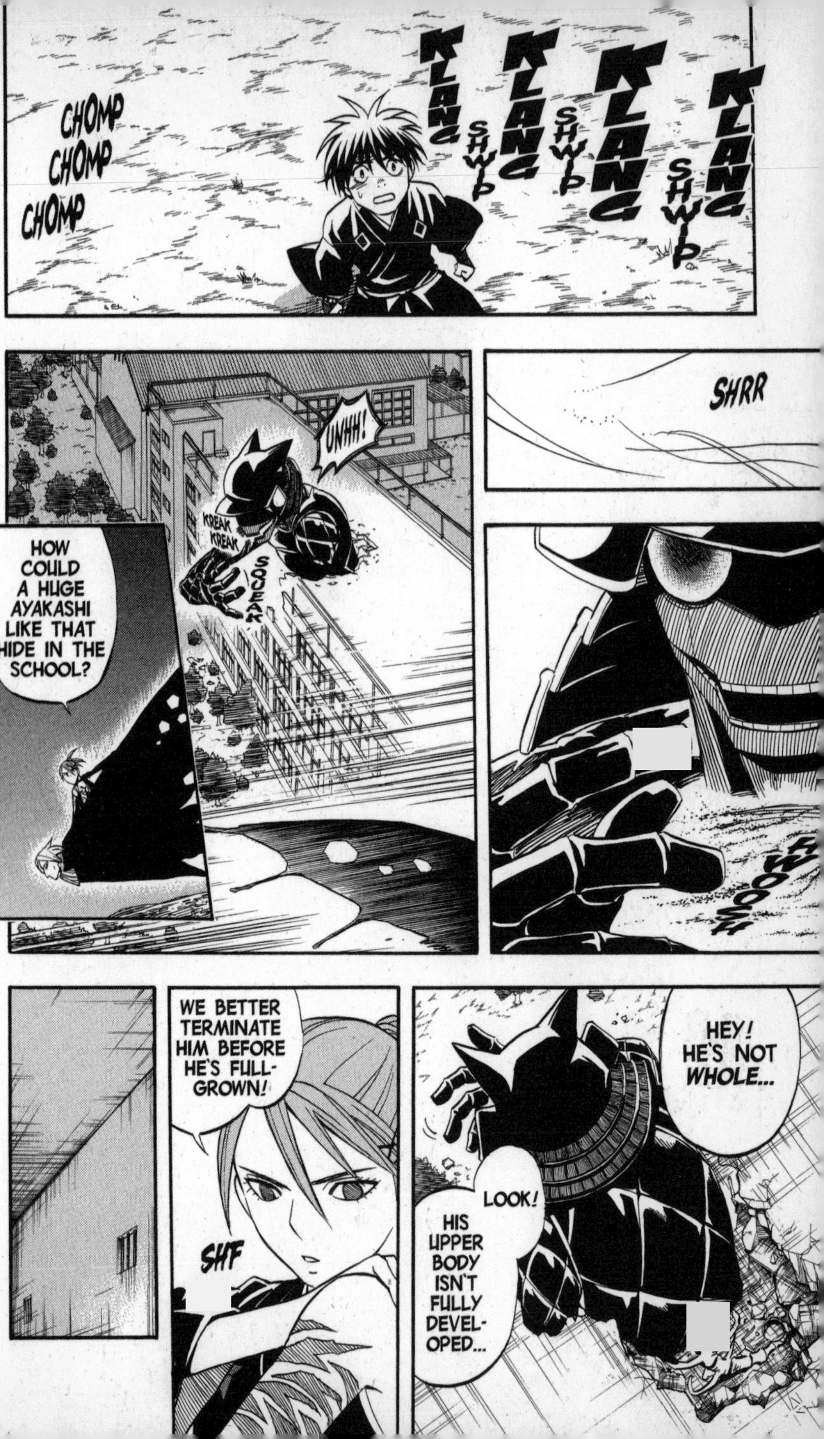
KLANG
SHWIP
KLANG
SHWIP
KLANG
SHWIP
KLANG
CHOMP CHOMP CHOMP
SHRR
WHOOSH
UNHH!
KREAK KREAK
SQUEAK
HOW COULD A HUGE AYAKASHI LIKE THAT HIDE IN THE SCHOOL?
HEY! HE'S NOT WHOLE...
LOOK!
HIS UPPER BODY ISN'T FULLY DEVEL-OPED...
WE BETTER TERMINATE HIM BEFORE HE'S FULL-GROWN!
SHF

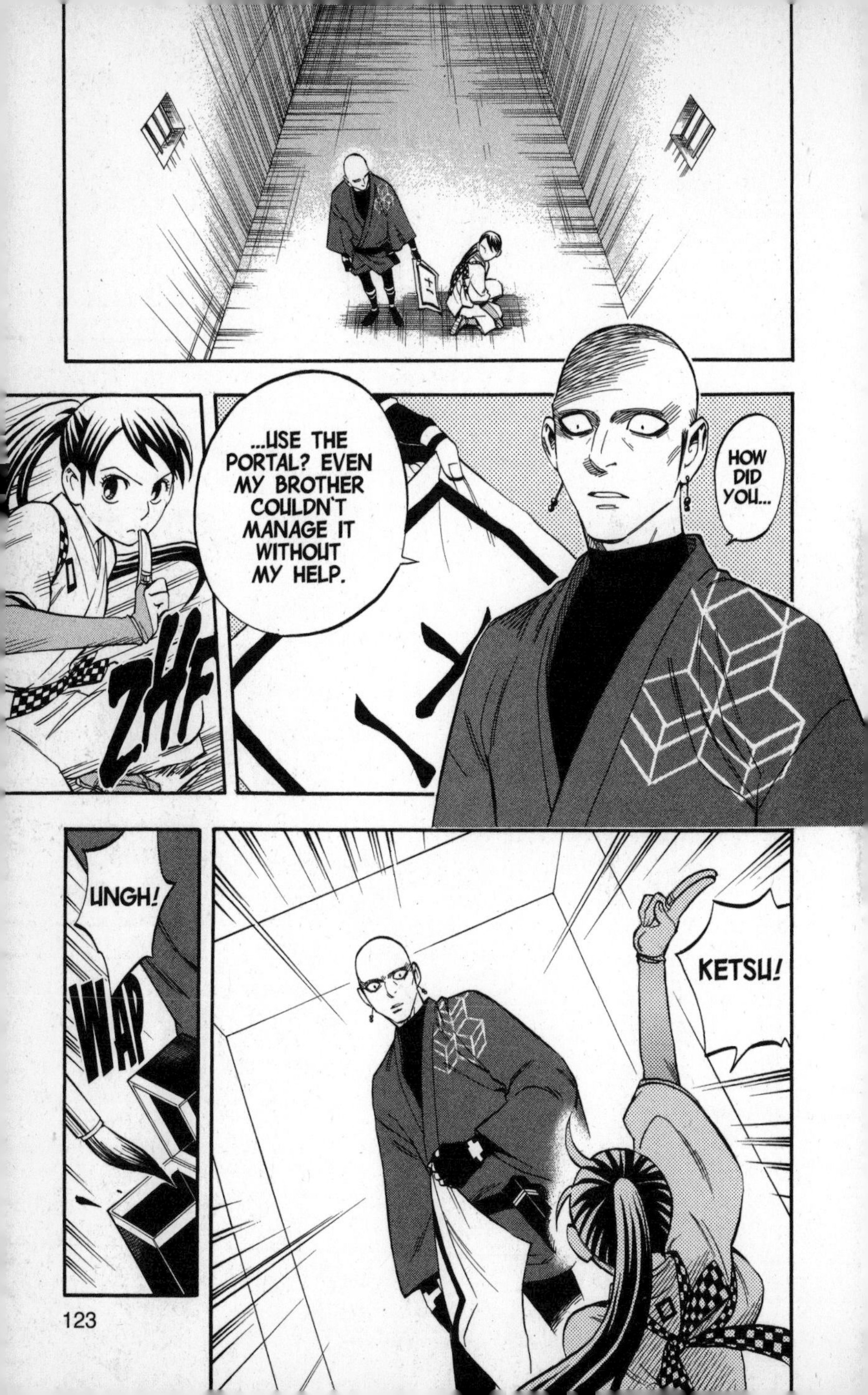
HOW DID YOU...
...USE THE PORTAL? EVEN MY BROTHER COULDN'T MANAGE IT WITHOUT MY HELP.
ZHF
KETSU!
UNGH!
WAP

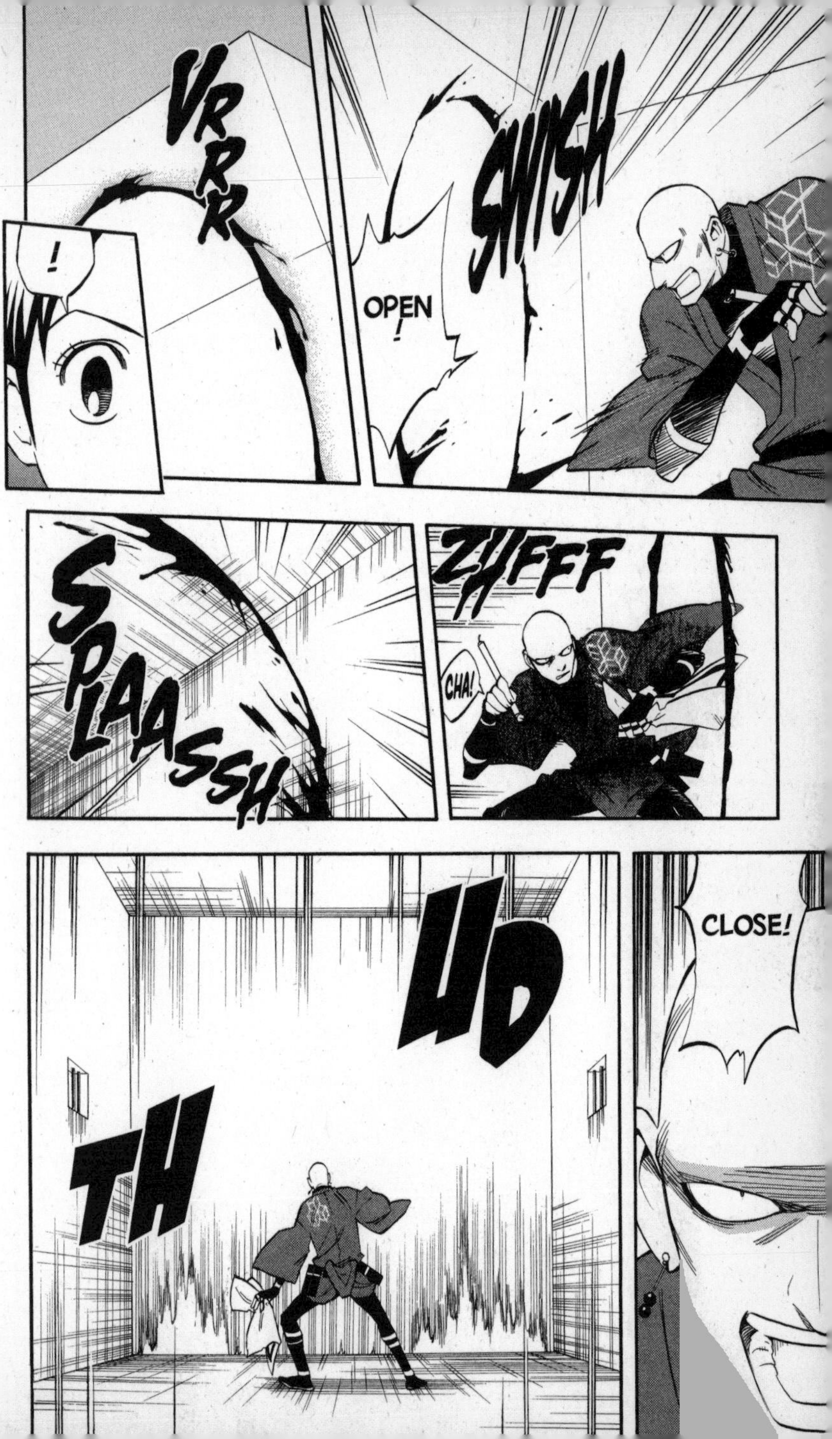
SWISH
OPEN!
VRRR
!
ZHFFF
CHA!
SPLAASSH
CLOSE!
THUD

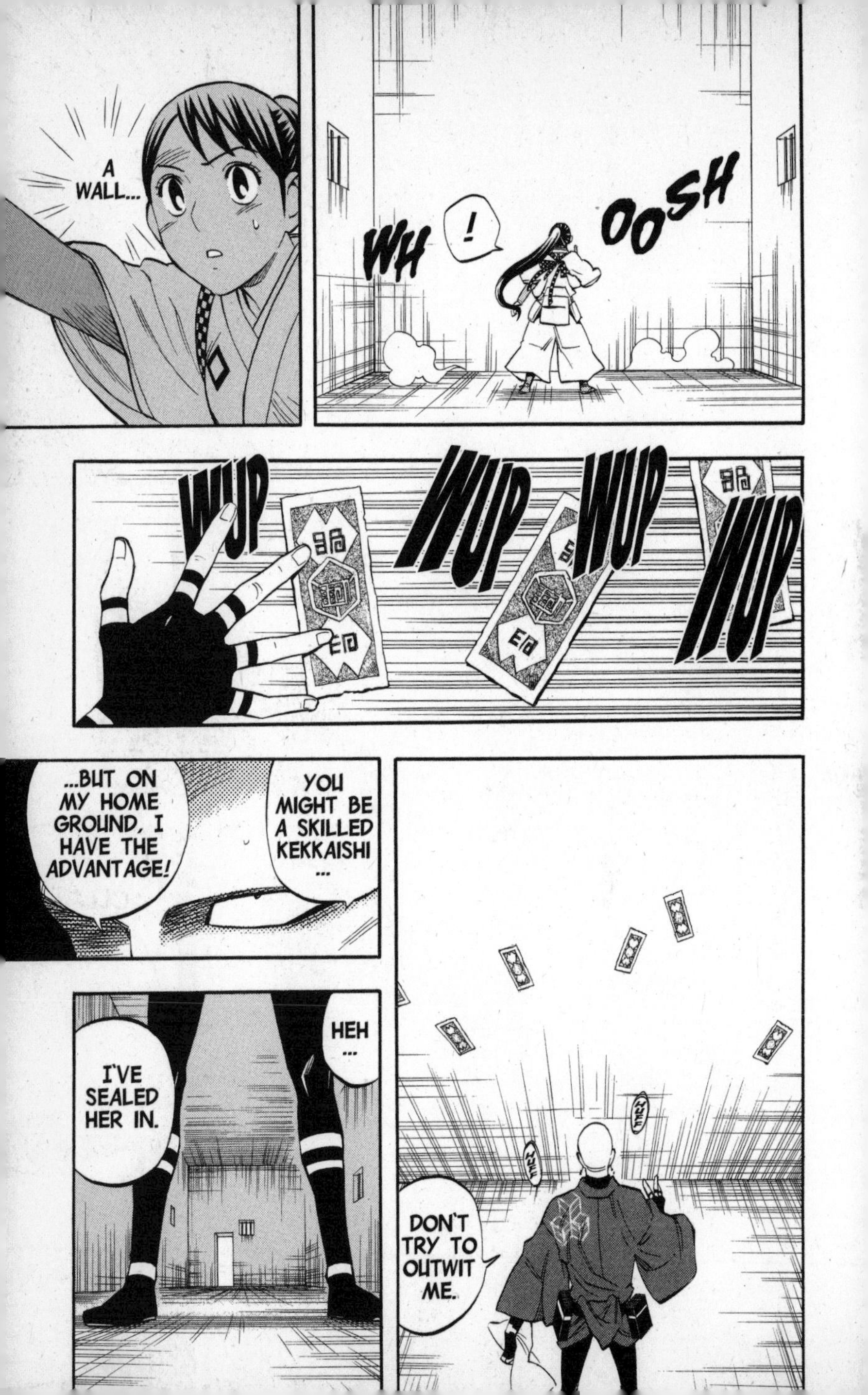
WH
!
OOSH
A WALL...
WUP
WUP
WUP
WUP
DON'T TRY TO OUTWIT ME.
YOU MIGHT BE A SKILLED KEKKAISHI...
...BUT ON MY HOME GROUND, I HAVE THE ADVANTAGE!
HEH...
I'VE SEALED HER IN.

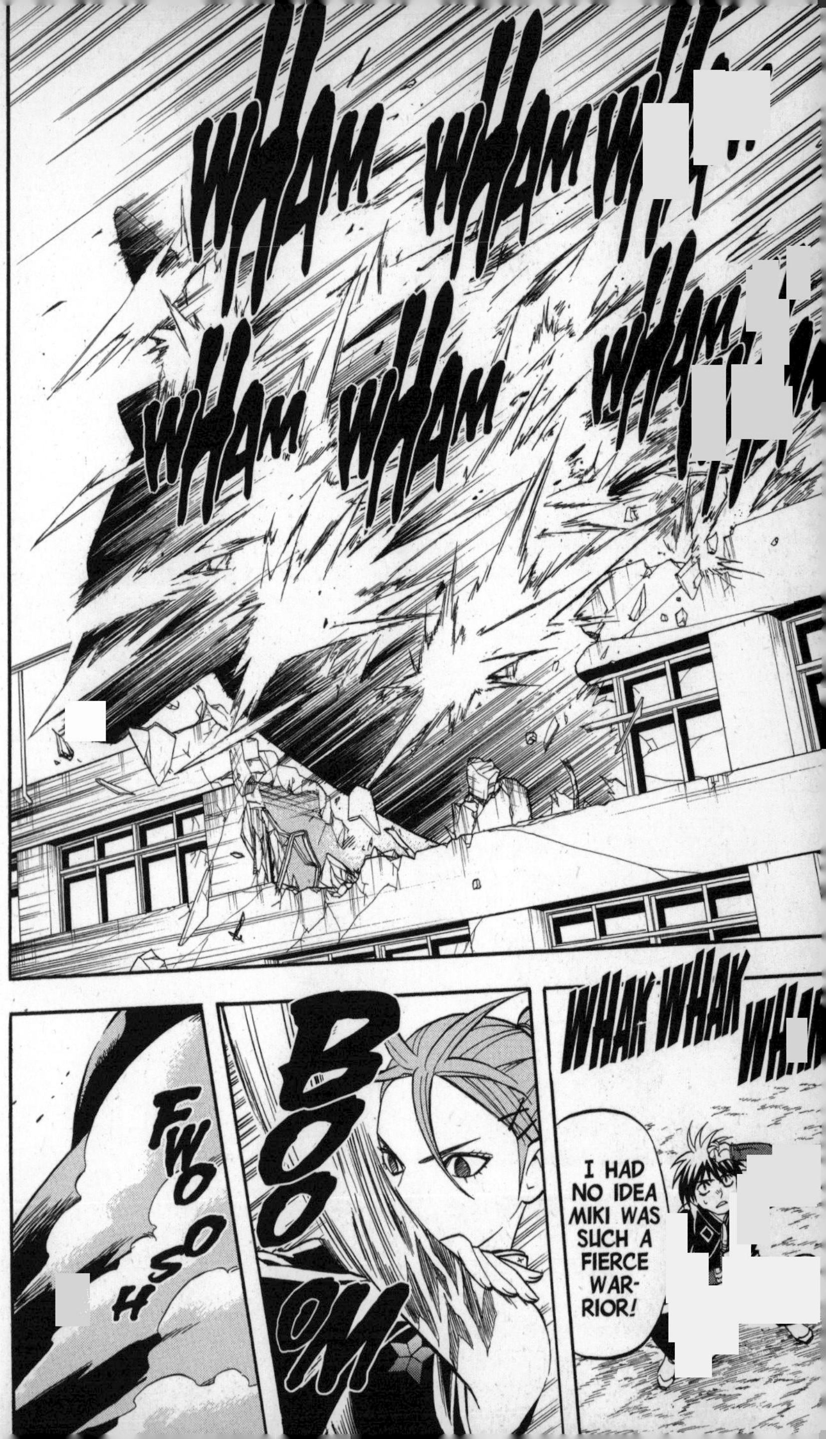
WHAM WHAM
WHAM WHAM WHAM
WHAK WHAK
I HAD NO IDEA MIKI WAS SUCH A FIERCE WARRIOR!
BOOM
FWOOSH

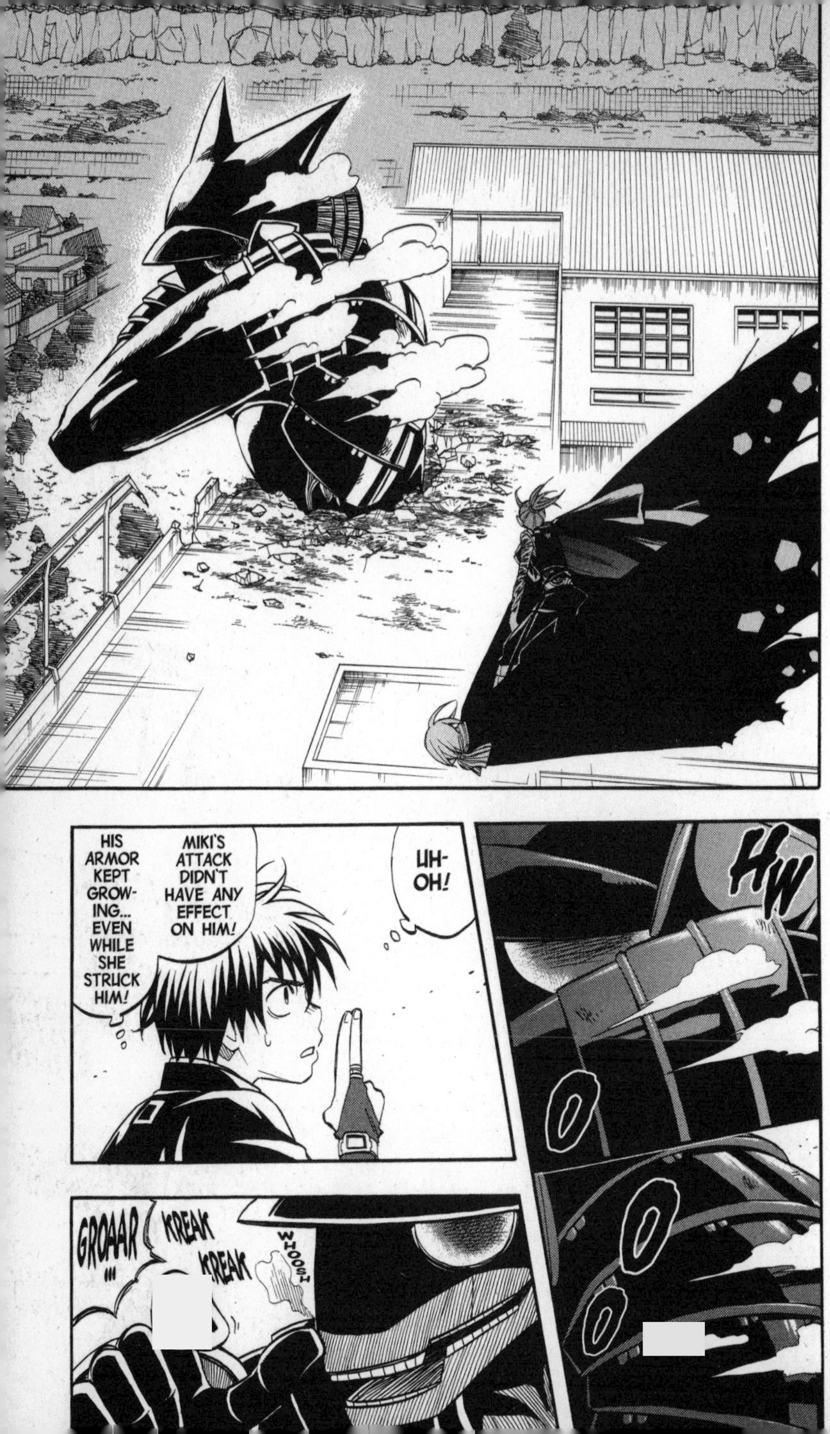
HW
UH-OH!
MIKI'S ATTACK DIDN'T HAVE ANY EFFECT ON HIM!
HIS ARMOR KEPT GROWING... EVEN WHILE SHE STRUCK HIM!
WHOOSH
KREAK KREAK
GROAAR!!!

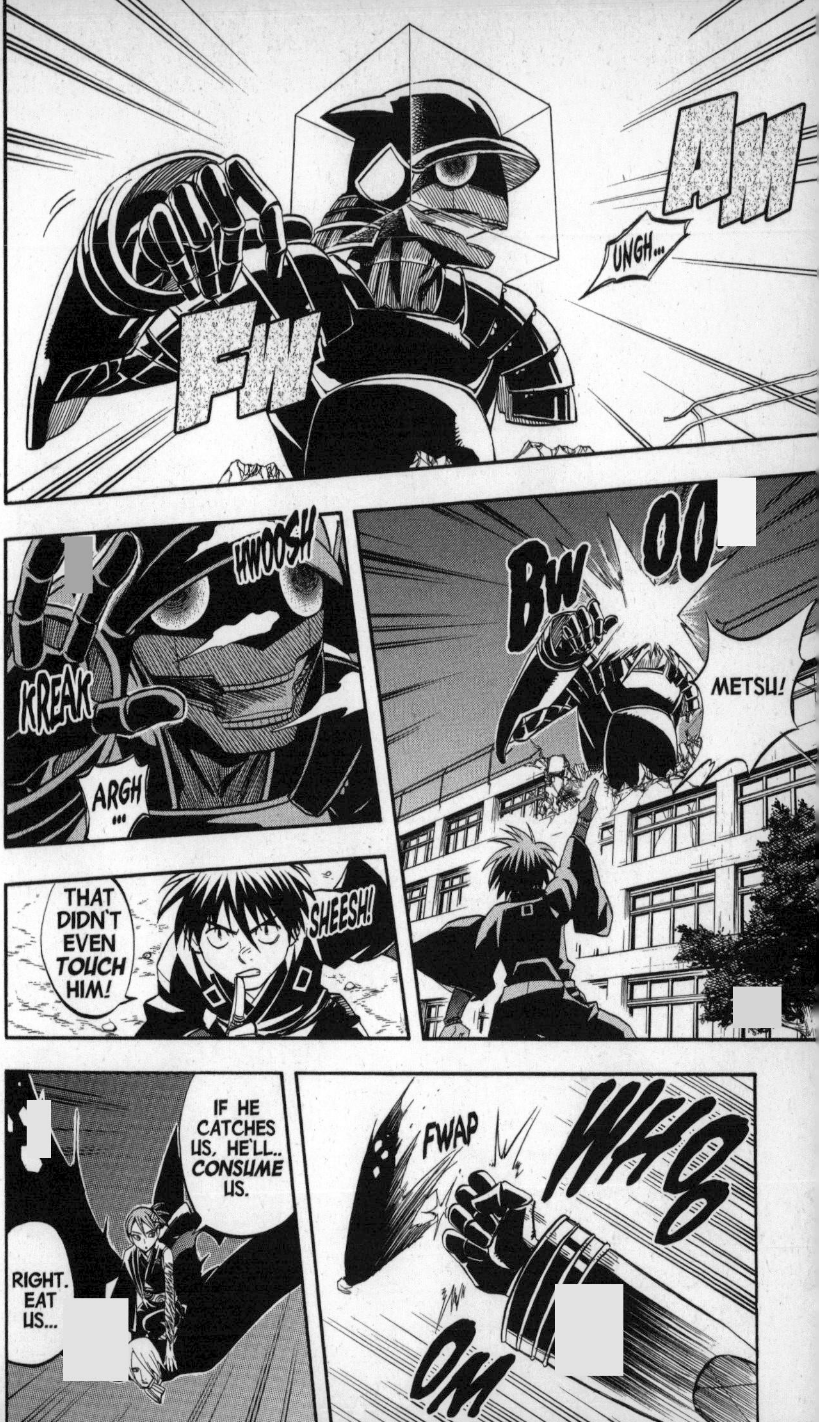
AM
UNGH...
FW
BW
OO
METSU!
HWOOSH
KREAK
ARGH...
SHEESH!
THAT DIDN'T EVEN TOUCH HIM!
WHO
FWAP
OM
IF HE CATCHES US, HE'LL.. CONSUME US.
RIGHT. EAT US...

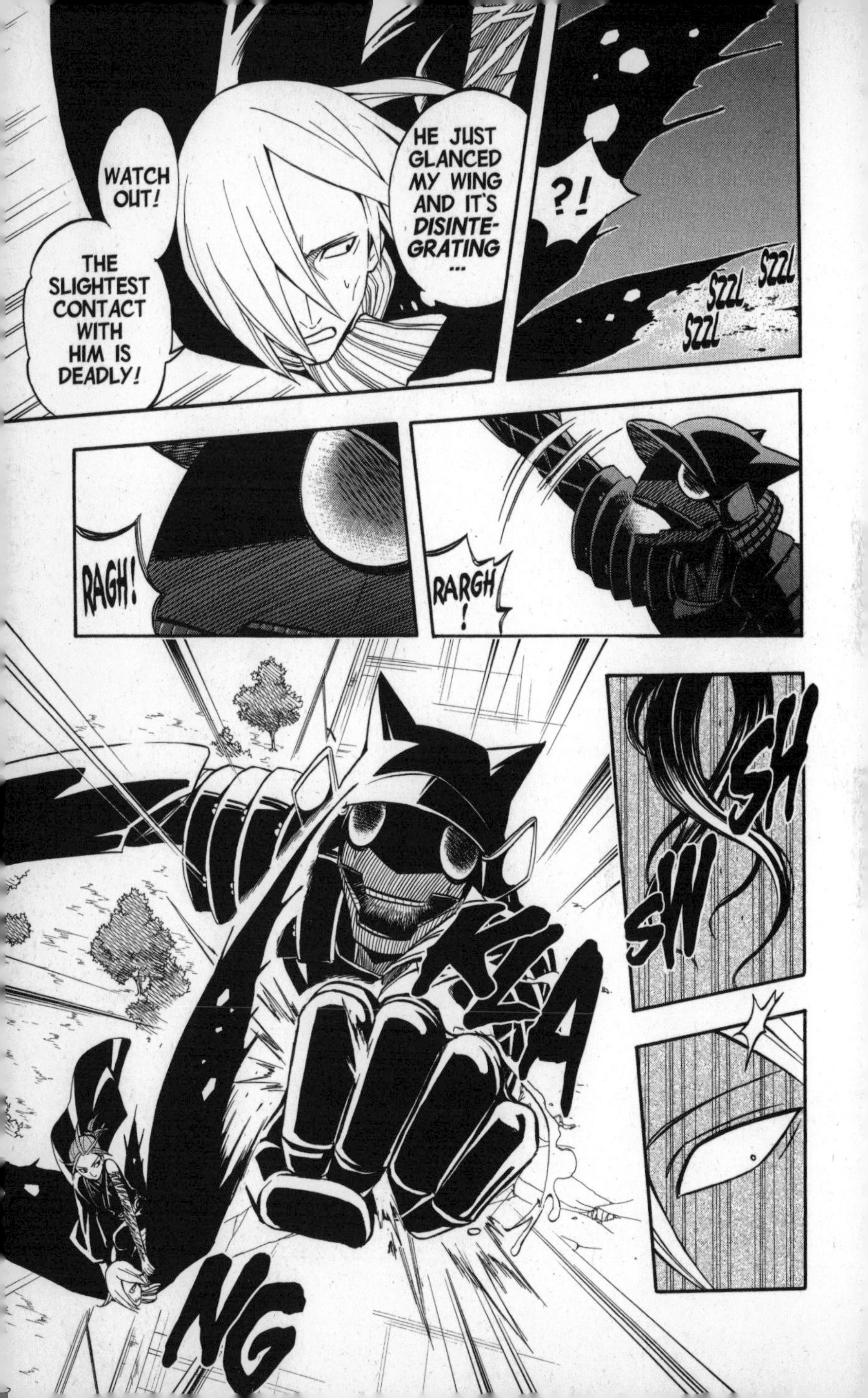
?!
SZZL
SZZL
SZZL
HE JUST GLANCED MY WING AND IT'S *DISINTEGRATING* ...
WATCH OUT!
THE SLIGHTEST CONTACT WITH HIM IS DEADLY!
RARGH!
RAGH!
SWSH
KANG

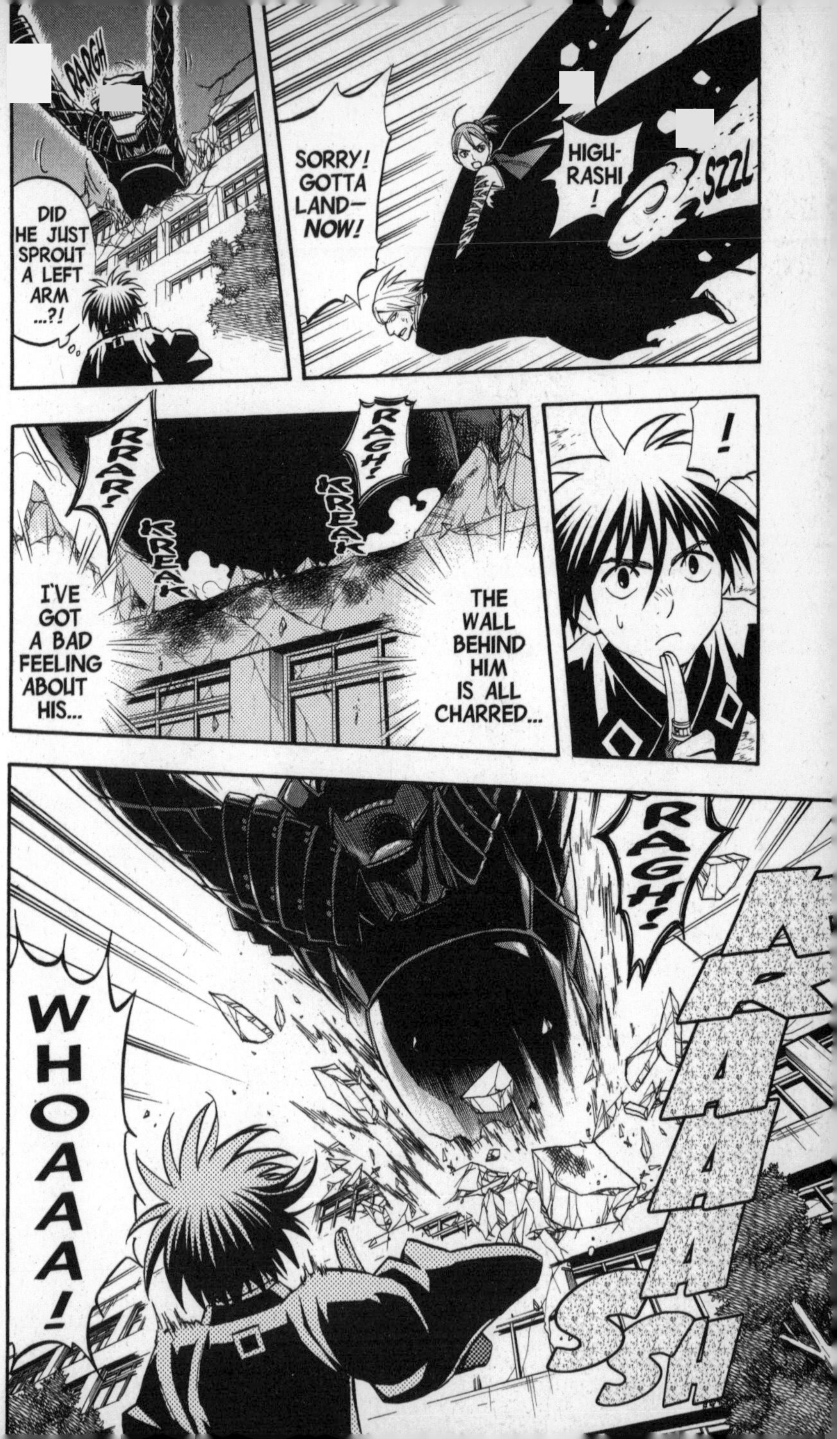
HIGU-RASHI!
SZZL
SORRY! GOTTA LAND—NOW!
RARGH
DID HE JUST SPROUT A LEFT ARM ...?!
!
RAGH!
KREAK
THE WALL BEHIND HIM IS ALL CHARRED...
RRAR!
KREAK
I'VE GOT A BAD FEELING ABOUT HIS...
RAGH!
WHOAAAA!

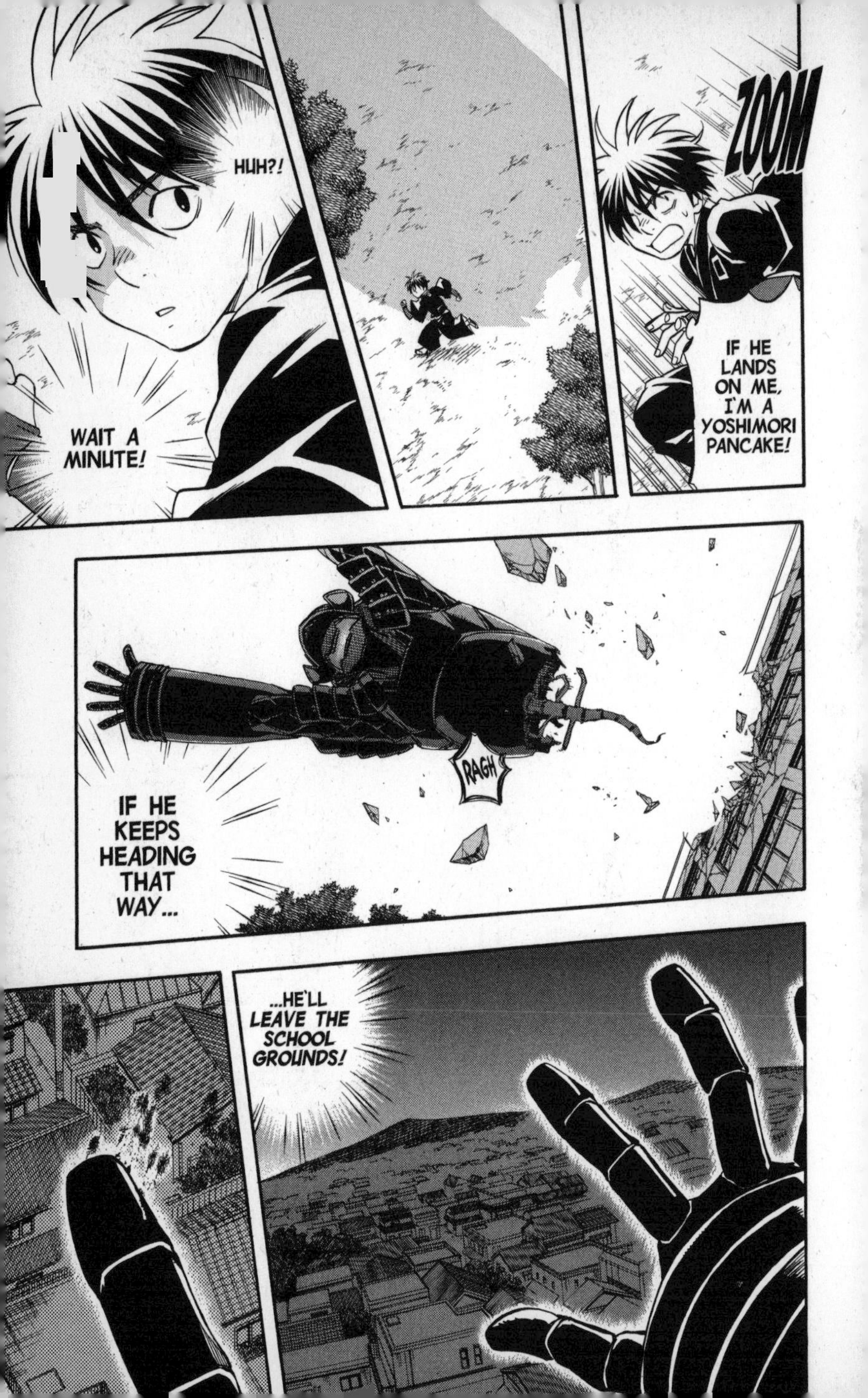
ZOOM
IF HE LANDS ON ME, I'M A YOSHIMORI PANCAKE!
HUH?!
WAIT A MINUTE!
RAGH
IF HE KEEPS HEADING THAT WAY...
...HE'LL LEAVE THE SCHOOL GROUNDS!

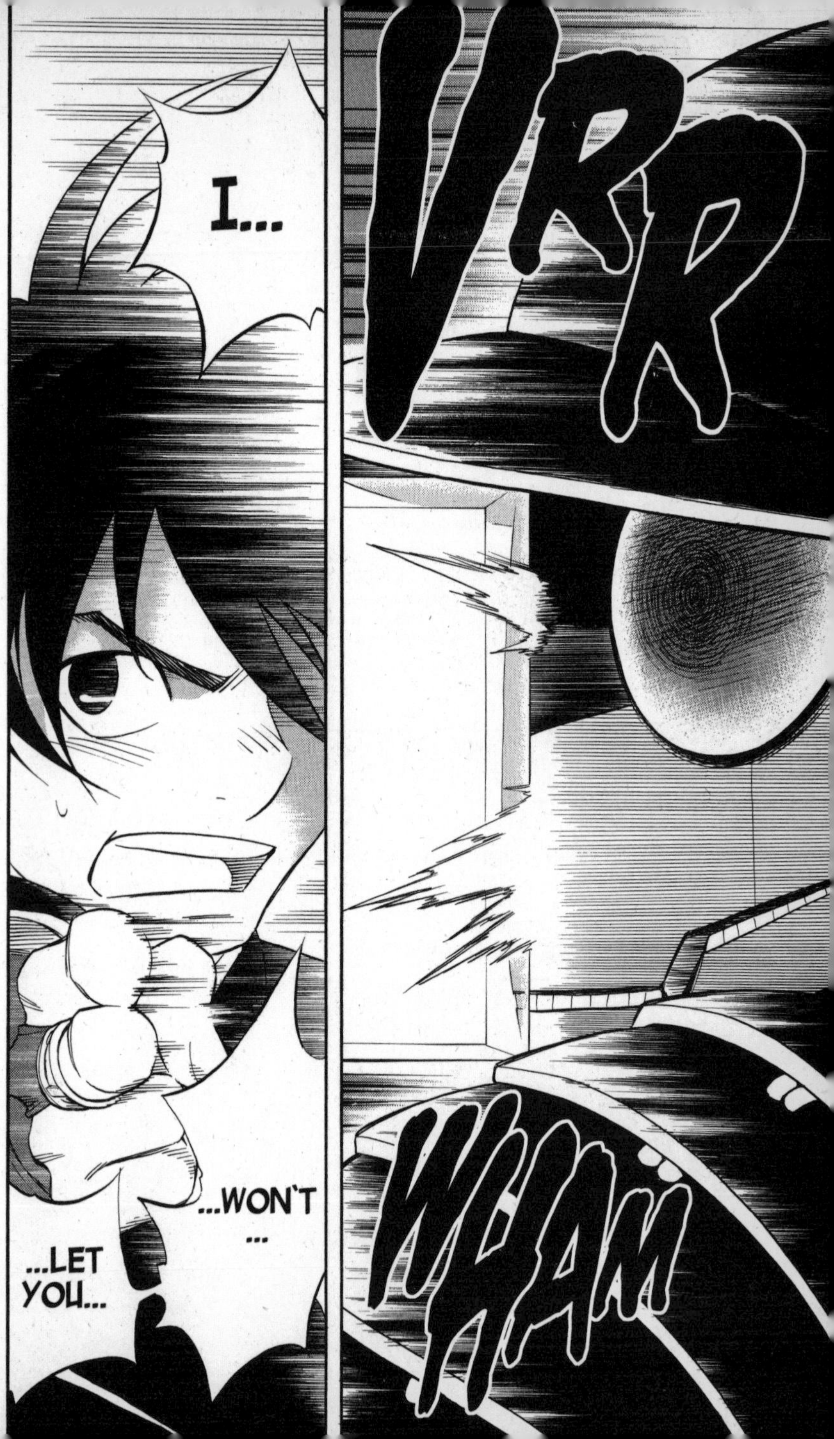
VRR
WHAM
I...
...WON'T ...
...LET YOU...

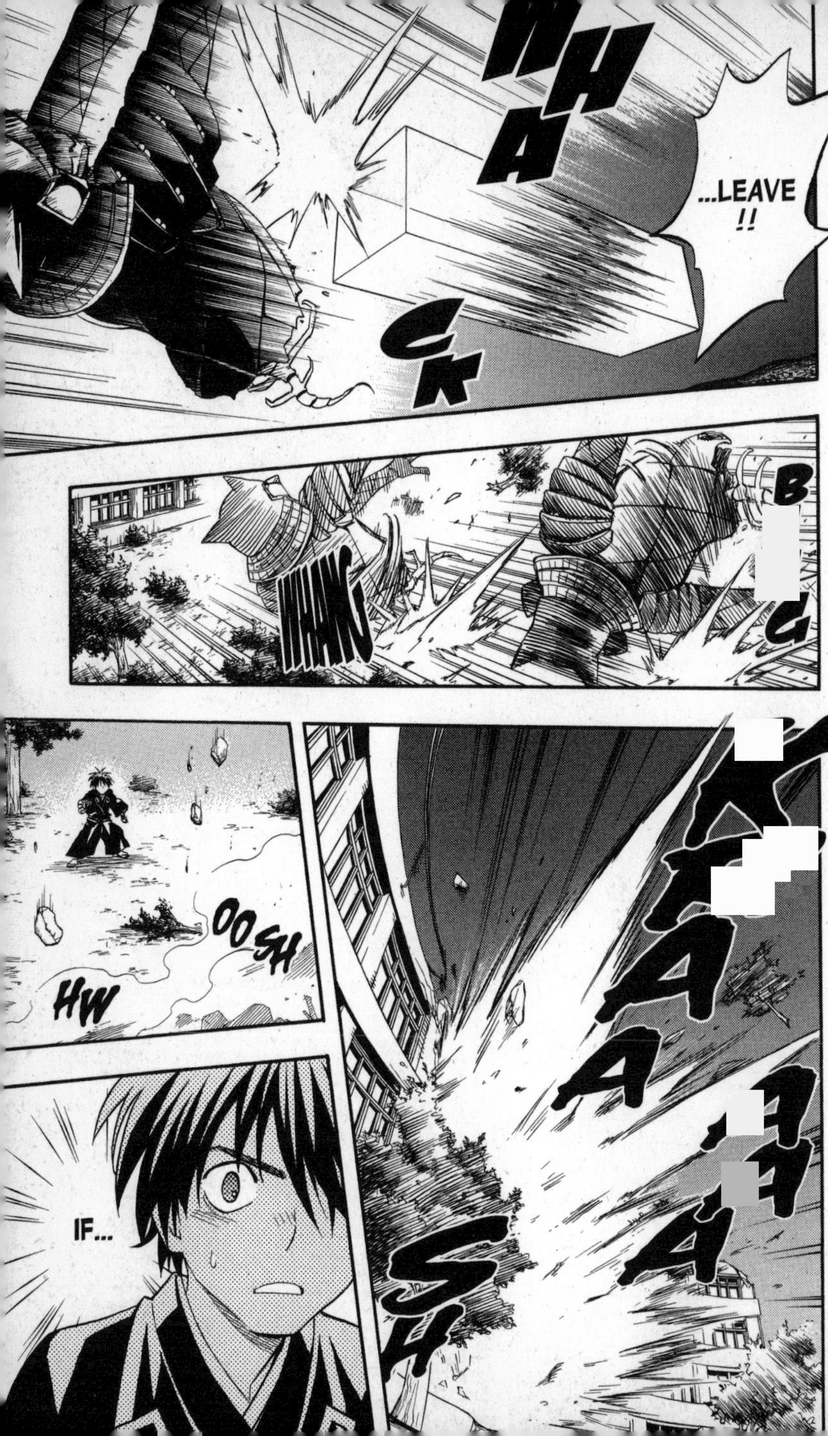
...LEAVE !!
WHA
CK
WHANG
OOSH
HW
IF...

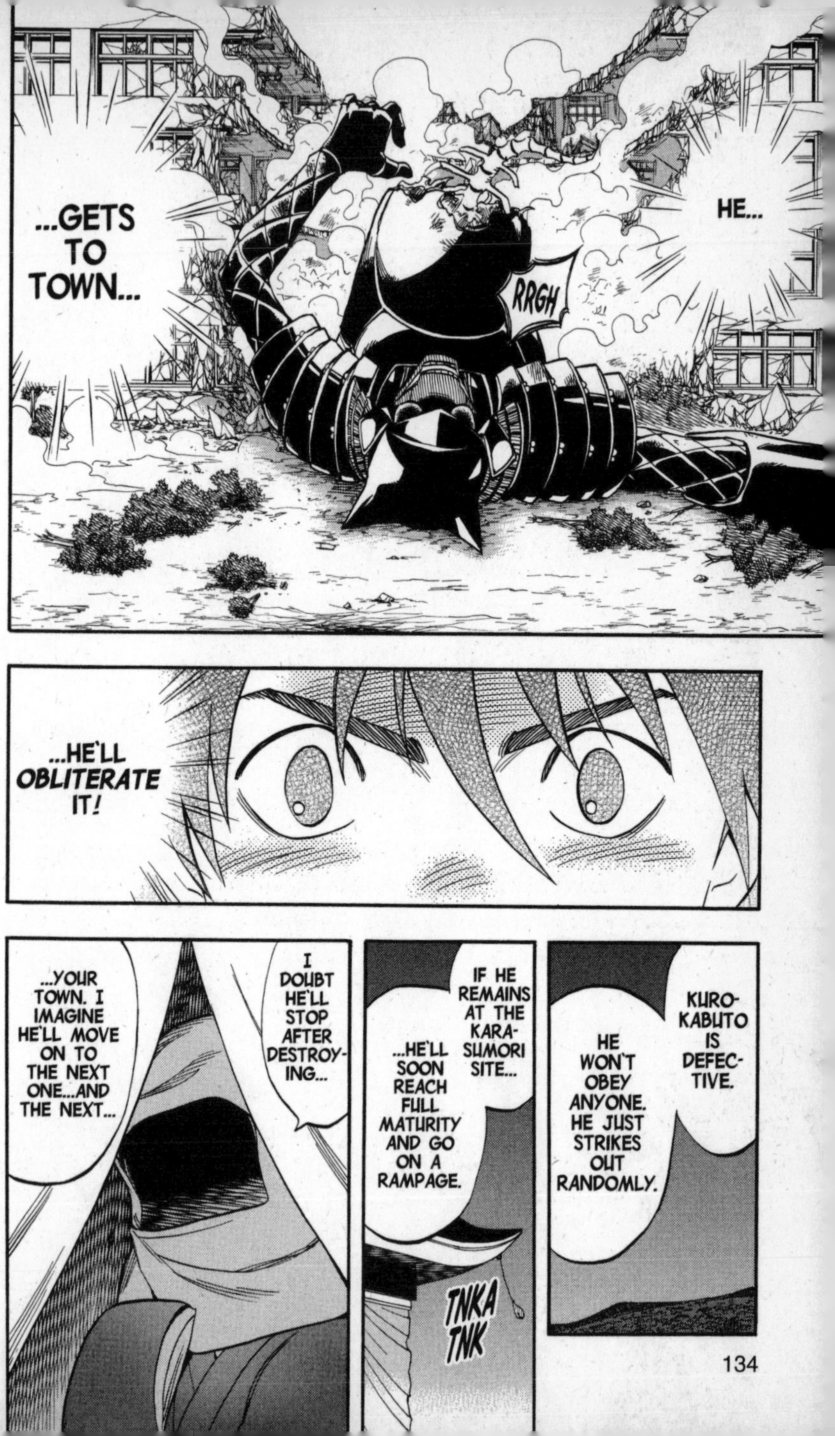
HE...
...GETS TO TOWN...
RRGH
...HE'LL *OBLITERATE* IT!
KURO-KABUTO IS DEFEC-TIVE.
HE WON'T OBEY ANYONE. HE JUST STRIKES OUT RANDOMLY.
IF HE REMAINS AT THE KARA-SUMORI SITE...
...HE'LL SOON REACH FULL MATURITY AND GO ON A RAMPAGE.
TNKA TNK
I DOUBT HE'LL STOP AFTER DESTROY-ING...
...YOUR TOWN. I IMAGINE HE'LL MOVE ON TO THE NEXT ONE...AND THE NEXT...

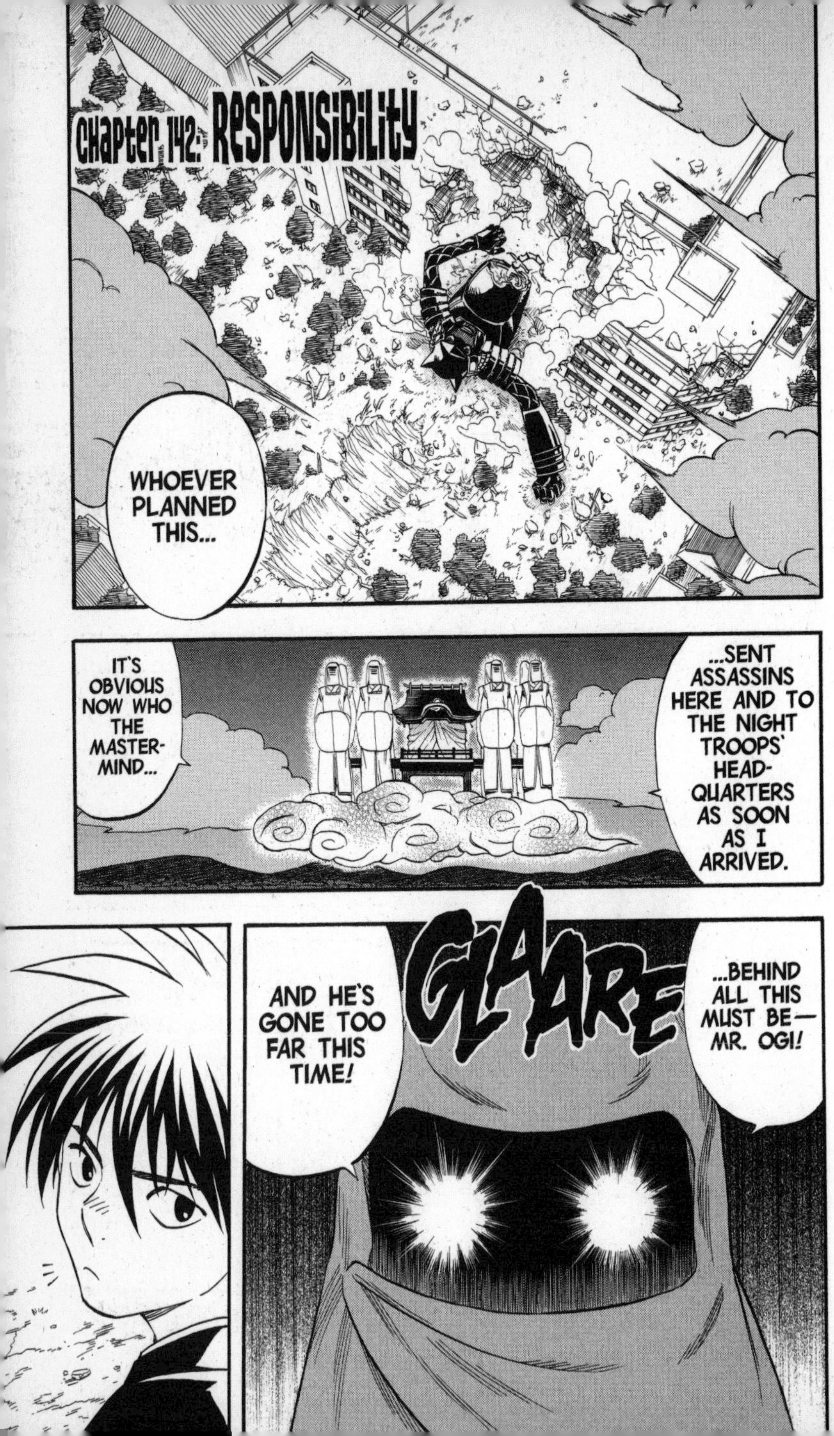
Chapter 142: Responsibility
WHOEVER PLANNED THIS...
...SENT ASSASSINS HERE AND TO THE NIGHT TROOPS' HEADQUARTERS AS SOON AS I ARRIVED.
IT'S OBVIOUS NOW WHO THE MASTERMIND...
...BEHIND ALL THIS MUST BE—MR. OGI!
GLAARE
AND HE'S GONE TOO FAR THIS TIME!

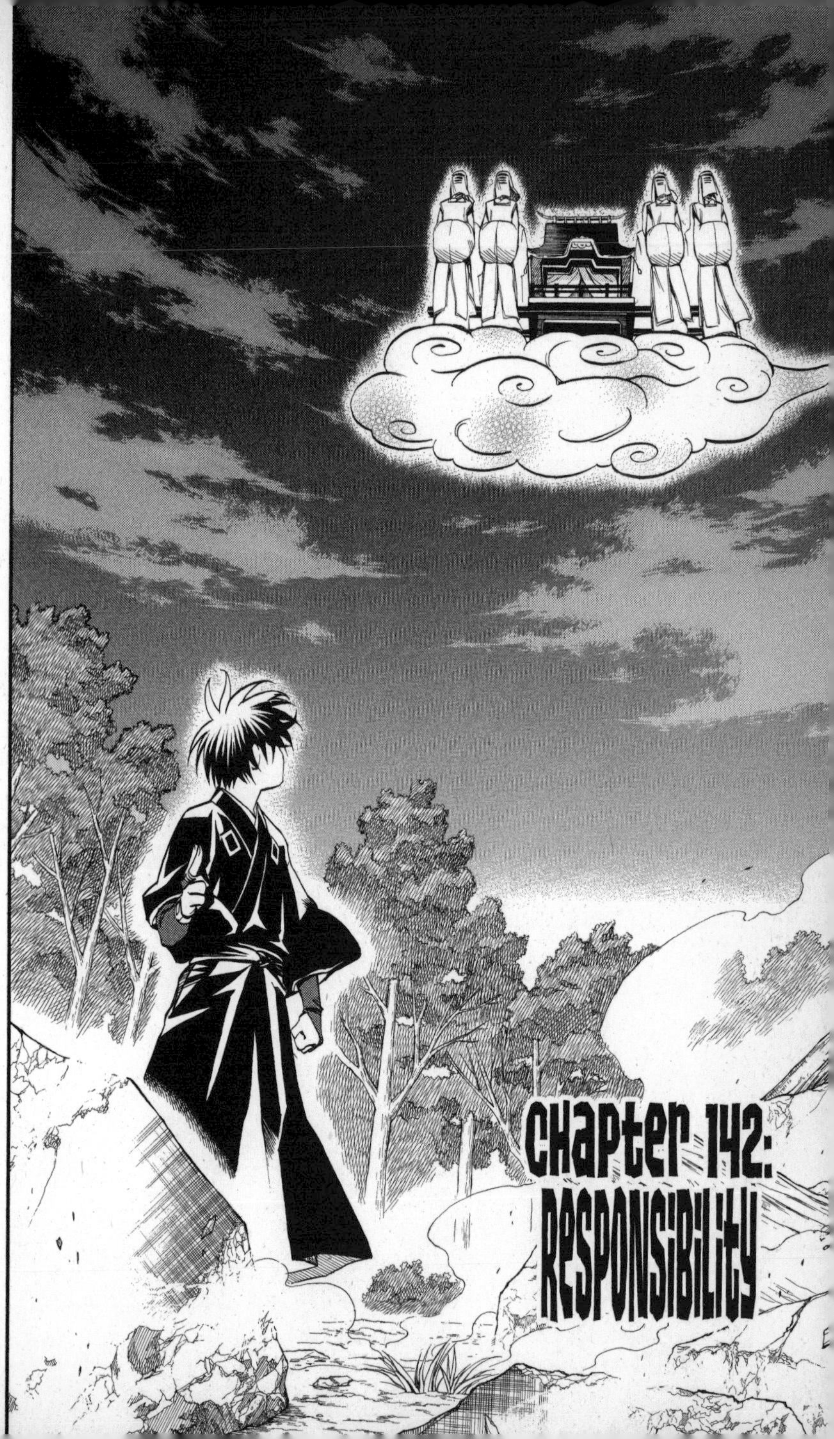

Chapter 142:
Responsibility

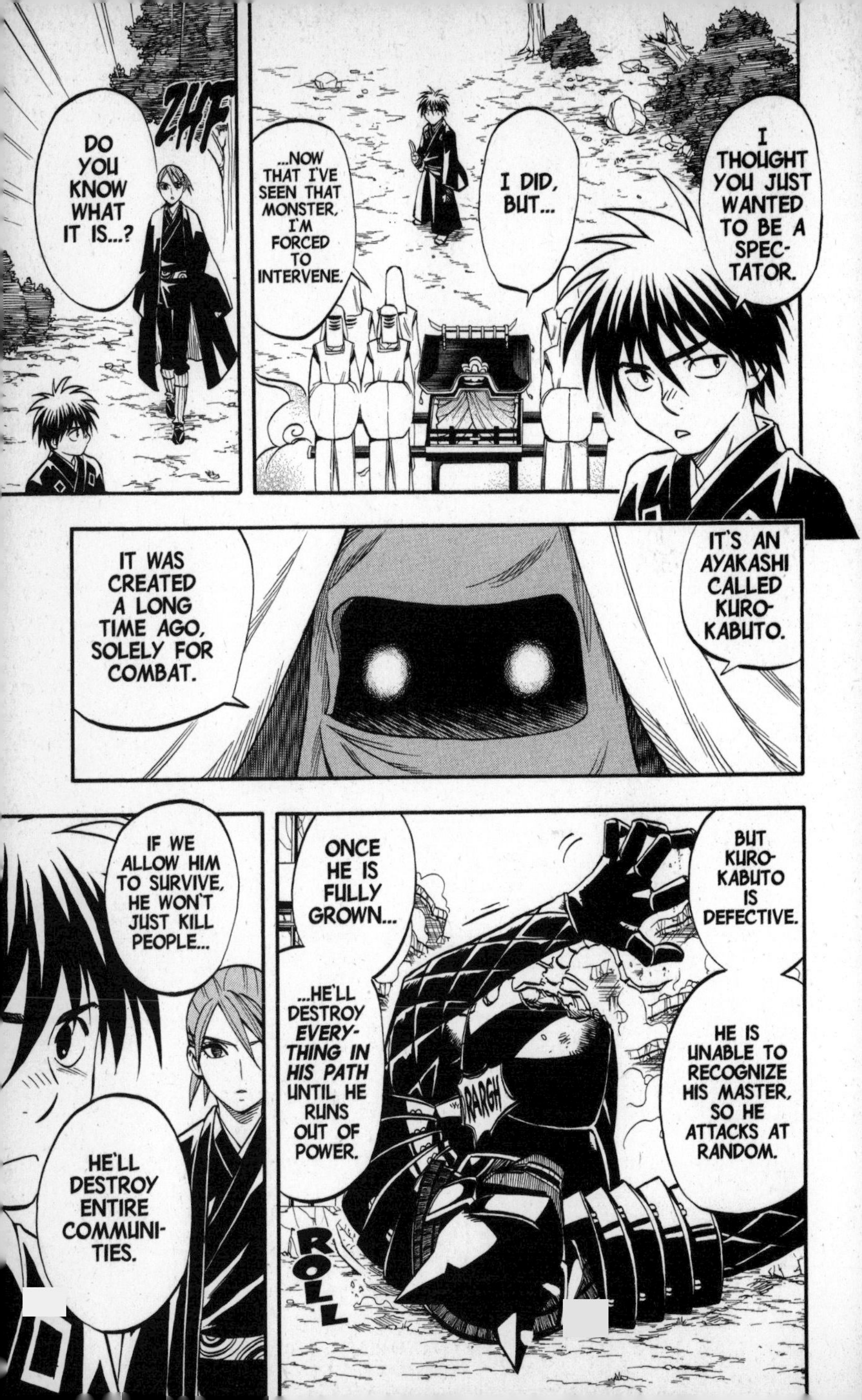
I THOUGHT YOU JUST WANTED TO BE A SPECTATOR.
I DID, BUT...
...NOW THAT I'VE SEEN THAT MONSTER, I'M FORCED TO INTERVENE.
ZHF
DO YOU KNOW WHAT IT IS...?
IT'S AN AYAKASHI CALLED KURO-KABUTO.
IT WAS CREATED A LONG TIME AGO, SOLELY FOR COMBAT.
BUT KURO-KABUTO IS DEFECTIVE.
HE IS UNABLE TO RECOGNIZE HIS MASTER, SO HE ATTACKS AT RANDOM.
RARGH
ONCE HE IS FULLY GROWN...
...HE'LL DESTROY *EVERYTHING* IN HIS PATH UNTIL HE RUNS OUT OF POWER.
ROLL
IF WE ALLOW HIM TO SURVIVE, HE WON'T JUST KILL PEOPLE...
HE'LL DESTROY ENTIRE COMMUNITIES.

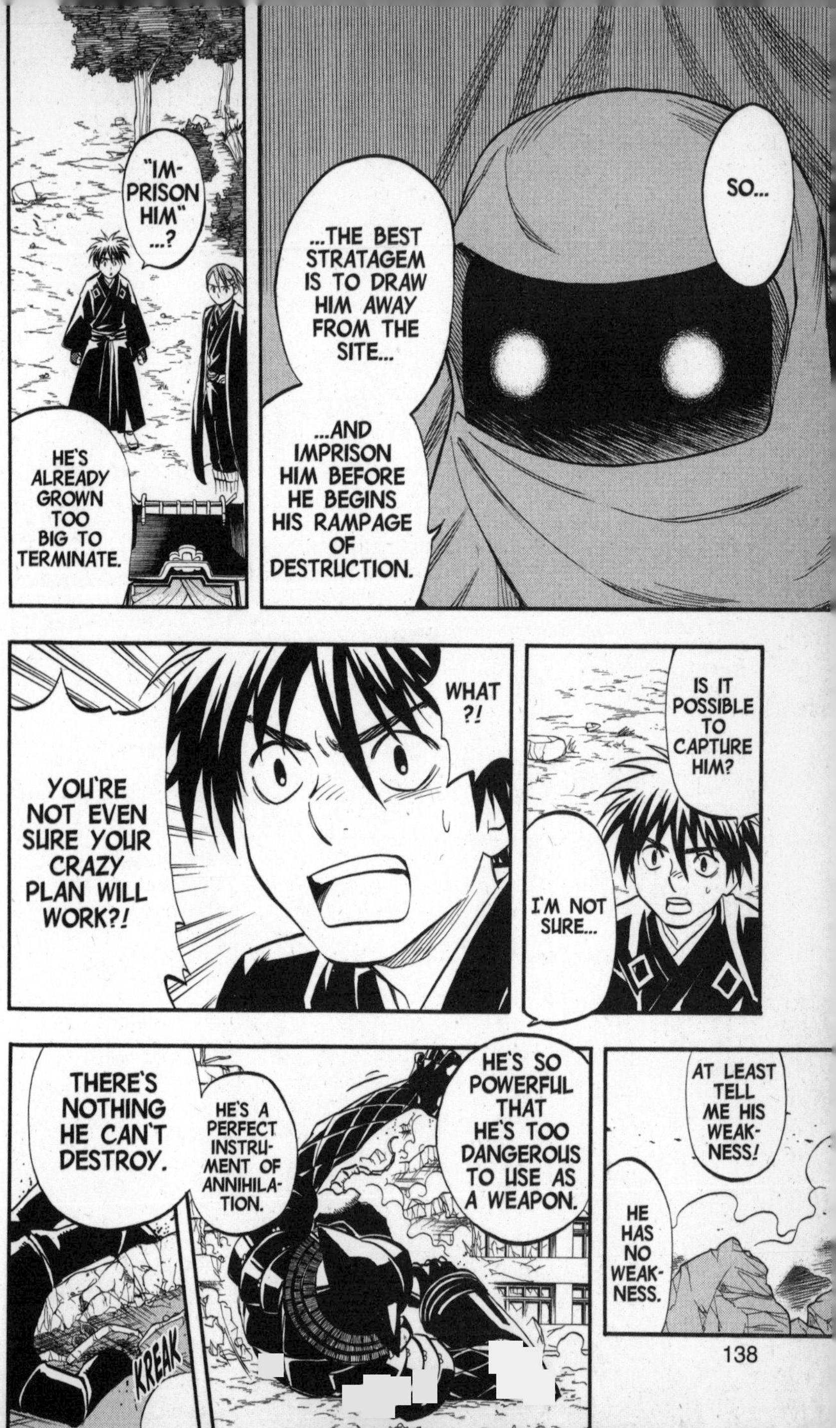
SO...
...THE BEST STRATAGEM IS TO DRAW HIM AWAY FROM THE SITE...
...AND IMPRISON HIM BEFORE HE BEGINS HIS RAMPAGE OF DESTRUCTION.
"IM-PRISON HIM" ...?
HE'S ALREADY GROWN TOO BIG TO TERMINATE.
IS IT POSSIBLE TO CAPTURE HIM?
I'M NOT SURE...
WHAT ?!
YOU'RE NOT EVEN SURE YOUR CRAZY PLAN WILL WORK?!
AT LEAST TELL ME HIS WEAK-NESS!
HE HAS NO WEAK-NESS.
HE'S SO POWERFUL THAT HE'S TOO DANGEROUS TO USE AS A WEAPON.
HE'S A PERFECT INSTRU-MENT OF ANNIHILA-TION.
THERE'S NOTHING HE CAN'T DESTROY.
KREAK

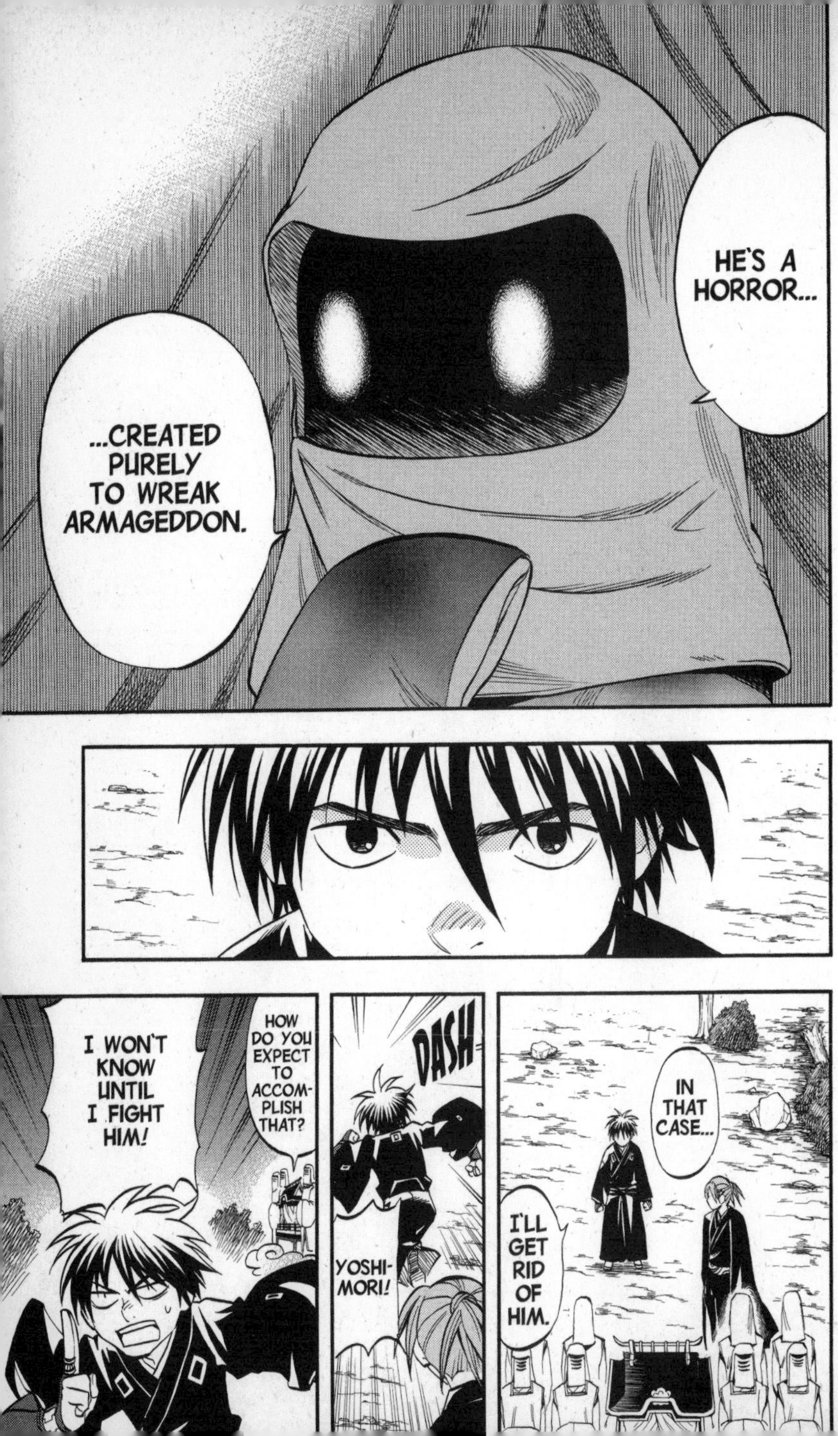
HE'S A HORROR...
...CREATED PURELY TO WREAK ARMAGEDDON.
IN THAT CASE...
I'LL GET RID OF HIM.
DASH
YOSHI-MORI!
HOW DO YOU EXPECT TO ACCOM-PLISH THAT?
I WON'T KNOW UNTIL I FIGHT HIM!

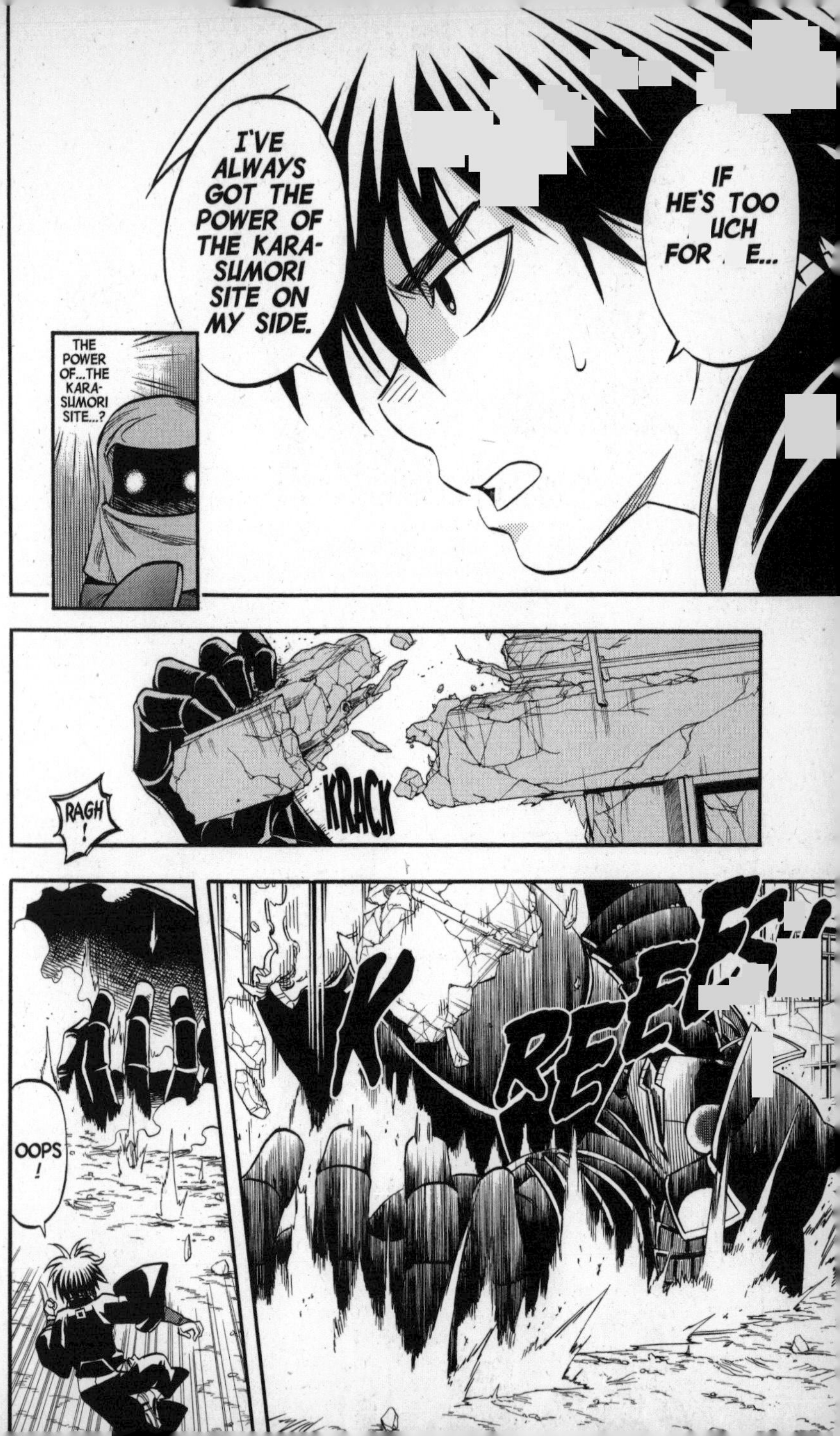
IF HE'S TOO UCH FOR E...
I'VE ALWAYS GOT THE POWER OF THE KARA-SUMORI SITE ON MY SIDE.
THE POWER OF...THE KARA-SUMORI SITE...?
KRACK
RAGH!
KREEEE
OOPS!

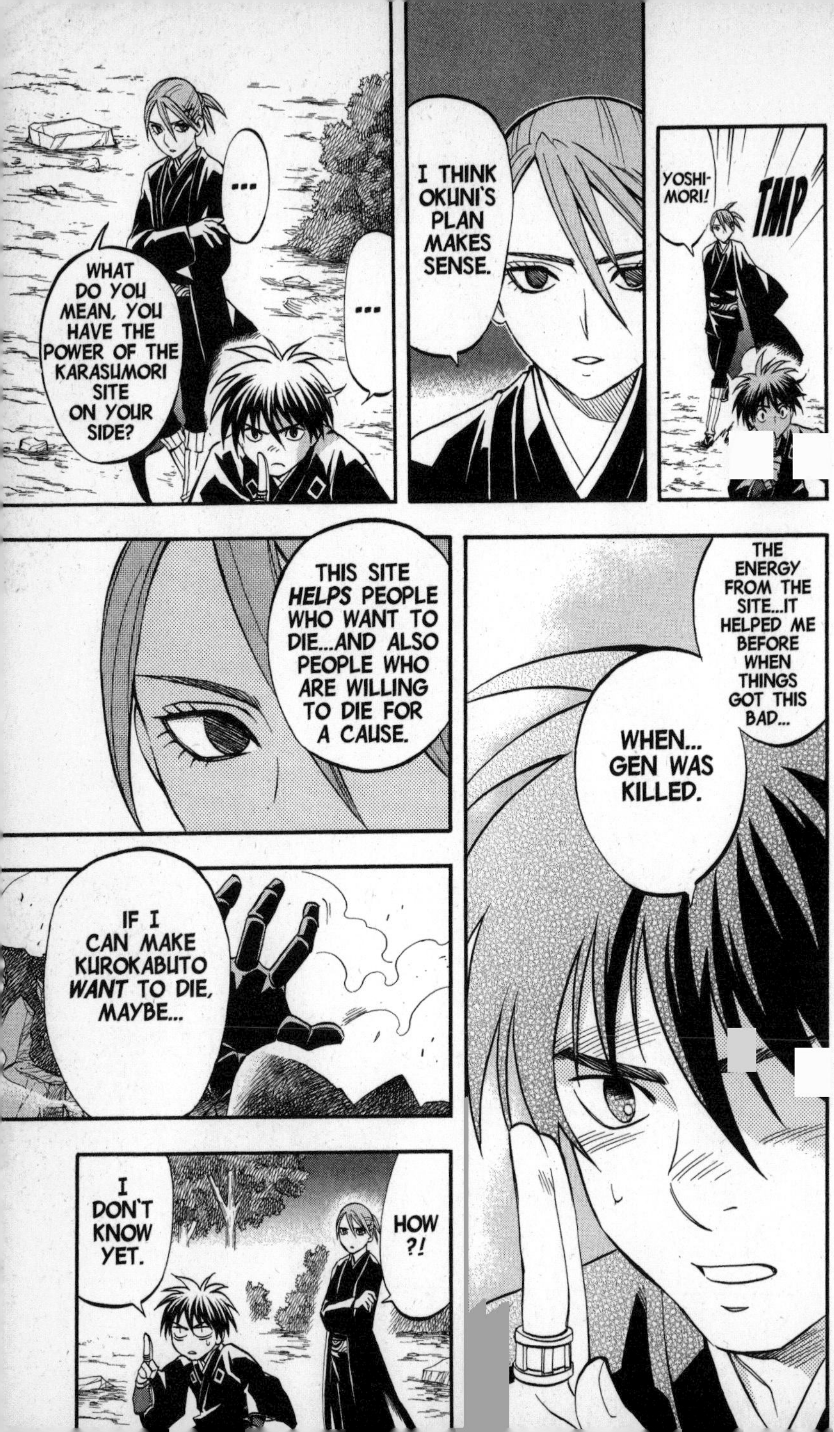
YOSHI-MORI!
TMP
I THINK OKUNI'S PLAN MAKES SENSE.
...
...
WHAT DO YOU MEAN, YOU HAVE THE POWER OF THE KARASUMORI SITE ON YOUR SIDE?
THE ENERGY FROM THE SITE...IT HELPED ME BEFORE WHEN THINGS GOT THIS BAD...
WHEN... GEN WAS KILLED.
THIS SITE *HELPS* PEOPLE WHO WANT TO DIE...AND ALSO PEOPLE WHO ARE WILLING TO DIE FOR A CAUSE.
IF I CAN MAKE KUROKABUTO *WANT* TO DIE, MAYBE...
HOW ?!
I DON'T KNOW YET.

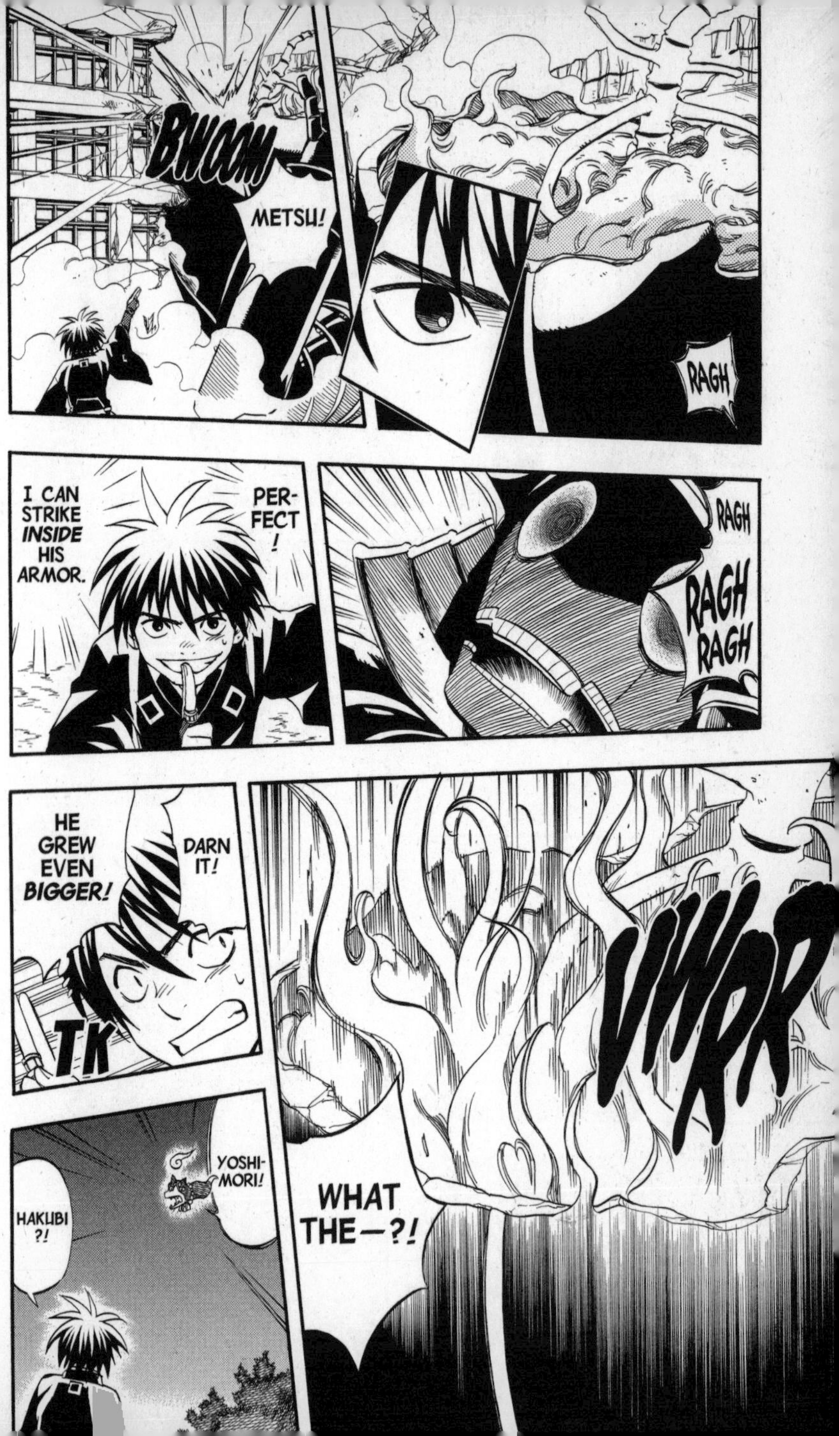
RAGH
METSU!
BWOOM
RAGH
RAGH RAGH
PERFECT!
I CAN STRIKE *INSIDE* HIS ARMOR.
VWRR
WHAT THE—?!
DARN IT!
HE GREW EVEN *BIGGER!*
TK
YOSHIMORI!
HAKUBI?!

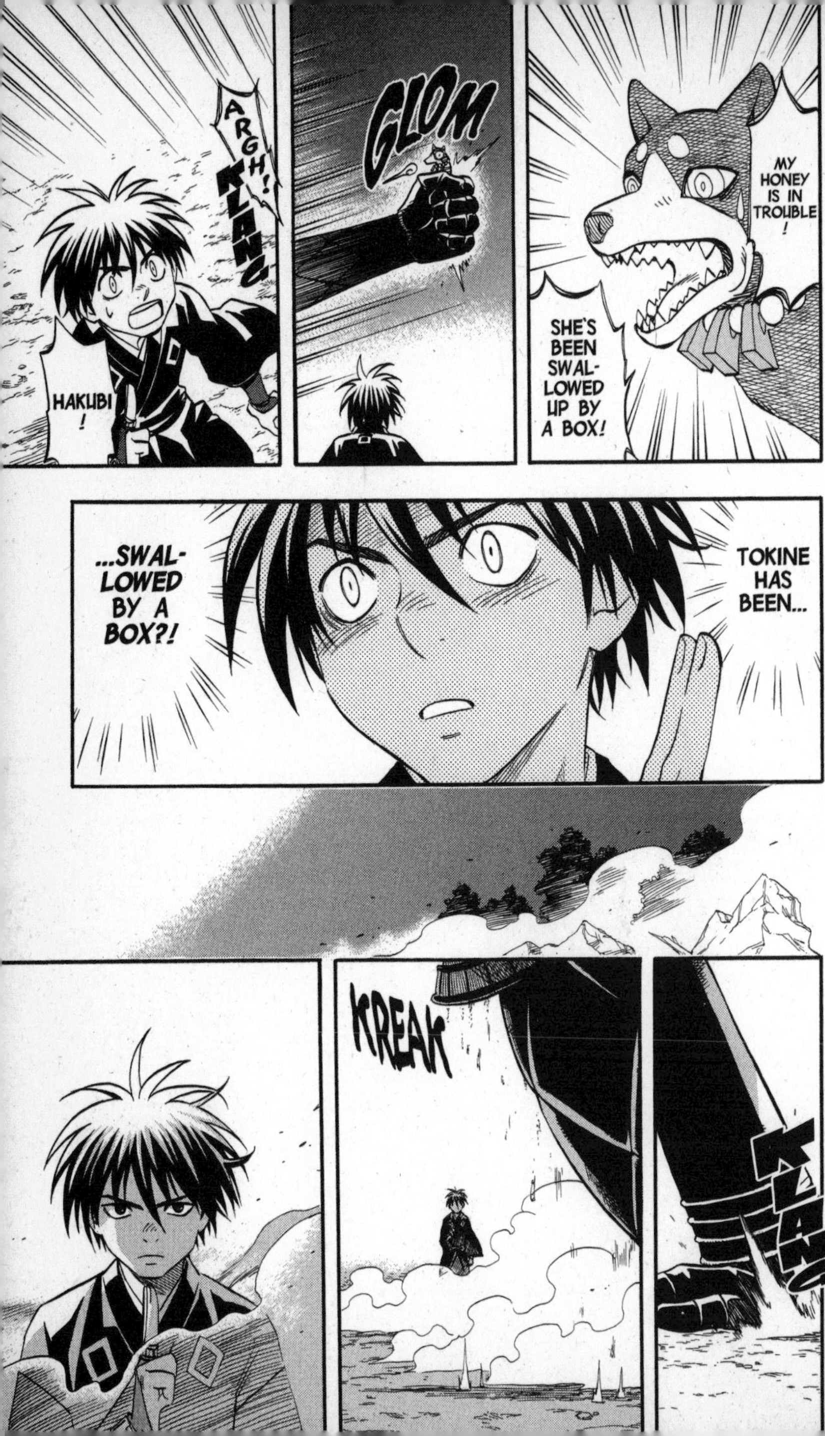
MY HONEY IS IN TROUBLE!
SHE'S BEEN SWAL-LOWED UP BY A BOX!
GLOM
ARGH!
KLANG
HAKUBI!
TOKINE HAS BEEN...
...SWAL-LOWED BY A BOX?!
KLANG
KREAK

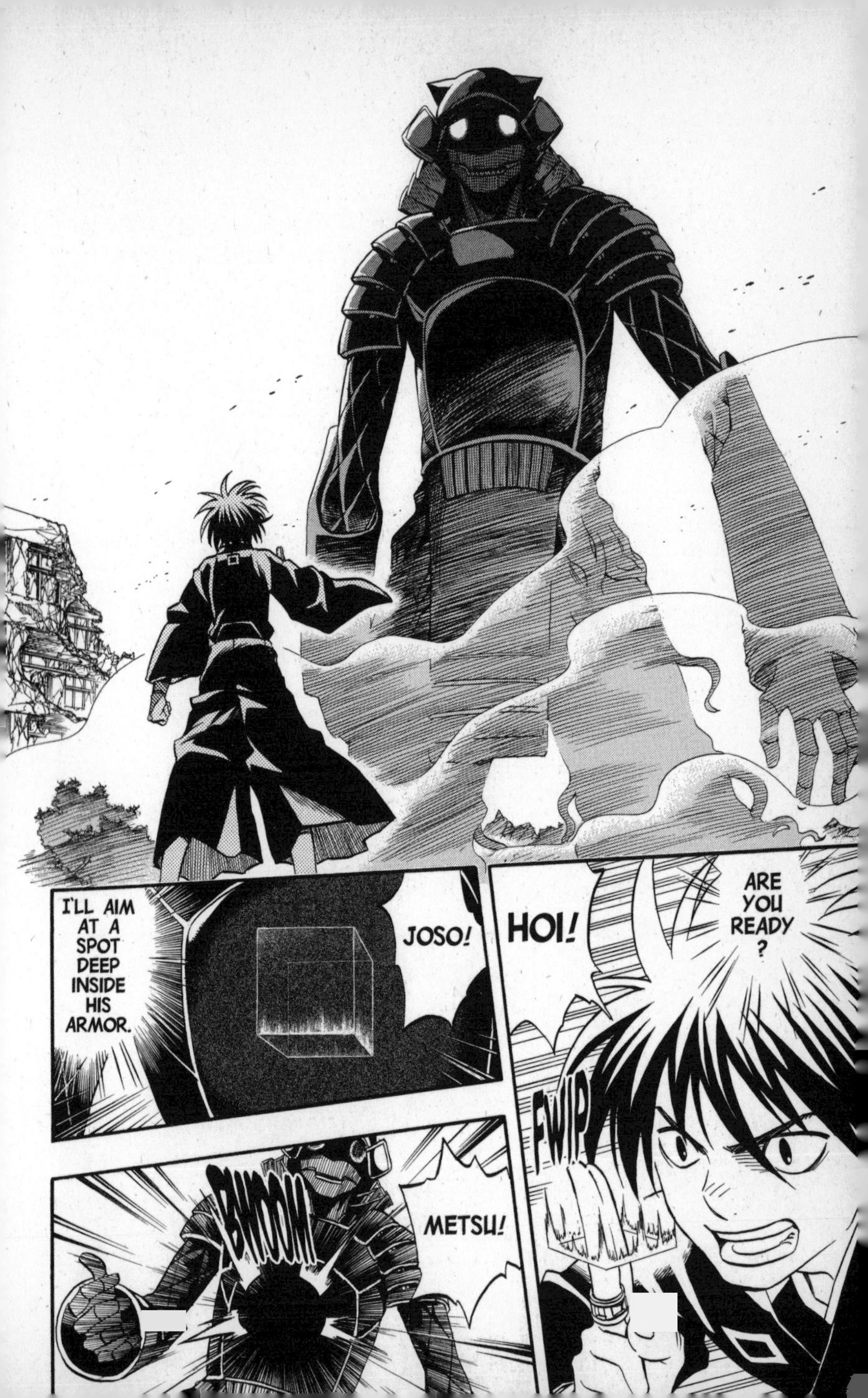
ARE YOU READY?
HOI!
FWIP
JOSO!
I'LL AIM AT A SPOT DEEP INSIDE HIS ARMOR.
METSU!
BHOOM

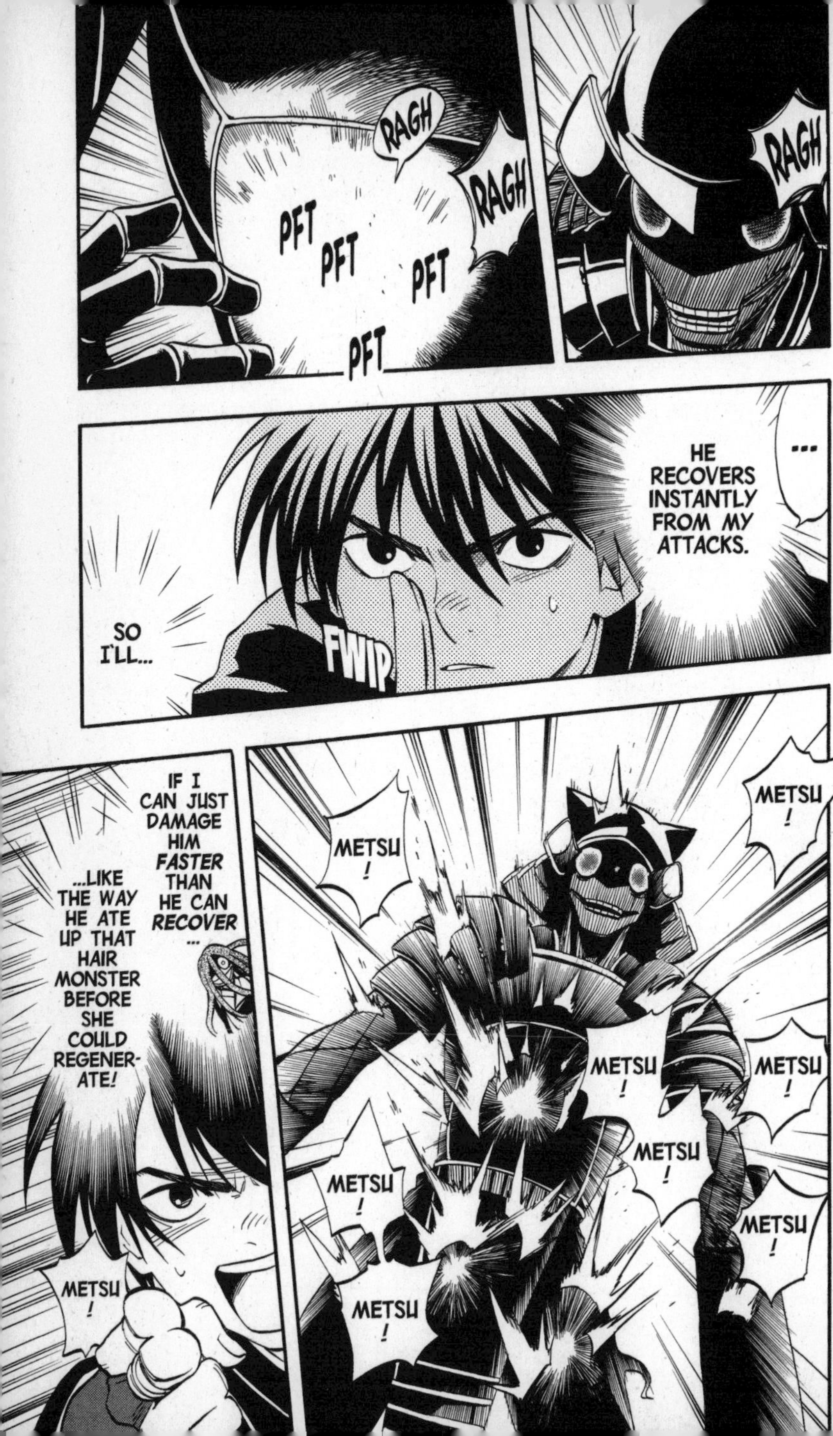
RAGH
RAGH
RAGH
PFT
PFT
PFT
PFT
...
HE RECOVERS INSTANTLY FROM MY ATTACKS.
FWIP
SO I'LL...
METSU!
METSU!
METSU!
METSU!
METSU!
METSU!
METSU!
METSU!
IF I CAN JUST DAMAGE HIM *FASTER* THAN HE CAN *RECOVER*...
...LIKE THE WAY HE ATE UP THAT HAIR MONSTER BEFORE SHE COULD REGENERATE!
METSU!

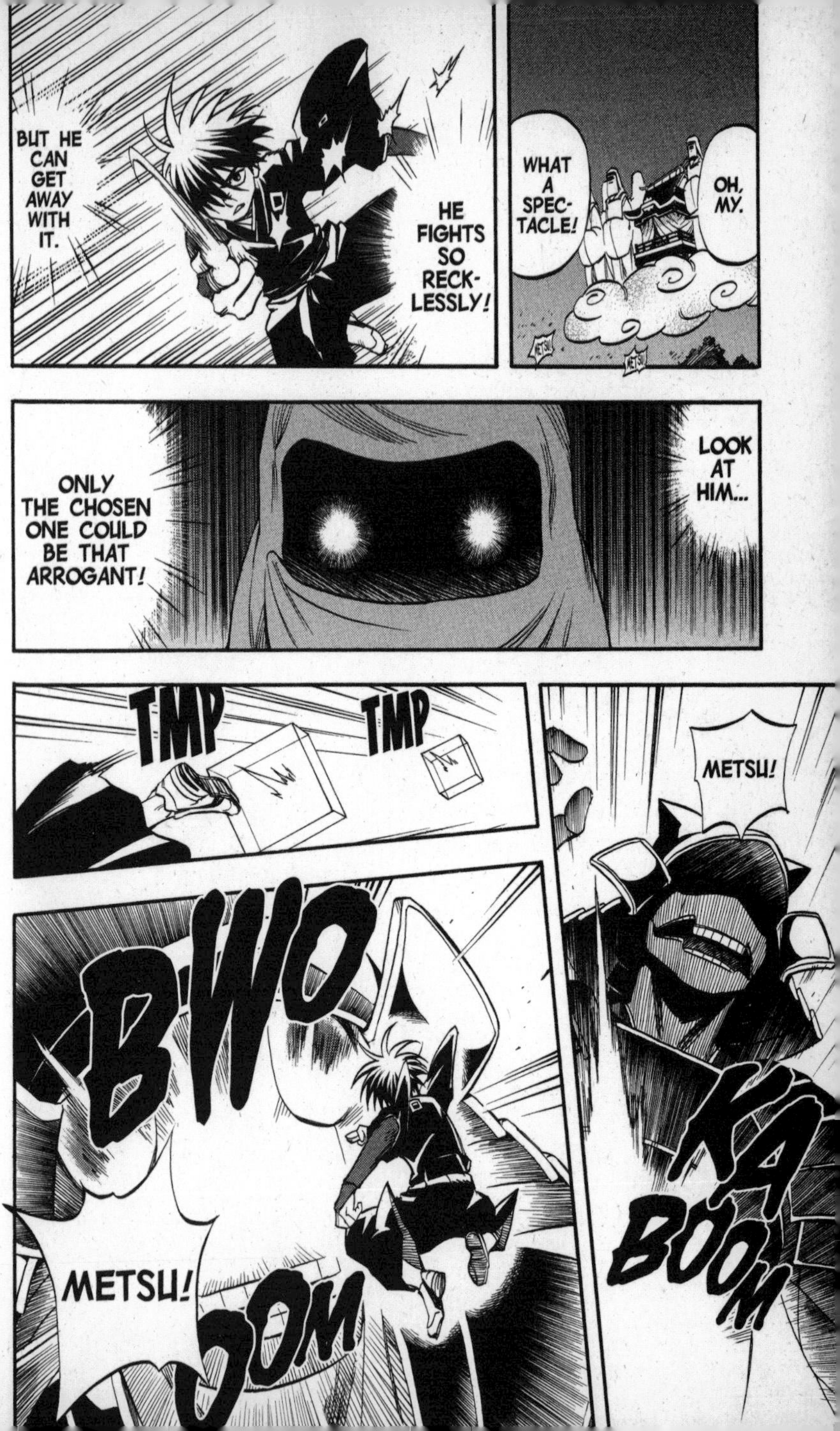
OH, MY.
WHAT A SPEC- TACLE!
METSU
METSU
HE FIGHTS SO RECK- LESSLY!
BUT HE CAN GET AWAY WITH IT.
LOOK AT HIM...
ONLY THE CHOSEN ONE COULD BE THAT ARROGANT!
METSU!
KA BOOM
TMP
TMP
BWO OM
METSU!

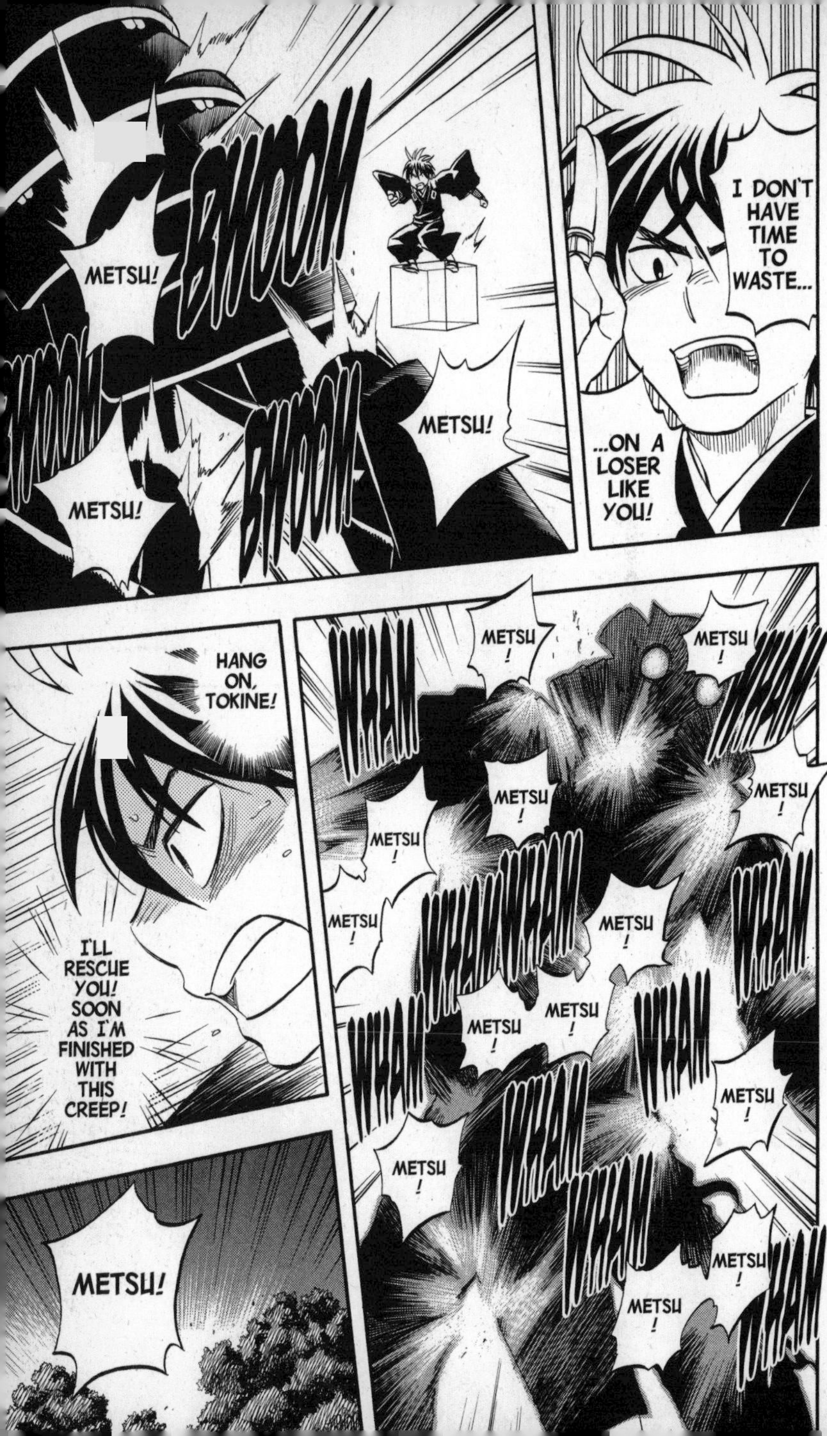
I DON'T HAVE TIME TO WASTE...
...ON A LOSER LIKE YOU!
BWOOM!
METSU!
METSU!
BWOOM
METSU!
METSU!
METSU!
WHAM
METSU!
METSU!
METSU!
METSU!
WHAM
METSU!
METSU!
METSU!
METSU!
METSU!
METSU!
HANG ON, TOKINE!
I'LL RESCUE YOU! SOON AS I'M FINISHED WITH THIS CREEP!
METSU!

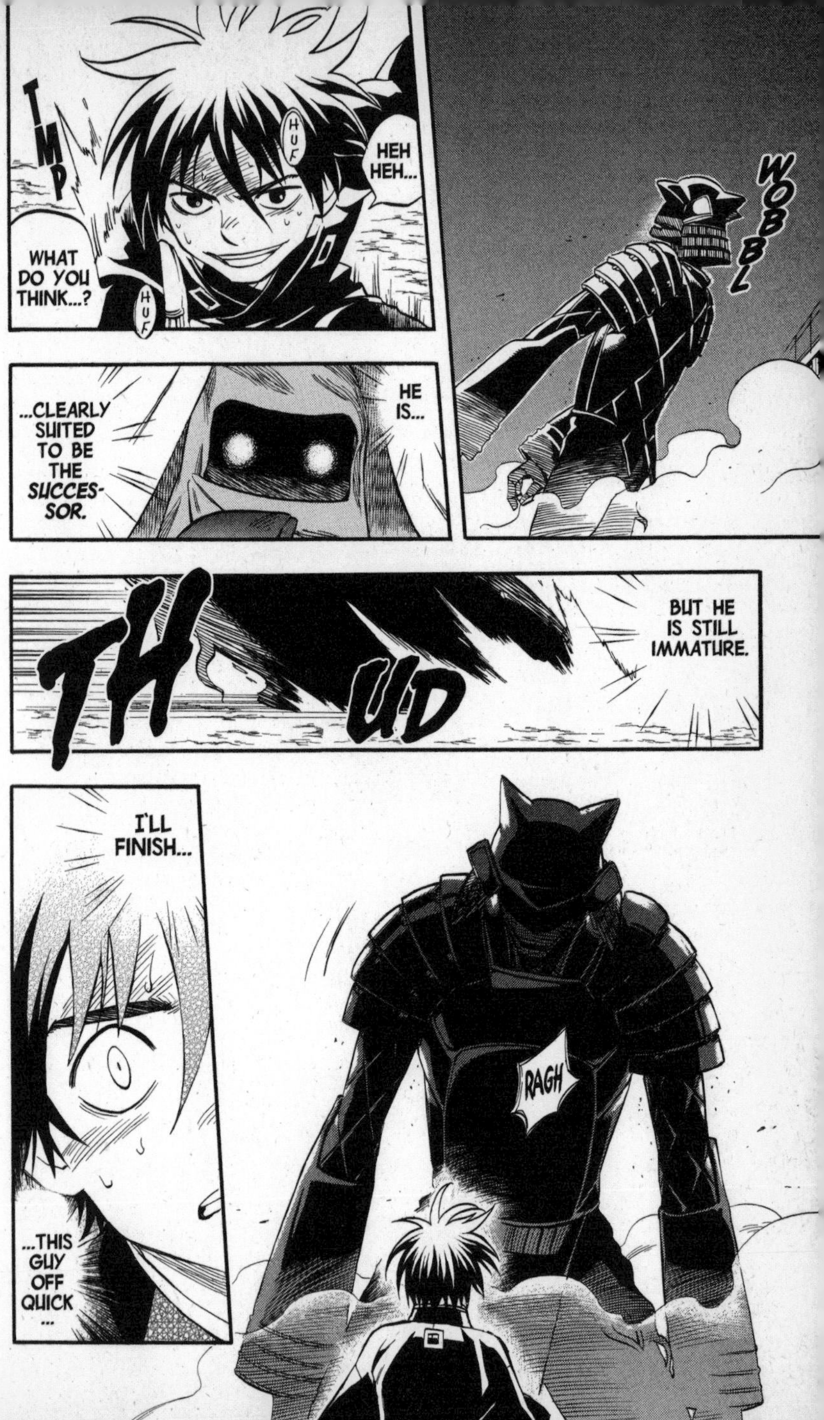
WOBBL
HEH HEH...
HUF
TMP
WHAT DO YOU THINK...?
HUF
HE IS...
...CLEARLY SUITED TO BE THE SUCCES-SOR.
BUT HE IS STILL IMMATURE.
THUD
RAGH
I'LL FINISH...
...THIS GUY OFF QUICK...

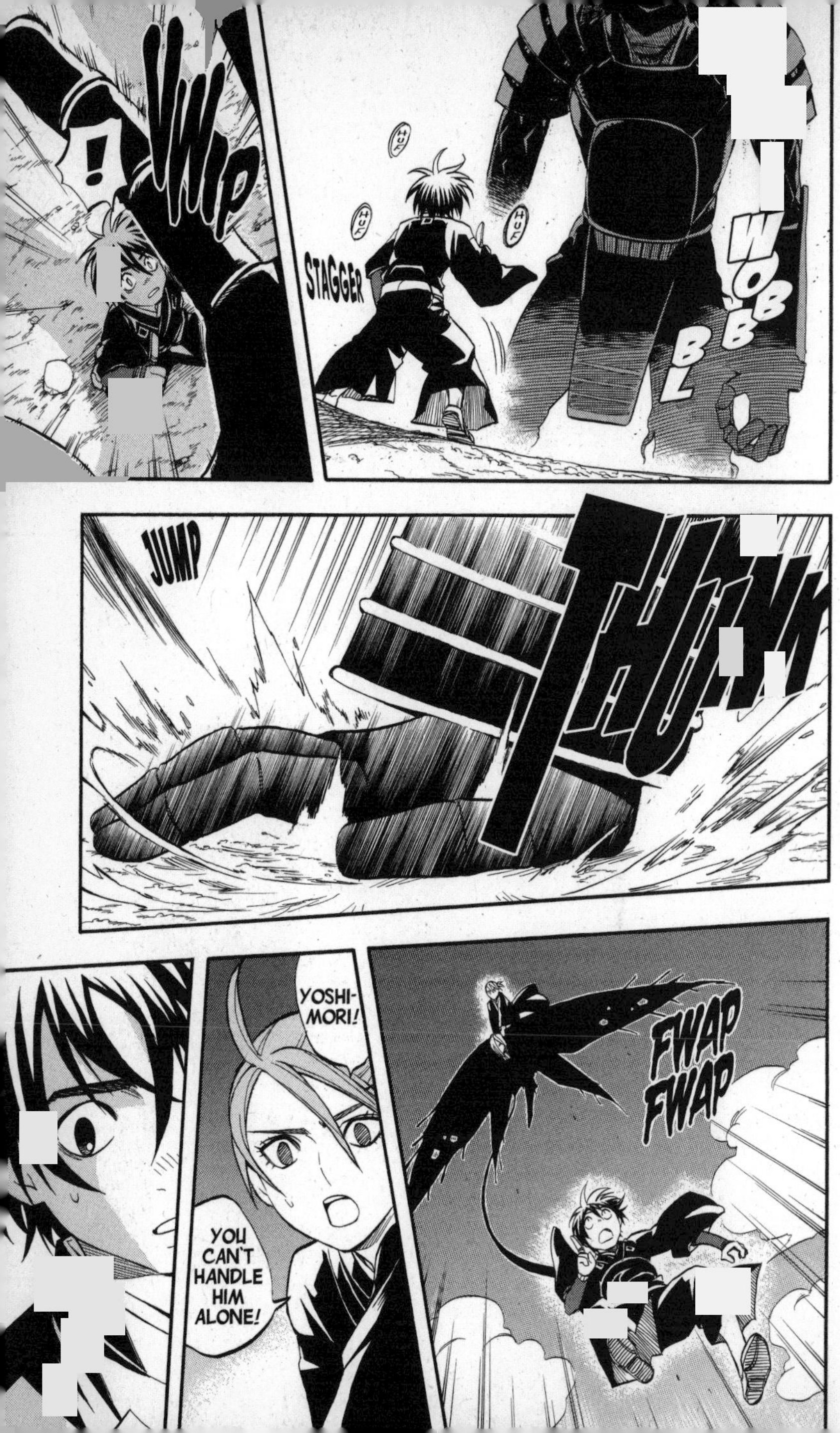
WOBBL
HUF
HUF
HUF
STAGGER
WHIP
!
THUNK
JUMP
FWAP FWAP
YOSHIMORI!
YOU CAN'T HANDLE HIM ALONE!

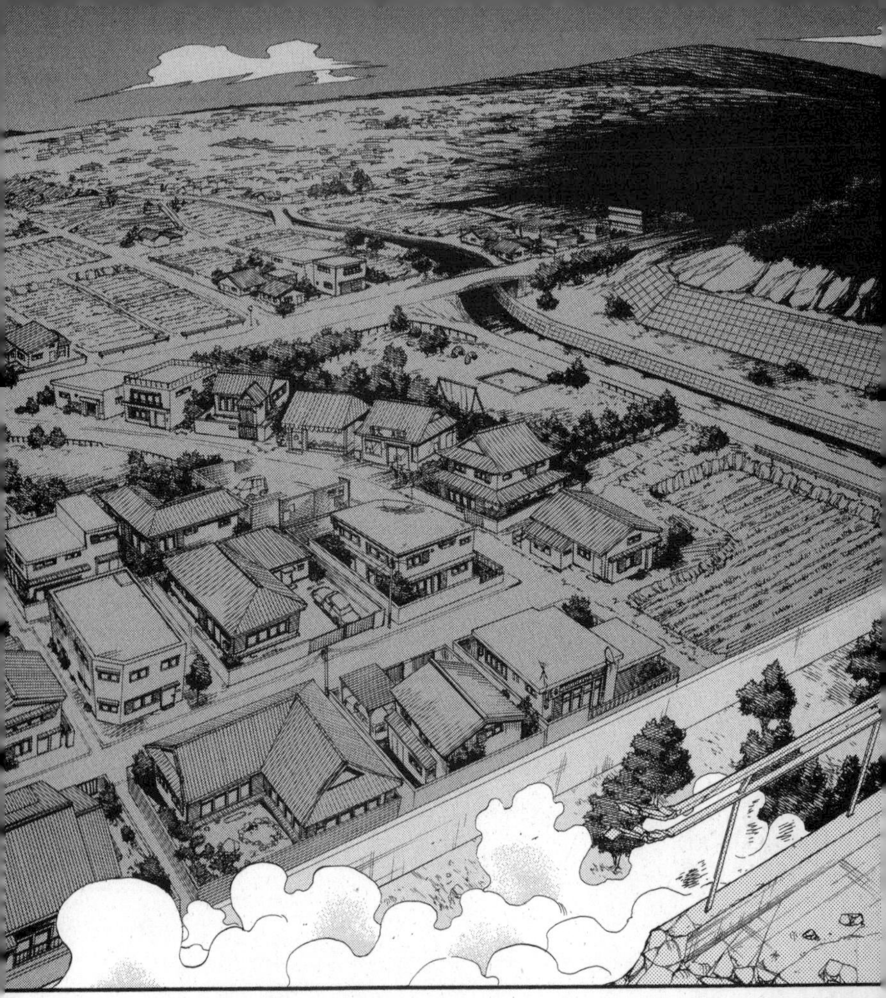
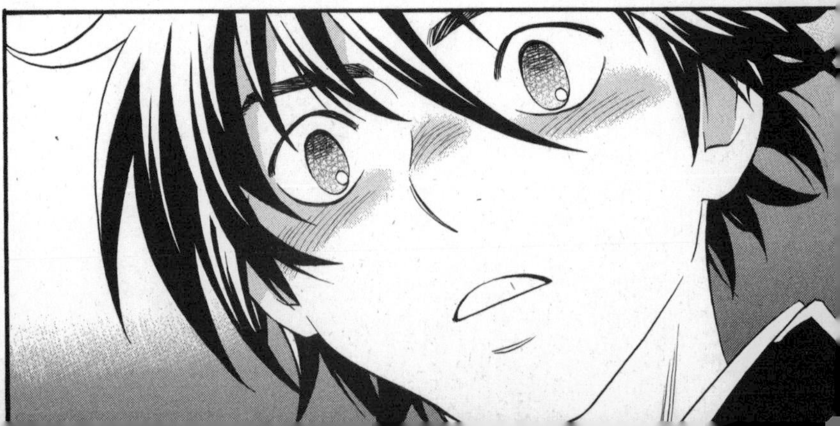

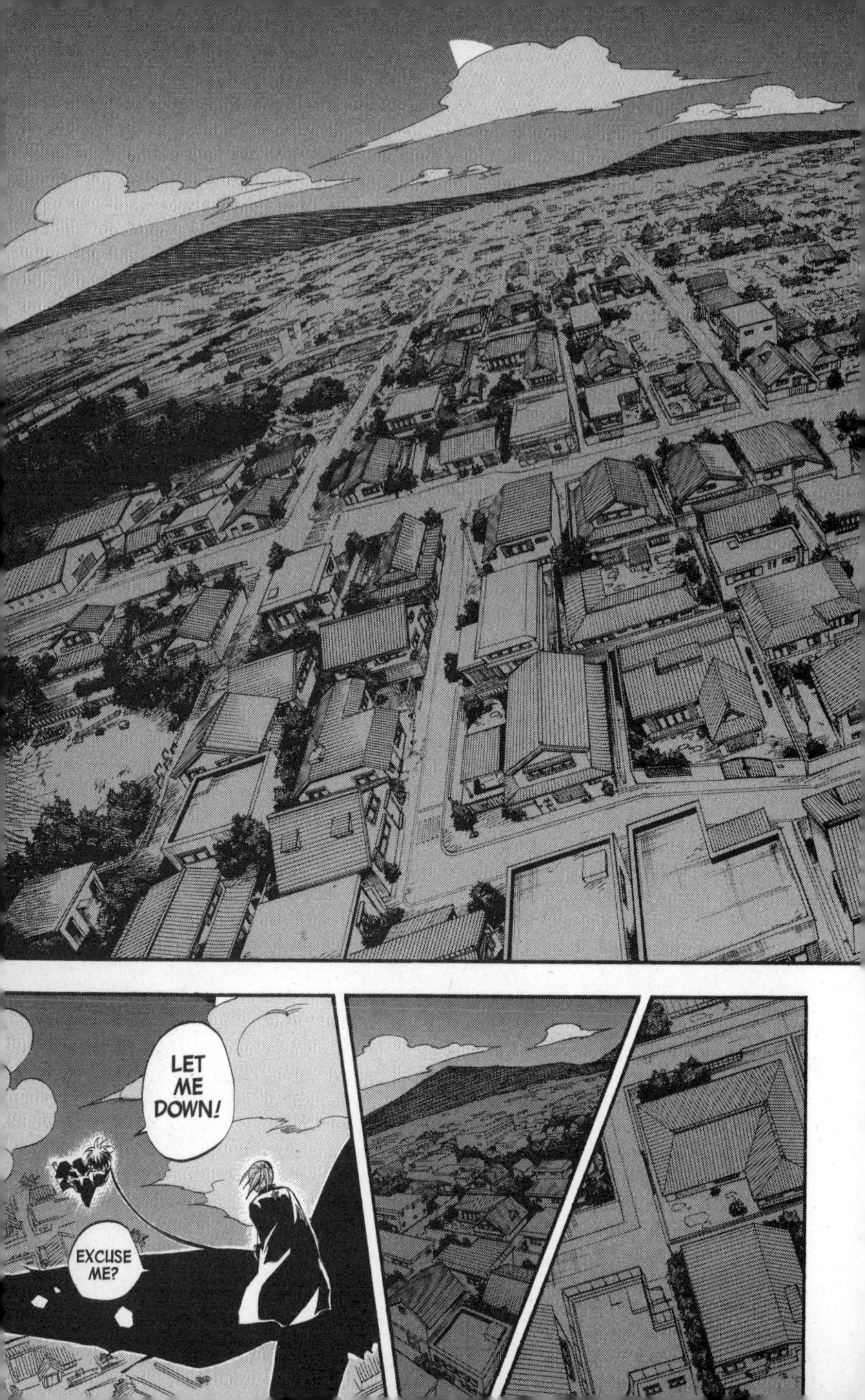
LET ME DOWN!
EXCUSE ME?

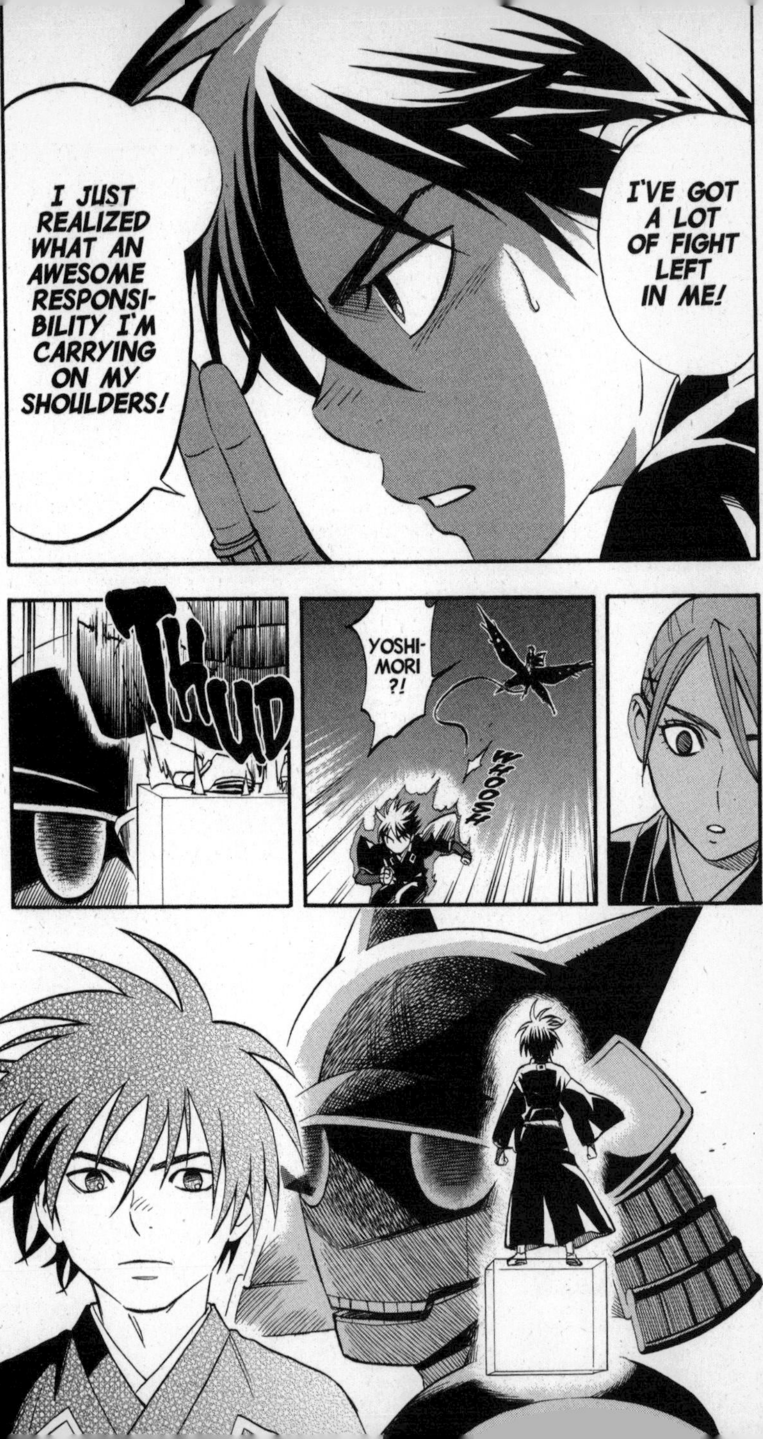
I'VE GOT A LOT OF FIGHT LEFT IN ME!
I JUST REALIZED WHAT AN AWESOME RESPONSI-BILITY I'M CARRYING ON MY SHOULDERS!
YOSHI-MORI?!
WHOOSH
THUD

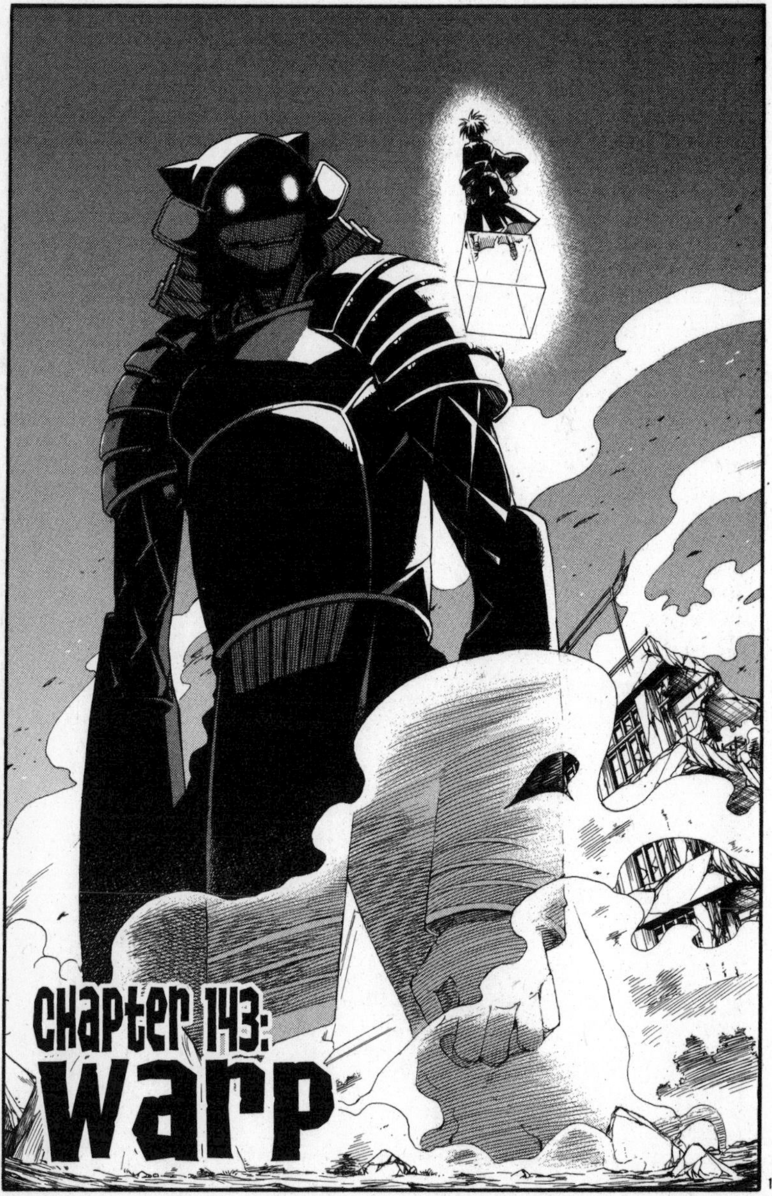
Chapter 143:
Warp

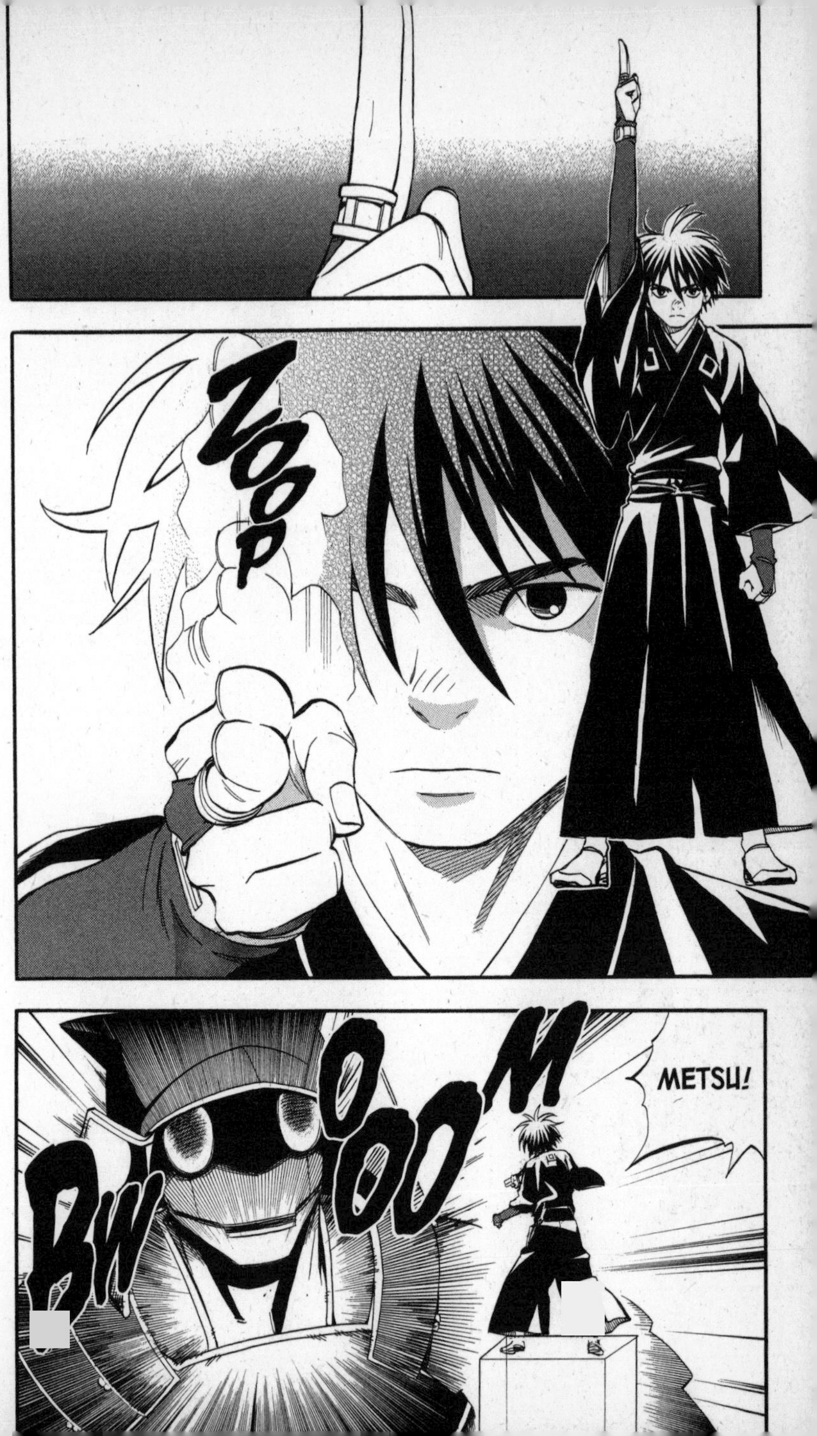
ZOOP
METSU!
BWOOOOM

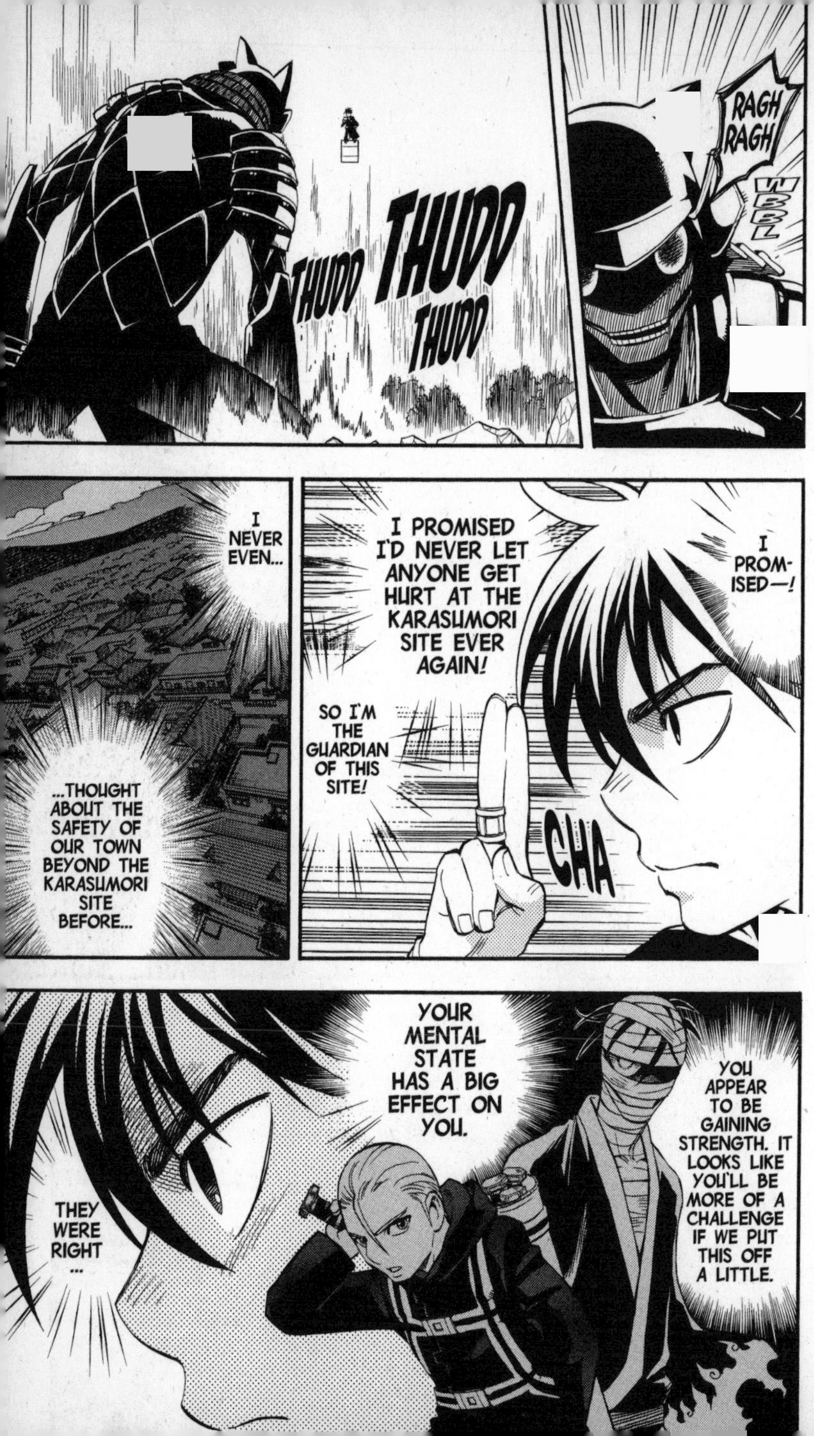
RAGH RAGH
WBBL
THUDD THUDD THUDD
I PROMISED—!
I PROMISED I'D NEVER LET ANYONE GET HURT AT THE KARASUMORI SITE EVER AGAIN!
SO I'M THE GUARDIAN OF THIS SITE!
CHA
I NEVER EVEN...
...THOUGHT ABOUT THE SAFETY OF OUR TOWN BEYOND THE KARASUMORI SITE BEFORE...
YOU APPEAR TO BE GAINING STRENGTH. IT LOOKS LIKE YOU'LL BE MORE OF A CHALLENGE IF WE PUT THIS OFF A LITTLE.
YOUR MENTAL STATE HAS A BIG EFFECT ON YOU.
THEY WERE RIGHT...

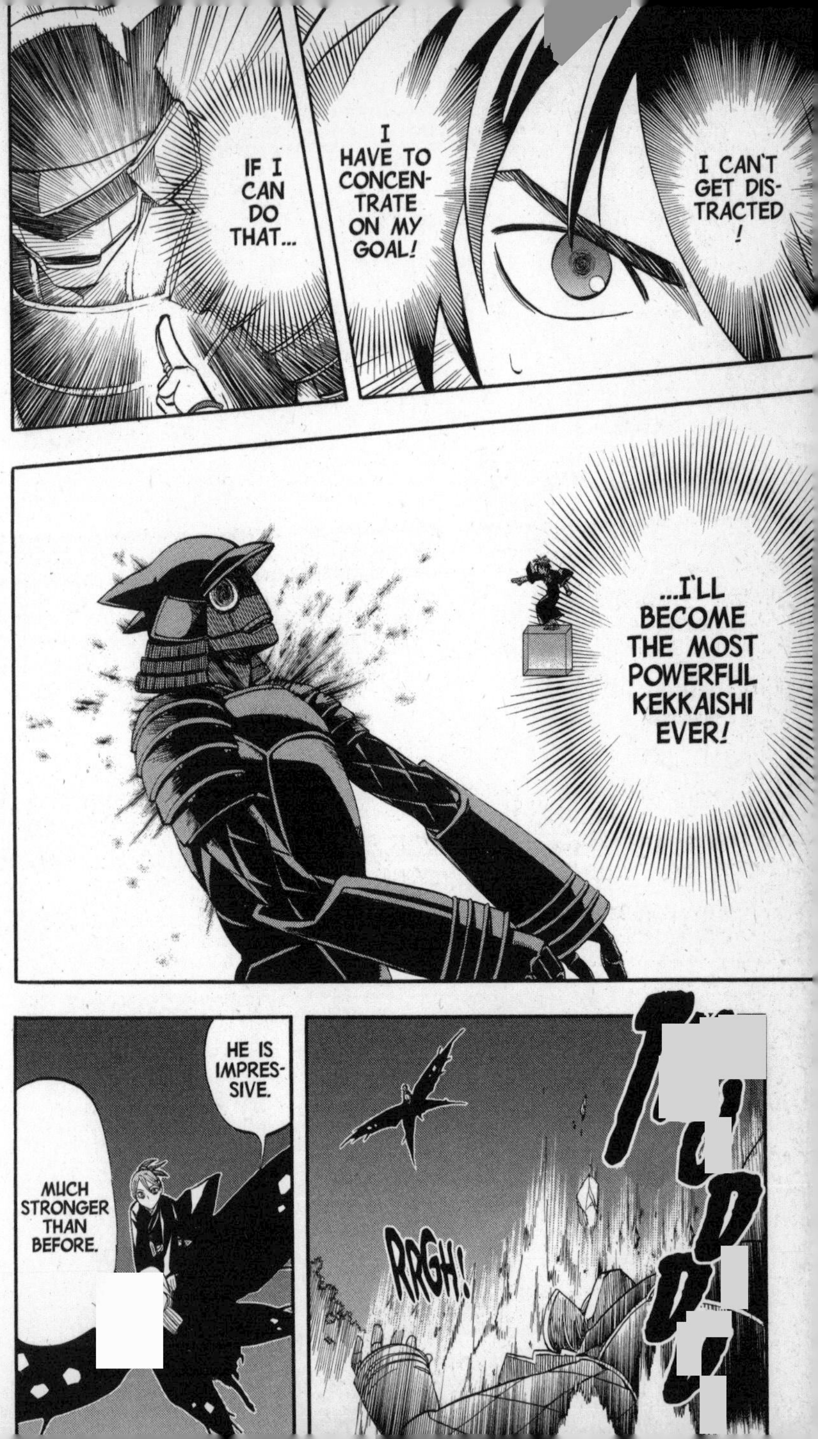
I CAN'T GET DISTRACTED!
I HAVE TO CONCENTRATE ON MY GOAL!
IF I CAN DO THAT...
...I'LL BECOME THE MOST POWERFUL KEKKAISHI EVER!
RRGH!
HE IS IMPRESSIVE.
MUCH STRONGER THAN BEFORE.

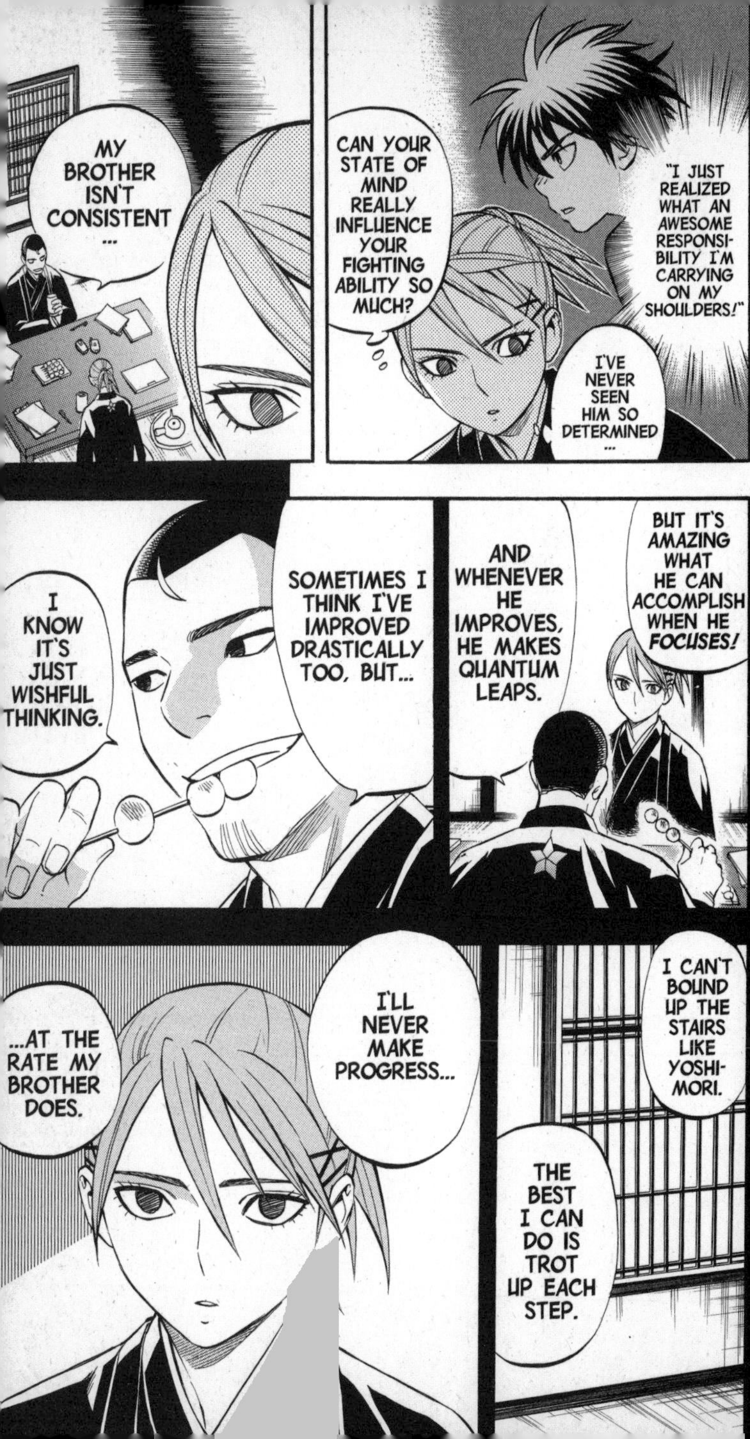
"I JUST REALIZED WHAT AN AWESOME RESPONSIBILITY I'M CARRYING ON MY SHOULDERS!"
I'VE NEVER SEEN HIM SO DETERMINED...
CAN YOUR STATE OF MIND REALLY INFLUENCE YOUR FIGHTING ABILITY SO MUCH?
MY BROTHER ISN'T CONSISTENT...
BUT IT'S AMAZING WHAT HE CAN ACCOMPLISH WHEN HE *FOCUSES!*
AND WHENEVER HE IMPROVES, HE MAKES QUANTUM LEAPS.
SOMETIMES I THINK I'VE IMPROVED DRASTICALLY TOO, BUT...
I KNOW IT'S JUST WISHFUL THINKING.
I CAN'T BOUND UP THE STAIRS LIKE YOSHIMORI.
THE BEST I CAN DO IS TROT UP EACH STEP.
I'LL NEVER MAKE PROGRESS...
...AT THE RATE MY BROTHER DOES.

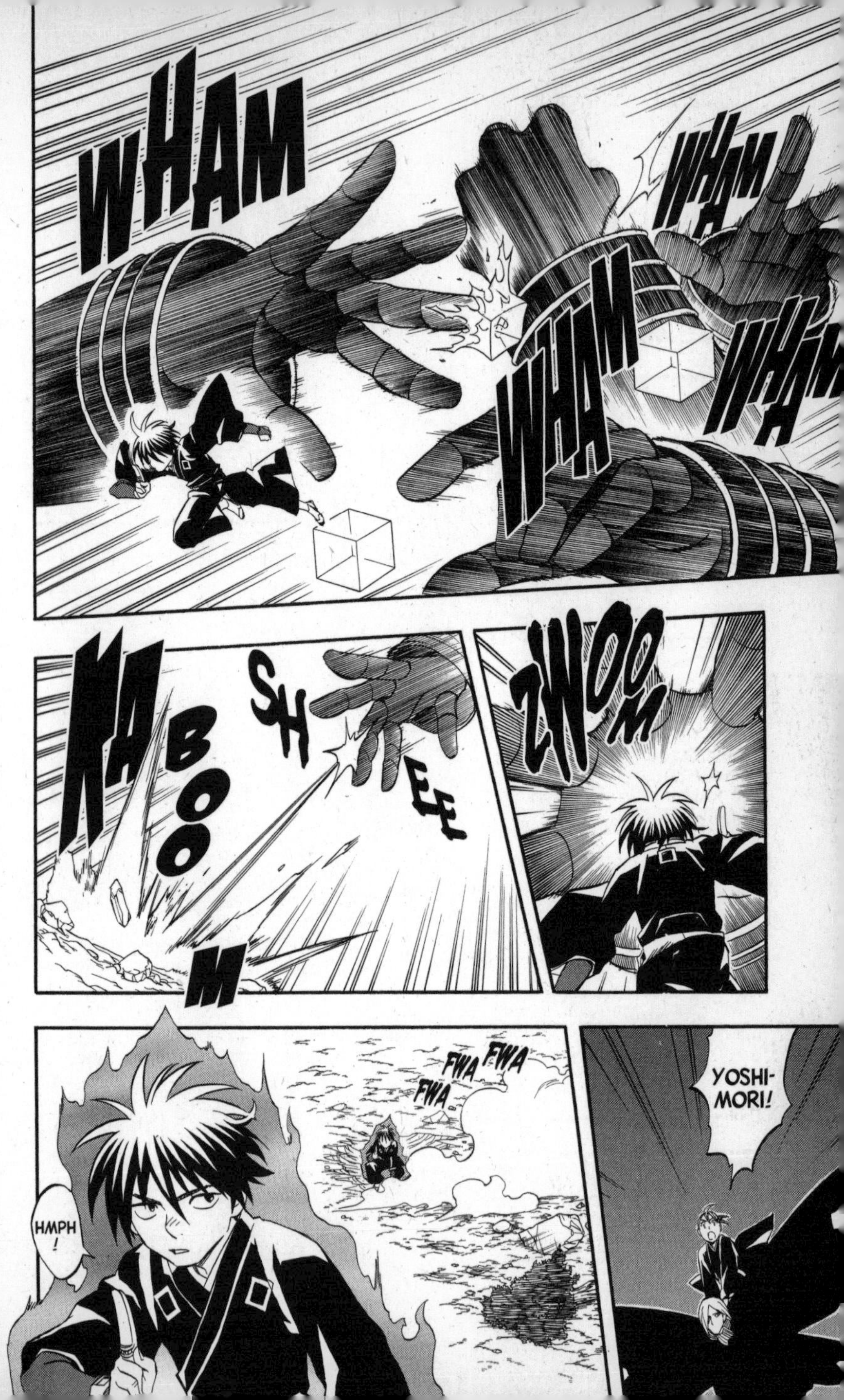

WHAM
WHAM
WHAM
WHAM
ZWOOM
KABOOOM
SHEEE
YOSHI-MORI!
FWA FWA FWA
HMPH!

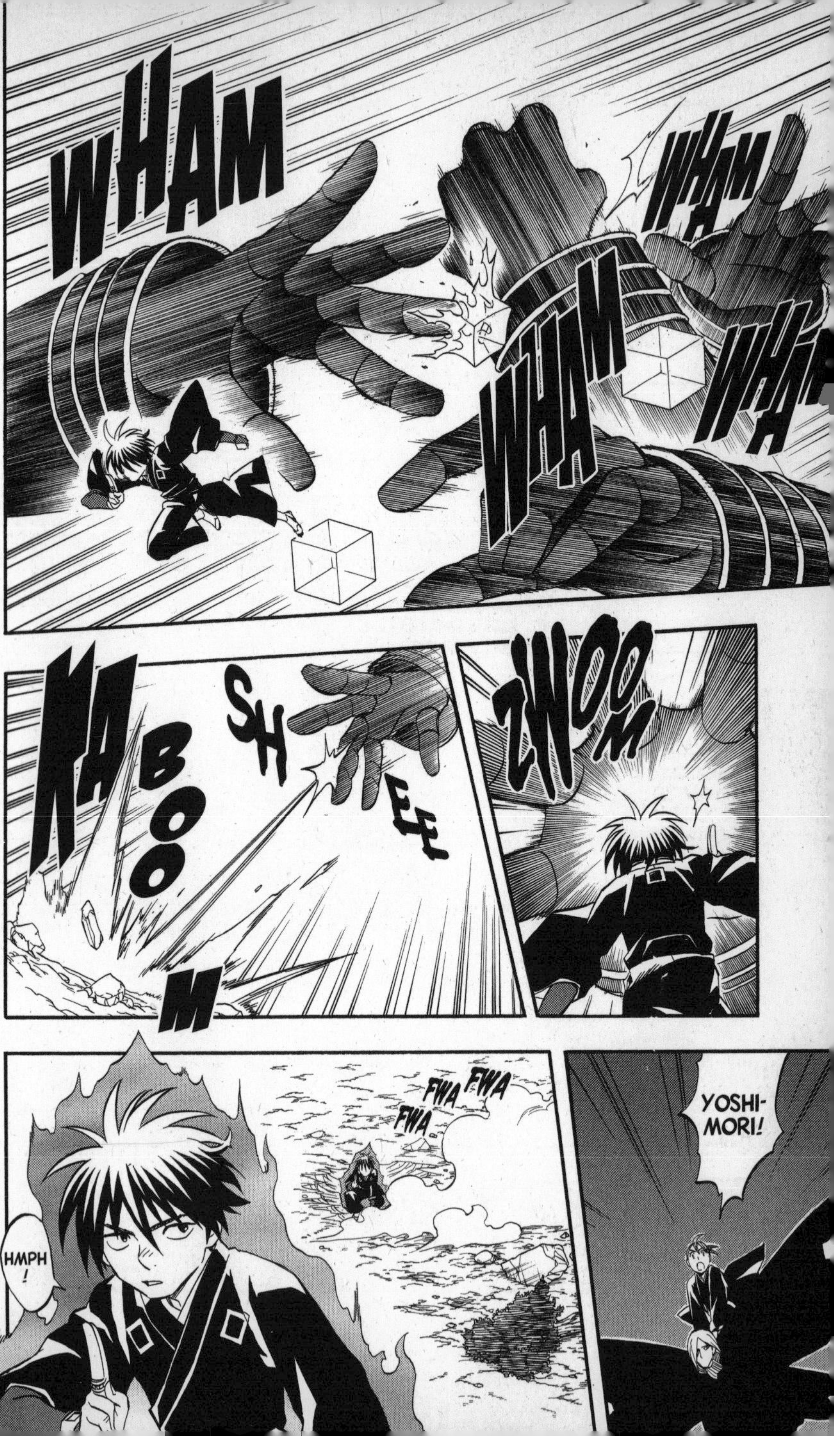
WHAM
WHA
WHAM
WHAM
ZWOOM
SHEE
KABOOM
YOSHI-MORI!
FWA FWA FWA
HMPH!

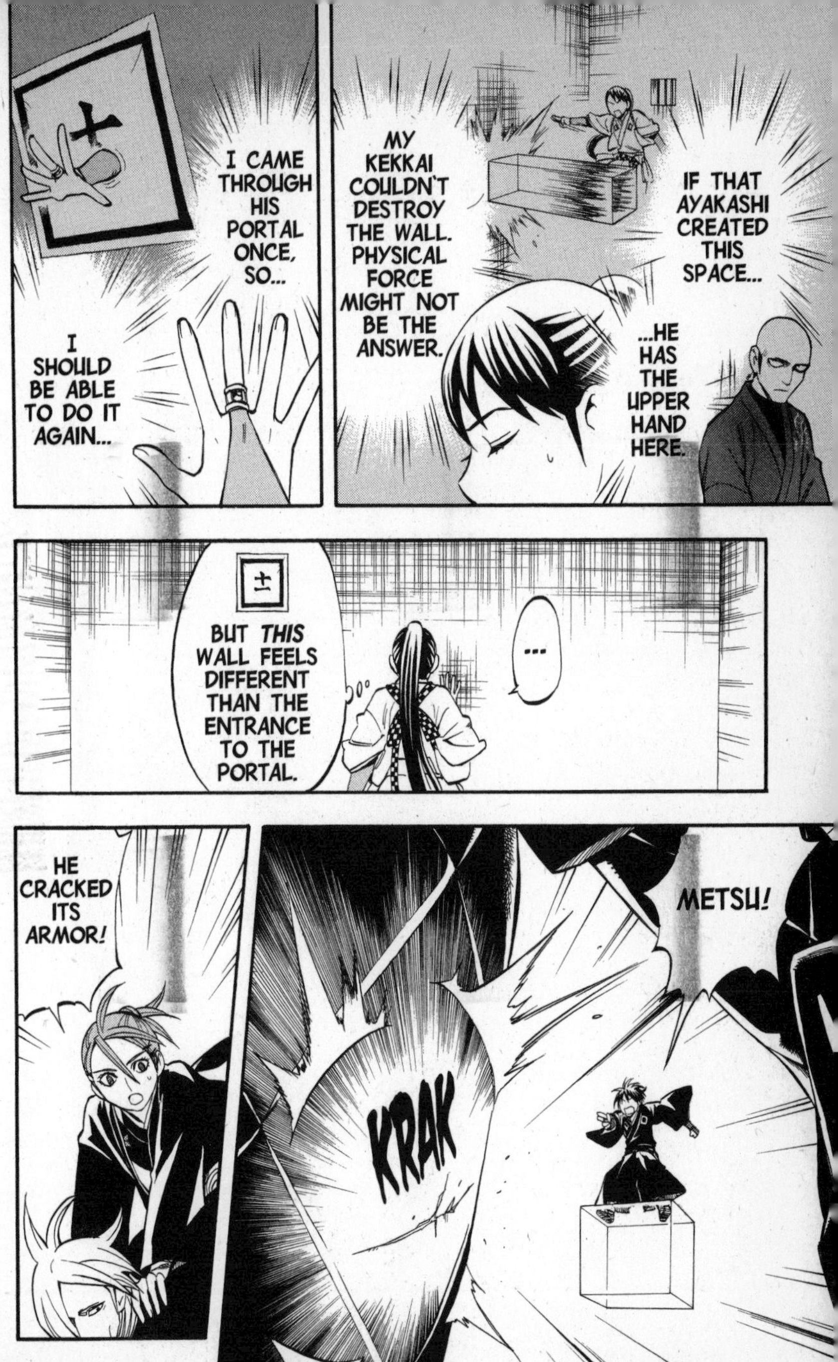
IF THAT AYAKASHI CREATED THIS SPACE...
...HE HAS THE UPPER HAND HERE.
MY KEKKAI COULDN'T DESTROY THE WALL. PHYSICAL FORCE MIGHT NOT BE THE ANSWER.
I CAME THROUGH HIS PORTAL ONCE, SO...
I SHOULD BE ABLE TO DO IT AGAIN...
...
BUT THIS WALL FEELS DIFFERENT THAN THE ENTRANCE TO THE PORTAL.
METSU!
KRAK
HE CRACKED ITS ARMOR!

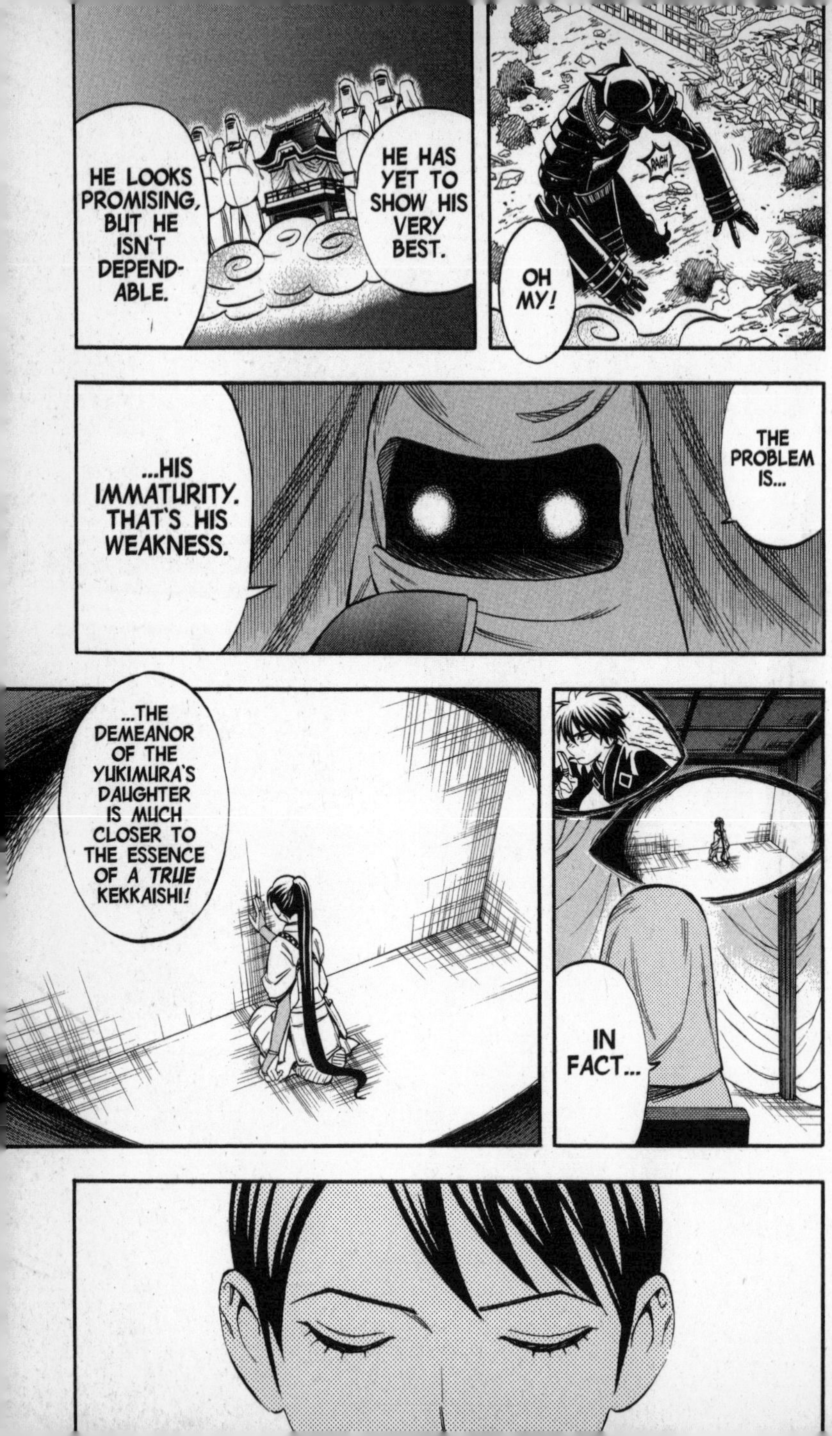
RAGH
OH MY!
HE HAS YET TO SHOW HIS VERY BEST.
HE LOOKS PROMISING, BUT HE ISN'T DEPENDABLE.
THE PROBLEM IS...
...HIS IMMATURITY. THAT'S HIS WEAKNESS.
IN FACT...
...THE DEMEANOR OF THE YUKIMURA'S DAUGHTER IS MUCH CLOSER TO THE ESSENCE OF A *TRUE* KEKKAISHI!

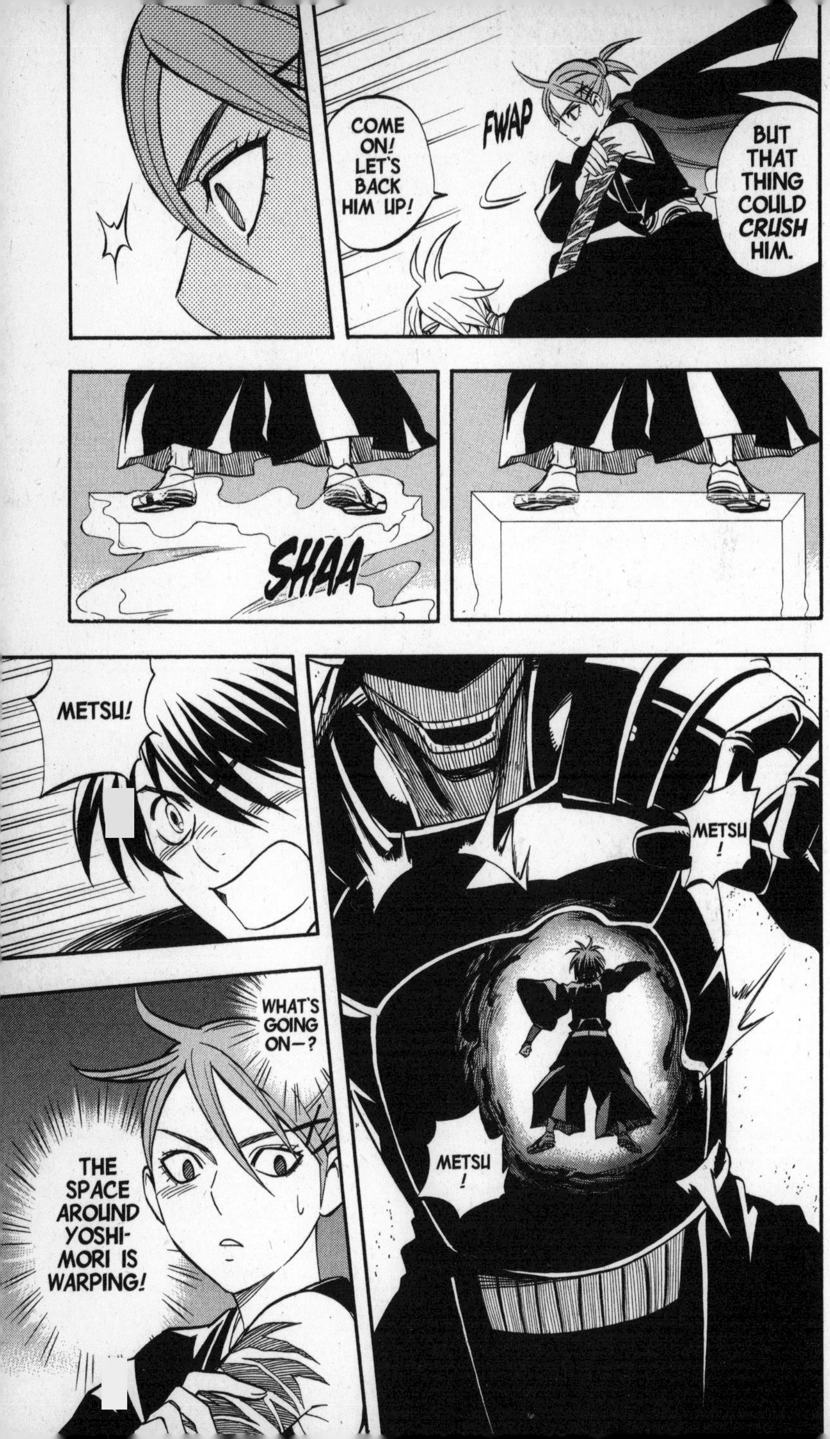
BUT THAT THING COULD CRUSH HIM.
FWAP
COME ON! LET'S BACK HIM UP!
SHAA
METSU !
METSU !
METSU!
WHAT'S GOING ON—?
THE SPACE AROUND YOSHI-MORI IS WARPING!

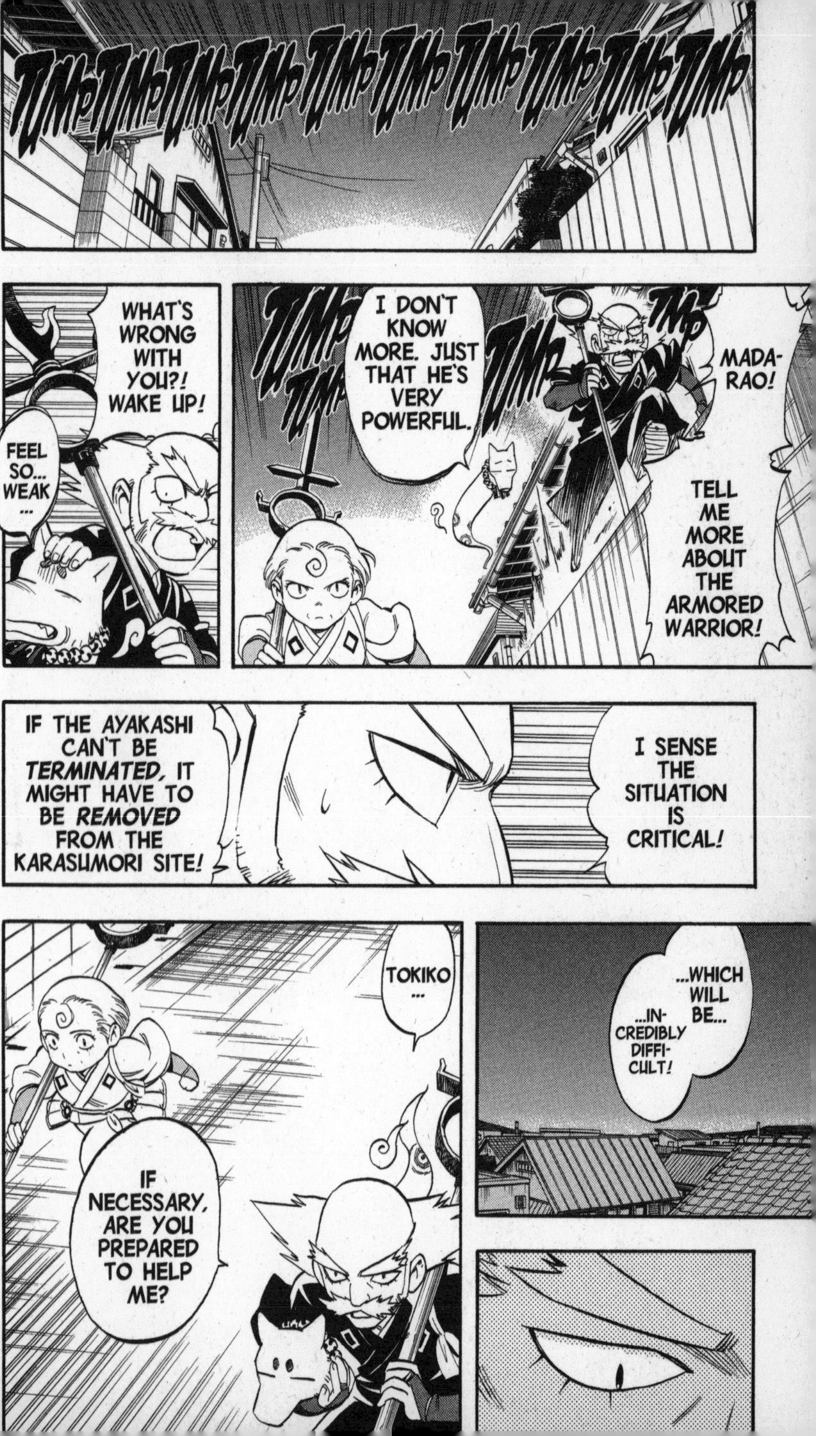
THMP THMP THMP THMP THMP THMP THMP THMP THMP THMP
THMP
MADA-RAO!
TELL ME MORE ABOUT THE ARMORED WARRIOR!
THMP
I DON'T KNOW MORE. JUST THAT HE'S VERY POWERFUL.
THMP THMP
WHAT'S WRONG WITH YOU?! WAKE UP!
FEEL SO... WEAK ...
I SENSE THE SITUATION IS CRITICAL!
IF THE *AYAKASHI* CAN'T BE *TERMINATED*, IT MIGHT HAVE TO BE *REMOVED* FROM THE KARASUMORI SITE!
...WHICH WILL BE...
...INCREDIBLY DIFFICULT!
TOKIKO ...
IF NECESSARY, ARE YOU PREPARED TO HELP ME?

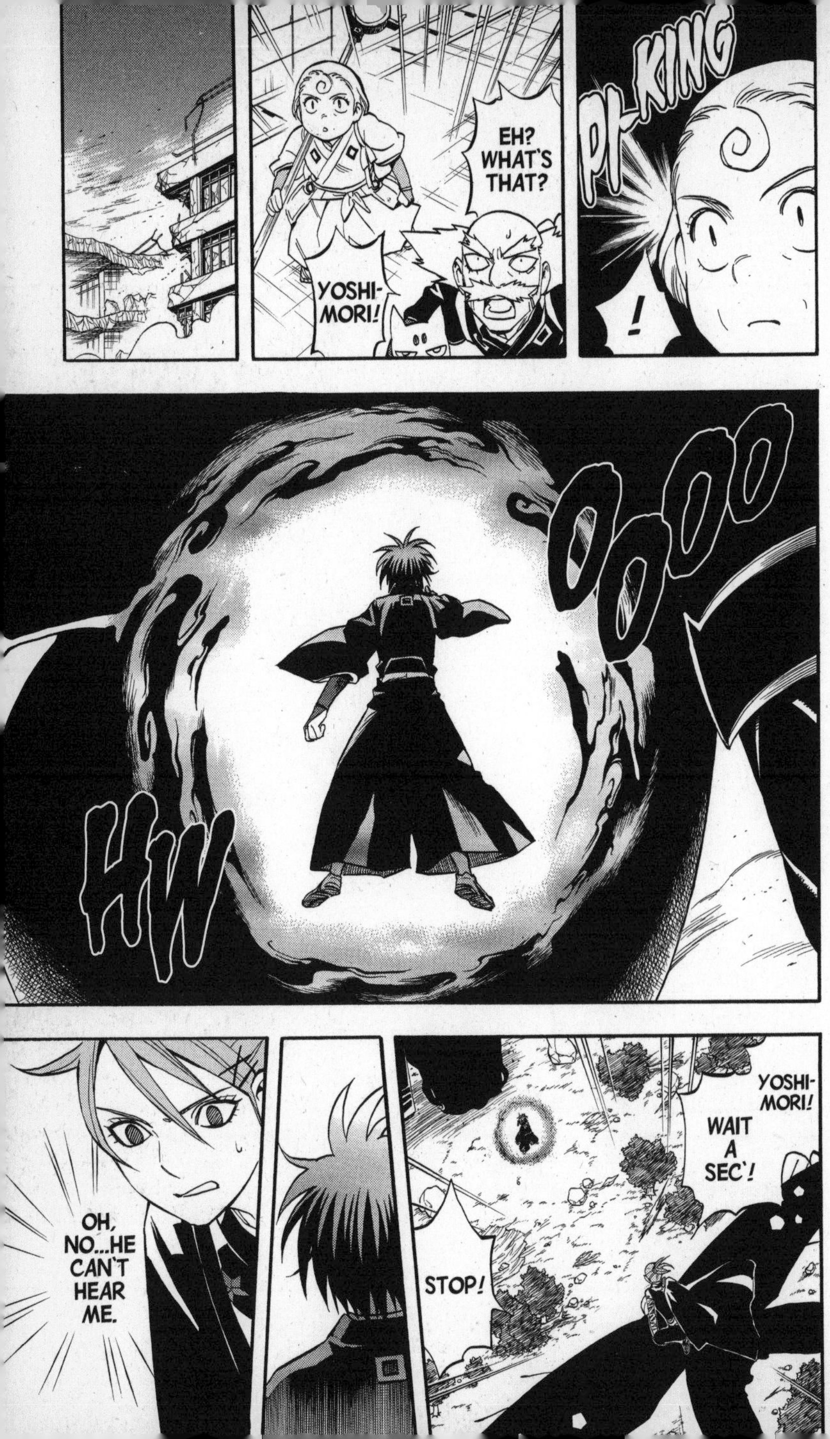
PI-KING
!
EH? WHAT'S THAT?
YOSHI-MORI!
OOOOO
HW
YOSHI-MORI!
WAIT A SEC'!
STOP!
OH, NO...HE CAN'T HEAR ME.

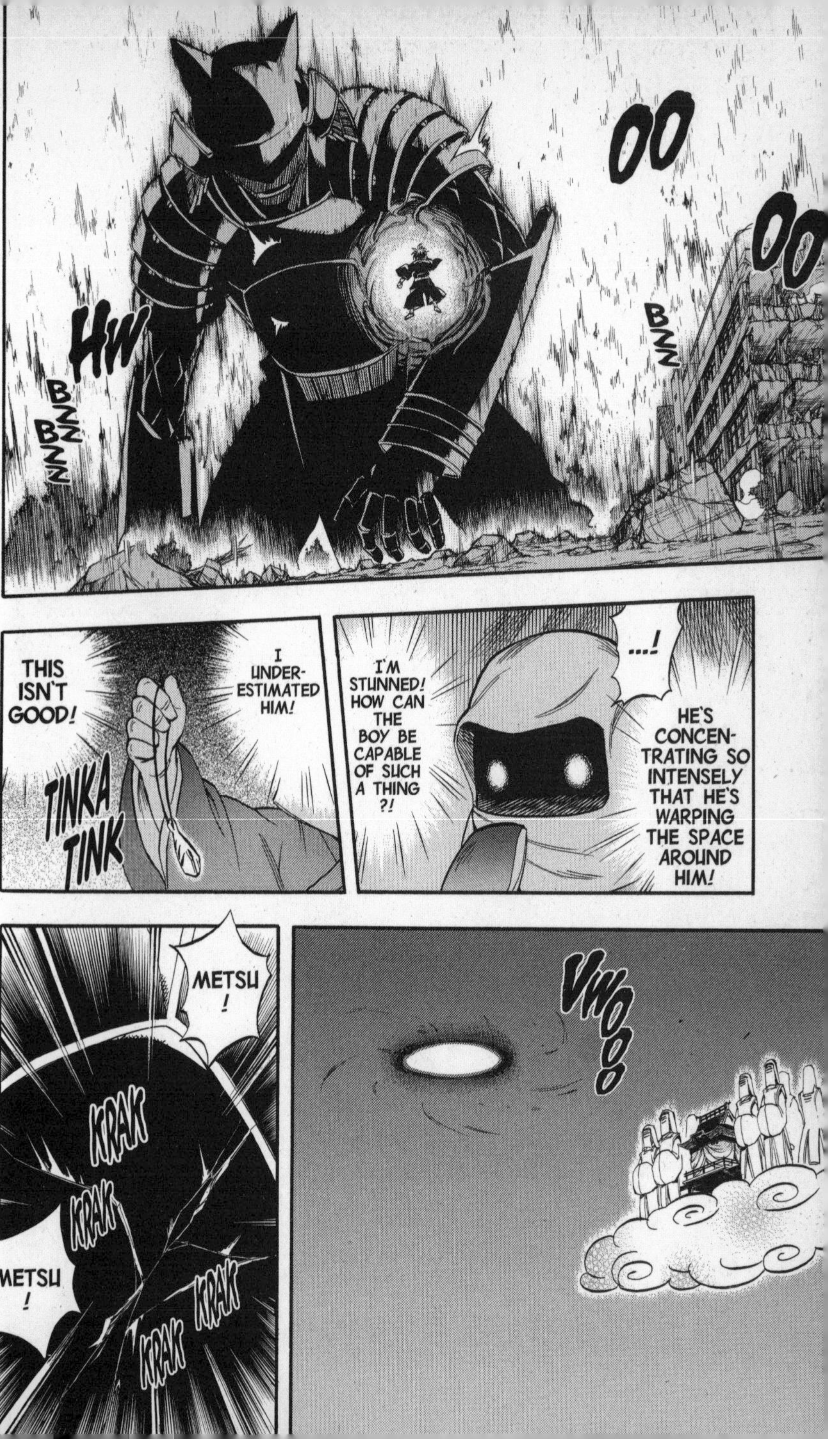
OO
OO
BZZ
HW
BZZ
BZZ
...!
HE'S CONCEN-TRATING SO INTENSELY THAT HE'S WARPING THE SPACE AROUND HIM!
I'M STUNNED! HOW CAN THE BOY BE CAPABLE OF SUCH A THING?!
I UNDER-ESTIMATED HIM!
THIS ISN'T GOOD!
TINKA TINK
VWOOOO
METSU!
KRAK
KRAK
METSU!
KRAK
KRAK

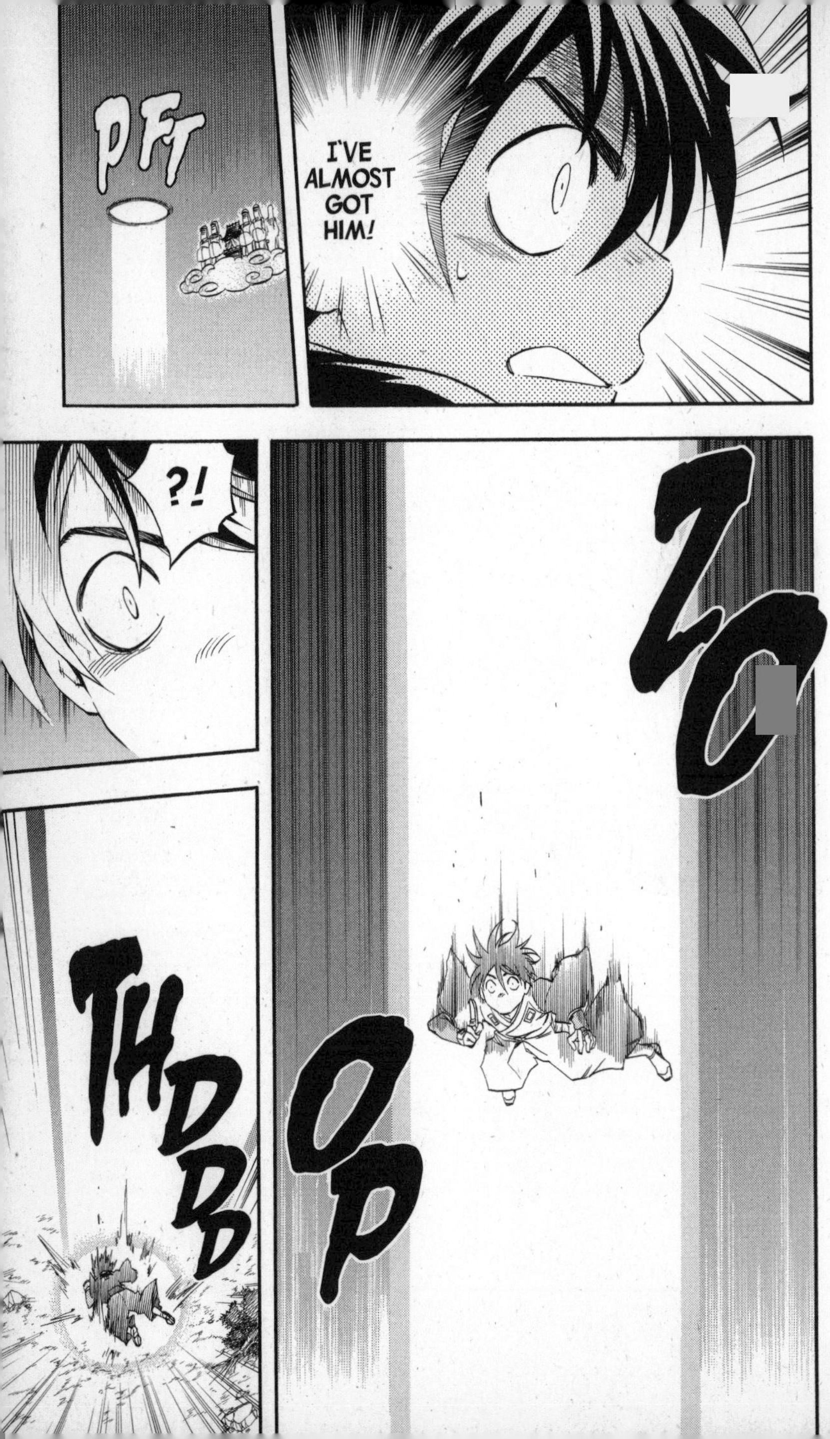
I'VE ALMOST GOT HIM!
PFT
ZOOP
?!
THDDD

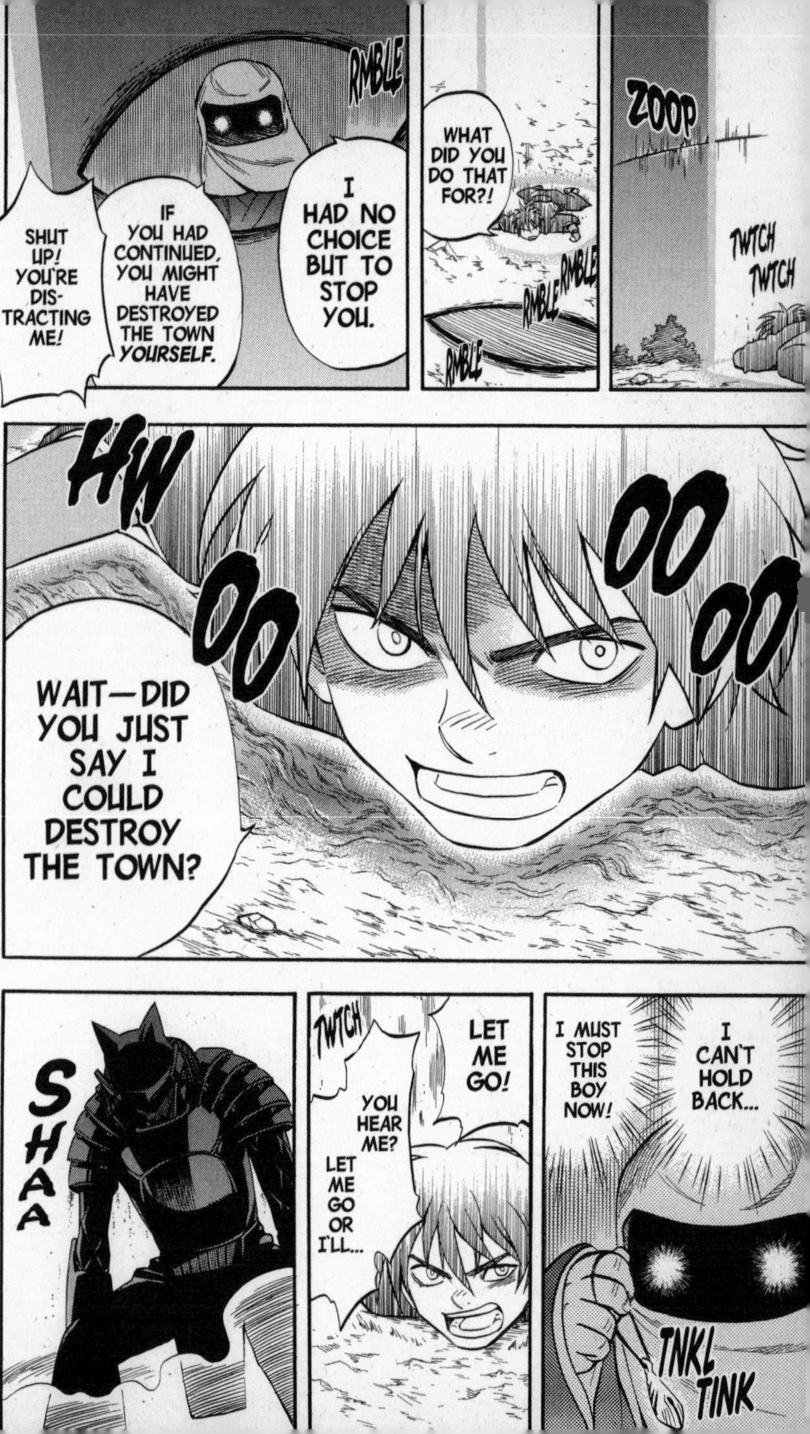
ZOOP
TWTCH TWTCH
WHAT DID YOU DO THAT FOR?!
RMBLE RMBLE
RMBLE
RMBLE
I HAD NO CHOICE BUT TO STOP YOU.
IF YOU HAD CONTINUED, YOU MIGHT HAVE DESTROYED THE TOWN YOURSELF.
SHUT UP! YOU'RE DIS-TRACTING ME!
HWOOOOOO
WAIT—DID YOU JUST SAY I COULD DESTROY THE TOWN?
I CAN'T HOLD BACK...
I MUST STOP THIS BOY NOW!
TNKL TINK
LET ME GO!
TWTCH
YOU HEAR ME? LET ME GO OR I'LL...
SHAA

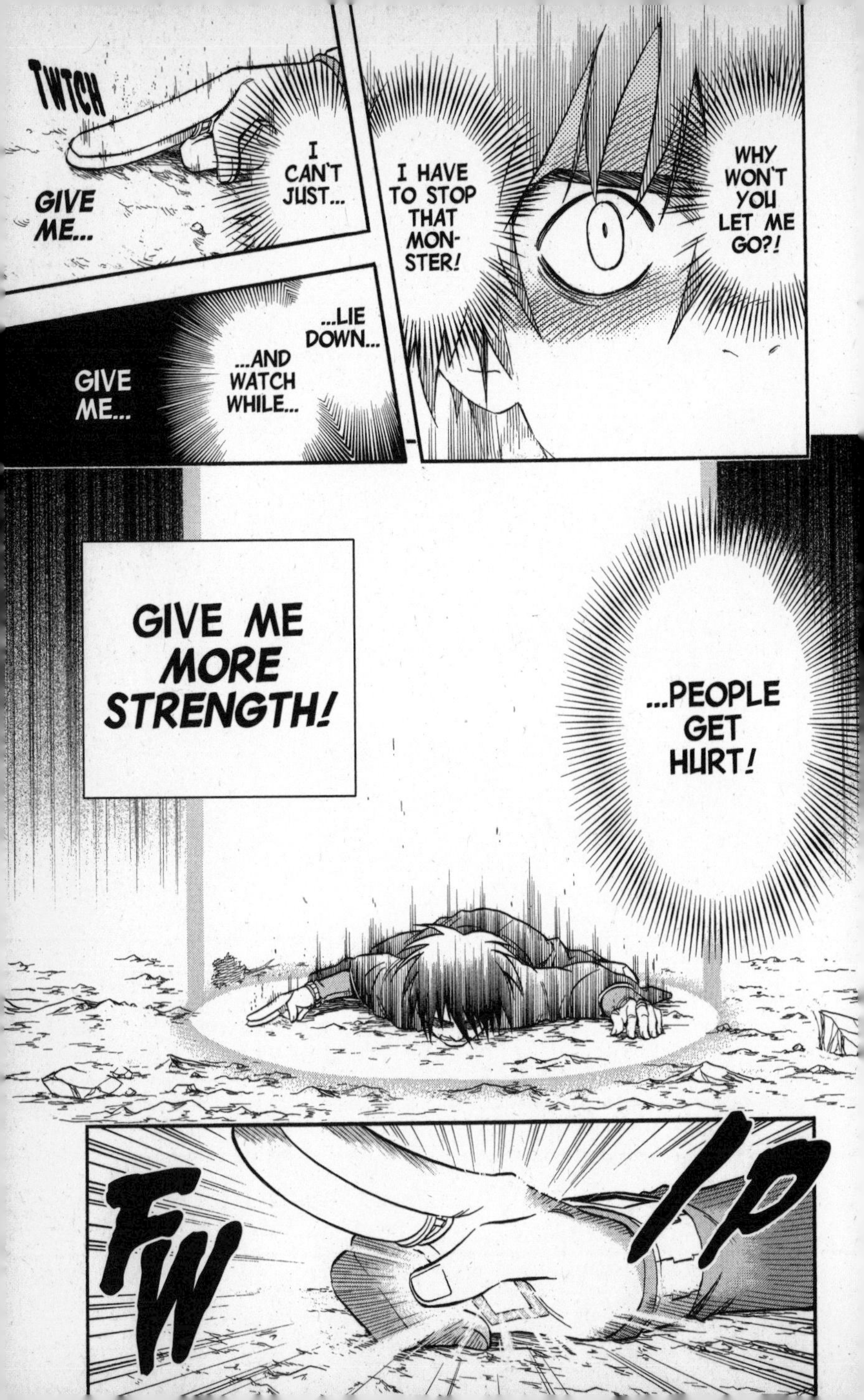
WHY WON'T YOU LET ME GO?!
I HAVE TO STOP THAT MONSTER!
I CAN'T JUST...
TWTCH
GIVE ME...
...LIE DOWN...
...AND WATCH WHILE...
GIVE ME...
...PEOPLE GET HURT!
GIVE ME MORE STRENGTH!
FWIP

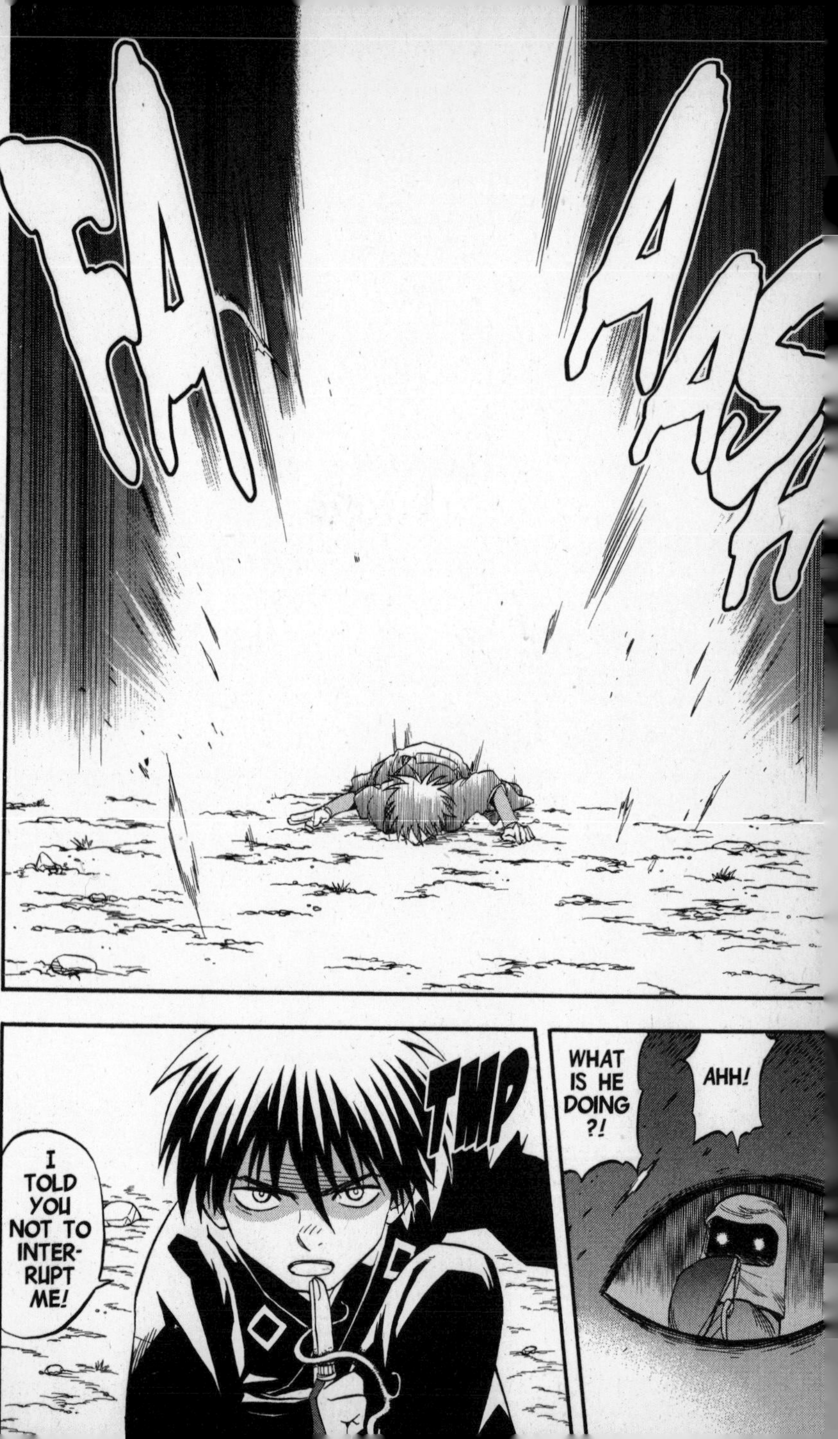
FAAAS
AHH!
WHAT IS HE DOING?!
TMP
I TOLD YOU NOT TO INTER-RUPT ME!

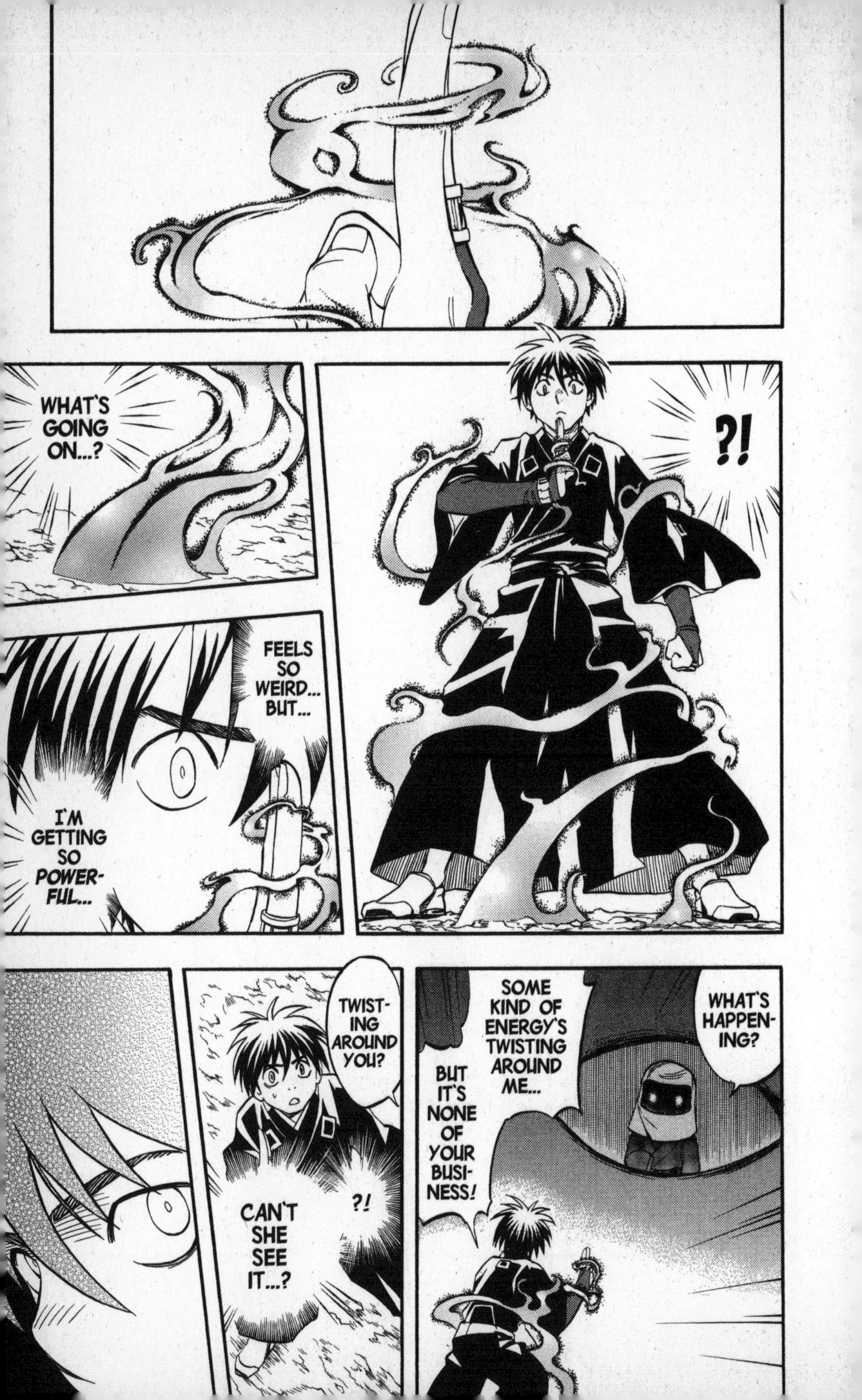
?!
WHAT'S GOING ON...?
FEELS SO WEIRD... BUT...
I'M GETTING SO POWERFUL...
WHAT'S HAPPENING?
SOME KIND OF ENERGY'S TWISTING AROUND ME...
BUT IT'S NONE OF YOUR BUSINESS!
TWISTING AROUND YOU?
?!
CAN'T SHE SEE IT...?

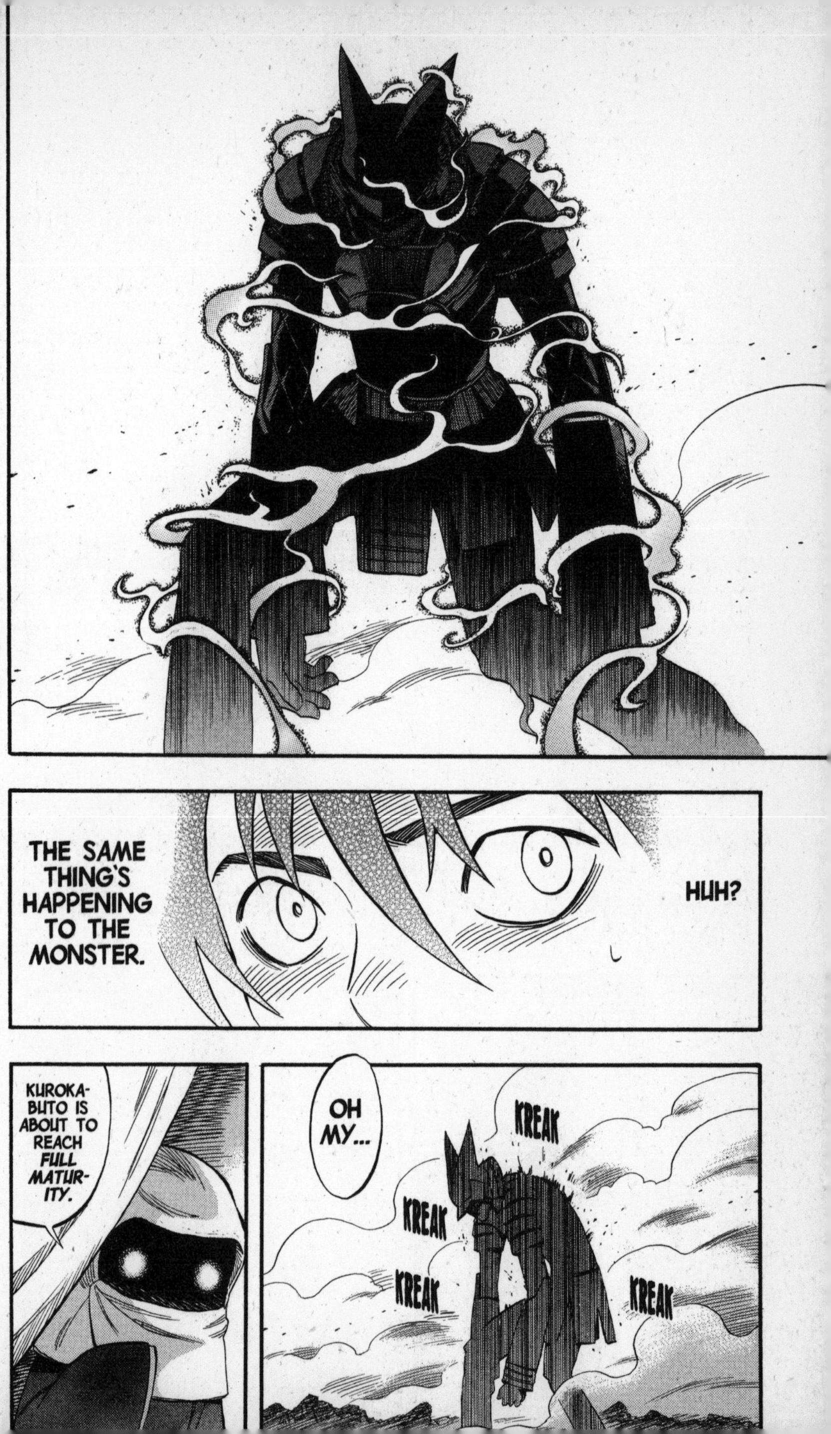
HUH?
THE SAME THING'S HAPPENING TO THE MONSTER.
OH MY...
KREAK
KREAK
KREAK
KREAK
KUROKA-BUTO IS ABOUT TO REACH FULL MATUR-ITY.

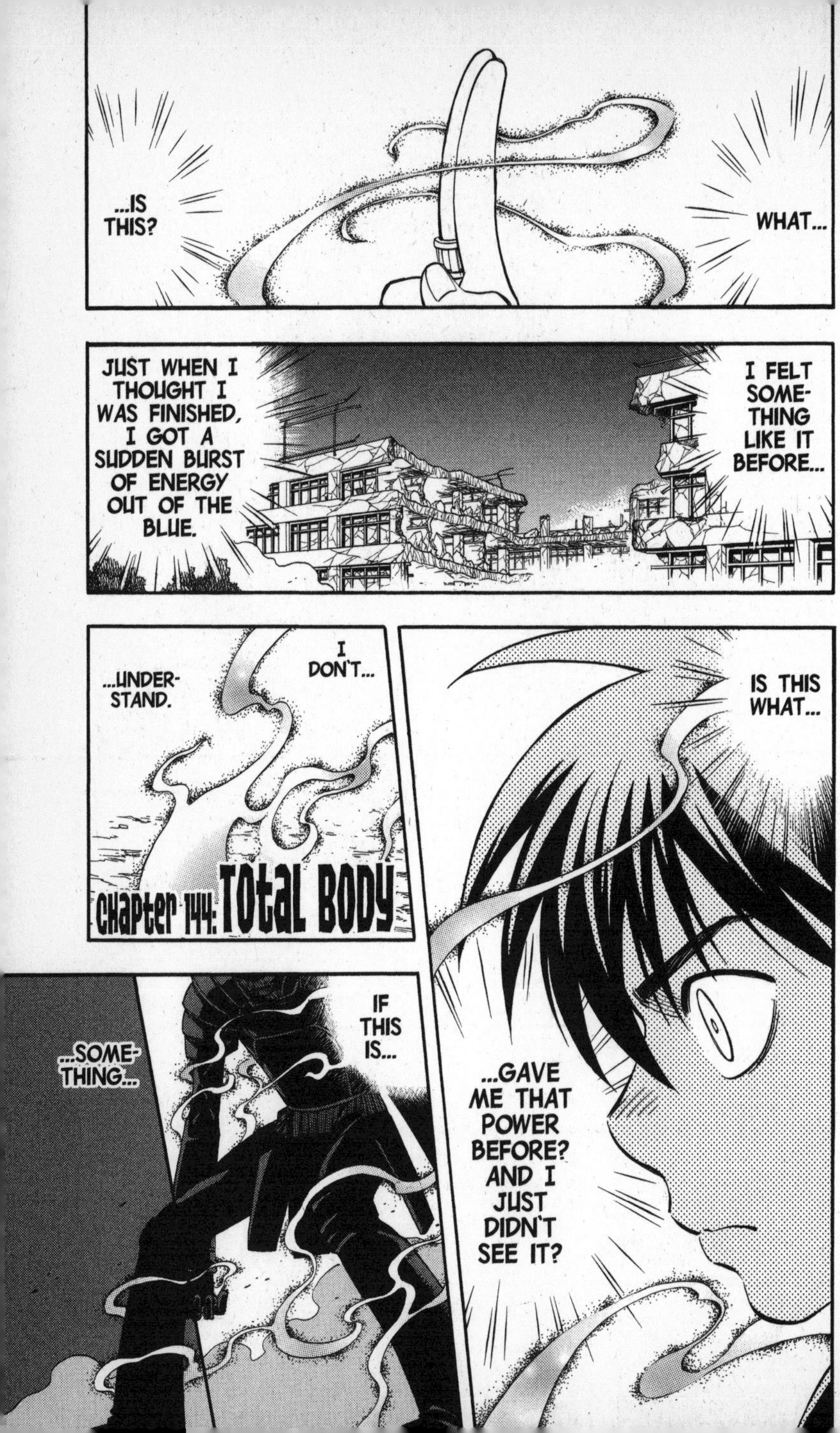
WHAT...
...IS THIS?
I FELT SOMETHING LIKE IT BEFORE...
JUST WHEN I THOUGHT I WAS FINISHED, I GOT A SUDDEN BURST OF ENERGY OUT OF THE BLUE.
IS THIS WHAT...
...GAVE ME THAT POWER BEFORE? AND I JUST DIDN'T SEE IT?
I DON'T...
...UNDERSTAND.
Chapter 144: Total Body
IF THIS IS...
...SOMETHING...

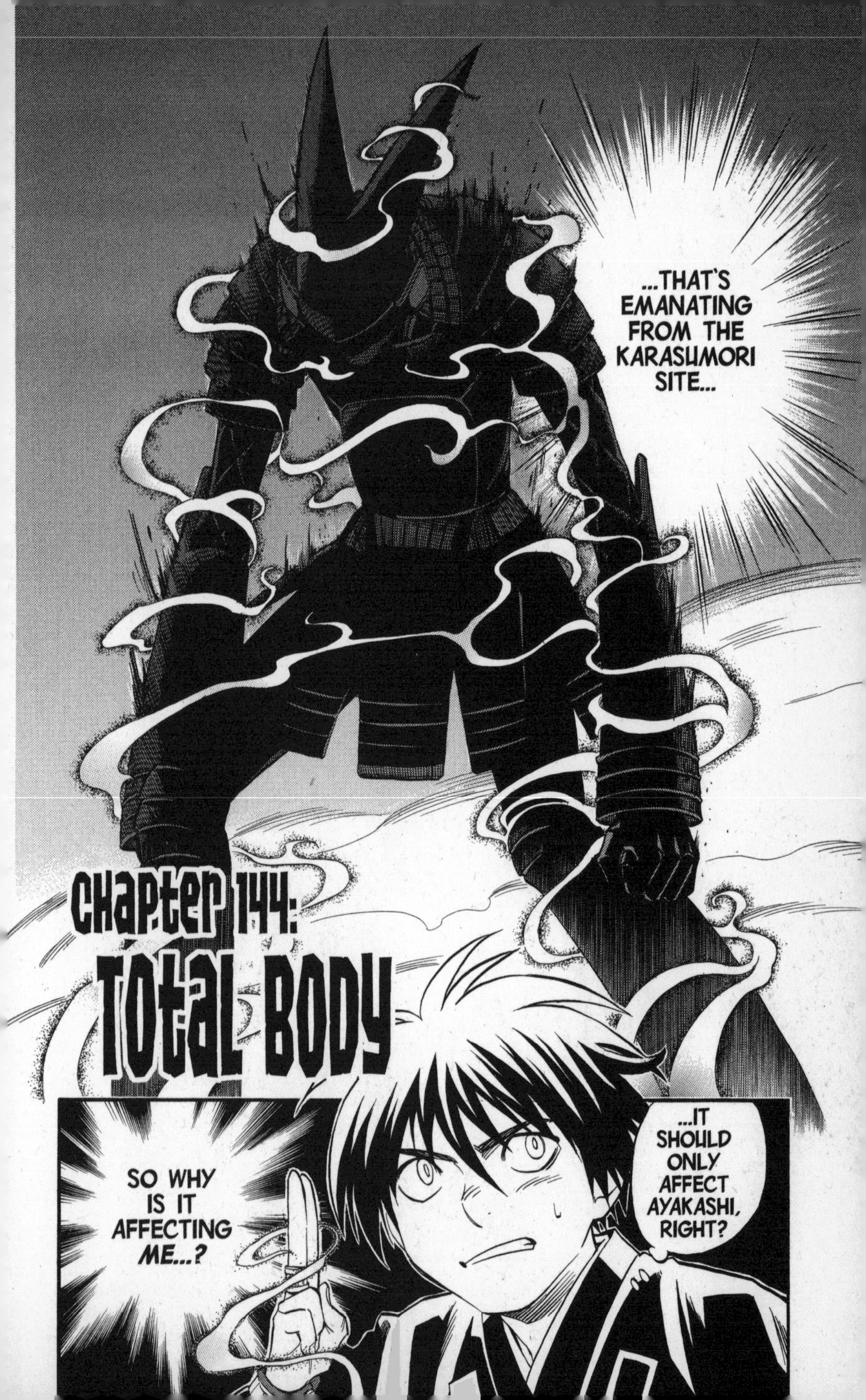
...THAT'S EMANATING FROM THE KARASUMORI SITE...
CHAPTER 144: TOTAL BODY
...IT SHOULD ONLY AFFECT AYAKASHI, RIGHT?
SO WHY IS IT AFFECTING *ME*...?

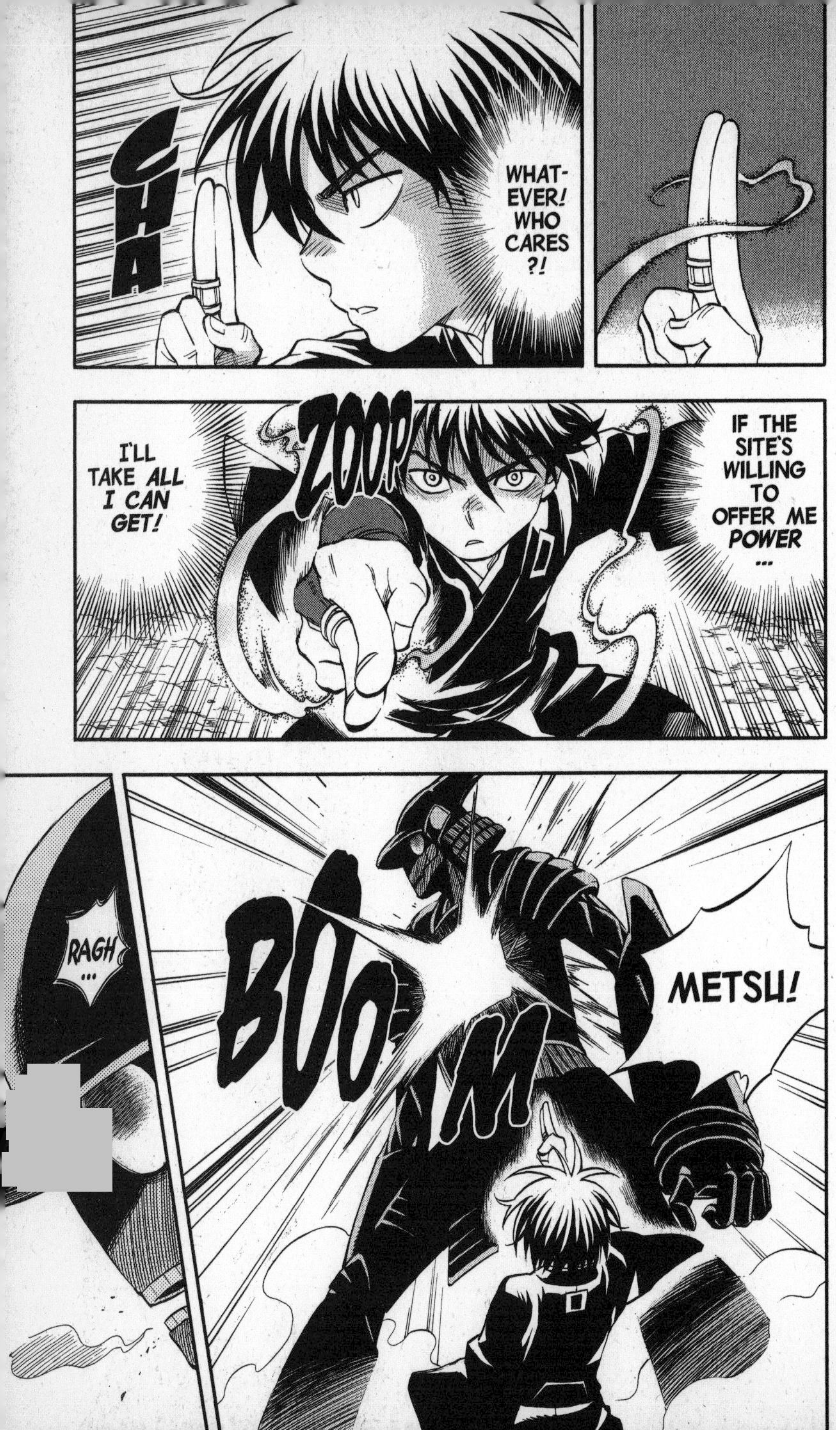
WHAT-EVER! WHO CARES?!
CHA
IF THE SITE'S WILLING TO OFFER ME POWER...
ZOOP
I'LL TAKE ALL I CAN GET!
METSU!
BOOM
RAGH...

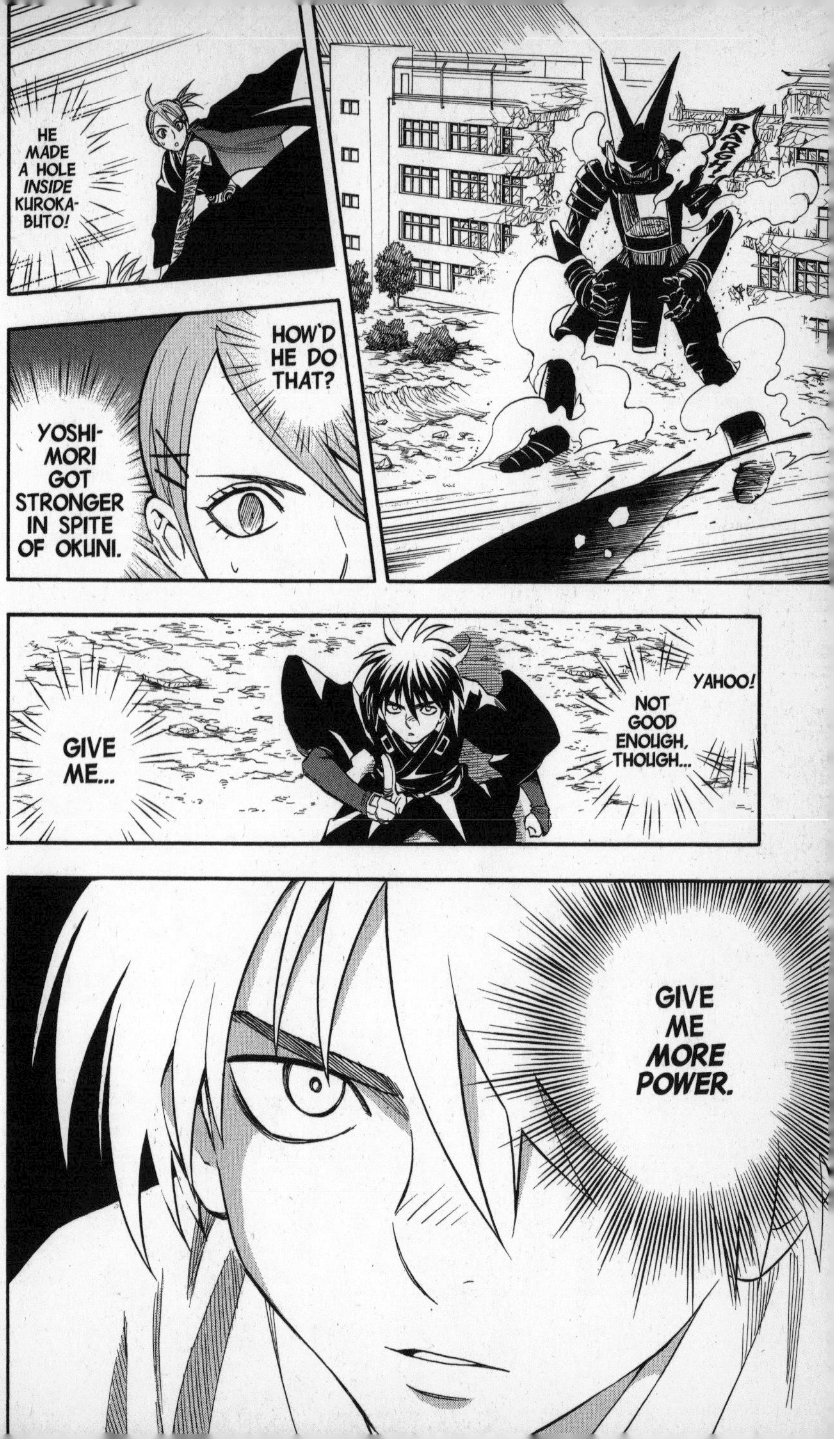
RAAGH!
HE MADE A HOLE INSIDE KUROKA-BUTO!
HOW'D HE DO THAT?
YOSHI-MORI GOT STRONGER IN SPITE OF OKUNI.
YAHOO!
NOT GOOD ENOUGH, THOUGH...
GIVE ME...
GIVE ME MORE POWER.

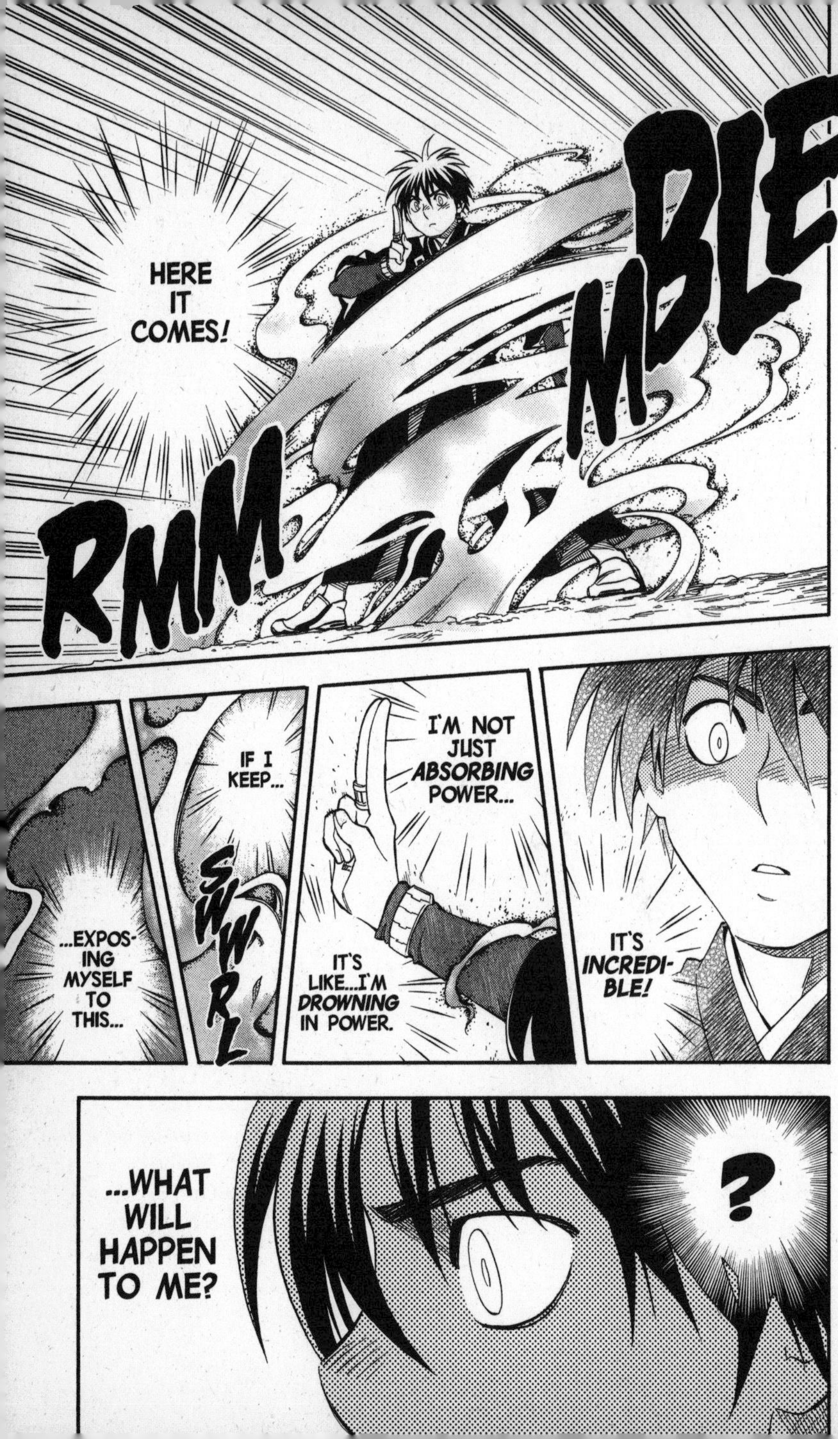
HERE IT COMES!
RMMMBLE
IT'S INCREDIBLE!
I'M NOT JUST ABSORBING POWER...
IT'S LIKE...I'M DROWNING IN POWER.
IF I KEEP...
SWWWRL
...EXPOSING MYSELF TO THIS...
?
...WHAT WILL HAPPEN TO ME?

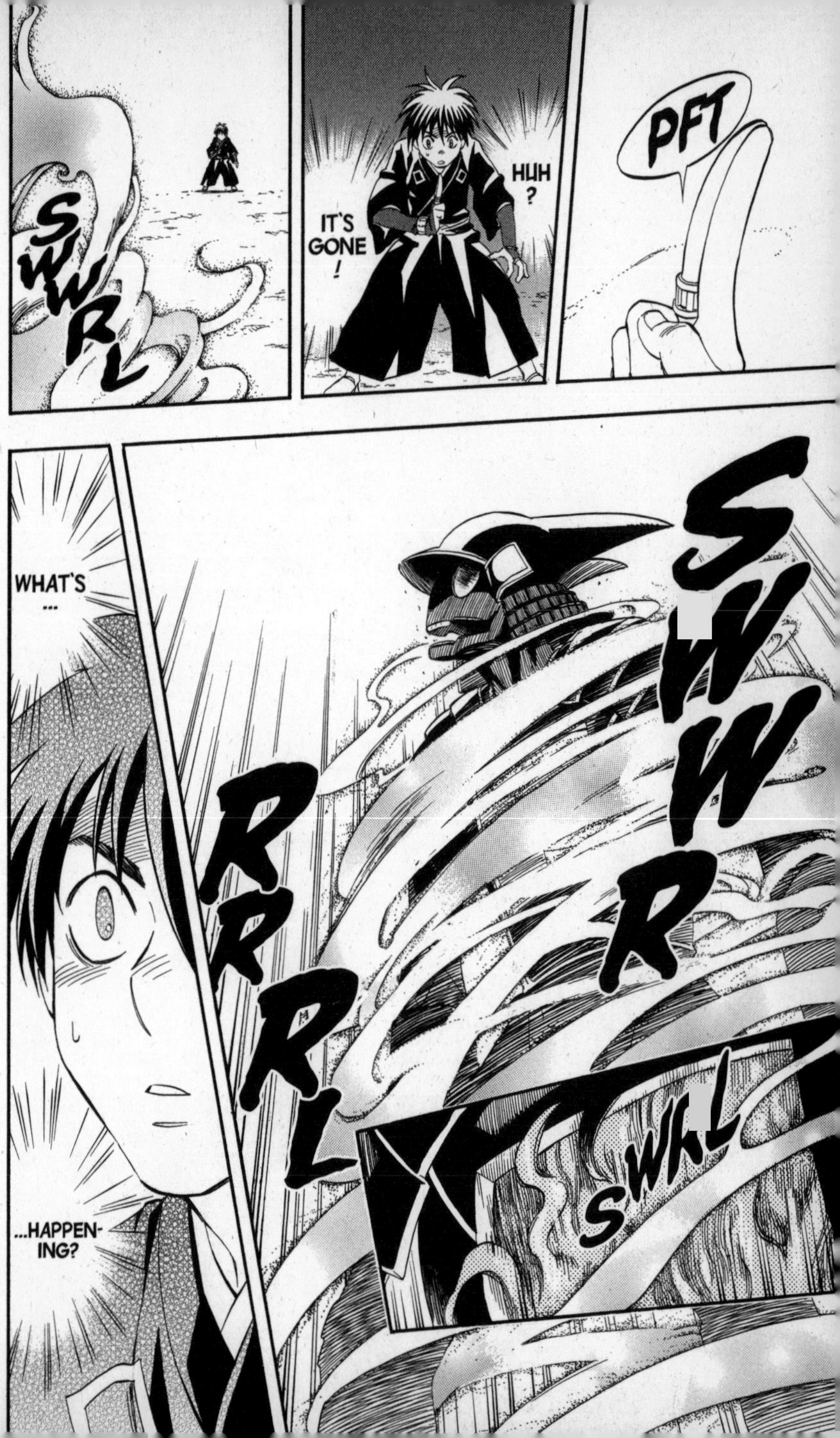
PFT
HUH?
IT'S GONE!
SWRL
SWWR
RRRL
SWRL
WHAT'S...
...HAPPENING?

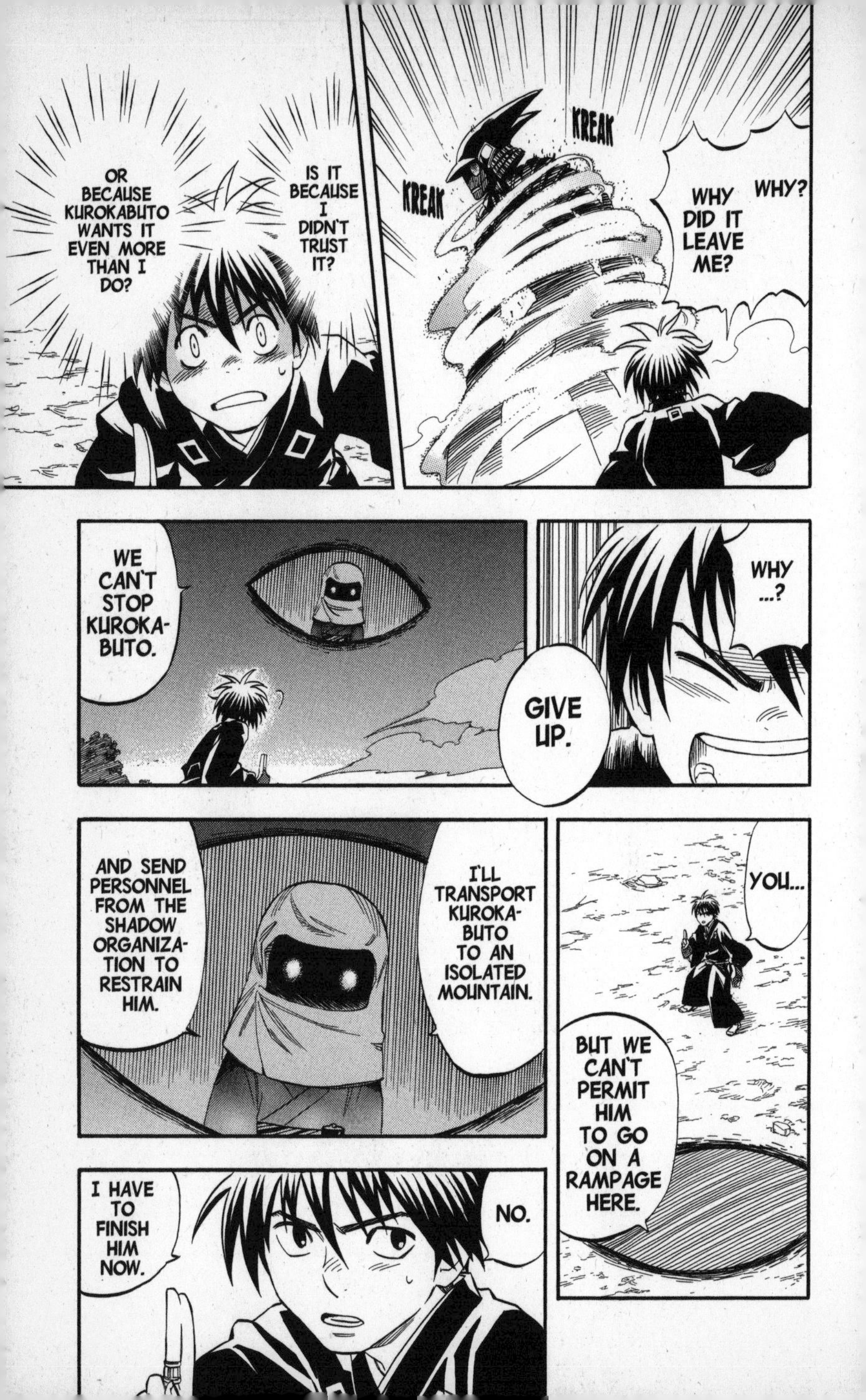
WHY?
WHY DID IT LEAVE ME?
KREAK
KREAK
IS IT BECAUSE I DIDN'T TRUST IT?
OR BECAUSE KUROKABUTO WANTS IT EVEN MORE THAN I DO?
WHY ...?
GIVE UP.
WE CAN'T STOP KUROKA-BUTO.
YOU...
BUT WE CAN'T PERMIT HIM TO GO ON A RAMPAGE HERE.
I'LL TRANSPORT KUROKA-BUTO TO AN ISOLATED MOUNTAIN.
AND SEND PERSONNEL FROM THE SHADOW ORGANIZA-TION TO RESTRAIN HIM.
NO.
I HAVE TO FINISH HIM NOW.

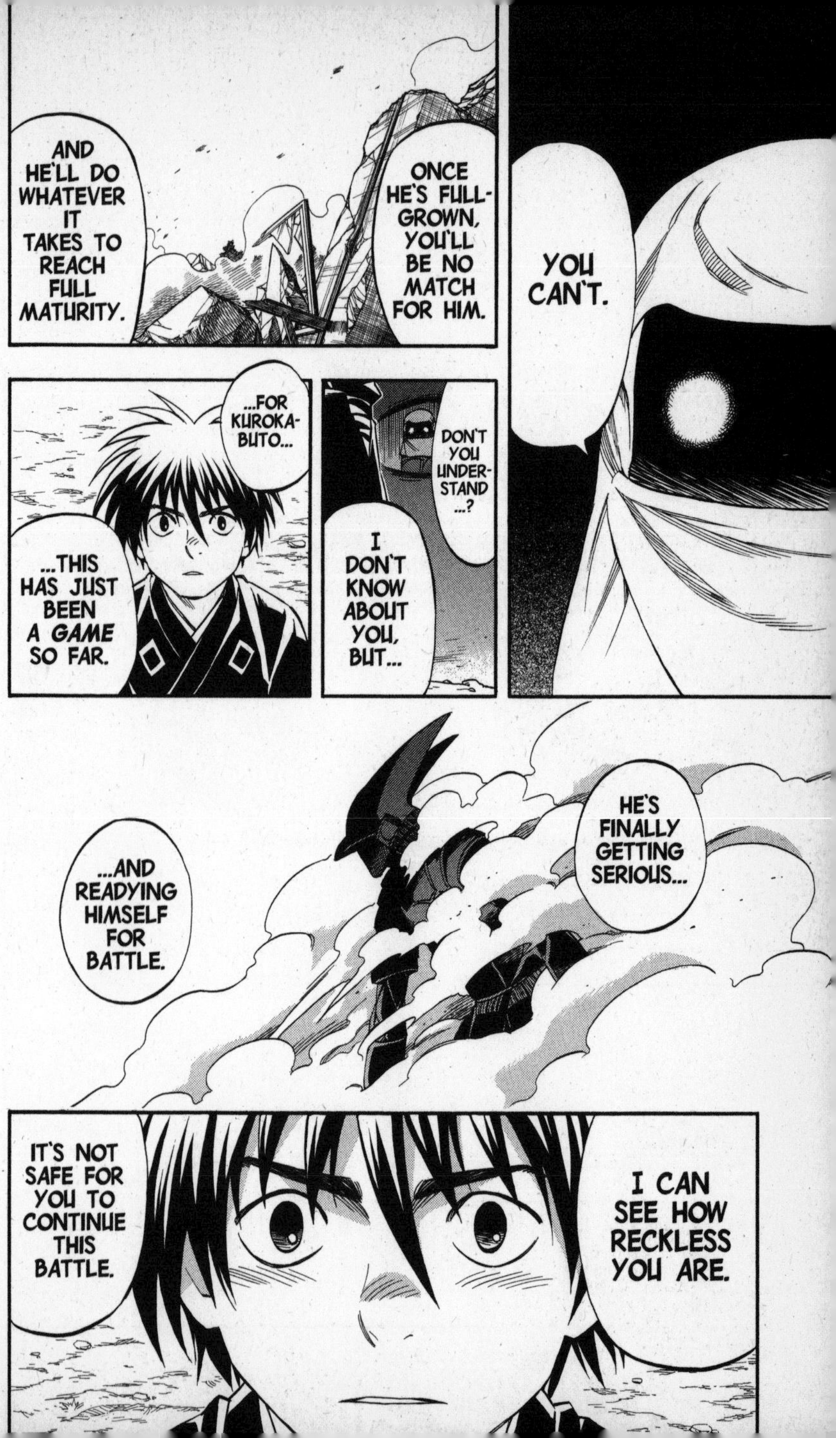
YOU CAN'T.
ONCE HE'S FULL-GROWN, YOU'LL BE NO MATCH FOR HIM.
AND HE'LL DO WHATEVER IT TAKES TO REACH FULL MATURITY.
DON'T YOU UNDERSTAND ...?
I DON'T KNOW ABOUT YOU, BUT...
...FOR KUROKABUTO...
...THIS HAS JUST BEEN A *GAME* SO FAR.
HE'S FINALLY GETTING SERIOUS...
...AND READYING HIMSELF FOR BATTLE.
I CAN SEE HOW RECKLESS YOU ARE.
IT'S NOT SAFE FOR YOU TO CONTINUE THIS BATTLE.

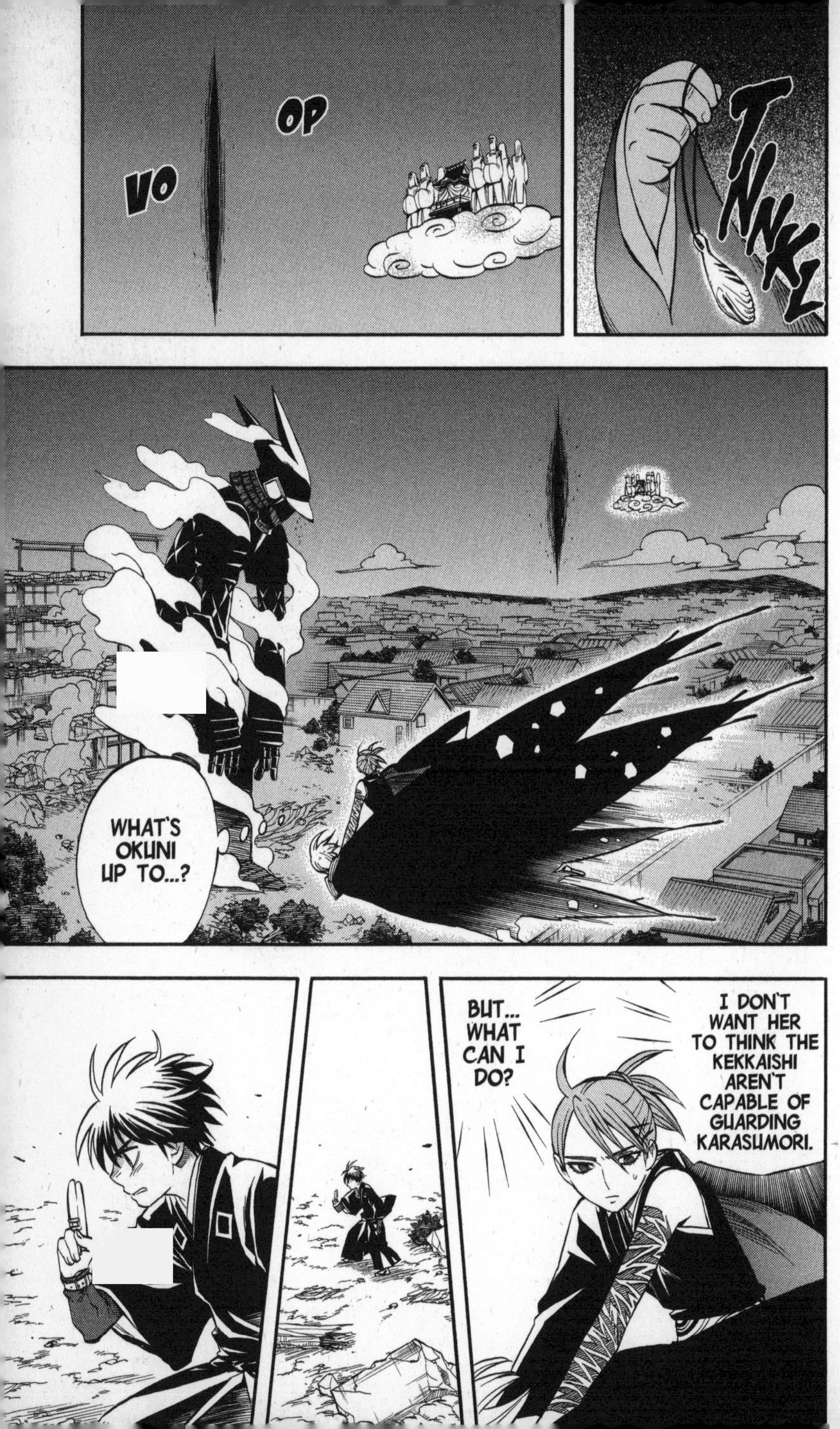
TINKL
VO OP
WHAT'S OKUNI UP TO...?
I DON'T WANT HER TO THINK THE KEKKAISHI AREN'T CAPABLE OF GUARDING KARASUMORI.
BUT... WHAT CAN I DO?

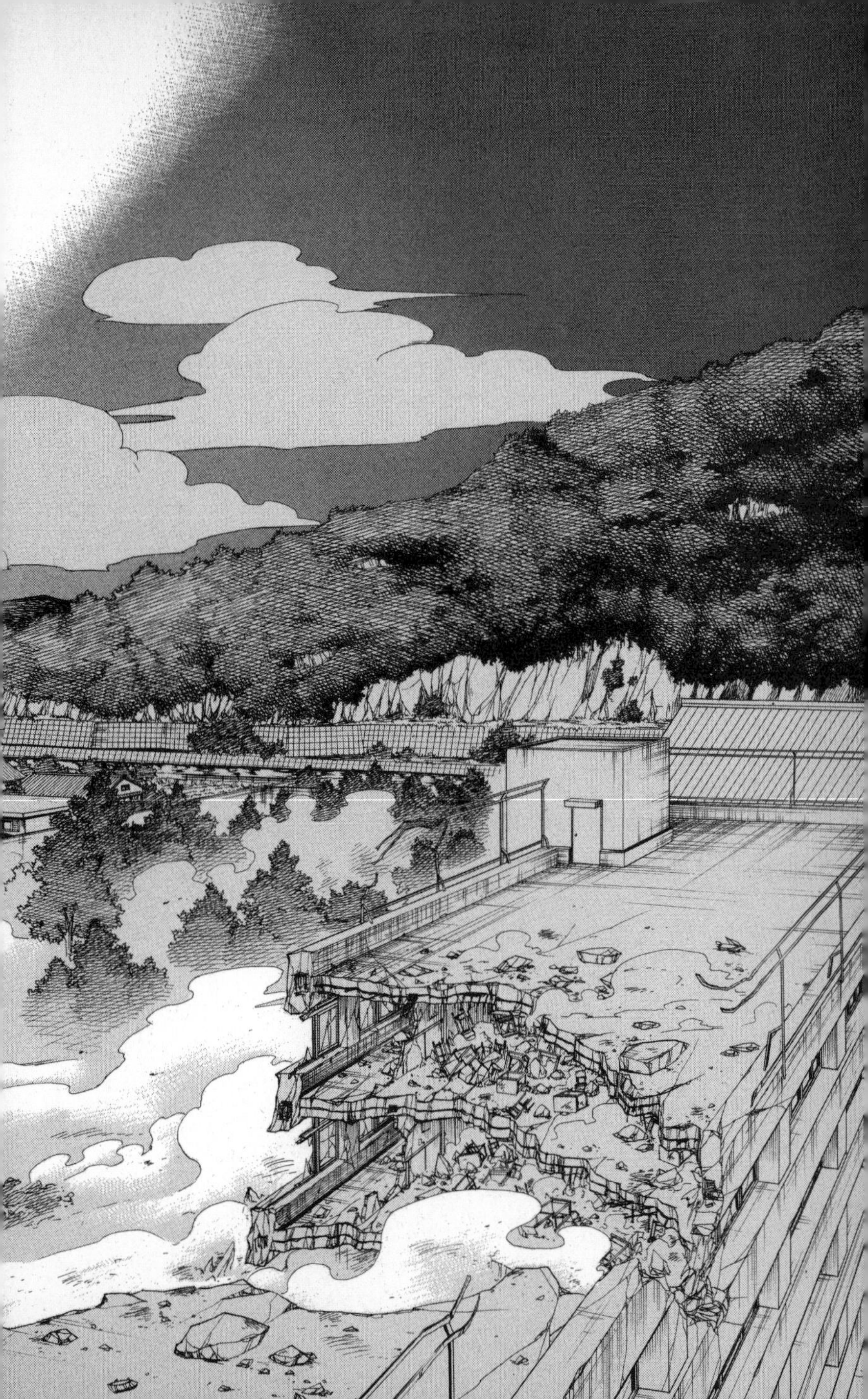

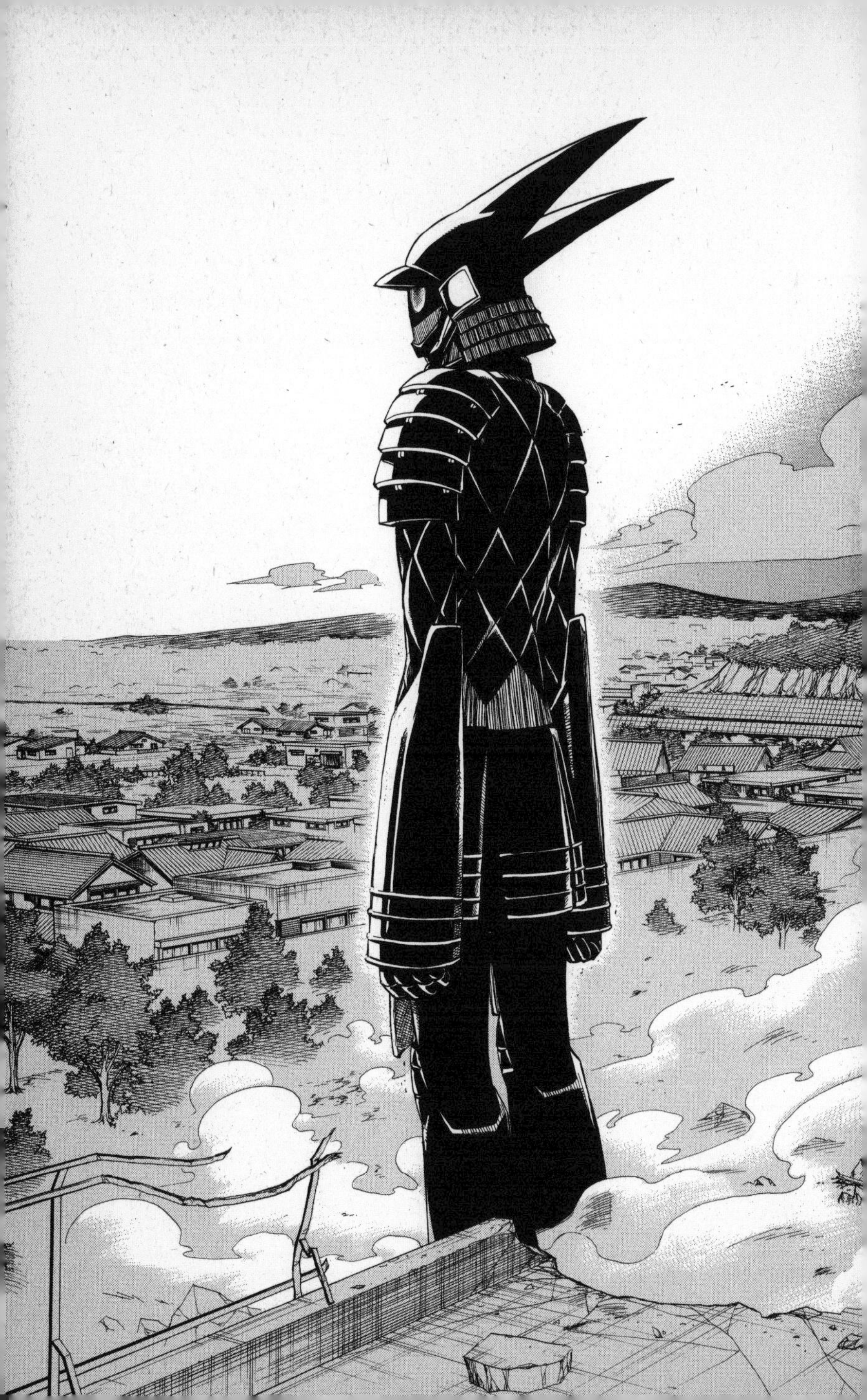

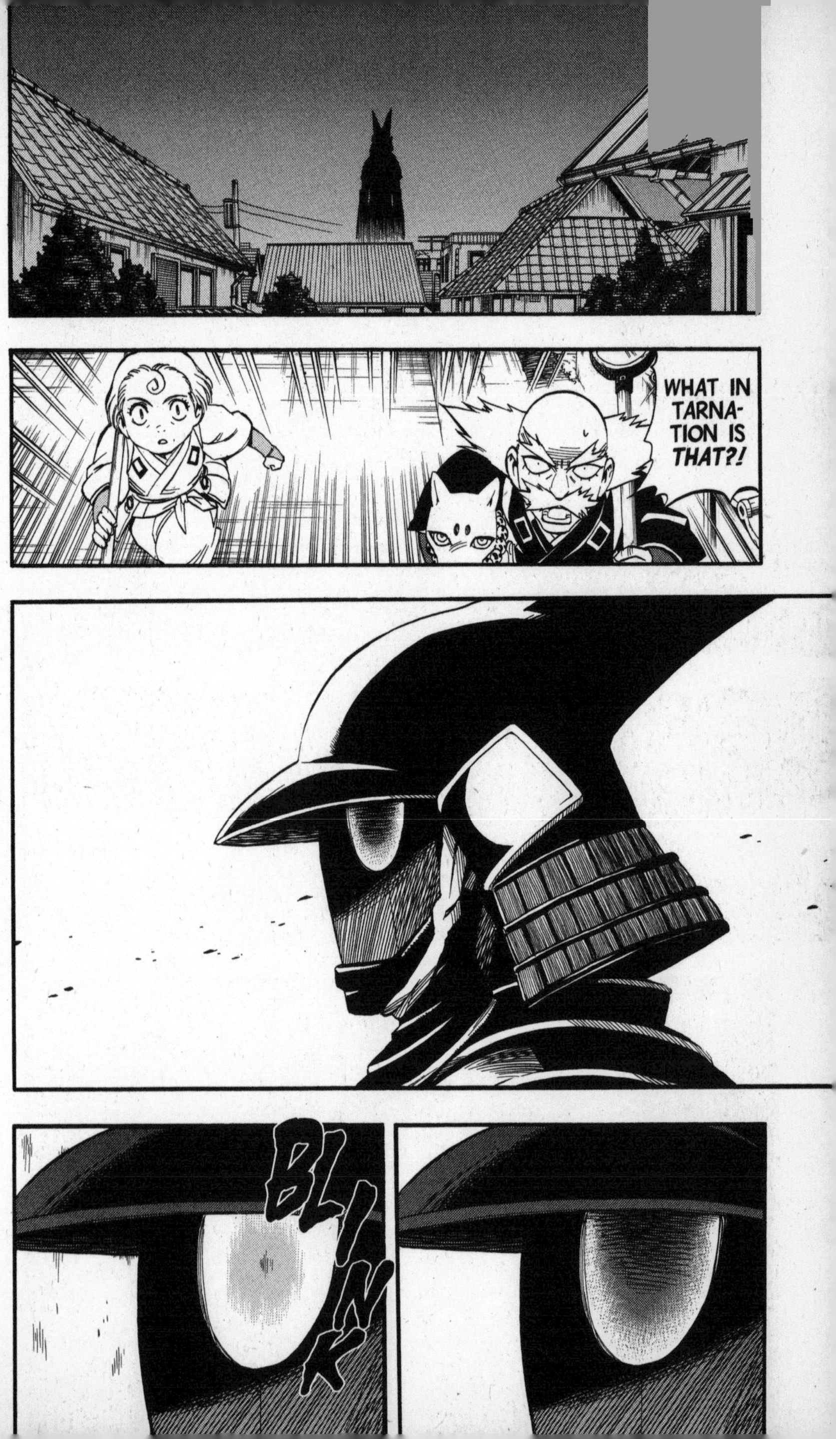
WHAT IN TARNA-TION IS THAT?!
BLINK

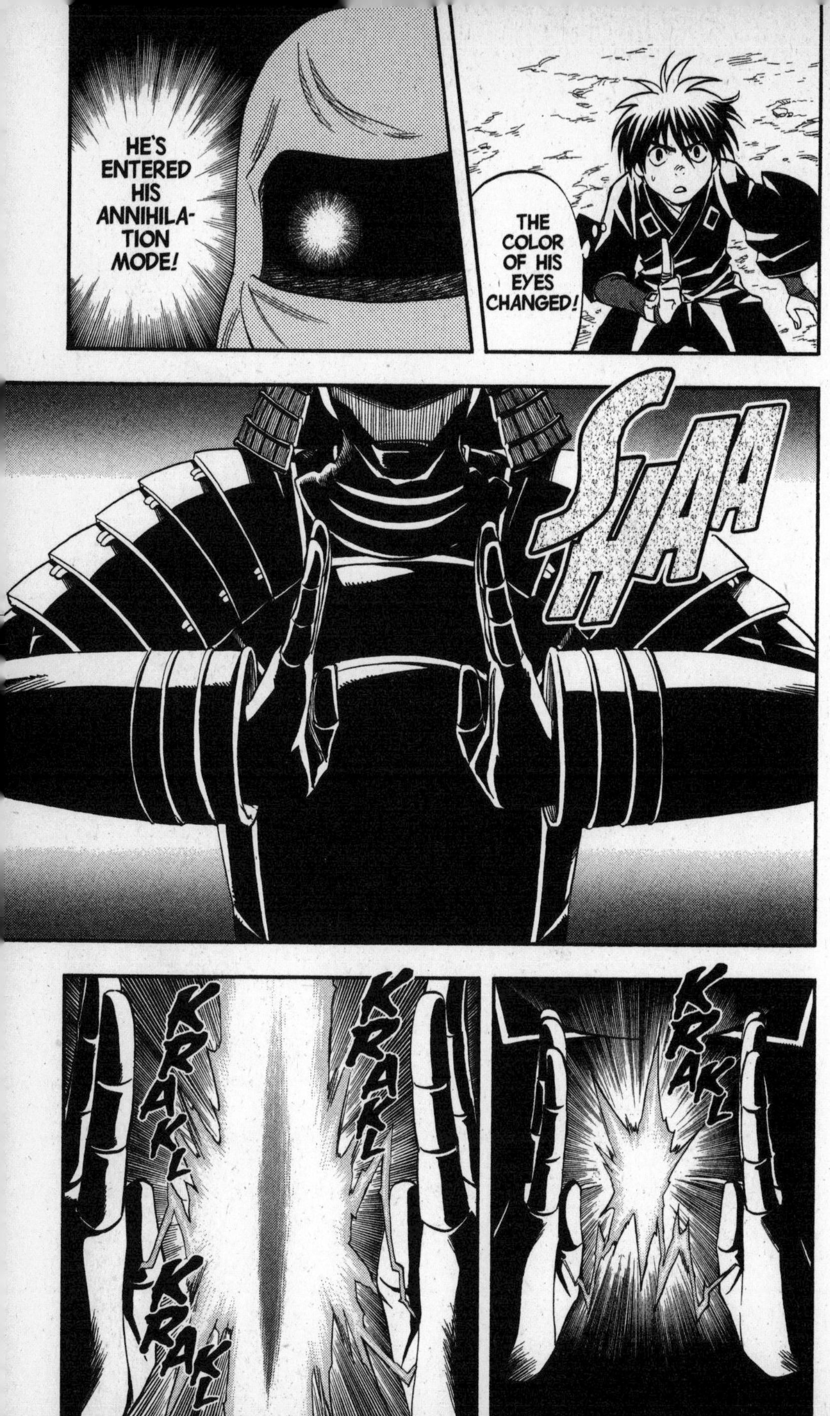
THE COLOR OF HIS EYES CHANGED!
HE'S ENTERED HIS ANNIHILA-TION MODE!
SHAA
KRAKL
KRAKL
KRAKL
KRAKL

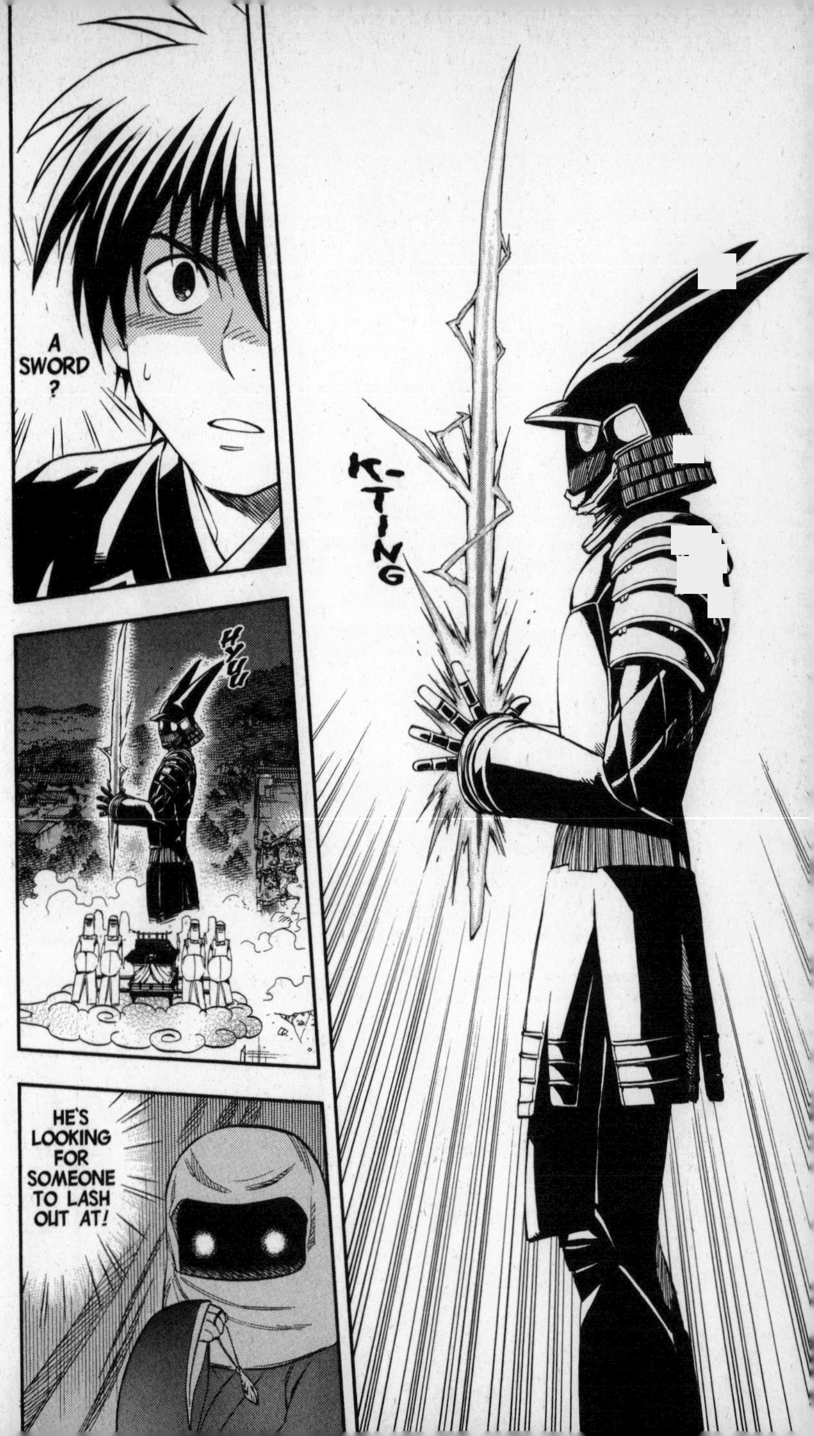
K-TING
A SWORD?
HYUU
HE'S LOOKING FOR SOMEONE TO LASH OUT AT!

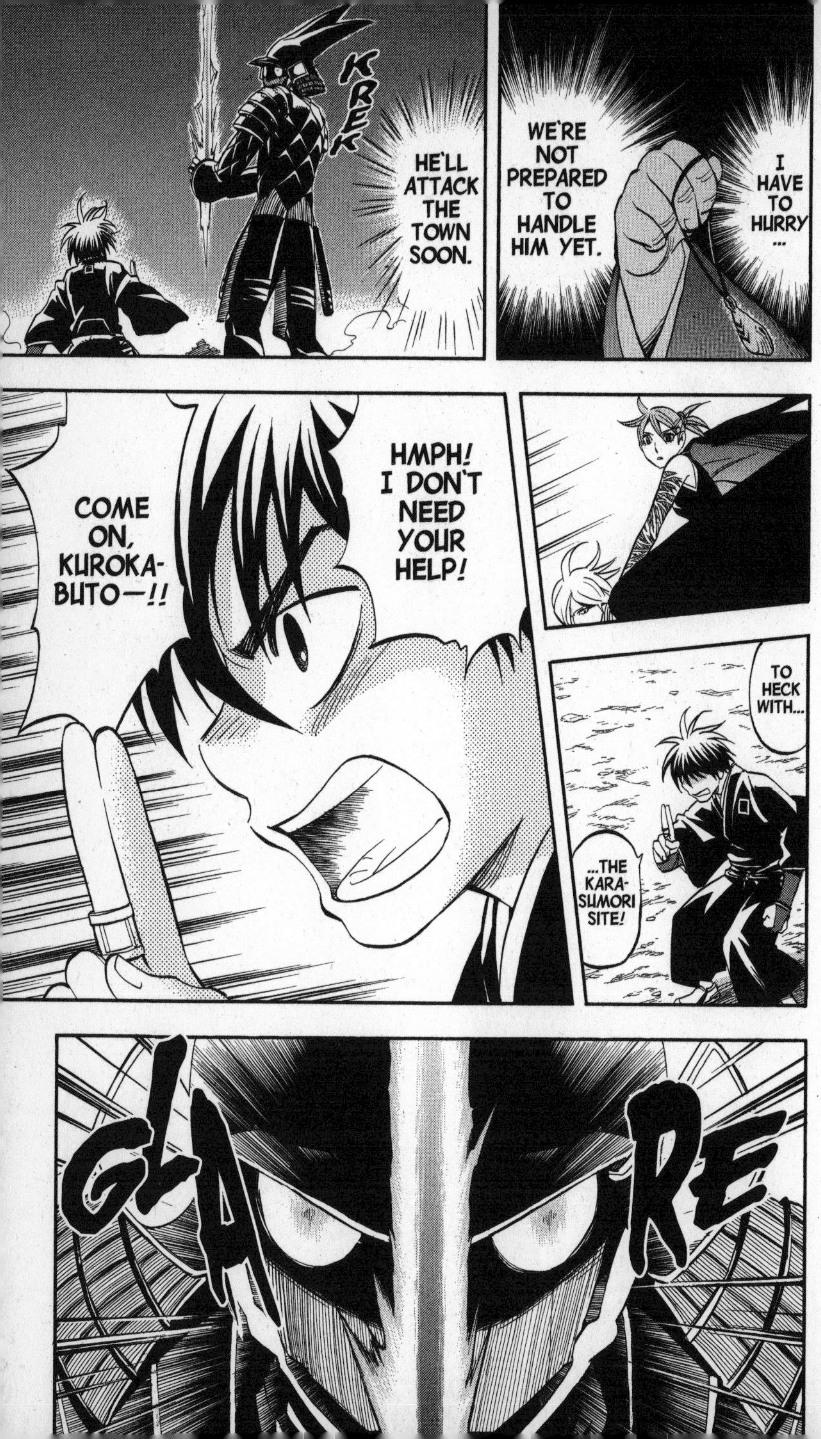
WE'RE NOT PREPARED TO HANDLE HIM YET.
I HAVE TO HURRY...
KREK
HE'LL ATTACK THE TOWN SOON.
TO HECK WITH...
...THE KARA-SUMORI SITE!
HMPH! I DON'T NEED YOUR HELP!
COME ON, KUROKA-BUTO—!!
GLARE

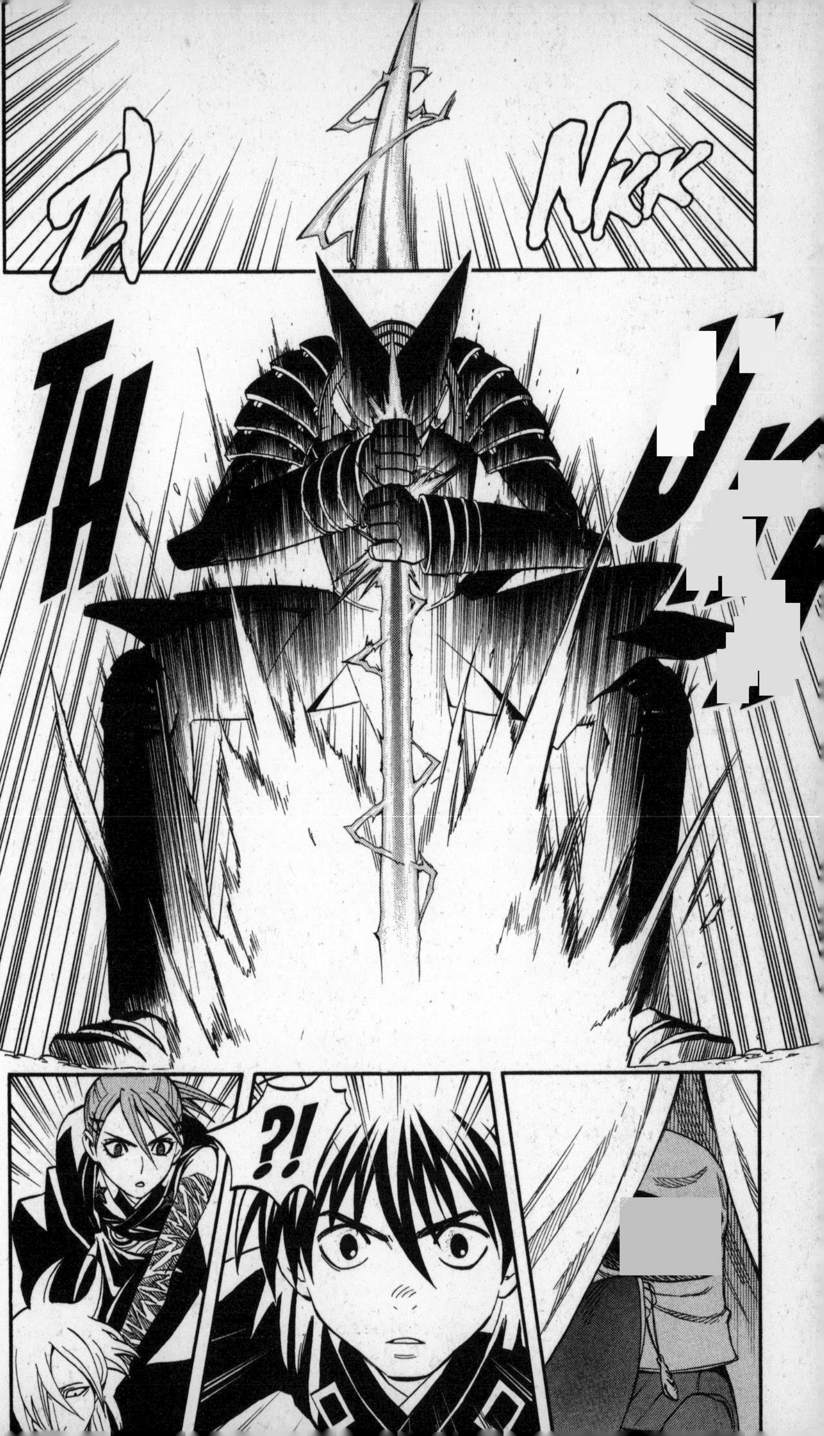
ZI
NKK
TH
?!

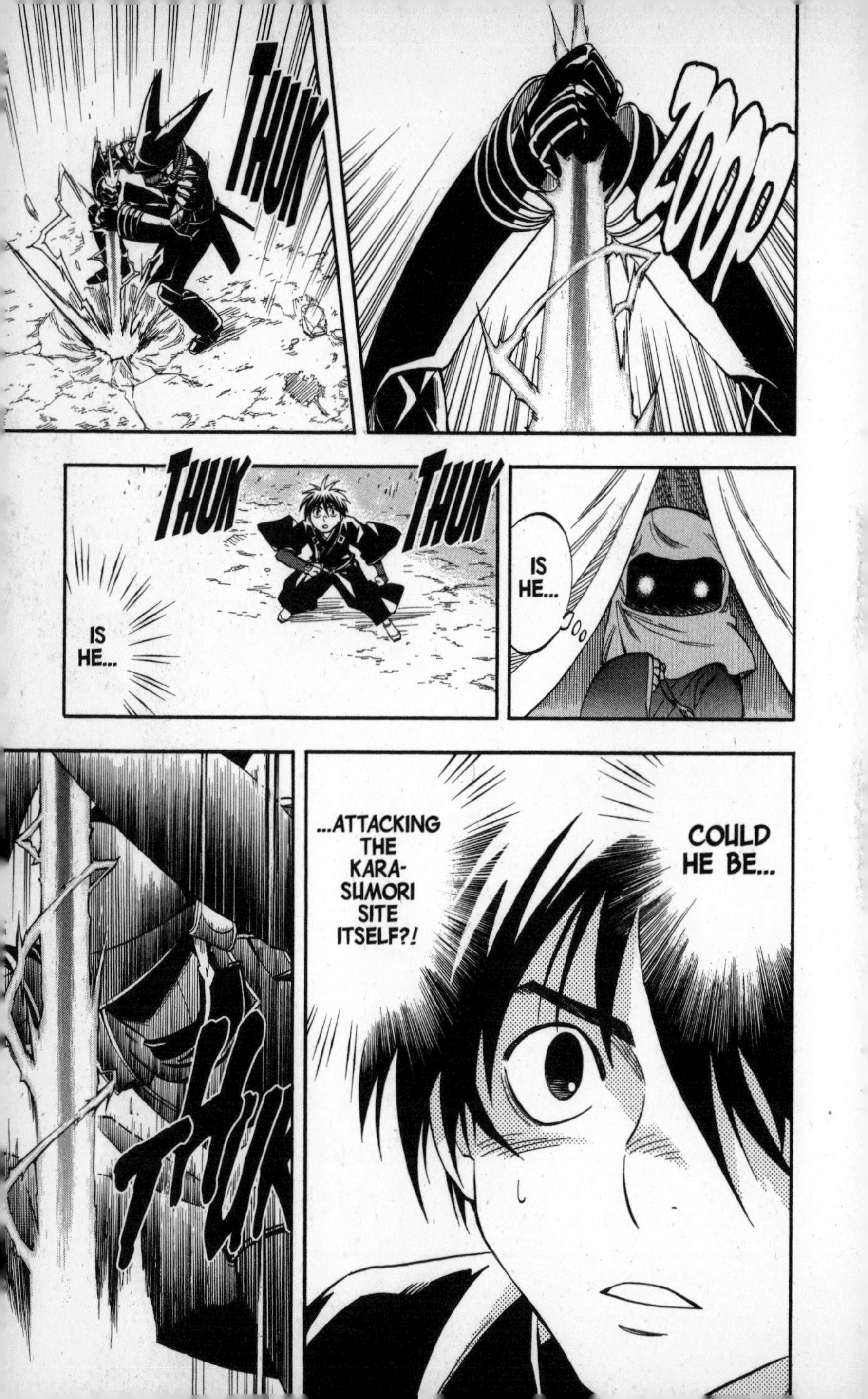
ZOOOP
THUK
IS HE...
THUK
THUK
IS HE...
COULD HE BE...
...ATTACKING THE KARA-SUMORI SITE ITSELF?!
THUK

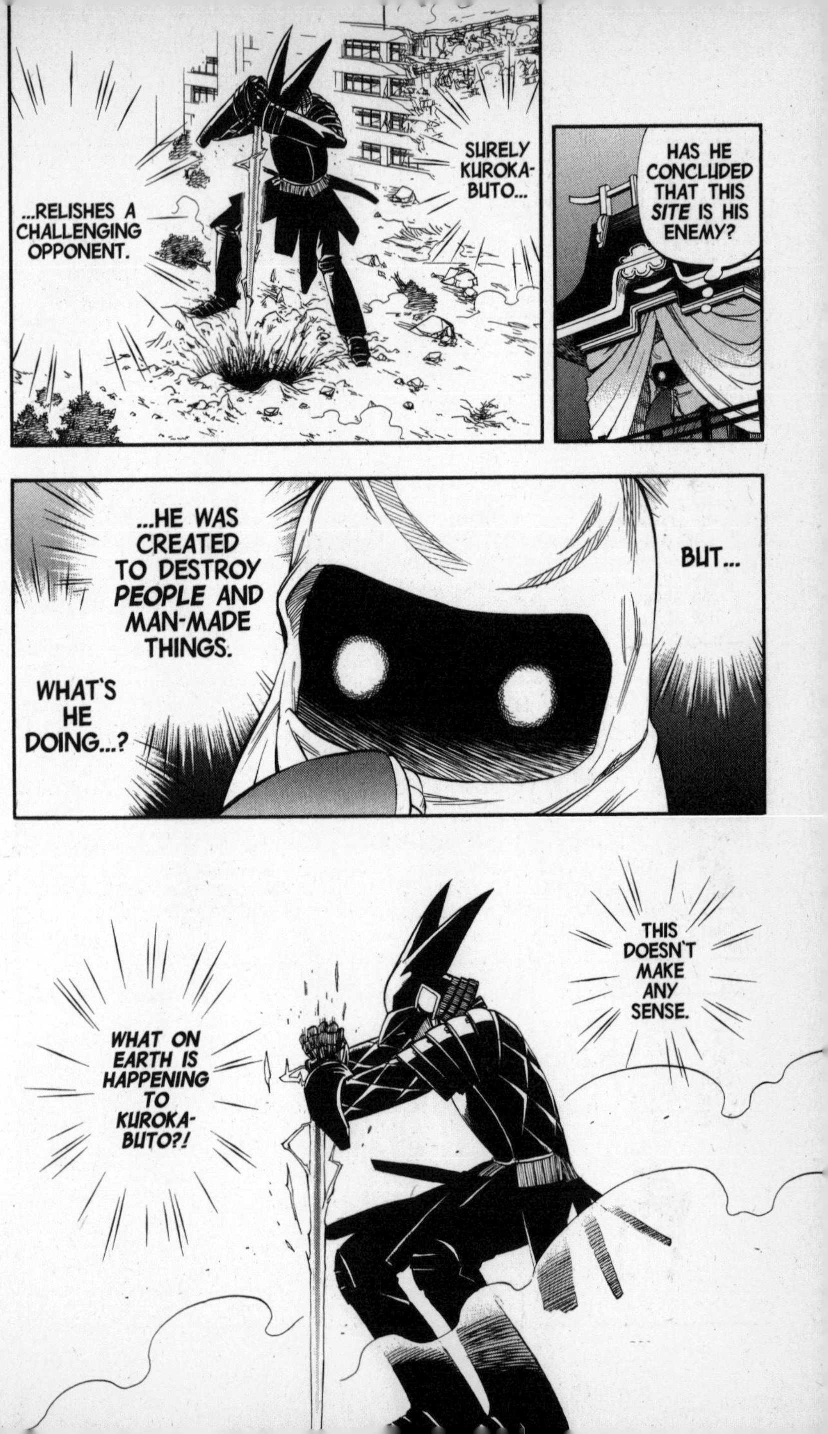
HAS HE CONCLUDED THAT THIS *SITE* IS HIS ENEMY?
SURELY KUROKA-BUTO...
...RELISHES A CHALLENGING OPPONENT.
BUT...
...HE WAS CREATED TO DESTROY *PEOPLE* AND MAN-MADE THINGS.
WHAT'S HE DOING...?
THIS DOESN'T MAKE ANY SENSE.
WHAT ON EARTH IS HAPPENING TO KUROKA-BUTO?!

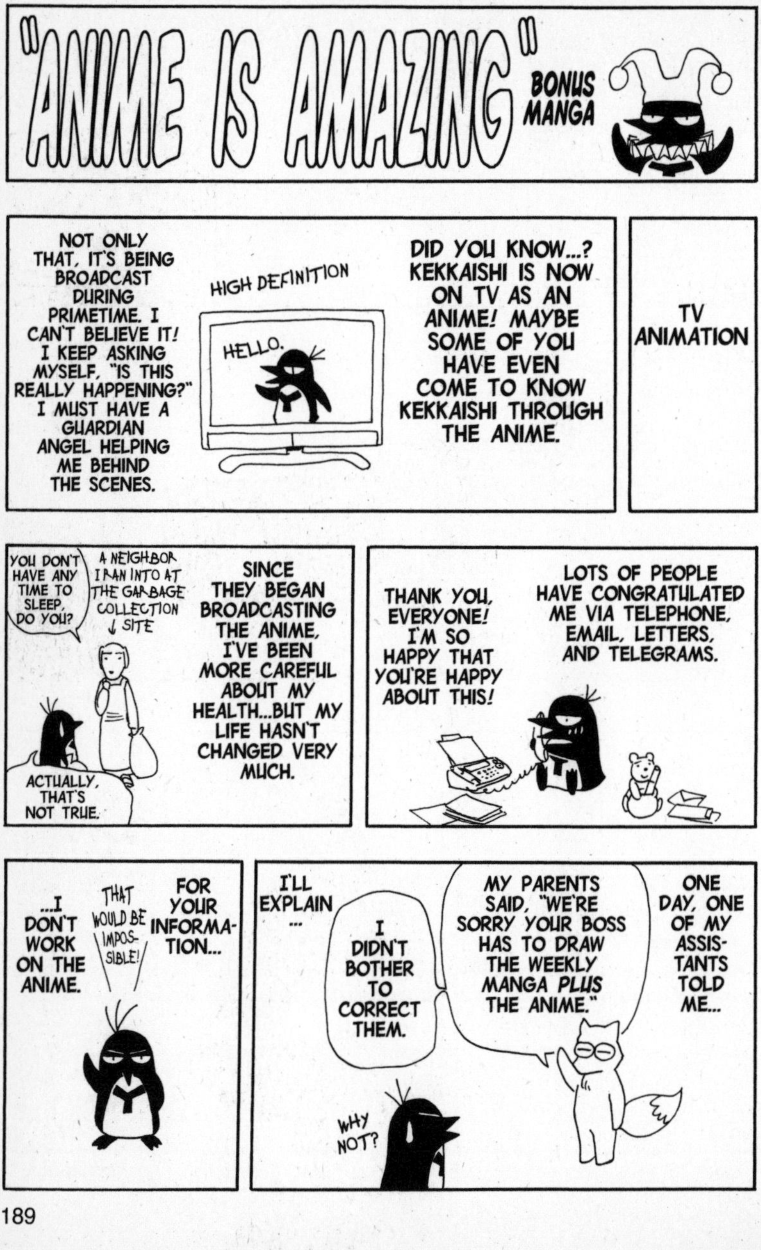

"ANIME IS AMAZING"
BONUS MANGA
TV ANIMATION
DID YOU KNOW...? KEKKAISHI IS NOW ON TV AS AN ANIME! MAYBE SOME OF YOU HAVE EVEN COME TO KNOW KEKKAISHI THROUGH THE ANIME.
HIGH DEFINITION
HELLO.
NOT ONLY THAT, IT'S BEING BROADCAST DURING PRIMETIME. I CAN'T BELIEVE IT! I KEEP ASKING MYSELF, "IS THIS REALLY HAPPENING?" I MUST HAVE A GUARDIAN ANGEL HELPING ME BEHIND THE SCENES.
LOTS OF PEOPLE HAVE CONGRATULATED ME VIA TELEPHONE, EMAIL, LETTERS, AND TELEGRAMS.
THANK YOU, EVERYONE! I'M SO HAPPY THAT YOU'RE HAPPY ABOUT THIS!
SINCE THEY BEGAN BROADCASTING THE ANIME, I'VE BEEN MORE CAREFUL ABOUT MY HEALTH...BUT MY LIFE HASN'T CHANGED VERY MUCH.
A NEIGHBOR I RAN INTO AT THE GARBAGE COLLECTION SITE
YOU DON'T HAVE ANY TIME TO SLEEP, DO YOU?
ACTUALLY, THAT'S NOT TRUE.
ONE DAY, ONE OF MY ASSISTANTS TOLD ME...
MY PARENTS SAID, "WE'RE SORRY YOUR BOSS HAS TO DRAW THE WEEKLY MANGA PLUS THE ANIME."
I DIDN'T BOTHER TO CORRECT THEM.
I'LL EXPLAIN...
WHY NOT?
FOR YOUR INFORMATION...
THAT WOULD BE IMPOSSIBLE!
...I DON'T WORK ON THE ANIME.

MANGA AND ANIME ARE CREATED IN COMPLETELY DIFFERENT WAYS. WHILE MANGA PRODUCTION ONLY REQUIRES A SMALL NUMBER OF PEOPLE, ANIME REQUIRES A LARGE STAFF.
REMEMBER ALL THE NAMES IN THE CREDITS AT THE OPENING OR ENDING OF THE TV SHOW? ALL THOSE PEOPLE PLAY A PART IN THE ANIME PRODUCTION.
SO MANY NAMES!
ACTUALLY, MY NAME APPEARS IN THE CREDITS TOO.
TV ANIMATION IS MORE THAN ANY SINGLE MANGA CREATOR COULD HANDLE.
ANIME IS MADE BY PROFESSIONALS WHO SPECIALIZE IN THE FIELD.
HONESTLY, THE WEEKLY MANGA KEEPS ME BUSY ENOUGH!
FILM IS OFTEN REFERRED TO AS A COMPOSITE ART. VISUAL IMAGES ACCOMPANY SOUNDS, COLORS, AND MOVEMENTS.
THEY LEAVE A DIFFERENT IMPRESSION THAN THE STATIC, ALMOST MONOCHROME IMAGES OF MANGA.
TO TELL YOU THE TRUTH, WHEN I SEE THOSE SPECTACULAR ACTION SEQUENCES WITH SOUND, COLOR, AND SPECIAL EFFECTS IN THE ANIME ON TV...
HMPH! I CAN'T DO THAT IN MY MANGA.
CHOMP CHOMP
...I GET JEALOUS.
BUT THEY CAN'T DO EVERYTHING I CAN DO IN MY MANGA—SUCH AS BREAKING UP A PAGE INTO A FEW LARGE PANELS AND THEN ARRANGING THOSE PANELS HOWEVER I WANT.
FROM TIME TO TIME, I FEEL LIKE I'M COMPETING WITH THE ANIME. BUT ONE OF THE ADVANTAGES OF MANGA MIGHT BE THAT IT LEAVES MORE ROOM FOR THE READER'S IMAGINATION.
IN CONCLUSION, LET ME JUST SAY THAT I'LL BE EXTREMELY HAPPY IF YOU ENJOY MY STORY IN *BOTH* FORMATS!
I APPRECIATE YOUR CONTINUING SUPPORT FOR KEKKAISHI!
I'VE NOTICED THAT THE PENGUIN MAKES FREQUENT APPEARANCES IN THE ANIME. WHEN HE DOES, I CAN'T HELP BUT FEEL A LITTLE SELF-CONSCIOUS...

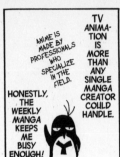

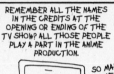

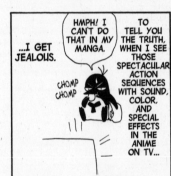

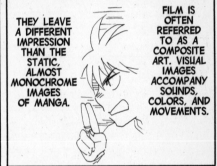

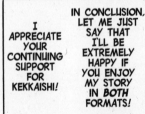

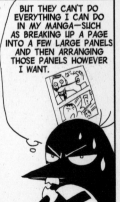

TA-DAH!

Don't stare!

Oh... Wow!

MESSAGE FROM YELLOW TANABE

Ever since the animated version of *Kekkaishi* came out, I've been coming across bookstore tables covered with piles of my manga laid out flat. These high profile displays of my work scare me. I mean, I'm very happy they're there, but at the same time, it freaks me out. When the first volume of *Kekkaishi* was printed, I remember I was just excited to see my book being sold at all, and I cheered, "Yay! That's my book!"

KEKKAISHI

VOLUME 15

VIZ MEDIA EDITION

STORY AND ART BY YELLOW TANABE

Translation/Yuko Sawada
Touch-up Art & Lettering/Stephen Dutro
Cover Design & Graphic Layout/Izumi Evers
Editor/Annette Roman

Editor in Chief, Books/Alvin Lu
Editor in Chief, Magazines/Marc Weidenbaum
VP of Publishing Licensing/Rika Inouye
VP of Sales/Gonzalo Ferreyra
Sr. VP of Marketing/Liza Coppola
Publisher/Hyoe Narita

Printed in the U.S.A.

Published by VIZ Media, LLC
P.O. Box 77010
San Francisco, CA 94107

VIZ Media Edition
10 9 8 7 6 5 4 3 2 1
First printing, November 2008

www.viz.com

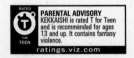

RATED T FOR TEEN
PARENTAL ADVISORY
KEKKAISHI is rated T for Teen and is recommended for ages 13 and up. It contains fantasy violence.
ratings.viz.com

store.viz.com

INUYASHA

Read the action from the start with the original manga series

Full color adaptation of the popular TV series

Art book with cel art, paintings, character profiles and more

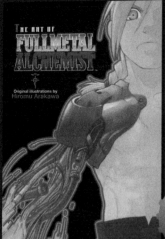

The Art of Fullmetal Alchemist

Contains all the manga artwork from 2001 to 2003!
- Gorgeously painted illustrations
- Color title pages, Japanese tankobon and promotional artwork
- Main character portraits and character designs from the video games

And a special two-page message from series creator Hiromu Arakawa!

Hardcover
$**19**99

The Art of Fullmetal Alchemist: The Anime

Includes art inspired by the popular anime series!
- Initial character designs
- Cel art
- Production notes

Plus, an interview with Yoshiyuki Ito, character designer for the anime!

Hardcover
$**19**99

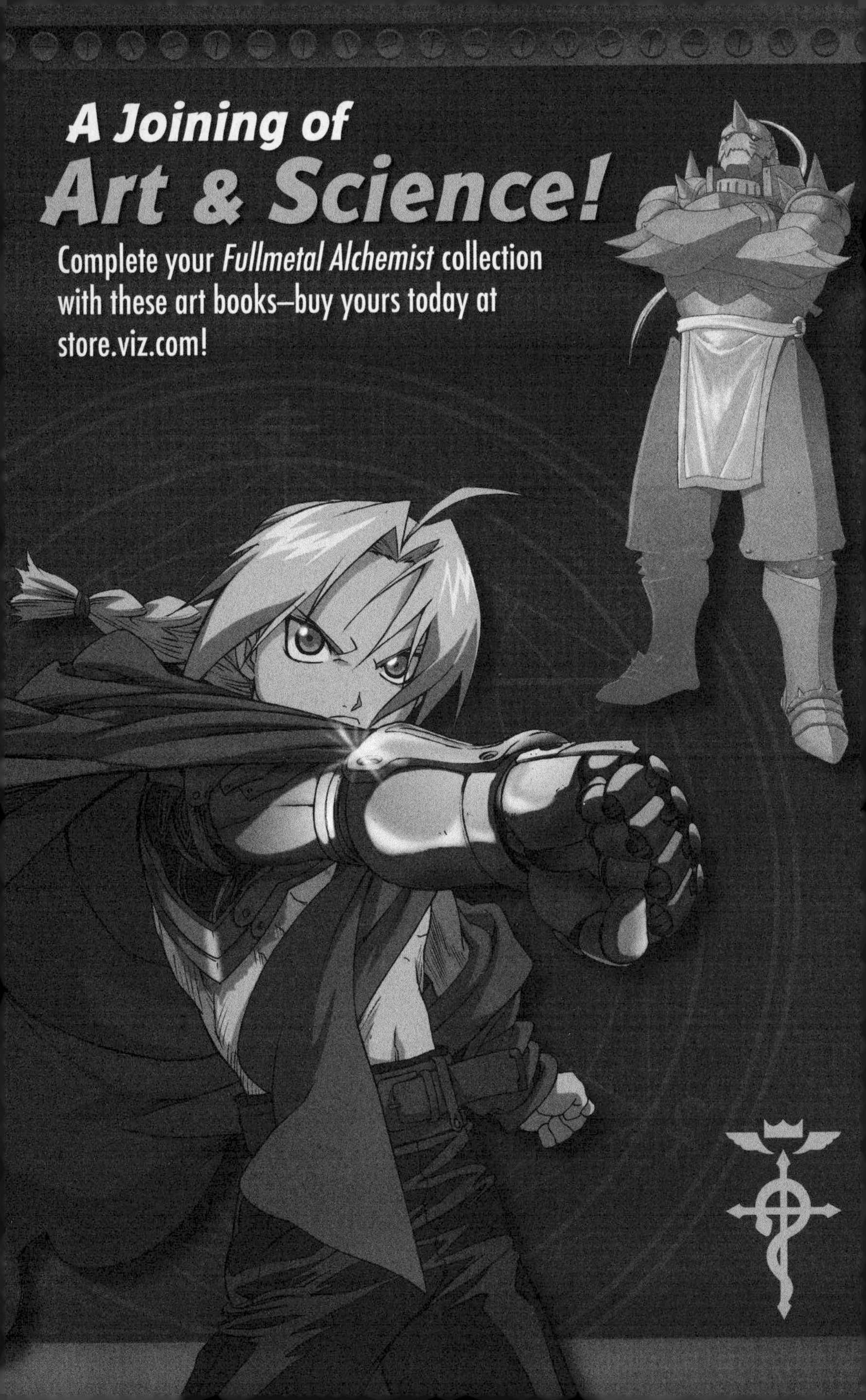
A Joining of
Art & Science!
Complete your Fullmetal Alchemist collection with these art books–buy yours today at store.viz.com!

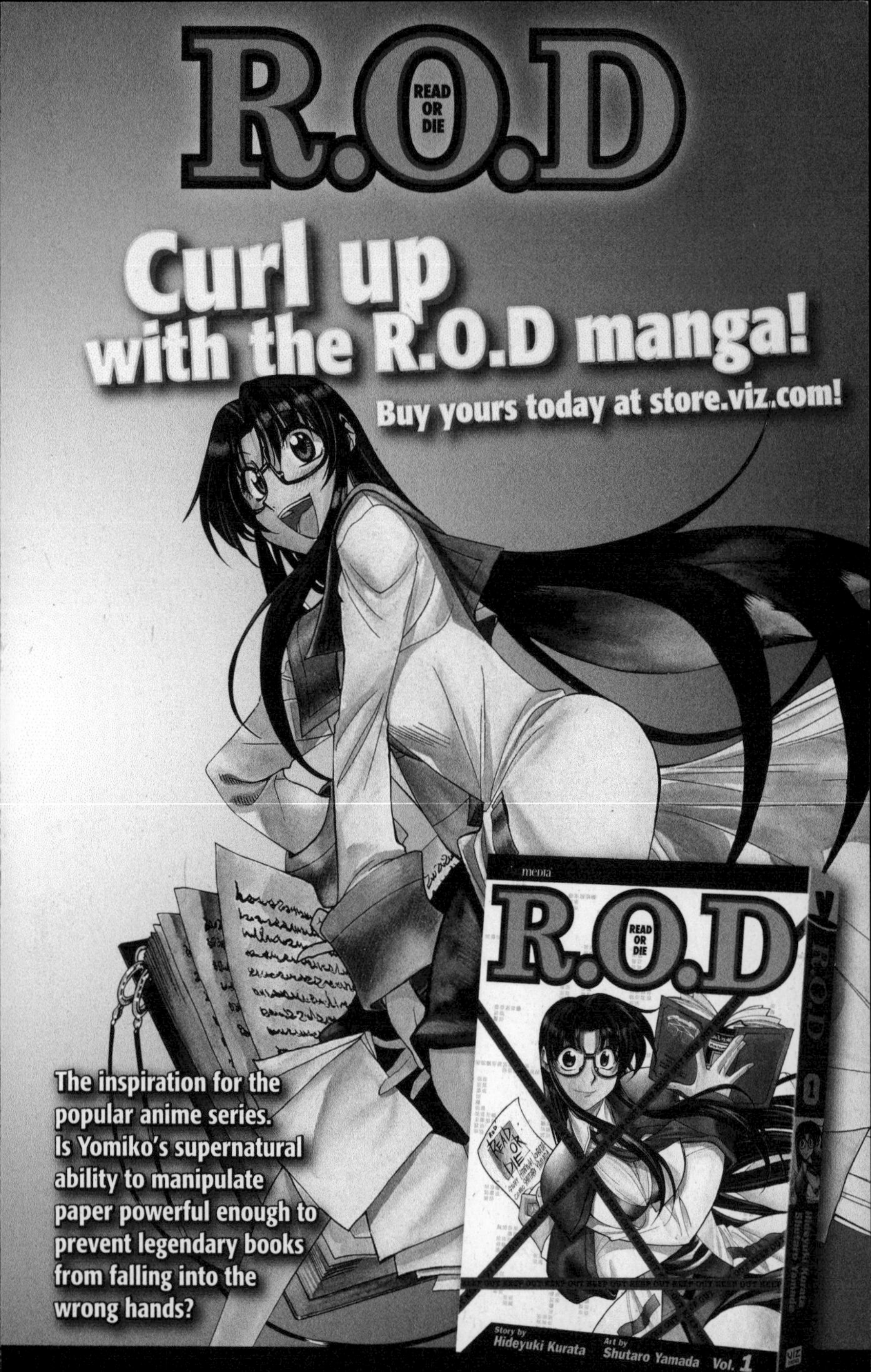
R.O.D
READ OR DIE
Curl up with the R.O.D manga!
Buy yours today at store.viz.com!
The inspiration for the popular anime series. Is Yomiko's supernatural ability to manipulate paper powerful enough to prevent legendary books from falling into the wrong hands?
media
R.O.D
READ OR DIE
Story by Hideyuki Kurata
Art by Shutaro Yamada
Vol. 1

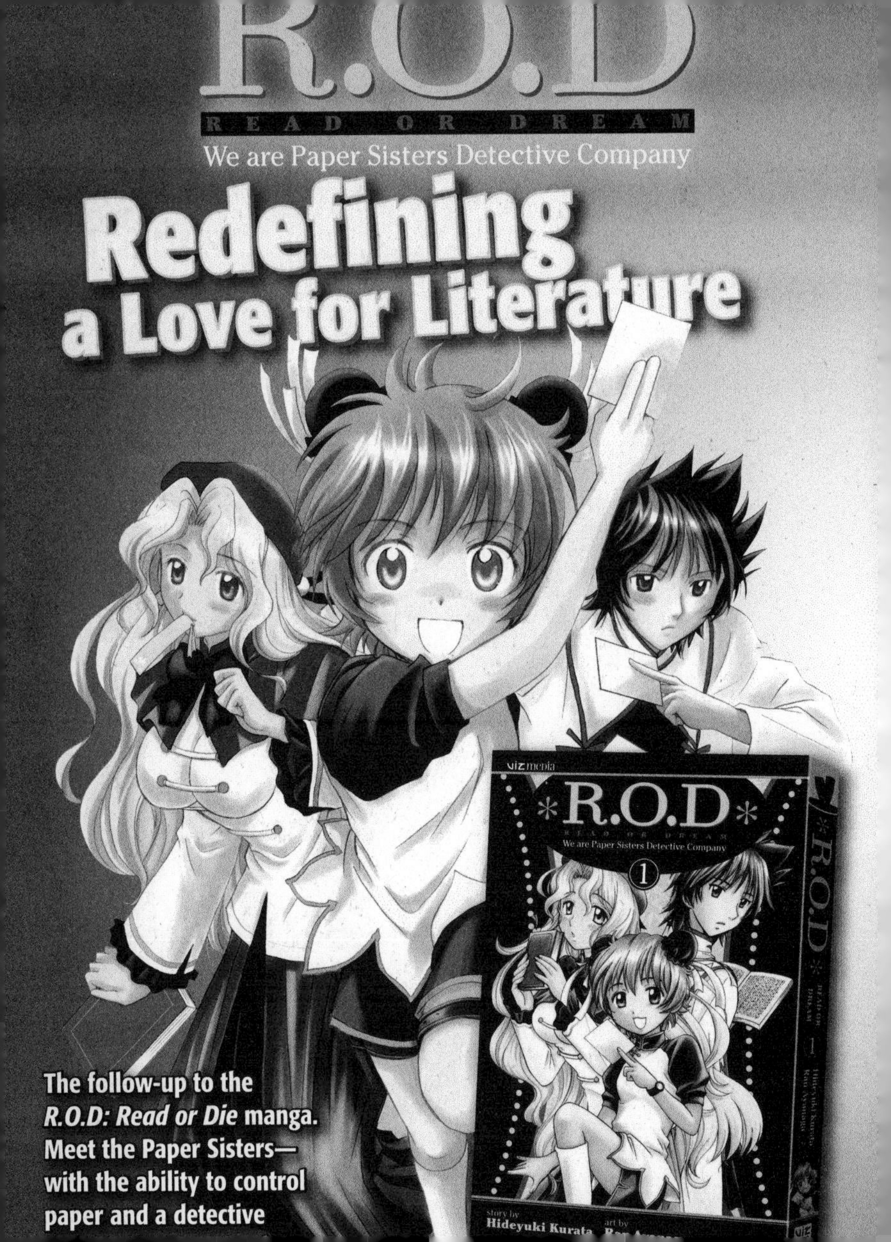

R.O.D
READ OR DREAM
We are Paper Sisters Detective Company
Redefining a Love for Literature
The follow-up to the *R.O.D: Read or Die* manga. Meet the Paper Sisters—with the ability to control paper and a detective
viz media
R.O.D
READ OR DREAM
We are Paper Sisters Detective Company
1
story by
Hideyuki Kurata
art by

LOVE MANGA?
LET US KNOW WHAT YOU THINK!

OUR MANGA SURVEY IS NOW
AVAILABLE ONLINE. PLEASE VISIT:
VIZ.COM/MANGASURVEY

HELP US MAKE THE MANGA